The Eclipse of Parliament

Appearance and Reality in British Politics since 1914

Bruce P. Lenman
Professor in Modern History, University of St Andrews

Edward Arnold
A division of Hodder & Stoughton
LONDON NEW YORK MELBOURNE AUCKLAND

In Piam Memoriam

Robert, Viscount Molesworth, a great Irishman

and

Andrew Fletcher of Saltoun, the patriot laird

© 1992 Bruce P. Lenman

First published in Great Britain 1992

Distributed in the USA by Routledge, Chapman and Hall, Inc.
29 West 35th Street, New York, NY 10001

British Library Cataloguing in Publication Data

Lenman, Bruce
  Eclipse of Parliament: Appearance and
  Reality in British Politics Since 1914
  I. Title
  320.941

  ISBN 0-340-49492-1

Typeset in 10/11pt Linotron Palatino by Rowland
Phototypesetting Limited, Bury St Edmunds, Suffolk.
Printed and bound in Great Britain for Edward Arnold,
a division of Hodder and Stoughton Limited, Mill Road,
Dunton Green, Sevenoaks, Kent TN13 2YA by
Biddles Limited, Guildford and King's Lynn.

Contents

Preface

In a work covering so large a sweep of history, I have necessarily leaned heavily on many standard texts. As I have tried to keep footnotes purely to document specific points or arguments, I would like here to record my deep gratitude to many authors whose work underpins mine, but whose influence it would be difficult fully to acknowledge even if it were possible.

To kind friends who read all or part of several chapters, to my great benefit, I am more grateful than I can here say. To Edenside Computing, that most intelligent and helpful of firms, I owe the processing of my manuscript with exemplary speed and professionalism.

To save space, I use 'Whitehall' as shorthand for the London-based policy-making élite of the UK bureaucracy and 'Westminster' for its central political organs.

Bruce P. Lenman
January 1992

1

Introduction:
In the bleak midwinter

It is names we want, not numbers—otherwise how can we have influence with the government or the foreign office?
> The secretary of the Anglo-German fellowship established 1935

Behold, I send you forth as sheep in the midst of wolves: be ye therefore wise as serpents, and harmless as doves.
> Matthew 10:16

In December 1978, Quintin Hogg, Lord Hailsham, trekked north to deliver an address on 'The Nation and the Constitution' in a Scottish university. By nature a great orator, his lordship provided his hosts with by far the liveliest of the lectures in a series entitled 'The Crown and the Thistle'. He waxed eloquent on the theme that, though until recently 'we have believed in (or at least have practised) a theory of limited government' which he believed to be a condition for the survival of democracy, these days were over. He and his audience now lived under 'elective dictatorship', and this was so because of the failure of British institutions:

> It is our existing institutions which are now in question. There has always been a danger inherent in our constitution that elective dictatorship would take over. The danger has not been obvious because in recent years we have seldom acted in such a way that it became real. We have not practised elective dictatorship because there used to be effective checks and balances . . . Increasingly during my lifetime these inherent safeguards have become eroded.[1]

He then went on to list factors such as the vast increase in the scale of the Government and of its patronage; the support of the Civil Service (whom he quaintly likened to eunuchs guarding a political harem: 'all political

---

[1] Lord Hailsham 'The Nation and the Constitution' in *The Crown and the Thistle: the Nature of Nationhood*, ed. Colin Maclean (Scottish Academic Press, Edinburgh 1979), pp. 73–4.

opinions have first been carefully removed'); and the ability of the Government to manipulate the economy to maximize effective use of the prerogative of dissolution. When to these powers was added the rigid internal discipline of the ruling party, Hailsham was sure that traditional democracy had ceased to function. He was clear that it was 'the House of Commons which is not doing its job and which is therefore in need of reform', and he added in words of insight that:

> There are suggestions for the reform of the House of Commons from time to time. But, alas, they all point the House of Commons more firmly in the direction of elective dictatorship. They are all, or nearly all, proposals for enabling government to get its business through more easily.[1]

It was all good stirring stuff. Nor was his lordship less daring in prescription than he had been fearless in diagnosing the disease. What was needed was radical institutional reconstruction. He wanted extensive devolution of powers to regional authorities, including of course several English regions. There would be a new federal constitution and at the centre a smaller but more powerful House of Commons, with a more developed committee system, would thoroughly vet a smaller volume of legislation. The Commons would be elected by the existing 'first-past-the-post' voting system, but Lord Hailsham wanted an elected second chamber chosen by proportional representation on a regional basis. Certain changes to entrenched categories of law were only to be valid after the legislation making the changes:

> . . . be subjected to referendum after the Act had reached the Royal Assent, and that the referenda should not be effective unless each part of the United Kingdom, or at least a majority of the provinces, voted favourably to the proposals, as well as a majority of the whole.[2]

Warmly applauded at the time and by subsequent reviewers, these proposals provoke the inevitable question 'but what good came of it at last?' It was and is a reasonable question, as Lord Hailsham was shortly to assume high office in the new 1979 administration formed by Mrs Thatcher. Alas, the answer is 'nothing at all'. Nor, with the benefit of hindsight was it ever likely that anything would come of it. Hailsham was going around in 1978–9 making speeches and writing articles which committed him apparently to such proposals as a written constitution and a bill of rights, but always as part of an 'armoury of weapons against elective dictatorship'. What his lordship meant by this, eccentrically enough, was that desperate measures were needed to save the lieges from the existing Government. It happened to be a Labour one led by the very conservative Jim Callaghan, and was propped up, greatly to Hailsham's anger, by a pact with the Liberal Party led by David Steel. This was necessary because the tiny majority which the previous Labour Premier, Harold Wilson, had bequeathed to Callaghan had shrunk by attrition to vanishing point. Anything less like an effective elective dictatorship than Callaghan's Government in the winter of 1978–9 would be difficult to find. A quite different school of Conservative thought interpreted the 1970s as a period when sheer anarchy

---

[1] *Ibid.*, p. 75.
[2] *Ibid.*, p. 77.

masterminded by Marxists in various guises was plunging Britain into the agony of ungovernability. One writer proposed that proportional representation be introduced to give a large 'moderate' block of voters power to hold the political balance as the first step towards 'the restoration of sovereign power to Parliament', a body which he feared was being replaced by pressure groups and special interests.[1] Hailsham, on the contrary, saw a fearful engine of tyranny already in place. His gloom was extravagant:

> For some years now, and especially since February 1974, I have been oppressed by a sinister foreboding. We are living in the City of Destruction, a dying country in a dying civilization, and across the plain there is no wicket gate offering a way of escape.[2]

Now in 1974 the Conservatives lost an election. That vexed his lordship, understandably, but his vexation was because he was counting on the disintegration of the Labour Party if it had lost. It was the presence of Labour in power which turned Hailsham into a Cassandra. There have been, in the twentieth-century UK, premiers who behaved like elective dictators, not necessarily during the whole of their tenure of the office. However, neither Callaghan nor Wilson between 1974 and 1979 even faintly approached that mode of operation. Though the concept is normally deeply flawed as an analogue of the position even of a powerful prime minister in peacetime, there was more to be said for applying it to Mrs Thatcher after 1979, at least in terms of style. Hailsham had met Mrs Thatcher's future Press Secretary Bernard Ingham in the early 1960s when, as Minister for the North East, his lordship relentlessly toured that depressed area in boots and a cloth cap, looking like nothing so much as the cartoon character, Andy Cap.[3] As the Prime Minister's Press Secretary (described as a 'Yorkshire Rasputin' by Tory MP John Biffen), Ingham had carried the process of manipulating news through the Lobby system of unascribable briefings to a pitch which many thought alarming. Technically a civil servant, and with a history of active Labour politics, Ingham became a fanatical Thatcher loyalist. From September 1979 until she fell in late 1990, Ingham fought for her through thick and thin, bullying the press ruthlessly. He was suspected of leaking whatever had to be leaked in certain cases, and he did much to prepare the way for the destruction of some of the 100 or so ministers she fired during the time he served her. Yet in this disconcerting atmosphere, Hailsham's worries never seem to have revived.

Teased ever so gently about this by Anthony Seldon in 1987, Hailsham eventually produced his answer:

> She is anti big government and not pro big government and therefore she was on my side as regards the fear of elective dictatorship. The fact that she enforces her opinions within the Cabinet, even when they are contentious, doesn't mean that she is a dictator. What I was talking about when I was talking about elective dictatorship was the power the Cabinet has of ruling

---

[1] Richard Clutterbuck *Britain in Agony: The Growth of Political Violence* (Faber and Faber, London 1978).

[2] Lord Hailsham *The Dilemma of Democracy: Diagnosis and Prescription* (Collins, London 1978), p. 15.

[3] Bernard Ingham *Kill the Messenger* (HarperCollins, London 1991), p. 63.

the country and intruding authority into one field after another of private lives and public organizations.[1]

So the brave phrases, the radical prescriptions, the apparently heroic rethinking were in fact covers for self-serving paranoia. His lordship simply could not accept a Labour Government, even one led by Callaghan and Healey, as legitimate. In the absence of a party capable of attaining office which did not differ very much from the Conservatives, legitimacy meant the Conservatives in power. However, the Hailsham critique of the way the political structure of the UK had developed had its own validity regardless of its author's tortuous motives. It had to, for Hailsham obviously veiled his motives when advancing it in order to attract support from those who did not necessarily share those motives.

There was also great significance in the fact that everyone who heard Hailsham wax eloquent on the theme of elective dictatorship assumed that he was talking about the prime minister. By 1978, there was already a substantial and controversial literature, not to mention a lively public debate, on the subject of the powers of that office and their impact on the nature of the political system in the United Kingdom of Great Britain and Northern Ireland. In theory, that political system was directly descended from the Glorious Revolution of 1688, when Prince William of Orange landed in England with a Dutch army and, with support from the English political class, overthrew the reigning King James II. William's reign, in the words of two recent commentators:

> . . . initiated the slow but steady transfer of real power from monarchy to Parliament. Thus were laid the foundations of two British institutions still admired and envied the world over: constitutional monarchy and Parliamentary democracy.[2]

This was a very Dutch view of what constituted the core of UK politics. No informed commentator in 1988 thought that British politics were particularly democratic. Their principal democratic sanction was an infrequent general election, but even that was heavily qualified by a voting system which regularly, in effect, disenfranchised not only third-party minorities with up to a quarter of the votes cast, but arguably a majority of all votes cast, because a majority regularly voted against the party which won power. It was also qualified, as Lord Hailsham pointed out, by the prerogative of arbitrary dissolution. Charter 88, a body founded to recall the 300th anniversary of the Glorious Revolution, and to press for some of the values it was supposed to have embodied, pointed out in the early summer of 1990 that the central democratic choice of the UK was entirely dependent on calculations of party advantage based on private polls and careful manipulation by the Chancellor of the perceived prosperity of the electorate. The electorate was usually only given a chance to elect a new government when somebody calculated it was likely to re-elect the old one, and in the words of Anthony Barnett: '. . . what we are witnessing has all the

---

[1] 'Prime Ministers and Near Prime Ministers', interview of Lord Hailsham by Anthony Seldon in *Contemporary Record*, Vol. 1, No. 3, Autumn 1987, p. 58.

[2] Henri and Barbara van der Zee *1688: Revolution in the Family* (Viking, London 1988), p. 240.

dignity of a punter waiting around outside a betting shop, eventually summoning the courage to go in.'[1]

As for the monarchy, nobody suffered from the illusion that its holder mattered greatly in the structure of UK politics. In so far as it was controversial, it was because radical commentators saw it as a machine for validating anachronistic and retrogressive social values. Non-radical commentators, after Malcolm Muggeridge had first made the point, saw it realistically as a long-running soap opera in which some of the younger family characters did not greatly appeal to viewers.[2] After the Lords had succumbed to the embrace of television, the Commons very reluctantly followed suit, on the grounds that if it did not allow itself to be televised, it would sink into obscurity. As it was, the most popular feature of its activity with viewers turned out to be yet another long-running soap opera: prime minister's question time. There was the world of difference between this and the deliberate use of the medium by the prime minister. John Biffen, a former Leader of the House of Commons sacked by Mrs Thatcher after her 1987 election victory, supported the televising of the Commons on the grounds that the executive was routinely using television news and current affairs programmes to outflank the House. Mrs Thatcher would announce major policy initiatives on television. Enormous effort went into the projection of the prime ministerial image on the television screen, some of it even drawing inspiration from the technique of the evangelist Billy Graham. This was the projection of real power, very little of which remained in the Commons.[3]

It still remained a highly contentious question as to exactly how the undoubted concentration of power in the figure of the prime minister could be described, and how it related to, and was limited by, other forms of power. The different schools of thought included one which used the word 'presidential' to describe it, using an analogy with the executive presidency of the USA. As a description, this was better on style than on substance. Presidential in the American sense the prime minister could, by definition, hardly be. The American federal political system was an eighteenth-century critique of the more alarming trends in contemporary Westminster and it was based on a system of checks and balances and division of powers which did not exist in the UK. Another school, which stressed the relative weakness of the premier, and the need for a premier to act as chairman of a cabinet from whose members came all detailed proposals was equally unsatisfactory. Its vision was valid, but very, very partial. The pattern of authority could and did work that way, but very often indeed it did not. Oddly, the most perceptive analysis was probably the one hammered out in semi-retirement from the power-game by Tony Benn. He had never been the shrewdest of practising politicians. Even allowing for the fact that after Harold Wilson, he was the politician most viciously smeared by the

[1] The phrase comes from a Newsletter issued in the summer of 1990 and signed by Anthony Barnett, Co-ordinator of Charter 88.

[2] Tom Nairn *The Enchanted Glass: Britain and Its Monarchy* (Radius, London 1988); Piers Brendon *Our Own Dear Queen* (Secker and Warburg, London 1986).

[3] Michael Cockerell *Live from Number 10: The Inside Story of the Prime Minister and Television* (Faber and Faber, London 1988).

media since 1945, his programmes in the 1970s had never had any serious chance of implementation. They remain rejected alternatives of some historical interest. Yet he did think his way through to the monarchical element in the position of the prime minister, and even grasped the key point that it was an absolute rather than a constitutional monarchy.[1] His specific proposals for coping with this problem, which included the election of the cabinet by the Parliamentary Labour Party in a future Labour Government were even when he first put them forward deemed unlikely to be accepted.[2] Nevertheless there is much to be said for his views as an analysis pivoting on the assumption that there is a monarchical element in the Westminster system; that it is a prime minister who has usurped nearly all the still-formidable prerogative powers of the Crown; and that this new personal monarchy is free of most of the checks and balances laboriously constructed to contain the hereditary monarchy (which survives as a fig-leaf for the system). After all, a most perceptive biography of the indispensable Bernard Ingham concluded that in his relationship with the Prime Minister:

> He was not really a Machiavelli or a Svengali or an *éminence grise* or any of the other (as he might put it) bloody foreigners to whom he was regularly compared. His role was much more that of an ultra-loyal servant; a courtier one might almost say . . .[3]

It would be wrong to suggest that this modern monarchy is either unique or secure. Many absolute monarchs have come to swift and sudden ends. After all, how else can one safely make an end of them? Secondly, because the term 'British' was and is still to some extent supra-national, the world has many former British territories in which not dissimilar political developments have occurred, though seldom in so extreme a form. Brian Mulroney, the Canadian Premier, himself occupying a Westminster-derived post, was 'almost shell-shocked' when he heard that Thatcher, after three election victories, was being pushed from her throne.[4]

There were very similar developments in the Irish Republic, despite a single transferable vote system in elections designed to limit executive capacity to impose initiatives on a conservative society, and a very sensible reluctance on the part of that society to give a large majority mandate to any party.[5] Charles J. Haughey, an opposition leader who had appeared 'weak, indecisive and apparently unable to come to terms with his new role'[6], unexpectedly achieved power early in 1982 in Dublin and went on to dominate the politics of the Republic for the rest of the decade with much the same charismatic mixture of assertive leadership and contro-

---

[1] There is a convenient summary of the different schools of thought in James Barber 'The Power of the Prime Minister', in *British Politics in Perspective*, eds. R. L. Borthwick and J. E. Spence (Leicester University Press, Leicester 1984), pp. 73–101.

[2] Philip Norton *The Constitution in Flux* (Martin Robertson, Oxford 1982), chap. 1.

[3] Robert Harris *Good and Faithful Servant: The Unauthorized Biography of Bernard Ingham* (Faber and Faber, London 1990), p. 5.

[4] Ingham *Kill the Messenger*, p. 392.

[5] Brian Farrell *Chairman or Chief: The Role of the Taoiseach in Irish Government* (Gill and Macmillan, Dublin 1971).

[6] Joe Joyce and Peter Murtagh *The Boss: Charles J. Haughey in Government* (Poolbeg Press, Swords, Co. Dublin 1983), p. 14.

versial pushing of power to its limits as Thatcher. Plots against him made his throne permanently shaky. He even had to vacate it from time to time. There were two differences between him and Thatcher. He survived in power until 1992. The other was that, though both clearly loved power, there had always been some doubt as to what Charlie Haughey wanted to do with it. Maggie Thatcher never had that problem.

The debate on the relative economic decline of the UK is not one which has produced many satisfactory answers.[1] Too many 'solutions' to a complex multi-factorial problem turn out to be glib and emotionally rather than intellectually satisfying. It is, therefore, only as a contribution to an analysis that any factor should be tentatively advanced. Nevertheless, it is surely worth noting that the UK political system transfers significant power to manipulate the economy to the Government and that even if the record shows more botching than success in the endeavour, attempts to secure political advantage by such manipulation are continuous and relatively unchecked, least of all by the legislature. The Dublin legislature has, if anything, a less impressive record in this respect that the Westminster one,[2] and the fact remains that, by Western European standards, the UK was in the late-twentieth century a very unsuccessful economy. Indeed, only the Republic of Ireland could be described as faring marginally worse. It remains to enquire historically how it came to pass that the twentieth-century United Kingdom ended up with the dubious blessings of an administration with such unbridled domestic authority.

The state in the UK denied the need for any kind of mediating powers between an executive which dominated the legislature, and the population. Such a position had arisen long before Lord Hailsham artfully tried to delegitimize non-Conservative governments by saying, rather than insinuating, that the problem of elective dictatorship had first become apparent in 1974, when the Labour Party unexpectedly captured power. In practice, his lordship's rhetoric was calculated to create a one-party state, by selling the idea that only Conservative government could be acceptable within the existing framework of power. By 1987 it was said that the planning department of a great international corporation had classified the UK (alongside Japan) as a 'one party democratic state', a view vindicated by the slender but decisive Conservative victory in the 1992 election.[3] The UK was therefore in the late twentieth century a state structure whose powerful central organs enabled a minority to monopolize all meaningful domestic power.

It was a remarkable development within a political tradition which had once prided itself on limiting the claims of over-mighty organs of governance. Sixteenth-century Englishmen really had no theory of the state. They had theories about how the various elements of society should relate to

---

[1] Alan Sked *Britain's Decline: Problems and Perspectives* (Basil Blackwell for the Historical Association, Oxford 1987) is a good overview.

[2] A comparative study which brings out the very limited role of the Westminster Commons and the Dublin Oireachtas compared with, say, the Swedish Riksdag is *Parliaments in Western Europe*, ed. Philip Norton (Frank Cass, London 1990)

[3] Gavyn Davis 'The Economics of a One-Party State', in *The Independent*, Business and City, Monday 13 April 1992, p. 21.

one another.[1] Their seventeenth-century descendants carried through two revolutions against what they perceived as the threat of an arbitrary expansion of the powers of their kings, for fear that they might end up subjects of a Continental-type monarchical absolutist state. Those revolutions, far more than the industrial revolution of the late eighteenth century, gave England its claim to significance in world history, especially when this robust hostility to excessive state power was transplanted to colonial America.

What will be argued in this study, is that the betrayal of these libertarian traditions was well under way by the eighteenth century, particularly after 1707, when the union of Scotland with England created a Kingdom of Great Britain in which the doctrine of 'parliamentary sovereignty' was used to undermine the elements of contract and accountability which had been underlined by popular perceptions of the Glorious Revolution of 1688 in England. All regional and municipal governments were relentlessly subordinated to the will of the Westminster parliament, especially after the extrusion from the British monarchy of those American Englishmen who most stoutly resisted this trend. Apart from infrequent general elections in which only a fraction of the seats were likely to change hands, such checks and balances as were left were internal to the triple-structured parliament in London: King, Lords and Commons.

With the collapse of real monarchy in the early nineteenth century, those balances began to crumble. Mass parties evolved in the later nineteenth century and enabled their leaders to tame both the electorate and the Commons. Executive power, working through a whipped majority, could dominate the lower house of the legislature. Such checking power as survived in the House of Lords was undermined by the increasingly archaic and indefensible nature of its membership, and then broken for ever by a hostile majority in the Commons in 1911 which forced through a statute removing the ability of the Lords seriously to block legislation. The upshot left the UK with an alarming concentration of power in the head of the executive, the prime minister. This office had evolved since the early eighteenth century, receiving two enormous accretions of power, first when it absorbed most of the powers of the monarchy, and later when its incumbent could count on the authority derived from leadership of a disciplined mass party. To wield the full potential of the office, a premier needed a reasonably homogenous and deferential electorate, which did not exist in the UK in 1914. Civil war would have broken out had not world events postponed it.

Thereafter the First and Second World Wars and the Cold War saw massive extensions not only of the apparatus of the state, but also of its claims to irresponsible power over the individual. With the removal of Catholic Ireland from the body politic in 1922, the UK electorate became homogeneous and deferential enough to accept first minority-based Conservative rule, and then a Conservative-dominated regime thinly disguised as a National Government which actually received majority support from voters. The only non-Conservative regime to enjoy power as distinct from

[1] Christopher Morris *Political Thought in England: Tyndale to Hooker* (Oxford University Press, London 1953), Introduction, p. 1.

office in the post-1945 era reversed none of the trends towards centralization and increased executive power over the inhabitants of the UK.
Indeed, its introduction of a bureaucratic welfare state and its passionate
commitment to the Cold War enhanced those trends. Greater patronage
made the premier even more formidable.

None of this meant that that the political system was assertively independent in an international context. Historically, the concept of the sovereignty
of parliament has tended to be a rhetoric used to prevent the inhabitants
of the UK from having serious influence on major policy decisions affecting
their lives. Foreign governments, including those representing peoples
who have escaped from the British political system, have throughout the
twentieth century been a major influence in the UK decision-taking process. Since 1940 the UK executive has only intermittently jibbed at this fact,
though there has been more protest from non-office-holding members of
parliament, for whom the loss of the fig-leaf of sovereignty has been a
repeated reminder and exposure of their fundamental powerlessness
within the system.

The office of prime minister by the late twentieth century resembled
nothing so much as the Continental absolute monarchies which the English
had once prided themselves on rejecting. Its style varied with different
reigns. Though the powers of the office were vast internally, it was an office
sustained by, and at the apex of a complex of vested interests, domestic and
foreign. Its function was to serve those interests, with some latitude of
choice, depending on circumstances, in the field of policy. Failure deemed
to be irrecoverable was followed by political assassination, but then most
absolutisms are tempered by assassination when they cease to serve the
purposes of those who have set them up, tolerated, or supported them.

In 1947 Penguin Books published *The Case for Conservatism* by the young
Quintin Hogg, the future Lord Hailsham. Hogg's work was exactly twice
the length originally specified by Penguin. He had much to say to the
electorate by way of warnings similar to his Cassandra-like speech of 1978.
One recurring theme in 1947, defended by quotations from Edmund Burke,
was that English liberties were a sacred trust to be claimed, asserted and
handed down to posterity. Hogg warned that after the Labour victory, the
UK teetered on the brink of becoming a one-party state. He was particularly
angry about the threat posed by the 'Socialist State' to the independence of
local governments, and their admirable 'public enterprises' which supplied
basic utilities to the community. He denounced with evangelical zeal the
subjection of the British people to regulations, directives, and other forms
of delegated legislation not subject to debate and scrutiny by the people's
representatives in parliament.[1]

This present study ends with a demonstration that even more under
Conservative administrations than Labour ones in the late twentieth century, all these trends accelerated. Much of the tidal wave of regulatory
directives did not even emanate from within the country, let alone receive
serious scrutiny there. Nor, it will be argued, was this surprising. It was in
the nature of the political system to trample on what an eighteenth-century

---

[1] Quintin Hogg *The Case for Conservatism* (Penguin Books, West Drayton 1948), esp.
pp. 67, 81–2, 88, and 304–5.

Englishman would have regarded as his essential liberties. Despite the windy rhetoric of politicians with liberty on their lips and power in their hearts, the UK government by the second half of the twentieth century was neither a parliamentary regime, nor a particularly democratic one.

2

Whatever happened to checks and balances?

There being three kinds of government among men, absolute monarchy, aristocracy and democracy, and all of these having their particular conveniences and inconveniences, the experience and wisdom of your ancestors hath so moulded this out of a mixture of these as to give to this kingdom (as far as human prudence can provide) the conveniences of all three, without the inconveniences of any one, as long as the balance hangs even between the three . . .

Charles I's answer to the Nineteen Propositions 18 June 1642

. . . But on Britannia's shore
Now present, I to raise my reign began
By raising the democracy, the third
And broadest bulwark of the guarded state.
Then was the full the perfect plan disclosed
Of Britain's matchless constitution, mixed
Of mutual checking and supporting powers,
King, lords, and commons; . . .

The voice of the Goddess of Liberty speaking in James Thomson's poem 'Liberty', first published in 1735–6

In so far as the modern political system of the UK may be said to have a legitimating historical root, that root was the Glorious Revolution of 1688 when William of Orange bloodlessly overthrew King James II in England. Elsewhere in the multiple kingdoms and provinces of an Atlantic-wide British monarchy, there were other revolutions, many far from bloodless, and all producing different interpretations of what had in fact happened. In England, the real revolution was dynastic and religious, not parliamentary. William of Orange had 'not come over to establish a Commonwealth', and he was emphatic that the Crown would 'not be the worse' because he wore it. He was able to move towards the physical possession of the throne because the Catholic James first sent his baby heir to France with his Queen, Mary of Modena, and then followed them himself. In the embar-

11

rassing vacuum which followed the first abortive flight of James, William dealt with not a parliament but a provisional government of peers led by the Earl of Rochester. That body upheld law and order in London, and arranged for the return of the captured King James. He soon fled again, tacitly encouraged by William. On the dubious grounds that James had 'abdicated' and the sounder one that the throne was vacant, a convention parliament offered the throne conjointly to William and his English Stuart wife, Mary, daughter of the deposed James. Thereby the English political nation did sundry very radical things like breaking the hereditary succession, distinguishing between the person and office of the monarch and making it clear that Protestantism was a prerequisite for occupancy of the throne.[1]

All of this however left the 'ancient constitution' of England untouched in terms of structures. The Glorious Revolution was seen as reinforcing these. Its best-known ideological statement, which is hardly such in reality, was the Bill of Rights of 1689. That document denounced specific behaviour by the late monarch which was seen as violating 'the known laws and statutes and freedom of this realm'.[2] By and large, the behaviour specified had violated the customs and usages of England, which were now vindicated. Balance was of the essence of the English view of their constitution. James had tipped it too far towards the monarchical element. Now it was to be restored to that universally-desired equilibrium which had been so eloquently praised by King Charles I in his Reply to the Nineteen Propositions on the eve of the outbreak of the great mid-seventeenth-century English civil war. Sovereignty was an attribute of monarchy, but the king's sovereignty could be expressed in different ways. It was expressed in his roles as fount of both honour and justice. Supremely, it was expressed in his management of the executive government and its armed forces, of both of which he was the head. However, for certain purposes for which he required the active assistance of the political nation, the highest expression of his sovereignty was as king in parliament. Parliament was a trinity of which the king was by far the most important part. For example, since a convention parliament was unknown to English law, the one which had offered William and Mary the Crown had to be retrospectively legalized by the new sovereigns in their high court of parliament.[3]

Everyone expected the monarch to be the active head of the executive, which William certainly was. The regularity and importance of parliamentary sittings in his reign was largely a function of his need to finance an almost intolerably expensive war against France between 1688 and 1697. In 1694, he was forced to agree to an act which required a dissolution of parliament every three years, and the issuing of writs (which meant an

---

[1] Robert Beddard 'The Unexpected Whig Revolution of 1688' in *The Revolutions of 1688*, ed. Robert Beddard (Clarendon, Oxford, 1991), pp. 11–101; and *A Kingdom without a King: The Journal of the Provisional Government in the Revolution* (Phaidon, Oxford 1988).

[2] The text of the Bill of Rights can conveniently be found in *The Eighteenth Century Constitution: Document and Commentary*, ed. E. N. Williams (Cambridge University Press, Cambridge 1970), doc. no. 10, pp. 26–33.

[3] 1 Gul. et Mar., cap 1, reprinted in *English Historical Documents Vol. VIII 1660–1714*, ed. Andrew Browning (Eyre and Spottiswood, London 1953), pp. 158–9.

election) for summoning a new one, but even this Triennial Act was justified by ancient usage in its preamble:

> Whereas by the ancient laws, and statutes of this kingdom frequent parlia-
> ments ought to be held; and whereas frequent and new parliaments tend very
> much to the happy union and good agreement of the King and people . . .[1]

Parliament was needed, for only in his parliament could William secure
new grants of taxation or add new penalties of body or goods to the penal
code. It is true that the Act of Settlement of 1701 was 'An act for the further
limitation of the crown and better securing the rights and liberties of the
subject', but it was drawn up to cope with the securing of the Protestant
succession by the importing of a foreign, Hanoverian dynasty, and most
of its specific provisions are attempts to cope with the novel problems
created by an unprecedented situation in which the sovereign might have
conflicting loyalties to two realms. Much of it was repealed before it became
operative.[2]

Eighteenth-century Englishmen were perfectly well aware of the danger
of abuse of power by the politicians in the other two parts of a parliament.
The high-handed treatment by the Commons of some gentlemen of Kent
who petitioned them aroused widespread anger in 1701, and inspired
anonymous satiric verse:

> Nature has left this tincture in the blood,
> That all men would be tyrants if they could,
> Not kings alone, not ecclesiastic pride
> But Parliaments, and all mankind beside
>
> ———
>
> Then why should we think strange the Parliament
> The people's late petitions should resent?
> 'Tis fatal to tyrannic pride when they
> Who should be ruined grumble to obey;[3]

Historians have sunk a great deal of ingenuity into showing that, in the
course of the conflict between the great new Whig and Tory parties in the
reign of Queen Anne, the Glorious Revolution was an embarrassment to
both. Whigs could never establish it as a revolutionary act and their attempt
to destroy Tory credibility by impeaching the Tory divine Dr Henry Sachev-
erell rebounded on them and showed that their concepts of a right of
resistance, and a social contract were unacceptable to a conservative political nation.[4] All this was true, but it did not affect the universal belief that
there had to be checks and balances against incipient tyranny on the part
of one of the three elements of the constitution.

Sir Robert Walpole, writing against the proposal by the Peerage Bill of
1719 to close the peerage to further creations, automatically fell into this
mode of discourse, saying that the nobility were a vital part of it:

> They know well they are intended the guardians as well as ornaments of the

[1] Text in *Eighteenth Century Constitution*, doc. no. 18, pp. 49–50.
[2] Text in *ibid.*, doc. no. 21, pp. 56–60.
[3] The anonymous satire is printed in *English Historical Documents VIII*, doc. no. 57,
pp. 170–2.
[4] J. P. Kenyon *Revolution Principles: The Politics of Party 1689–1720* (Cambridge University Press, Cambridge 1977).

monarchy, an essential prerogative of which it must be to add to, and augment their number in such proportion as to render them a proper balance against the democratic part of our constitution, without being formidable to the monarchy itself, the support of which is the reason of their institution.[1]

It was ironic that by the 1740s, Walpole himself was being accused of unbalancing the constitution by engrossing the royal power and corrupting the legislature by bullying and bribery. His critic, Mr Sandys, thundered:

> According to our constitution, we can have no sole and prime minister: we ought always to have several prime ministers or officers of state: every such officer has his own proper department; and no officer ought to meddle in the affairs belonging to the department of another.[2]

Sir Robert of course indignantly repudiated the encroachment on the prerogative of the Crown implied in this 'chimerical authority' and added: 'I unequivocally deny that I am the sole and prime minister, and that to my influence and direction all the measures of government must be attributed . . .'[3]

The very name prime minister was a term of abuse, in that it implied an improper monopoly of royal favour. The accession of George III in 1760 undoubtedly marked a resurgence in royal will to participate actively in politics and administration. The supine nature of George I and George II can be greatly exaggerated, but George III was the first politician in the realm and was seen to be such. The inevitable price he paid was rancour and abuse from politicians whom he discarded or failed to chose when exercising his undoubted right to select his ministers (provided they were generally acceptable to the legislature). In particular, the Rockingham Whig faction, to which C. J. Fox was attached, developed a deep dislike of the monarch after he removed it from office in 1766, and through its fugleman Edmund Burke, built up an absurd mythology to justify its view that the king should appoint it to office and keep it there for ever. Even the more extreme branch of the Whigs, the 'Old' or 'True' Whigs, who had clung to the radical core of revolution principles and believed in contract, resistance and spreading the fruits of the Revolution to wider circles in the community than the aristocratic élite, were staunch upholders of the need for balance. Algernon Sidney, who with John Locke was regarded by Thomas Jefferson as one of the two main sources for American understanding of the principles of liberty, and who had been martyred by Charles II, has a section in his *Discourse Concerning Government* headed 'The best Governments of the World have been composed of Monarchy, Aristocracy, and Democracy'.[4]

That was the balance which preserved liberty and, to advanced Whigs (often called Commonwealthmen), a people which defended its liberty would demand respect at home; triumph in competition abroad; and

[1] Cited in A. S. Turberville *The House of Lords in the Reign of William III* (Greenwood, Westport, CT n.d.), p. 238.

[2] Speech by Mr Sandys. Text in *Eighteenth Century Constitution*, doc. no. 71, pp. 126–8.

[3] Reply by Walpole. Text in *ibid.*, doc. no. 72, pp. 128–30.

[4] Algernon Sidney *Discourses Concerning Government*, ed. Thomas G. West (Liberty Classics, Indianapolis, IN 1990), Section 16, p. 166.

prosper, for tyranny, slavery, and poverty marched together. Freemen trampled all three.[1] So what, one may ask, went wrong? One answer is that increasingly a more conservative ideology was becoming preponderant in ruling circles in late eighteenth-century Great Britain. This was the doctrine of 'the sovereignty of parliament'. As H. T. Dickinson has shown, this was cultivated as an antidote to the radical implications of classic Whig doctrines and as a bulwark of the propertied interest which had a very large measure of access to parliamentary influence.[2] Then the separation of powers between executive, judiciary and legislature, so admired by the great French observer and theorist Montesquieu and by many English thinkers deeply influenced by him, turned out to be an illusion. The executive by the late-eighteenth century deeply penetrated the legislature and vice versa and the doctrine of absolute 'parliamentary sovereignty' was bound in the end to subject English Common Law to its empire.[3] After the most radical section of the English nation had left the monarchy to become Americans, Charles J. Fox made the first truly determined bid to annexe the powers of the sovereign to the prime minister and to reduce the king to a figurehead. In a traumatic constitutional crisis in 1782–4, he failed because the bulk of the political nation were appalled, and rightly so, at the thought of 'Caro Khan' usurping George III.[4]

Yet what Fox sought was more or less achieved by the man brought in to save the monarchy: the Younger Pitt. Partly it happened because of the fits of insanity which afflicted George III, but in the Regency Crisis of 1788–9, it became clear that he was prepared to deprive a Prince Regent politically hostile to him of basic royal powers, even at the cost of an extremely dangerous clash with the still-independent Irish parliament, which had followed the laws, customs and usages of both realms in being prepared to give the Prince of Wales full powers. The recovery of King George terminated the crisis but by the second decade of the nineteenth century, it was clear that the monarchy, like the Anglican church-state of which it was the anointed head, was collapsing.[5] It did not help that the Prince Regent, later George IV, was latterly a mental, moral and physical slob, and that he had in law forfeited his right of succession by marrying Mrs Fitzherbert illegally and secretly in 1785. By the 1820s, he was a public relations figure sent by the Cabinet on unspeakably vulgar (and hugely successful) public tours to Edinburgh and Dublin.

---

[1] The best introduction to the Commonwealthmen is still Caroline Robbins *The Eighteenth-Century Commonwealthman* (Harvard University Press, Cambridge, MA 1961).
[2] H. T. Dickinson *Liberty and Property: Political Ideology in Eighteenth-Century Britain* (Methuen, London 1977); Paul Langford *Public Life and the Propertied Englishman 1689–1798* (Clarendon Press, Oxford 1991), shows a parliament very willing to absorb and oblige concentrations of property.
[3] F. T. H. Fletcher *Montesquieu and English Politics (1750–1800)* (Porcupine Press, Philadelphia 1980 reprint), Chap. VIII.
[4] John Cannon *The Fox-North coalition: Crisis of the Constitution 1782–4* (Cambridge University Press, Cambridge 1969). Professor Cannon is somewhat kinder to Fox than most contemporaries.
[5] J. C. D. Clark *English Society 1688–1832* (Cambridge University Press, Cambridge 1985), remains the classic analysis of the collapse of the Anglican church-state and its monarchy.

What had happened was not that the prime minister had successfully usurped royal prerogatives. They had been taken over by a committee. There was indeed a Prime Minister, in the shape of Lord Liverpool from 1815 to 1827, but he was no dominating bully. He was indispensable because only he had the tact and standing to hold together in the Cabinet a committee of able but difficult aristocratic politicians who ran the state. On his deathbed in 1830, George IV was praised by the Whig lawyer Lord Campbell as 'the model of a constitutional king of England . . . He has stood by and let the country govern itself'. Campbell was not entirely just. George IV was in practice a detached member of the ruling committee who occasionally displayed royal powers, and there were spasms of doubt as in September 1821 as to 'who commanded the Cabinet's first loyalty—the King or his Prime Minister'.[1] After the franchise extensions of 1832, such a question became unthinkable. The breaking of the link between Commons and Lords provided by the control of blocs of MPs by peers, symbolized the widening of the political nation beyond the aristocratically-dominated hierarchy which had been prepared to accede to reasonable royal initiative.

In practice, the rapid collapse of the extremes of polarization induced by the struggle to secure the widening of the franchise in 1832 created a period in which party structures were weak and the Government had great difficulty controlling the Commons. It could also have problems with the Lords. Government tended to be genuine Cabinet government, but even in choosing his Cabinet, a premier might have to make allowances for the feelings of the House. Both the Whig Melbourne and the Tory Peel expressed worries about the weakness of the executive in the face of a Commons full of independent MPs, whom Lord Derby defined acidly but accurately as MPs who could not be relied upon. The Cabinet's capacity to lead the House of Commons was in fact very limited. The threat of a dissolution if the Government could not have its way on a specific issue was neither sensible nor usual. MPs did not like general elections, less because they feared defeat than because of the expense and effort they involved. Parliaments were expected to run for a decent five or six years and there had to be a substantial reason for a dissolution. There were indeed five or six occasions between 1832 and 1868 when the defeat of a government was followed by a dissolution, but there were eight examples in the same period when defeated cabinets chose simply to resign, and untold examples of cabinets which swallowed their pride after a defeat and carried on. It followed that it was very important for the bulk of a cabinet to turn up to the Commons, to show solidarity, and to support the Government's measures. Resignation or visible disaffection could shake an administration's grip on power. Nor were there many able men around to fill a cabinet. Of over 650 MPs, only 200 or so would speak on any scale during a session. Discounting those in opposition to the Government, it is clear that most premiers were willing to regard very modest talents indeed on the part of an acceptable member of the ruling class in either Lords or Commons as qualifying him for a cabinet post. The Lords, who had for a

[1] J. E. Cookson *Lord Liverpool's Administration 1815–1822* (Scottish Academic Press, Edinburgh 1975), pp. 324–5.

long time been disqualified from voting on financial measures, were not on the whole as difficult as the Commons between 1832 and 1867. They never, for example, tried to vote down a Government simply because they disliked the composition of the Cabinet.[1]

There was one very strong Prime Minister in this era in the shape of Sir Robert Peel, whose administration between 1841 and 1845 was a *tour de force* based on the personal ascendancy of an extremely able, hard-working, and immensely proud man, a survivor from the pre-1832 regime, who did not so much see himself as leading the Government or chairing Cabinet as embodying Government. So far was he from creating the Conservative Party that when Conservative members grouped round him, they were annoyed to find just how far he considered this gave him the right to command their allegiance and obedience. As early as 1841 he had, in publicly discussing the position of prime minister, laid enormous stress on his personal opinions, and threatened to resign if he could not have his way on matters he thought important.

> I will propose those measures: and I do with confidence assure this House, that no consideration of mere political support shall induce me to alter them. I will not hold office by the servile tenure which would compel me to be the instrument of carrying other men's opinions into effect.[2]

Over the repeal of the corn laws, there came the parting of the ways with the most important part of his own party, so in due course Peel went. Less imperious premiers exploited their ability to use the royal prerogative. Lord Melbourne, who was extremely kind and patient towards the not-very-bright young Queen Victoria, was wryly amusing about his own chores as distributor of honours and maker of bishops. Lord Palmerston, socially an outrageous survival of the Regency, and an Irishman to boot, survived for ten years as Premier by shrewdly exploiting the room for manoeuvre which prerogative powers gave him in foreign affairs, whilst allowing associates like Lord John Russell to discredit themselves in the difficult mire of domestic affairs. Pam did not bother, to the great anger of Queen Victoria and Prince Albert, even to pretend that he need take them seriously when wielding the royal prerogative.[3]

The House of Commons had, in the mid-nineteenth century, vastly greater powers than it was to have in the twentieth. Between the 1830s and 1880s, party cohesion was very low. On less than 30 per cent of all issues did 90 per cent of either of the main parties vote together. Governments were sacked. Legislation was made and revised on the floor of the House. Individual ministers were hounded from office without the Government even daring to threaten a dissolution. The Commons controlled a very substantial part of its own timetable and it could be as tough with the bureaucracy as with the Cabinet. For example, it could compel the Foreign Office to divulge in Blue Books the details of negotiations with

[1] John P. Mackintosh *The British Cabinet* (Steven and Sons, 3rd edn, London 1977), Chap. 3.
[2] 'Peel on the Position of Prime Minister, 1841', printed in *Documents of Modern History: The Age of Peel*, ed. Norman Gash (Edward Arnold, London 1968), pp. 86–8.
[3] Cecil Woodham-Smith *Queen Victoria: Her Life and Times. Volume I 1819–1861* (Hamish Hamilton, London 1972).

foreign powers, to allow the House to have meaningful debates on foreign policy.[1] The very idea would make a twentieth-century Foreign Office mandarin sick. In fact, the heavens did not fall. This was W. L. Burn's 'Age of Equipoise', balanced between town and country; aristocracy and democracy; discipline and *laissez-faire*.[2] Preponderantly, it was also a period of peace and mounting prosperity, but change eroded its social base.

The reassertion of executive control over the legislature came with the rise of organized mass parties in the later nineteenth-century, starting with the final coming together of various groups under the leadership of William Gladstone to form the Liberal Party in 1867–8. Of this event, John Vincent has shrewdly said: 'Oratory apart, Gladstone did not so much create the circumstances of the 1860s as make good administrative use of the opportunities given by popular support, to reassert the authority of the State over Parliament.'[3] Inevitably, the Conservatives followed behind rapidly. The Irish Home Rulers, exploiting the unique solidarity of Catholic Ireland, created the first severely disciplined, coherent parliamentary party, most of whose MPs were crucially dependent on it for financial support. It was responsive to a mass electorate and a charismatic leader in Charles Stewart Parnell. More than most, he displayed two corollaries of the new situation. One was that such party leaders had a frequent tendency towards a dictatorial style of leadership. The other, proved by his fall in 1890–1, was that, however dictatorial (and it was no accident that Parnell called his favourite horse Dictator), if their leadership offered their party only the prospect of electoral defeat, they would be ditched. As one scholar has remarked, the period after 1868 was one in which 'parliamentary government' was demolished and a 'two-party' system constructed. Actually, it was a three-party system, but his further insight is wholly valid: 'Acting on an electoral mandate, parties became the autonomous institutions within the constitution, rather than Parliament itself.'[4]

Triggered by Home Rule Party obstruction of business, there was a systematic and successful campaign for the Government to take over control of the parliamentary timetable. As the different parties came to represent bitterly hostile regional, religious and economic interests what Lord Salisbury called a 'state of bloodless civil war' began to reign. It reached destructive levels after the split in the Liberal Party over Gladstone's unexpected public announcement of his conversion to Irish Home Rule, and his unsuccessful sponsorship of the first Home Rule Bill in 1886, which in fact ushered in a long period of Conservative (aided by Liberal Unionist) ascendancy. Party discipline in parliamentary voting was spectacularly greater, which is one reason why Arthur Balfour, that most philosophically detached of Tories, was able in 1902 to carry his procedural reforms which completed the structure of a 'parliamentary railway timetable', enabling a

---

[1] John P. Mackintosh *The Government and Politics of Britain* (Hutchinson University Library, pbk edn, London 1970), pp. 26–9.

[2] W. L. Burn *The Age of Equipoise* (George Allen and Unwin, London 1964).

[3] John Vincent *The Formation of the British Liberal Party 1857–68* (Longman, Penguin edn, London 1972), p. 289.

[4] Angus Hawkins '"Parliamentary Government" and Victorian Political Parties, c. 1830–c. 1880', *English Historical Review* (CIV, 1989), p. 668.

Government with even a thin majority to railroad measures through the Commons.

The sole surviving check on executive power was one which was indefensible both in its composition and latterly in the use it made of its power. The House of Lords was Tory-dominated and hereditary by definition. Provoked by Lloyd George's 'People's Budget' of 1909, and denounced as 'Mr Balfour's Poodle', it was manoeuvred into a false position, and had its powers to impose more than a modest delay on government measures withdrawn by the Parliament Act of 1911. Despite public assurances by the Liberal Premier, Herbert H. Asquith, that basic reform of the second chamber was an urgent matter, there was little likelihood of any such thing. Apart from the difficulty of securing agreement on any proposal, a weak, politically indefensible second chamber suited a premier with a majority in the Commons only too well. The doctrine of the absolute sovereignty of parliament (at least over its domestic subjects) had been developing relentlessly from eighteenth-century thinkers like Sir William Blackstone, to the very conservative Victorian jurist John Austin, to bloom as lushly, if not rankly in the writings of such mid-twentieth century writers as Sir Ivor Jennings. What the later commentators failed to allow for was the reality of UK politics.

The best-known historian of the 1909–11 House of Lords crisis concludes that the passage of the Parliament Act made remarkably little difference.[1] It was an odd conclusion, because its passage cleared the way for civil war. Men like Asquith were asserting claims to exercise absolute power over situations, such as that which existed in the North of Ireland, which they neither understood nor would have sympathized with had they had a clearer understanding of it. Their worlds were Westminster and Whitehall. Nothing outside was real, in the sense that they expected everything within the jurisdiction of the Crown to be dealt with in accordance with what was administratively convenient in the light of a ritualized party ballet culminating in legislation. The fact that Nationalists and Unionists in Ireland were by 1914 armed, organized and mutually incompatible did not seem to penetrate the official mind with sufficient impact. Party structures narrowed sympathies rather than broadened them. Irish parties were just an extreme case, but there were indeed extreme. Of the politician who was to exercise by far the most sustained electoral appeal in twentieth-century Ireland, it had been said as early as 1918; 'If Ireland as a nation means what de Valera means by it, then Ulster is not part of that nation.'[2] The zero-sum game of Westminster politics, which was effectively to be transferred to Dublin and Belfast after 1922, had already failed disastrously before 1914. In the words of an authority:

> The final test of a constitution is whether it works. To put it another way, a successful constitution contains a 'rule of recognition', accepted by those to whom governance is confided, which determines whether actions are regarded as having authority. It is doubtful, to put it no higher, whether the British constitution passed that test in the years immediately before the

---

[1] Roy Jenkins *Mr Balfour's Poodle* (Collins, London 1968 edn), p. 269.
[2] Stephen Gwynn cited in John Bowman *De Valera and the Ulster Question 1917–1973* (Oxford University Press, pbk edn, Oxford 1983), p. 338.

outbreak of the Great War. It could be asked whether Britain still possessed the minimum conditions necessary for parliamentary government.[1]

The only possible criticism of this wholly wise summary of the situation is that it does not grasp that 'parliamentary government' had not existed for decades before 1914.

Not that this fact seems to have impinged as decisively as it should have on the deeply self-satisfied mind of Mr H. H. Asquith. He had enjoyed an 'assured succession' to Sir Henry Campbell-Bannerman as leader of the Liberal Party and Prime Minister in 1908. The Government had been faring badly in by-elections before his accession. By 1910, it had lost its overall majority in the Commons, being totally dependent on the support of the Irish Home Rule Party for survival. That fact decisively changed the hitherto profoundly confused situation which had followed from Gladstone's conversion to Home Rule for Ireland in 1885–86. Panicked into decision by unrealistic and alarmist reports of near anarchy in Ireland, Gladstone had then pressed for Home Rule with a degree of commitment far greater than that of the majority of the Liberal Party which rather reluctantly accepted his lead, and with an unrealistic urgency which exceeded that of contemporary Irish Home Rulers.[2] By 1910, what was at issue was the survival of the Government. It had to pass legislation acceptable to the Irish Home Rule Party to survive.

High policy was therefore predetermined and unlikely to be modified even by pressure from within the Liberal Party. Backbenchers had virtually no influence over the Cabinet. Asquith left the party whips to discipline the rankers. His style was deeply élitist, and be ran a 'highly departmentalised' Cabinet which could be, and in 1913–4 was, kept in ignorance of vitally important Irish and European negotiations conducted by the Premier and a few colleagues. Unfortunately, Asquith's grasp of Irish realities was no deeper than Gladstone's. His policy 'depended on the continued control of Home Rule policy by politicians at Westminster'.[3] By 1914, Nationalist and Unionist communities in Ireland were preparing for civil war, and British factions were on the edge of joining in the fight. Only the outbreak of the First World War in August 1914 averted the slide into chaos.

---

[1] G. H. L. Le May *The Victorian Constitution* (Duckworth, London 1979), p. 189.

[2] James Loughlin *Gladstone, Home Rule and the Ulster Question 1882–93* (Humanities Press, Atlantic Highlands, NJ 1987).

[3] Patricia Jalland *The Liberals and Ireland: The Ulster Question in British Politics to 1914* (Harvester Press, Brighton 1980), pp. 15 and 206.

3

The rich rewards of incompetence:
*Asquith and the saving of the sovereign
premiership 1914–16*

Mr Asquith, do you take an interest in the War?'

Lady Maud Tree

In this new experience you may find temptations both in wine and women.
You must entirely resist both temptations, and, while treating all women
with perfect courtesy, you should avoid any intimacy.
  from *Lord Kitchener's Advice*, to the British Expeditionary Force, 1914

There can be few more striking examples of the way in which Westminster
politicians tend to think in terms of their own claustrophobic but compulsive political ballet than the self-satisfaction which Asquith contrived to
carry from peace to war in the summer of 1914. It has been said that he
'did not make the mistake of regarding himself as indispensable', but this
was not really so. On a philosophical plane he could recognize that the
political system with which he was so familiar would inevitably generate
another prime minister if he were suddenly to drop dead. Though he knew
he had a good, well-trained mind, he was perfectly well aware that he was
no mental, let alone spiritual, giant. This he was happy to admit to himself
in a literary conceit which he penned to amuse himself in the early stages
of the war. In another sense, this was all false modesty, for he simply took
it for granted that the talents he had brought to the premiership, the office
itself, and the qualities which he believed himself to have developed in
that office and through holding it, rendered it unthinkable that he could
or would be ousted in the foreseeable future.
  As Prime Minister, Asquith felt that he 'had, or acquired a rather
specialized faculty of insight and manipulation in dealing with diversities
of character and temperament'. He was however well aware of the rule of
'Luck' in bringing him to the top of the greasy pole. Among the unforeseen
opportunities which had assisted his career he listed 'the disappearance of
possible competitors' and 'the special political conditions of your time'.
Most interesting of all was his view of the sudden outbreak of 'the Great

War', for he clearly saw it as yet another stroke of luck 'at a most critical and fateful moment in your career'. This latter phrase is perhaps as close as he ever came to facing up to the fact that he had led the United Kingdom of Great Britain and Ireland to the verge of bloody civil war, but at the time he penned it his mind was in fact in self-congratulatory mode, benignly conscious of the way in which his patient, judicious and generous mind, allied to 'the substantial advantage of personality and authority' had won for him not just the affectionate support of old friends such as R. B. Haldane, Edward Grey and Lord Crewe, but also 'the loyal attachment of men so diverse as Lloyd George and Winston Churchill, as Illingworth, McKenna and Montagu'. The names, however eminent some were or were to become, matter less than the tone of this Asquithian reverie.

He had no serious doubts about his hold over his colleagues, or his ability to maintain it indefinitely. They, in their turn, tended to feed his self-esteem. On one occasion in March 1915, Edwin Montagu, a political intimate who had been Financial Secretary to the Treasury from February 1914 and who had entered the Cabinet as Chancellor of the Duchy of Lancaster in February 1915, assured him that if there was any question of pressure on Asquith to resign, the whole Cabinet, including its two most self-obsessed opportunists, Lloyd George and Winston Churchill, would resign *en masse* to make it clear that there was no alternative to Asquith for the premiership. Asquith genuinely regarded himself, as long as his health and wits were unimpaired, as the indispensable father-figure without whom his team of colleagues could scarcely function. When he pointed out to a quarrelling Lloyd George and Reginald McKenna, also in March 1915, how difficult their tantrums were making his life, that pair promptly chanted the mantra about the way Asquith upheld the political cosmos and how, if he disappeared, the Cabinet was as dust.[1]

If he was a little too confident of his grip on his colleagues, Asquith was quite shrewd enough to grasp that if he wanted a continuous enjoyment of the respect and authority which, in his undemonstrative way, he assumed was his right, he needed to hold on to his office. He had already held it through a series of increasingly violent political storms. By nature he was, as his second wife later said, blessed with 'marvellously calm temper and even spirits', but there was calculation behind his surprisingly positive response to the UK's entry into a war which he would have preferred, of course, never to see, or to be able to keep at arm's length. In the previous crises of his reign in office, he had found that he could keep control of the largest party in a bitterly divided Commons, and of the premiership which that party made accessible to him. His own authority as effective head of the state, not to say the calm eye of the hurricane, had tended to emerge stronger rather than weaker in purely Westminster terms. This certainly happened in August 1914. The fashionable crowd in the Gallery of the House of Commons took it for granted that 'the Irish will be fighting each other this very night' when Asquith stood up and announced the indefinite shelving of the Amending Bill, which was the symbol of some hope of compromise over the Ulster obstacle to the third

---

[1] The text of Asquith's play, in which a recently-demised Asquith appears before Rhadamanthus, stern judge of Hades, is printed in Jenkins *Asquith*, pp. 373–6.

Irish Home Rule Bill. Margot Asquith, 'as if in a dream', told them crushingly that 'we are on the verge of a European War'. Asquith himself, though anxious, could see that British entry into the conflict would not only enable him to shelve the dangerous and insoluble Irish issue, but also precipitate a surge of support across party lines for the Government and, above all, the Premier.

Not much wonder that he displayed Olympian amusement at the panic he found when he met leaders of the City of London on the eve of war. He categorized the worried plutocrats as 'the greatest ninnies I have ever had to tackle', and claimed that he had found them 'in a state of funk, like old women chattering over tea cups in a Cathedral town'. The only serious worry Asquith had was that the decision to enter the war might gravely divide the Liberal Party. Here, with some massive assistance from the German invasion of Belgium, he was lucky. The wave of indignation which German behaviour provoked helped to ensure that only two ministers resigned: John Morley and John Burns. Neither carried a great deal of political weight, though Morley, as the author of the official biography of Gladstone, could with some effort be depicted as guardian of the Gladstonian Ark of the Covenant. Asquith accepted their decisions with characteristic generosity, and retained occasional social relations with both, to the eternal credit of all involved. Asquith said, after reading Morley's letter of resignation, that he would miss him very much, and that Morley was 'one of the most distinguished men living'. It was scarcely true, but then mutual puffery was *de rigueur* amongst the Liberal mandarinate.[1]

Thereafter, the political impact of the Great War domestically was all the Prime Minister could have hoped for, and indeed more. All the political parties, including both the Irish ones, rallied behind Asquith in a way which would have been inconceivable a week or two before. The mass of public opinion, in so far as it could be judged, seemed to move the same way. Ministers like Winston Churchill as First Lord of the Admiralty, and Grey, the Foreign Secretary, were able to greatly enhance their public stature by their actions and words as war broke out. Grey even coined his only memorable phrase in a lifetime of speaking for a living, when he referred to the lights going out all over Europe. The appointment of a reluctant Field Marshal Lord Kitchener to the War Office proved a tremendously successful piece of public relations. It hardly mattered that thereafter it rapidly became apparent to his senior colleagues that his appointment was a disaster in administrative terms. He formed the compelling image which made up that most famous of all recruiting posters ('Your Country Needs You'), but the Great Poster himself had no capacity whatever to run the sort of bureaucratic machinery required to raise and supply armies for a major European war. He did very rarely have a flash of irrational but penetrating insight, like the one which told him that the war was likely to last much longer than most people expected, but he was incapable of delegating authority or decisions; tended to wreck rather than build up organizations; and retained the penny-pinching habits on which,

---

[1] The quotations from Asquith and Margot Asquith are drawn from *The Autobiography of Margot Asquith* ed. Mark Bonham Carter (Eyre and Spottiswoode, London 1962), pp. 282–3 and 294.

rather than on tactical flair—for he had none—he had built his early reputation as a general.

Reverses and absurdities occurred, but they were often balanced by
victories, and they appeared to do little to shake the government's image.
After his impressively vigorous mobilization of the fleet for war, Winston
Churchill, for example, had involved himself in, indeed to some extent
created, the tragi-comedy of the defence of Antwerp. Before the war, his
addiction to reading lives of Napoleon had sent a tingle of apprehension
through his colleagues. War brought out at once the delusions of military
genius which surged within this Major of Hussars. He inserted himself
within the besieged Belgian port of Antwerp, where he became an embarrassment to the high command of the doomed garrison and an object of
considerable annoyance to the troops. He bombarded his long-suffering
Cabinet colleagues with telegrams in which he offered to resign as First
Lord of the Admiralty if they would grant him the high military rank
necessary to launch him on his glittering military career. Kitchener, bizarrely, offered to make him a lieutenant-general, but the rest of the Cabinet
was merely provoked to Homeric laughter, whilst Asquith sensibly ordered
him home to the Admiralty.[1]

The loss of a large part of the Royal Naval Division, which Churchill had
ill-advisedly thrown into Antwerp (much of it spent the war in internment
in the neutral Holland to which it had retreated), provoked a howl of
abuse, especially in the Tory press. However, Churchill was *sui generis*.
Even Bonar Law, whose response to the whole episode was the perfectly
rational one of saying that it merely confirmed his view that Churchill had
an unbalanced mind, added that Winston was unusual and had ability.
The political rally behind the government went on. The long retreat of the
allied armies after the battle of Mons finally came to a halt with the
undoubted allied victory at the battle of the Marne, which made it clear
that Paris would not fall. The only sizeable German naval squadron at
large, commanded by Admiral von Spee, crossed the Pacific from China
to sink a British cruiser force commanded by Admiral 'Kit' Craddock off
the Chilean port of Coronel on the first day of November 1914. Two British
cruisers went down with all hands, but retribution came quickly as Churchill and Fisher (who had been called out of retirement at age 74 in October
to serve as First Sea Lord) despatched two of the new battle-cruisers, with
supporting cruiser units, to the South Atlantic. Von Spee had the bad luck
to blunder into them in the Falkland Islands, where he was promptly
annihilated. The British public was unaware that Admiral Sir Frederick
Doveton Sturdee's victory had displayed grave deficiencies in the design
of the battle-cruisers, and spectacularly inefficient long-range gunnery by
the Royal Navy. The moral symmetry of the Coronel-Falklands episode
was deeply satisfying. Even the emergence in the winter of 1914–15 of

---

[1] The extraordinary tale of Churchill's sub-Napoleonic antics in Antwerp is well told
in Ted Morgan *Churchill: The rise to failure 1874–1915* (Triad Panther edn, London 1984),
pp. 458–67. He makes the fair point that they had, initially, the endorsement of the
Cabinet.

deadlocked trench warfare all along the Western Front did not immediately shake support for the government.[1]

Though it was Harold Wilson many decades later who coined the phrase that a week was a long time in politics, Asquith acted tacitly on the same assumption in 1914–15, treating the march of events as something of an exercise in serendipity. It was not so much that he found convenient events, as that he was able gratefully to seize on convenient aspects of events which found him. Thus the fact that the version of the Schlieffen plan which guided German strategy at the start of hostilities involved an immediate violation of Belgian neutrality, in order to outflank the French armies, not only helped Asquith greatly in domestic politics, but also enabled him to avoid any definition of war aims. Apart from the odd military lunatic like General Sir Henry Wilson,[2] few members of the ruling élites in the pre-1914 UK actually wanted to fight Germany more or less for the sake of fighting. It is however very clear that Asquith, Grey, Crewe and the other members of the inner circle of the Liberal government were committed to at least trying to bring the UK into any outright Franco-German clash, on the French side of course, but subject to political feasibility in the precariously-balanced and venomous atmosphere of contemporary Westminster politics. This would have been true whether Germany had invaded Belgium or not, so it is clear that the British Expeditionary Force was fighting for much more than Belgium. Nevertheless, for a long time, the only specific British war aim was the restoration of Belgium. Asquith made a series of speeches in the first weeks of the war in London, Dublin, and Cardiff, in which there was much stress on Belgium and the rights of small nations, but precious little else, apart from vague and bombastic verbiage about the need to 'crush Prussian militarism'.

The latter two words—Prussian militarism—were thereby sent into orbit in the English-speaking world where they proved one of those echoing clichés which reverberate misleadingly down the decades because they spare the user much thought and effort to understand something much disliked. They were still being used, in the highest circles, at the end of the Second World War. In many ways, the trouble was that the old Prussia, the 'little Great Power' with its traditions of limited aims, prudent government and economical use of force, had committed suicide by swallowing so much of Central Europe in the late nineteenth century to form the Wilhelminian Reich. The Third Reich, for all Hitler's cult of Frederick the Great, was a very un-Prussian affair.

Asquith was lucky enough to die in 1928 before he could see Hitler's Germany, but even in 1914 he was not by nature inclined to the vague,

---

[1] Glyn Williams and John Ramsden *Ruling Britannia: a political history of Britain 1688–1988* (Longman pbk edn, London 1990), p. 364, makes the point about the rally of support behind the Asquith government very succinctly.

[2] In 1911, whilst touring the Metz battlefields of the 1870–1 Franco-Prussian war, Wilson had laid and left a map showing the proposed areas of concentration of a future British Expeditionary Force in France at the feet of a statue symbolizing France at Mars-la-Tour. Insanity is the kindest explanation of this irresponsible gesture recounted in Major-General Sir C. E. Caldwell *Field Marshall Sir Henry Wilson* (2 vols., Cassell, London 1927), I, 105.

the inflammatory and the inelegant. Yet he increasingly seemed to regard these few speeches as Holy Writ, deprecating any questions on the subject of British war aims by curt references to those speeches. For nearly three years the peoples of the United Kingdom were asked to accept these increasingly dated records of ephemeral performances as sufficient explanation for the monstrous toll which war was taking of their sons. Political convenience was of course the basic reason for Asquith's position. Any clear definition of war aims would have required long and difficult negotiations with major allies. A series of secret agreements were building up on specific issues with France, Italy and Russia, which he was pledged not to reveal. He probably had few concrete ideas of his own, and could certainly see little point in formulating them before a decisive military defeat of Germany. More sinister was the fact that bipartisan support for war terms was not available in Westminster. As late as April 1915, when Harcourt, the Liberal Colonial Secretary, asked the Tory leaders in the Commons and Lords, Bonar Law and Lansdowne, to comment on a memorandum he had significantly entitled 'Spoils', they flatly refused, for they were hoping that a Liberal government might split over future peace terms, and they obviously meant to try to detach Liberal hard-liners. There was no damn nonsense in the Unionist Party about ceasing to pursue party advantage during a war. It had agreed to a partial suspension of parliamentary confrontation because it rightly saw the war as a priceless opportunity for the party.[1]

So there was bipartisan support for not telling anyone what the United Kingdom's war aims were, which suited Asquith very well. It also suited his Foreign Secretary Grey, since even the most banal platitude about upholding the European balance would have rung very hollow in the light of what he was preparing secretly to concede to Russia, and what a victorious Russia would take anyway. Reinforcing this bipartisan understanding that the less said about the purposes of the war the better, was a formal machinery of press control and censorship. In the early days of the conflict, two government agencies were hastily invented: the Press Bureau and the Foreign Office News Department. In fact the latter, given the Foreign Office tradition of extreme secrecy, was never more pervasive or paranoid than under Sir Edward Grey and with good reason. Autonomous, though connected with the Press Bureau, the Foreign Office News Department was designed mainly to manipulate foreign journalists. It disgorged information erratically, reluctantly and selectively, which still meant that slightly more was known publicly than would otherwise have been the case.[2] The Press Bureau, though mild compared with its Continental equivalents, was able, with the help of strict censorship of army communications and a ban on war correspondents in the BEF lines, to control the flow of information about the fighting, mainly by suppressing it totally. The upshot was often grotesque. There were two strange consequences to the battle of Mons. One was that British newspapers had no option but to

---

[1] V. H. Rothwell *British War Aims and Peace Diplomacy 1914–1918* (Clarendon Press, Oxford 1971), pp. 18–20.

[2] Stephen Koss *The Rise and Fall of the Political Press in Britain* (2 vols., Hamish Hamilton, London 1984), II, pp. 240–1.

report it on the basis of accounts issued in Berlin, which were available to them. The other was that this day's fighting, which cost the BEF 1,600 casualties and held up the superior forces of von Kluck by a day, rapidly entered the realm of legend, complete with divine manifestation in the shape of the Angels of Mons.[1]

Even before August 1914, there had been evidence that the Prime Minister's contact with reality was dangerously tenuous. After the outbreak of war, his short-term success in neutralizing threats to his position cocooned him in a profoundly unreal world of his own making. His own official biographer, J. A. Spender, referred in the memoirs he published in 1925 to 'the virtual suspension of Parliament' after 1914.[2] The bulk of MPs had become even more irrelevant as individuals than usual when the Unionist and Liberal front benches started to operate in tacit collusion. In nine months of remaining Liberal government, Asquith gave one speech surveying the development of the war. It was in March 1915, was not debated and did not mention France. Churchill, who with characteristic frankness, did try to initiate discussions of war policy a couple of times in this period, merely embarrassed the House of Commons. The Unionist and Liberal Whips rapidly negotiated a party truce which ensured that the parties would not compete against one another in by-elections, so the appalling possibility that segments of the electorate might have a voice in the political process was rapidly eliminated. Since Kitchener sat in the Lords, the upper chamber did regularly discuss the war, on the basis of a monthly statement from that not very articulate warrior. War aims were a forbidden topic. Much military information was suppressed. Collusion between the party élites was so pervasive that Austen Chamberlain, with his unfortunate gift for honesty which did him so much harm in the company he kept, speculated privately how shocked the public would be if they knew what was going on.[3]

They would have been even more shocked, especially after the publicity given to Lord Kitchener's sombre appeal to the members of the BEF to shun wine and women, if they had been fully cognizant of the Premier's life style. Of course, it was easy enough for Kitchener, whose sexual tastes were homoerotic, to talk about forswearing an opposite sex to which he was not attracted. Lloyd George, whose hobby was copulation, would no doubt have contended that indulging his over-active libido positively sustained his work drive and political ambition. It would be very difficult to make a similar case for Asquith. As befitted a competent barrister, he had the ability to shift a great deal of paperwork quickly and efficiently within a finite time. His capacity to delegate to able colleagues, and the excellence of the chairmanship he offered them in the Cabinet were beyond question, but he had always been self-indulgent as well as quietly self-satisfied. He drank heavily, to the point where he was of an evening occasionally decidedly unsteady in the House of Commons; hence his derisory nickname 'Squiffy'. This behaviour did not change with the

[1] Barbara W. Tuchman *August 1914* (Constable, London 1962) pp. 275–80.
[2] J. A. Spender *The Public Life* (2 vols., Cassell, London 1925) II, p. 122.
[3] A. J. P. Taylor 'Politics in the First World War' in A. J. P. Taylor *Essays in English History* (Hamish Hamilton, London 1976), pp. 220–2.

advent of war, any more than did the Prime Minister's penchant for frequent games of bridge and long restorative automobile rides in Kent. After the early spasm of vague speechifying across the breadth of the UK these rides were about the only regular journeys he made. He did not, for example, go near his constituency.

What he did do, with great frequency and on occasion at considerable length, was write to Venetia Stanley, the youngest child of Lord Sheffield, a young woman in her late twenties with whom he had fallen deeply in love. He both received letters from and wrote letters to her during Cabinet meetings, to the not inconsiderable vexation of some of his colleagues. Emotionally, this unconsummated affair helped stabilize Asquith until in July 1915 Venetia unexpectedly married his intimate colleague Edwin Montagu. The content of the letters is alarming, for in order to attract her, Asquith not only leaked Cabinet secrets like a sieve, but also enclosed on occasion highly classified original military documents, not to mention detailed military information. During the first three months of 1915, the Premier was writing to Miss Stanley an average of nearly fifty letters a month. Four in one day was the record. To contend that this involvement was no more an impediment to efficiency than Lloyd George's habit of singing Welsh hymns is unconvincing. Asquith was losing his grip.

Perceptive Liberals had realized at an early stage that the mere outbreak of war pushed their party to the verge of disaster. They could even see the stages by which the party might topple into irreversible ruin. Attorney-General Sir John Simon said in August 1914 that a coalition government 'would assuredly be the grave of Liberalism'. He was right, yet within nine months, and against his own declared preference and instincts, Asquith had dismantled his Liberal administration to form a coalition with his former Unionist enemies. By September 1914, internal politics had been reduced at the highest level to a duel between a sexagenarian Premier of self-indulgent tastes, and a spectrum of Unionist politicians ranging from the glumly cooperative Bonar Law to such rabidly hostile extreme right-wing MPs as W. Joynson Hicks. It was a struggle which Asquith steadily lost on two fronts: propaganda and intrigue.

He conspicuously failed to uphold Liberal principles in the face of vituperative Tory press campaigns designed to force him into inconsistent and impossible positions. His response, at the time and later, was to complain bitterly about the failure of the Unionist press to accept the party truce which had reduced the legislature to total insignificance. This was unrealistic, for one effect of closing down formal political debate in Westminster was bound to be to drive it into a highly politicized metropolitan press. The political and journalistic élites were intertwined to the point where Asquith's contempt for even the Liberal press ('written by boobies for boobies') was ill-advised. Furthermore, the Unionist press was bigger, better-funded and commercially more viable than its Liberal equivalent. Its sustained whipping-up of anti-German hysteria, quite deliberately linked with attacks on Liberal appointees and ministers as 'pro-German', was one of the most degrading episodes in modern British history, and Asquith offered little resistance to it.

Lord Chancellor R. B. Haldane was denounced as deliberately sabotaging the early despatch of the BEF, which as Secretary for War he had done more than anyone to design specifically for service in France. He was alleged to have described Germany as his 'spiritual home' (which he had not), and campaigns in the Harmsworth and other Unionist press produced abusive letters by the thousand. Sent to Haldane's house in sacks, they were appropriately disposed of by the kitchenmaid.[1] The Home Secretary, Reginald McKenna, was denounced for alleged softness in rounding up aliens. Prince Louis of Battenberg, on the strength of his German name was hounded out of his post as First Sea Lord. Ironically, Asquith paid very heavily for his departure. By recalling Lord Fisher to the post, the government yoked together a young autocrat, Winston Churchill as First Lord of the Admiralty, and an old and irascible one, Fisher. When, in May 1915, Fisher executed a characteristically perverse and eccentric resignation, it helped to push Asquith into a political crisis.

Given the outrageous demands for freedom from all political control which Fisher made as a condition for withdrawing his resignation, not to mention his crazy schemes for using the Royal Navy to land forces on the Baltic coast of Germany, his resignation was as much a public blessing as Kitchener's eventual drowning. It was characteristic of Asquith to send J. A. Spender, his confidant and the editor of the *Westminster Gazette*, to try to persuade the sulking Fisher to remain in office by assuring him that Winston Churchill was to be replaced at the Admiralty by A. J. Balfour. Spender recorded that Fisher 'stated in emphatic and somewhat racy language that he was even more unwilling to serve with Mr Balfour than with Mr Churchill'. Equally characteristic of the Unionist leadership was the letter which Bonar Law penned to Asquith on 17 May 1915, saying that he and Lansdowne had heard 'with dismay' that Fisher had resigned and that if the desperately undesirable possibility of 'a controversial discussion in the House of Commons' was to be avoided 'some change in the constitution of the Government seems to us inevitable'.[2] Yet again, politics were the game of manipulating a Premier who could be threatened with 'a controversial discussion' in the Commons, as the ultimate deterrent.

Others had played, or tried to play this game since the outbreak of the war. John Redmond, the Irish Home Rule Party leader, had applied pressure to Asquith to try to keep the lightweight and politically inept Lord and Lady Aberdeen in the Viceregal Lodge in Dublin. Asquith had had enough of them. Redmond was anxious to retain Augustine Birrell as Chief Secretary of Ireland. He was an Asquith crony who did indeed serve, to the permanent detriment of his reputation, until 1916. After a coalition was formed in 1915, Redmond even tried to veto the inclusion in the government, which he decline to join, of his arch-rival in Ireland, Edward Carson. The cooperation between the Liberals and Unionists had in fact deprived Redmond of his pre-war power to deprive Asquith of a majority. The Unionist leaders, on the other hand, had become essential for Asquith's peaceful tenure of Number Ten Downing Street. Their acquiescence was essential for the indefinite postponement of the General Election

---

[1] Dudley Sommer *Haldane of Cloan: his life and times 1856–1928* (Allen and Unwin, London 1960) pp. 315–9.

[2] J. A. Spender and Cyril Asquith *Life of Herbert Henry Asquith, Lord Oxford and Asquith* (2 vols., Hutchison, London 1932) II, pp. 164–5.

originally due in 1915. From day to day they could help keep the legislature in a state of suspended animation.

Bonar Law certainly thought that he had Asquith over a barrel though he did not exploit his advantage for purely personal advancement. Fisher's resignation was tied up with the general recognition that the attempt to force the Dardanelles, at first purely with naval forces, but later by combined operations, had failed and had become not, as designed, an alternative to the bloody stalemate on the Western Front, but another stalemate on the Gallipoli Peninsula. Though the plan had originated with Kitchener and enjoyed full Cabinet backing, the blame for its failure had come to rest, to an unfair degree, on the man who in the end had admittedly become its most vociferous advocate: Winston Churchill. In many ways, it was the least indefensible of a string of episodes which enabled the Unionists, who hated him as a political turncoat anyway, to denounce Churchill as an impulsive and unbalanced menace. If Admiral de Robeck had been less deterred by his heavy battleship losses at an earlier stage, and if General Ian Hamilton had shown more drive at the time of the first landings, the scheme might well have succeeded; knocked Turkey out of the war; greatly assisted Russia; and provided some alternative to the costly deadlock which was all the British high command offered in France. As it was, it failed, and on top of Antwerp and his role in precipitating the Curragh incident, it was bound to damage Churchill. A habitual gambler cannot afford that amount of bad luck.

Although some historians have tried to deny it, Asquith himself was clear that the crisis precipitated by Fisher was all the more visceral because it intermeshed with one which had been festering for some time: the so-called 'shell scandal'. Kitchener was notoriously unenthusiastic about the squandering of vast amounts of ammunition by British generals, which did not stop the BEF from firing off more shells in the battle of Neuve Chapelle in March 1915 than had been expended in nearly three years of the Boer War. When it had run its unsatisfactory course, Sir John French, commander of the BEF saw fit to feed criticisms of Asquith and Kitchener (whom he clearly regarded as an honorary civilian) to the press. By the time French was contemplating the failure of his infantry assaults at the battle of Festubert, he had convinced himself that failure was the fault of, as he later wrote, 'the Government as then constituted'. The phrase dates from 1919, when French published a disingenuous account of the events of 1915, but it clearly reflects his contemporary mood, for he sent his ADC, Captain Guest MP, to England to lay a documented case against Asquith's government before sympathetic politicians like Balfour and Bonar Law and, very significantly, Lloyd George. The material was leaked to Charles à Court Repington, 'the Gorgeous Wreckington', military correspondent of *The Times*. Failure to organize adequate supplies of shell to permit victory and breakthroughs in France added to Asquith's deficiencies in his enemies' eyes.

The trouble with this issue is that it just possibly was grossly exaggerated from start to finish. The British generals of the Great War were a varied crew. The spectrum ranged from Sir Douglas Haig, the highly-educated but uncommunicative scion of a Scottish whisky dynasty, to 'Wully' Robertson, the English ranker who rose to be Field Marshal Sir William

Robertson, Kitchener's semi-official keeper. Robertson dropped his 'h's' to the bitter end. In between the spectrum passed through the virtually ineducable Sir Henry Wilson who, despite being a Wilson of Currygrane, looked, talked and acted like a stage Irishman, which is what in many ways he was. He had flunked the entry exams to Woolwich (Royal Artillery) twice, Sandhurst three times, and sneaked into the army via a commission in the Irish Militia. What this band of brothers had in common was an invincible reluctance to admit they ever made a mistake, allied to an iron conviction that failure, especially bloody and pointless failure, meant that someone else was at fault. Churning the battlefield with a thousand more rounds per gun, however, was demonstrably not the answer. Significantly the ever more incompetent Russian generals, generated by what has justly been called the baroque manpower policies of Tsarist Russia, sang the same song on the Eastern Front.[1]

From Gallipoli to France in the spring of 1915, the performance of British generals had been dismal. In the Middle East, at the head of the Persian Gulf, where two Indian Army brigades had seized control of Basra from the Turks at the end of November 1914, a fresh disaster was brewing. A 'forward' faction in the ill-equipped Indian Army, supported by its elderly Commander-in-Chief, Sir Beauchamp Duff, was hell-bent on trying to conquer Mesopotamia with forces which the principal field commander, Major Charles Townshend, thought dangerously inadequate. The brutal fact was that the senior ranks of the Edwardian British Army were as skilful at backstairs politics as they were uninspired when faced with unpalatable problems on the battlefield. They were, after all, part of a self-conscious ruling élite. Kitchener had become one of the victims of the situation, but he had himself shown feline skills as a political manipulator some years earlier. As Commander-in-Chief India, he had defeated and driven from office no less a viceroy than Lord Curzon. Despite the exaggerated language used in his private diary by a soldier like Sir Henry Wilson, which suggested a deep division between 'brass-hats' and 'frocks' (i.e. military and civilians) the problem was that there was no sharp line between the military and civilian sections of the UK élite. The political generals all had networks of contacts with the press and the politicians. Without exception, their political sympathies were strongly Unionist. A Unionist prime minister with a clear majority could conceivably have brought them to heel, but in the course of the Great War they faced Liberal premiers who either could not or, in the cast of Asquith in 1914–5, would not challenge the Unionist Party to a showdown on military issues. As a result, the generals became in practice a militant conservative trade union capable of sustaining an essentially political relationship with the Government, in the sense that there existed between them an unstable balance of power. Solidarity, job-protection, and resistance to radical re-thinking of approaches to work were, naturally, prominent features of the military posture.

Asquith could still impose his will on an extremely unhappy Liberal Party. He could have faced Bonar Law's challenge in the Commons and

---

[1] Norman Stone *The Eastern Front 1914–1917* (Hodder and Stoughton, London 1975), esp. Chap. 1 and pp. 245–63.

almost certainly survived. He had enough Liberal, Labour and Irish Home Rule Party votes behind him. Instead, he chose to form a coalition in May 1915. A meeting of over a hundred Liberal MPs was only deterred from passing a resolution hostile to the decision by a twenty-minute harangue from Asquith concluding with a straight threat of resignation if the motion were passed. Unlike Gladstone, Asquith was not an incontinent wielder of bogus resignations. He meant what he said, and by repeating that threat he reduced his party to impotence in 1915–6. They were prisoners of the prestige and power of initiative in the office of prime minister. Of the Cabinet this was as true as of the rank and file. Though Asquith cut a very favourable deal with his new partners, the ruthless dismissal of Haldane, and the much less surprising demotion of Churchill marked, along with the entry of a significant Unionist minority into the Cabinet, yet another step along the path which led to the irreversible emasculation of the Liberal Party as a force in British politics.

At a superficial level, Asquith did notably well in keeping the Unionist leader, Bonar Law, to the minor post of Colonial Secretary. A Glasgow Ulsterman born in Canada who had never been to Oxford was, in Asquith's condescending metropolitan eyes, an 'ill-bred' troglodyte from realms of outer darkness. It was apparently quite deliberate policy, to judge by a contemporary Asquith memorandum, '. . . to prevent B. Law taking the office of either Munitions or the Exchequer'.[1] The Exchequer went, despite violent Unionist hostility, to R. B. McKenna, one of Asquith's closest Liberal colleagues, while Lloyd George moved to the Ministry of Munitions, which had been created to take the munitions issue out of Kitchener's hands. Though it is fashionable to cite contemporary forecasts of doom and gloom for the first occupant of this new job, it is clear that many insiders deemed it a priceless opportunity for any competent administrator. Both Balfour and Kitchener, neither of whom wished Bonar Law ill at this juncture, wanted him to take it, and Austen Chamberlain, the most straightforward of his colleagues, argued that the first two reasons for Bonar Law doing it were:

1. Because it is the biggest thing you can do in this country
2. Because it can *now* be made a success[2]

Asquith was laying a rod in pickle for himself by handing that opportunity to Lloyd George, even if the latter had at the time no intention of challenging his grip on the premiership. Asquith's consistent underestimation of Bonar Law was almost as dangerous. Law might have a negative mind, but it was very shrewd, and unlike so many self-styled 'brilliant' members of the political élite, he was hard-working, and not consumed with conceit.

Amongst those whom Asquith regarded with more benevolent condescension was his nominal monarch, George V. Asquith found the royal humour ('such as it is') pedestrian, while the royal mind appeared to the Premier to be full of views of such banality that it probably provided a fair mirror of the mind of 'the man in the tube', which was the Asquithian

---

[1] Memorandum by Asquith, 26 May 1915, cited in full in Robert Blake *The Unknown Prime Minister*, p. 251.
[2] Cited in *ibid.*, p. 250.

updated version of the man on the Clapham omnibus.[1] In practice, Asquith not only understood intellectually that the prime minister was the reigning monarch of the UK, but also increasingly felt that he himself reigned by divine right. This did not mean that he lost his political cunning. On the contrary, since his own retention of office was an absolute good in his mind, he displayed infinite flexibility in avoiding the head-on clashes with powerful groups which might have curtailed that tenure. His own followers in the Liberal Party at Westminster hardly ranked as such a group and the former Liberal chief Whip Lord Murray of Elibank was not the only one to deplore the Premier's increasing neglect of them. It was the right wing of the Liberal Party, of whom Lloyd George had become, paradoxically, the standard-bearer, and above all the Unionists who could put pressure on Asquith. The barriers between those two groups were already eroding as the Northcliffe press called for Lloyd George to head a new coalition. It is true that close contact with Lloyd George's egotism, trickiness, and self-seeking came as something of a shock to the mainstream Unionist leadership. They even began to recognize sterling qualities in Reginald McKenna. However, the logic of events, partially laid down in theory as early as 1910, was to overcome personal preferences. The *Manchester Guardian* perceptively remarked, a fortnight after the formation of the new government that 'The attempt to stampede the country into conscription is now in full swing'.[2]

That an acceptance of conscription, even 'for the duration', would eat the heart out of the Liberal Party was a fact of which the Unionist politicians and press were acutely aware. That was why they had been so attracted by the concept ever since 1906. By 1915, the passionate proponents of conscription within the Cabinet knew that they could blackmail their opponents with the brute fact that the life of the Commons automatically terminated at the end of January 1916 unless it was extended by legislation which required the agreement of the Lords. Given the huge Unionist majority in the Lords, that agreement was not likely to be forthcoming without critical concessions to conscriptionist pressure. That the Unionists would win an election was fairly clear. It had not been the Labour Party which had been steadily undermining the Liberals, particularly in local elections before 1914, it had been the Unionists. The undoubted loss of prestige by Asquith's administration in 1914–5 would merely have accentuated an established trend: the 'strange revival of a Tory England'.[3] Of this Bonar Law was well aware, but both as a patriot and as a fully paid-up (if at times intellectually detached) member of the British Establishment, he must have been appalled by the prospect of the amount of dirty linen which would have to be washed in public, if there was an election. Far

[1] Asquith to Venetia Stanley, 18 March 1915, in *Asquith Letters to Venetia Stanley* No. 355, pp. 487–8.
[2] Cited in Trevor Wilson *The Downfall of the Liberal Party* (Collins, Fontana edn, London 1968) p. 69. This work provides an excellent overview of Liberalism in 1915–6, even if it does ascribe more conscious Machiavellianism to Lloyd George than the record appears to warrant.
[3] Chris Cook, 'Labour and the downfall of the Liberal Party, 1906–14' in Alan Sked and Chris Cook, eds *Crisis and Controversy: essays in honour of A. J. P. Taylor* (Macmillan, London 1976) pp. 38–65.

better to keep the public in ignorance of just what a shambles the Great War had become even by 1915, especially if he could get his way by other means.

Asquith did not disappoint him, though privately it is clear that he detested conscription; knew that there was profound hostility to it in both the Liberal Party and Labour; and very shrewdly suspected that at least in the short run it might not produce as good results as the voluntary system. Nevertheless, he slithered towards it with a series of 'compromises' which were patently bogus and which sold the pass of principle. The Derby recruiting scheme of October 1915 was nominally a bid to retain voluntarism, but so barbed with threats of compulsion if it failed that the next step, in November, which was an open threat to coerce unmarried men disguised as a pledge to married men, seemed natural. With Lloyd George threatening resignation by December, Asquith introduced conscription for 'unmarried slackers' in January 1916, and their lordships, strangely slow to deal with the bill prolonging the life of the Commons, were pleased to pass it, after the Commons accepted the conscription measure.

The Premier's argument that he was still an opponent of general conscription rang hollow. By March, Lloyd George was on the rampage demanding conscription of married men. There was a strong case for the Liberal Party pinning an anti-conscription flag to its mast, and going down to defeat in an election. At a time when issues like temperance, denominational education, home rule and even free trade were losing their grip on the core UK electorate—the English one—the Liberal Party desperately needed to offer alternatives relevant to contemporary problems. The Liberals would certainly have had strong support from Irish Home Rulers. They could have fought with every chance of success for the soul of Labour, and they could have hoped to emerge as a hard-hitting opposition. They would have been denounced as 'unpatriotic', but then in the Unionist vocabulary, that term had been interchangeable with 'Liberal' for decades. Instead, Asquith staggered on with more and more disreputable 'compromises', hounded by Lloyd George, by press barons like Northcliffe and Rothermere, and by a vociferous band of Unionist hard-liners led by Carson. The latter had stalked out of office after five months to challenge both Asquith and the more moderate Unionist leadership, which wanted to play along with Asquith.

The Prime Minister's endless prevarication in the face of issues which might cost him office not only appalled all the Liberal factions, but also earned him the contempt of his Unionist allies. The second Earl of Selborne, who was in the Cabinet as President of the Board of Agriculture 1915–6, recorded his amusement in October 1915 when Asquith, faced with a Cabinet where he would have to come off the fence one way or another over a conscription issue, simply sent his colleagues a message saying he was ill. Selborne's amusement was greatly increased by that rarest of phenomena: a Kitchener wisecrack. Kitchener said to Selborne: 'He is a great man; I thought he had exhausted all possible sources of delay; I never thought of the diarrhoea.'[1] By the latter part of 1916,

---

[1] Selborne to Robert Palmer, 20 October 1915, printed in George Boyce ed., *The Crisis of British Unionism* p. 152.

Asquith's position was impossible. Having surrendered virtually every point of principle, he needed military success to keep his coalition going. Instead, he was staring at a mixture of failure, tragedy and farce.

The Russian offensive under Brusilov against the Austro-Hungarian forces in Galicia in June was the beginning of a period of optimism, when the allies appeared to have the initiative on every front. By August, when they bribed Romania into entering the war by means of lavish promises of Austro-Hungarian territory, the situation looked even better for the allies, though Haig and Robertson continued their fanatical opposition to any diversion of troops or resources to the Balkans from their own offensive on the Somme, designed decisively to defeat Germany in the decisive theatre. Thereafter, everything went sour. The Brusilov offensive stalled. The Germans were able to use the railways of Central Europe to concentrate forces capable not only of repulsing the Romanian offensive, but also of crushing Romania. All that country's treacherous attack on Austria-Hungary did was make Romanian oil and grain available to Germany on easier terms whilst adding the need to prop up a residual Romanian front to the burdens of an overstrained Russian army. Serbia had already been destroyed. The Bulgarians proved capable of containing the allied forces concentrated at Salonika, whose advance might have relieved the Romanians. Faced with a stubborn refusal by King Constantine of Greece to declare war on Bulgaria, Franco-British manipulation of Greece behind the mask of a cooperative politician—Venizelos—became patently contemptuous of 'the rights of small nations', which had featured so prominently in their early war propaganda.

December saw the evacuation of British forces from their positions along the Dardanelles, after Kitchener, during a personal inspection in November, had decided that the Gallipoli campaign was doomed. Asquith was left with a Royal Commission into the fiasco, as he was with the parallel fiasco in Mesapotamia. There the Indian Army's *folie de grandeur* had culminated in the cutting-off, besieging and surrender of General Townshend in Kut. The Turks severely defeated several relief attempts. The Muslim element in Townshend's force proved unreliable in the face of Turkish propaganda. Kurdish irregular guards subjected captured British troops from the UK to predictable atrocities. On the Somme Haig, though always promising an imminent German collapse, was throwing away the New Armies of highly-motivated volunteers raised by Kitchener, with a prodigal hand, yielding neither strategic nor tactical gains of any consequence. As early as August 1916, F. E. Smith, then Attorney General, circulated to the Cabinet a memo by Winston Churchill (who had left to seek death or glory in France in late 1915) arguing that the offensive was destructive and pointless and should be called off. 'Wully' Robertson denounced it as a 'damnable paper'. He would.[1]

Asquith's last political lifebelt, oddly enough, had been the Easter Rebellion in Dublin in 1916. This was a deeply confused and confusing event. It would have been impossible without the heritage of political

[1] Cited in David French *British Strategy and War Aims 1914–16* (Allen and Unwin, London 1986), p. 205. This book is by far the best guide to the paradoxical position of the UK (unable to afford either to lose or win) by 1916.

deadlock and paramilitary organization which Ireland carried into the Great War from its pre-war crisis. Most non-Irish politicians at Westminster were relieved to forget that nightmare when the guns of August boomed out in Europe, and they could tell themselves they had a greater and more desperate crisis with which to wrestle, but the men who commanded (in so far as they could be commanded) the Irish volunteers thought differently. After a fall in numbers earlier in the war, recruiting had picked up, and there were 16,000 admittedly very poorly armed men by April 1916, all of whom regarded any attempt by Westminster to disband or disarm them, or impose general conscription, as a *casus belli*. If such justifications for violence did not arise during the war, the leadership of the Irish Volunteers saw their role primarily as a post-war pressure group for Home Rule, but they drilled openly and practised for future guerrilla warfare in an emotion-laden atmosphere of which an embarrassing number of extremist groups tried to take advantage. Up to a point, they were remarkably contradictory groups. The one most remote from reality and from the others was probably the Irish Socialist Republican Party led by the former Edinburgh carter James Connolly. Connolly had come out of the great Dublin labour dispute or lockout of 1913 with a 200-man Irish Citizen Army which appeared at first almost as absurd as its leader's theories about Ireland spearheading a socialist revolution in the West. Though automatically canonized not only by Catholic Ireland but also by Marxists after his death in the rebellion, Connolly's thought was little short of daft, and his attempt to will away the abyss between socialism and the Catholic Irish Nationalism he wanted to make its bedfellow was doomed.

None of this mattered compared with his passionate commitment to violence in 1916, though of course he was not the high priest of a vision of redemptive blood-sacrifice. That position by sheer strength of mind and personality went to Patrick Henry Pearse, an alarming young man whose welcome of war in 1914 had been as gushing as that of the sillier romantic poets in England, and had struck some of his future associates in 1916 as blithering idiocy. That it was, but Pearse was no idiot. Rather was he a cunning, passionate man who set out to parallel the path to Calvary in the hope that through self-sacrifice he could become a national messiah, or rather that God would let him achieve that role. Though Chief Secretary Birrell and indeed most Westminster politicians were mere triflers in comparison to Pearse, it has to be added that compared with his divine madness, they were sane. The bloody business which convulsed central Dublin from Easter Monday 24 April 1916 until the 29th of the same month was a shambles in every sense. It was triggered off by small groups of men out of control of larger nominal command structures. Even the Irish Republican Brotherhood, the oldest conspiratorial extreme Nationalist group, had apparently lost control of sub-groups formed within it as it tried to penetrate and take over the Volunteers. Attempts to co-ordinate the rising with German arms and aid would have been funny, if they had not been so tragic. They culminated in the capture by Crown forces of Sir Roger Casement, an upper-class Irishman who had by 1916 developed into a crashing bore of doubtful mental stability with one over-simply dominant idea in his head. His variety of Irish Nationalism was venomously hostile to the other peoples of the United Kingdom, for his vision of an independent

Ireland included it systematically cooperating with any foe of 'England'. Yet he had come, in a German submarine, to call off the rising.

Chief Secretary Birrell, who had had plenty of warnings about impending trouble, but had chosen to ignore them, was automatically driven to resignation by the fiasco. His Permanent Under-Secretary, Sir Matthew Nathan, resigned reluctantly. The Viceroy, Lord Wimborne, was pressed to resign by Asquith, but stubbornly and successfully resisted. In May, Asquith went over to Dublin and, because of his inability to find an alternative Chief Secretary, calmly shouldered the routine burdens himself. Of constructive ideas, he had no more than usual. Like virtually every other Westminster politician who was not Irish, he was happy to use the Lord Lieutenancy (admittedly an anachronism in a nominally United Kingdom) as a scapegoat for the mess. It was to go. In fact, anachronism or not, it corresponded with reality a good deal more than the pretence of a 'unitary' state. In the end, it survived because nobody could think of any better structure which was a feasible proposition. Despite the execution of the leaders of the rising by General Sir John Maxwell acting under martial law, it is difficult to think of any European state which would not have executed many more under similar circumstances. Though the dead men were potent martyrs in retrospect, the example of the sole significant leader who survived, De Valera, is a reminder that they would all have been formidable problems for Westminster had they lived. The trial of Sir Roger Casement for treason in June 1916 was ill-advised, especially since F. E. Smith, the Attorney-General, prosecuted, but once Casement's defence counsel, Mr Serjeant Sullivan, refused to go along with pressure from Smith for a plea of insanity, it was impossible to avoid a death-sentence. Serjeant Sullivan broke down through overstrain during the understandably fraught hearings. Well he might, for his defence was transparent and flimsy, however verbose. The decision to proceed to execution in August 1916 was deeply inhumane and politically crass.

By the late summer of 1916, the only talent Asquith was undoubtedly displaying was the one he had already developed to a disconcerting degree before 1914: a talent for painting himself into corners. His inertia was massive. His once rightly admired gift of chairmanship had withered. Cabinet meetings were intolerably protracted. They did not get through essential business. Backlogs mounted relentlessly. Partly this was because the Cabinet was too large and contained too many strong, conflicting personalities. Nevertheless, Asquith was clearly failing to improve a bad situation. After his return from Dublin, he tried to pass the poisoned chalice of the Chief Secretaryship for Ireland to Lloyd George. The Welshman was too shrewd to accept it. He did go to try to negotiate a settlement. Of course, the chances of a reasonable settlement by sincere agreement were zero. The witch's brew compounded of Westminster rule and denominationally-rooted culture clash in Ireland ruled such an event out at once. Nor was the normal negotiation between a well-meaning English minister and Irish politicians usually more than a protracted waste of time, since the latter, fearful of loss of support in their own community by the slightest sign of compromise, merely reiterated, over and over again, the maximum demands, or fantasies, of their respective communities.

But the little Welshman had one enormous advantage. With the admission of Unionists into the Cabinet in 1915, the Irish Home Rule Party had understandably become very worried indeed about the ability of Asquith to deliver Home Rule. Their disquiet reached paranoid levels when it came to Lloyd George. In June 1915, T. P. O'Connor, an influential Nationalist MP and editor, was not mincing words on the subject, for he '. . . spoke openly of their dislike of Lloyd George who would sell them or anyone else on the slightest provocation if only the price was high enough'.[1] The Home Rulers were thoroughly frightened by close contact with a far more Celtic personality than any they were in the habit of dealing with, and this provided the basis for a much healthier relationship, rooted in realistic fear and distrust rather than patronizing contempt on both sides. Very rapidly, Lloyd George reached an agreement with J. E. Redmond and Lord Carson. The Home Rule Act would be brought into operation immediately but the six Ulster counties were to be excluded by an Amending Act, nominally pending an Imperial Conference after the war which was to reconsider the government of the Empire, including Ireland. Since that conference was highly unlikely to reach any positive conclusions about the Empire, let alone Ireland, it is hardly surprising that Lloyd George had to give Carson written assurances against future coercion. It was no great deal: coercion of Ulster had proven impractical. Both Carson and Redmond effectively sold out their minorities in south and north respectively, though with Irish MPs remaining at Westminster in the meantime, the more extreme inconveniences caused by arbitrary division of either the British Isles or Ireland might have been averted by appropriate negotiations and arrangements.

It was the only available Irish settlement. Its outlines had already been identifiable before 1914. Asquith himself recognized this, for in trying to persuade the Cabinet to accept the proposal he pointed out, in his own words that: '. . . The proposed settlement would in his opinion have been accepted on all sides before the war and would be accepted with equal equanimity after the war'. The 'equanimity' was optimistic, but otherwise the argument was sound, and was supported by the two leading Unionist Cabinet members, Bonar Law and A. J. Balfour. It was, however, bitterly opposed by Lord Lansdowne and Walter Long. Rather than force those two Unionists to resign, which might destabilize the government and lead to 'the worst of evils—a General Election', Asquith allowed the proposal to die, congratulating himself on the fact that only Lord Selborne had resigned, an outcome which Asquith deemed 'very satisfactory'.[2] Selborne had resigned as soon as he heard the proposed deal, on the valid ground that it made even more irrelevant what few scraps of parliamentary democracy remained. He had always argued that the castration of the Lords effectively transferred sovereignty to the premier in Cabinet. Now the Cabinet was being downgraded by being presented with a *fait accompli* on

---

[1] Reported in the diary entry for 22 June 1915, by Charles Hobhouse, a Gladstonian Liberal who was in Asquith's Cabinet until 1915. It is printed in *Inside Asquith's Cabinet: from the diaries of Charles Hobhouse* ed. Edward David (John Murray, London 1977) pp. 248–9.
[2] Quotations are from the account in Spender and Asquith *Life of Asquith* II, pp. 220–1.

a major issue, and asked to approve a decision taken by a committee of three, authorized by the Premier, but including only one Cabinet member.[1] To wriggle out of the contradiction is not necessary. The deal was both sensible in content and offensive in implication.

Thereafter, it was only a question of time before the Premier was challenged. His retention of ultimate decision in his own hands was serving no discernible purposes other than his own negative and selfish ones. Yet there was no widespread desire to deprive him of the office of Prime Minister. Bonar Law was certainly becoming worried about Carson's increasing grip on the Unionist party, to the point where he believed something needed to be done to answer Carson's charges of slack and inefficient management of the war. On the other hand, most members of the Cabinet other than Asquith probably felt that some change was essential by the end of 1916, and Bonar Law was genuinely anxious to retain Asquith as Premier. The exact position of Lloyd George is a matter of much debate. In her diary for 14 November 1916, his mistress-secretary Frances Stevenson recorded a breakfast conversation with Lloyd George in which she summarized his response to the suggestion that he become Premier:

> . . . He said he wouldn't think of being responsible for a Ministry to run the war at this stage. There is nothing but disaster ahead. Had they asked him, some months ago, he said, it would have been a different matter: but now, he would simply get blamed for losing the war, and have the negotiating of an unfavourable peace. Nevertheless I pointed out to him that in the event of his being offered the Premiership he would be bound to accept—he could not refuse to do his best to save the country, whatever the odds against it.[2]

Even if the views recorded here represented only one side of Lloyd George's mind (and Frances Stevenson's response probably articulated the other side), they ring true.

In any case, Lloyd George's proposal for a small War Committee which would be composed of three members, not including Asquith, was not intended to drive Asquith from the premiership, and as late as early December 1916 it did not appear likely that it would. Asquith did not like the idea, but he realized that Unionist disillusionment with his style had reached the point where he had to make tactical concessions. Lloyd George was willing to compromise to the extent of acknowledging the Premier's 'supreme and effective control of war policy'; to Asquith having the right to sit in on the War Committee on specific occasions of interest to him; and indeed to a prime-ministerial veto over its decisions. If implemented, these proposals would in practice have substantially reduced the sovereign powers associated with the prime minister. The main business of government—war—would have been conducted by Lloyd George, Carson, Bonar Law and Arthur Henderson, the Labour Party leader whose adherence was thought to be socially and politically desirable. The Premier would have lost the right of initiative, and given the complex political situation, could only have used his reserve powers with care and discrimination. There was much logic in the proposal: the effect of an over-concentration of

[1] *Crisis of British Unionism* ed. Boyce, pp. 170–85.
[2] Entry of 14 November 1916 in *Lloyd George A Diary by Frances Stevenson* ed. A. J. P. Taylor (Hutchison, London 1971), p. 123.

power in the hands of Asquith had been, literally, paralytic. The proposals would have distributed power, in a checked and balanced way, for Asquith would have been in a position to take advantage of blatant failure on the part of the War Committee, all the more so since he would have distanced himself from responsibility for their policies.

It appears to have been a combination of personal animus against Lloyd George, and violent spleen as the result of reading a *Times* editorial which rubbed salt in the wound of his proposed removal from direct oversight of the war, which made Asquith repudiate the agreed compromise. After that, he was doomed.[1] In a paradoxical way, Asquith's idea of the premiership ultimately mastered his political judgement. Instead of his inadequacy leading to an overdue reaction against his office as he had developed it, his egotism ultimately made him resign, leaving the office as it was at the disposal of a man he detested. He had saved the sovereign premiership.

[1] John Grigg *Lloyd George: from peace to war 1912–16* (Methuen, London 1985), pp. 442–67.

4

A crowned but tethered goat: The resistible rise of Lloyd George 1916–19

The great actor stood just inside the doorway, close to the platform, and was absolutely fascinated by the speaker, hardly moving a muscle all the time the orator was speaking. When Mr Lloyd George ended, Sir Henry Irving drew a long deep breath and muttered 'Very fine! Very fine!' and returned to the theatre.

Anecdote from David Williamson, *Lloyd George: A Man of the People*
(G. H. Doran Co., New York, 1917), p. 11

Then came all the tribes of Israel to David unto Hebron, and spake, saying, Behold, we are thy bone and thy flesh.

Also in time past . . . thou wast he that leddest out and broughtest in Israel: and the Lord said to thee, Thou shalt feed my people Israel, and thou shalt be a captain over Israel.

II Samuel, 5, verses 1–2 (Authorized Version)

It was not surprising that the latter part of 1916 saw a major reconstruction of the Westminster Government. What was remarkable was the way Asquith had been able to put that reconstruction off for so long by a policy of aimiable drifts and politic concessions on specific issues. The war was not going at all well. In May 1916 the great naval battle between the British and German fleets off Jutland had failed to produce the hoped-for British tactical victory. Indeed, tactically it was more of a German victory, though the final flight of the German fleet made it a British strategic success, in the sense that the German surface fleet remained bottled-up. In the east, the Germans had crushed Romania, just as they had crushed Serbia in 1915. On the western front, it could be argued that the protracted carnage of the battles of Verdun and the Somme represented relative failure for the policies developed by the German Chief of Staff, General Falkenhayn, which preached economy of German soldiers' lives and the slaughter of the enemy by massed artillery. His forces lost slightly fewer men than the French at Verdun, possibly slightly more than the British on the Somme. However, General Sir Douglas Haig, Commander-in-Chief of the BEF, had undoubtedly begun his offensive expecting to achieve a decisive break-through. He failed, and began to talk of a war of attrition designed to break the German will to fight. By 18 November, some 600,000 British casualties later, Haig had broken neither the German line nor the German fighting spirit. The summer tonic of the success of the Russian General Brusilov's offensive against the Austro-Hungarians was more than counterbalanced by the surrender of a British army to the Turks at Kut in April, and the final evacuation of Gallipoli in December.

The predictable effect of such a sequence of events had been to unleash a barrage of criticism. It by no means came from one point of view. Loudest was the criticism of those like Lloyd George who called for a more dynamic conduct of the war in order to inflict a 'knock-out blow'. Wiser men than he, such as Lord Lansdowne, the elderly but spry Unionist leader in the Lords, were beginning to ask whether the concept of the 'knock-out' was not self-defeating. In a memorandum of November 1916 which anticipated the much better-known 'peace letter' which he published a year later, Lansdowne had argued that with casualties already over 1,100,000 and a debt increasing daily by £5,000,000, it was imperative to consider ways of avoiding needless prolongation of so profitless a struggle. Yet both extremes, and most opinion between them in the Government, agreed on one thing: there had to be significant change. Lansdowne retired, by no means reluctantly, as part of the reconstruction. In a letter written at this time to Lord Buckmaster he said: 'Changes were, I am convinced, inevitable, but I certainly did not expect this particular *dénouement*'[1]. That probably summed the situation up for most people, including the main participants. The outcome was the product of an accidental and unpredictable combination of circumstances and character clashes.

Lloyd George, for example, did not intend to become premier. On the contrary, he meant by means of the new War Committee to reduce the premier to a mere *roi fainéant*. Asquith's interpretation of the Committee's proposed role, and of his relationship to it, was naturally quite different, which suggests that the apparent compromise reached between Asquith and Lloyd George was flawed and unstable, even before newspaper comment blew it apart. That does not mean that it could not have been implemented; only that it would have been the prelude to another internal power struggle over its terms. Once Asquith had resigned, nobody could be sure who would emerge as prime minister, not least because, had Asquith been willing to serve under another person, he could have chosen his premier. Such was the anxiety to keep the prestige of his name within the Government that the Unionists would have accepted his choice between the two or three top candidates: Bonar Law, Arthur Balfour and Lloyd George.

The process of misrepresentation whereby a shambolic succession was mythologized into the ascent to predestined greatness of a man-god was deliberate, and flowed from the fluent pen of Max Aitken, Lord Beaverbrook. Though he has been described, quite unfairly, as a Canadian gift to British nationalism, Max Aitken was no such thing. From start to finish, he was driven by a relentless and increasingly impractical bee in his bonnet

---

[1] Lord Lansdowne to Lord Buckmaster, 16 December 1916, printed in Lord Newton *Lord Lansdowne: a biography* (Macmillan, London 1929), pp. 461–2.

on the subject of Imperial unity and tariff reform. He brought to British politics something of the impish spirit of the Canadian con-man. Most British press-barons were competent exclusively as businessmen, and, in the course of systematically abusing the editorial monopolies which their money gave them, usually displayed no talent for editorship and less for writing. Max Aitken, however, wrote quite brilliantly. He made a hobby of collecting the primary sources, so his capacity to set the trend of interpretation was formidable. Unfortunately, he had become a fairly typical British mainstream journalist, so his sympathy with fact was very limited. In two columns on Politicians and the War, 1914–1916 which he published in London in 1928 and 1932, Aitken set a pattern which has since been followed, often without acknowledgement, by the bulk of the subsequent literature.[1]

Many of the leading politicians of the Great War era launched into self-serving memoirs during the interwar period. Of these, the most engaging was Winston Churchill's *The World Crisis*, of which the first volume appeared, understandably enough, in April 1923, shortly after he had lost office with the collapse of the Lloyd George coalition in October 1922. Churchill's immediate personal objective was to justify his much-criticized conduct during the Dardanelles campaign. He also needed money, and the series made a great deal. The author's advance on the first volume was £4,000 against a 33.3% royalty. Eventually the work stretched to no less than five volumes, the last of which appeared in 1931. Though not unfairly described as autobiography thinly disguised as world history, the egotism behind the rolling periods which Churchill dictated was so colossal and unselfconscious as almost to cease to be offensive. Furthermore, he had a case to argue over the Dardanelles, as Clement Attlee, his future Labour opponent, was always ready to agree. There was, however, another and an openly-avowed propaganda purpose behind the writing of *The World Crisis*. As Churchill said, by 1923 there had already been a vast volume of publication on the Great War, much of it partisan, much of it critical of decisions taken or not taken by the political and military leadership of the UK. Lack of reverence towards the Westminster-based political system always alarmed and angered Churchill. Without a suitable core of peoples in the British Isles who were conditioned into a high degree of automatic deference towards it, there was no basis for his chosen career, no spring-board for his ambition. He therefore stated emphatically that:

> I hope that this account may be agreeable to those at least who wish to think well of our country, of its naval service, of its governing institutions, of its political life and public men; and that they will feel that perhaps after all Britain and her Empire have not been so ill-guided through the great con-vulsions as it is customary to declare[2]

Lloyd George over time showed less reverence for anything outside his own ego and career. One of his problems as a politician was that his

---

[1] J. M. McEwen 'The struggle for mastery in Britain: Lloyd George versus Asquith, December, 1916' *The Journal of British Studies* (XVIII, 1978), pp. 131–56.

[2] Winston S. Churchill *The World Crisis 1911–14* (Thornton Butterworth, London 1923), Preface, p. 8. For details about its publication, see Henry Pelling *Winston Churchill* (Book Club Associates, London 1974), pp. 333–4.

behaviour made this development disconcertingly clear. His decision, which became known in 1919, to sell his memoirs to the *Daily Telegraph* for no less than £90,000 (a vast sum in those days) caused a howl of public indignation so loud that he had to declare that the proceeds of the work would of course go to war charities. In the event, he did not return to work on the project for a decade, and needless to say, the proceeds did not go to charity, war or otherwise.[1] When Lloyd George did begin to publish his *War Memoirs* in 1933, they very meticulously followed the Beaverbrook account of the overthrow of Asquith, which Lloyd George had read and understandably liked, for it was very flattering towards him, as the supportive Miss Stevenson pointed out. Beaverbrook's central aim was in fact to give an exaggerated view of his own contemporary importance. He does seem to have held these delusions of grandeur at the time. Despite being an undistinguished Tory backbencher, with no real expertise in government administration, let alone policy, he unrealistically hoped to become President of the Board of Trade in December 1916, and had to be paid off for his limited services with a peerage.

The fact that it was Lloyd George rather than, say, Bonar Law, who emerged as premier, did not in any sense change the main thrust of events. Any successor to the much-criticized Asquith was going to set up a small War Cabinet or Committee, and any successor was likely to be in the grip of those predominantly Unionist political forces which were shouting for a hard line on peace terms plus a more vigorous pursuit of a knock-out victory by 'men of push and go'. Lloyd George had indicated his availability for high office in a Unionist-dominated government by means of his original call for a 'knock-out' victory, a call which was deliberately designed to scupper all consideration of a negotiated peace. He was doubly attractive to some, though not all, Unionists, as he had the capacity to inflict a deep, possibly mortal, split within the Liberal Party, and he was much likelier to be able to persuade Labour to play along than either Balfour or Bonar Law. Yet, in the last analysis, Bonar Law could have insisted on a dissolution; almost certainly, if characteristically reluctantly, won a big majority by exploiting war hysteria; and governed in the same general direction as followed Lloyd George's accession. He was a tough, formidable operator.

It is true that the waters were temporarily slightly muddied by a freak revival of sovereign attributes other than the purely social in the unlikely person of George V. With Asquith clearly finished and no premier designate to hand, George V declined to guarantee a dissolution to Bonar Law before he even accepted the office the prime minister and tried to form a government. Bonar Law attached no importance to this episode. If he had wanted a dissolution after kissing hands and acceding to prime ministerial office, he would clearly have insisted on one. George V knew his place.

To appease Max Aitken, and to get him out of the House of Commons in order to clear a seat for Sir Albert Stanley, a railway tycoon whom Lloyd George had preferred to the Presidency of the Board of Trade, and despite the fact that he was not even an MP, Bonar Law and Lloyd George were determined to give the Canadian newspaperman a peerage, as Viscount

[1] Lord Beaverbrook *Men and Power 1917–1918* (Hutchinson, London 1956), pp. 327–8 (esp. note on latter).

Beaverbrook. They had not consulted Lord Derby, the Unionist manager and uncrowned king of Lancashire, who was furious at the effect of an arbitrary promotion to the peerage of one of his junior Lancashire MPs. By definition it confused his own carefully-graded system of rewards for a combination of seniority and docility. Bonar Law and Lloyd George eventually decided to ride roughshod over Derby. George V they had not even bothered to inform. The Welshman simply had no respect for the decencies of the British Establishment. Bonar Law did, but on honours he had a blindness which was on balance to his credit. He found the greed and shamelessness with which members of his own party in particular pursued titles quite incomprehensible. Yet the rules of the game had been cruelly violated. The UK had just moved from an absolute monarchy not unlike that of Louis XV in *ancien régime* France, with an inactive monarch, Asquith, who still retained ultimate powers of decision, patronage and initiative, to a rather different system. It had some analogies with that of Ancient Sparta, for it was a warrior state ruled by not one, but two sovereigns: Lloyd George and Bonar Law. Under both systems, it was the job of George V to distract attention from the realities of power, but it was very difficult for him to do this with any morale and conviction unless the other parties to the charade, the real sovereigns, pretended in his presence that they believed the fairy story which made George V a person of some consequence. His secretary, Lord Stamfordham, indignantly protested that his master had not been informed about a peerage offered to a man who, even amongst the over-peeraged clique of newspaper barons, seemed to have little claim to the sort of 'public services' which would normally be used to justify or excuse ennoblement. Lord Stamfordham was roundly informed that the offer had been made and preparations were under way for a by-election at Ashton-under-Lyne: George V would have to bite on the bullet. He bit.[1]

Though Lloyd George undoubtedly inherited a difficult situation, once he had established so good a rapport with Bonar Law it was not exactly a difficult job to form the new government, given the patronage at his disposal. Unionists with insight into the realities of political power were clear that they would not be required to tolerate 'a dictatorship'. On the contrary, Earl Curzon, who had been Lord Privy Seal in Asquith's last Cabinet, loftily informed his fellow-Unionist Lord Lansdowne that 'His Government will be dictated to him by others, not shaped exclusively by himself.'[2] That was, perhaps, too confident a view, but there was a core of truth to it.

And the argument advanced by Bonar Law's distinguished biographer —that Bonar Law was, from December 1916 until his temporary retirement in 1921 'in effect a second Prime Minister'—is simply irrefutable. Bonar Law became Chancellor of the Exchequer, the second-ranking post in the political pecking order, but he was also leader of the Unionist Party, and the Leader of the House of Commons, a place to which Lloyd George resorted less and less, partly because of the weight of his outside commit-

---

[1] Robert Blake *The unknown Prime Minister: the life and times of Andrew Bonar Law* (Eyre and Spottiswoode, London 1955), pp. 342–50.

[2] Lord Curzon to Lord Lansdowne, Confidential, 3 December 1916, printed in Newton *Lansdowne*, pp. 452–3.

ments, and partly because it had become a place where nothing very much happened. It had, for example, remained profoundly passive during all the changes and reconstruction of late 1916. There were a mere handful of occasions like the so-called Maurice debate of May 1918, when a serious threat to the Government seemed to surface, and Lloyd George would then turn up determined to uphold his reputation and crush his critics. Usually, there was little opposition worthy of the name. The Home Rule Party had lost its leverage and was having trouble with its domestic power-base. Labour was split, with the larger section supporting Lloyd George. The Unionists were behind him, with significant Liberal backing, and Asquith led (if that be the word) the dissident Liberals with a mixture of lassitude and restraint, spiced occasionally, as in the Maurice debate, with a rare spasm of energy deriving from enduring personal resentment. Since Lloyd George, first thing every normal morning, moved along the passage between Nos. 10 and 11 Downing Street to spend a good hour in deep discussion in the Chancellor's study, it is safe to assume, despite the absence of written record, that most major proposals which subsequently emerged from the Prime Minister had been very thoroughly discussed with Bonar Law.

MPs, many of whom were of course in uniform by 1916, were held in reserve by party chieftains who bargained with one another behind closed doors over major policy decisions. Decent chaps, particularly if they were Unionist, tended to regard criticism of the Government in public session of the legislature as verging on the obscene. When, for example, Austen Chamberlain, the Liberal Unionist Secretary of State for India, resigned in the aftermath of the Kut débacle and the publication of the report of the Mesapotamian Commission, he realized that he might tend to be regarded as a possible rallying point for discontented MPs, so he stayed away from the House of Commons completely for a spell. Even in normal times, he was an unenthusiastic attender, as his constituents complained. Under such like circumstances, it was difficult to say what 'public opinion' was.

There had been no election since that of 1910, which had underlined the deep and bitter divisions between the groups which made up the UK electorate. The press barons tended to assume that public opinion was what they said it was. They were vitally important components in the ruling élite, but the top politicians, despite their assiduous cultivation of press magnates, were emphatic that the role of the latter must be secondary to their own genius and initiative. When Winston Churchill was passionately resisting his own ousting from the Admiralty in 1915, he wrote a letter to Bonar Law, appealing for support he did not receive. It includes the striking phrase: 'We are coming together not to work on public opinion but to wage war: and by waging successful war we shall dominate public opinion.'[1] That summed it up. Ideally, the élite hoped to dominate public opinion through solidarity, success and massive support from the press. There was however a very clear unwritten rule that the press potentates must not reach out directly for the levers of executive power. Even the mild Austen Chamberlain bridled and complained publicly in the

[1] Winston S. Churchill to Bonar Law, 21 May 1915, printed in Lord Beaverbrook *Politicians and the War 1914–16* (Thornton Butterworth, London 1928), pp. 126–9.

Commons when Lloyd George created a Ministry of Information under Beaverbrook, and offered a post to Lord Northcliffe. Austen Chamberlain openly denounced this manipulation of the press and the presence of newspaper moguls in government as an assault on the agreed margins of acceptable political manoeuvre. Typically, Lloyd George shut him up before he could become too embarrassing by offering him a job as Minister without Portfolio, but in the War Cabinet.[1]

Loyd George owed a great deal of his rise to power to two newspaper-men: Lord Northcliffe and Sir William Robertson Nicoll, editor of *The British Weekly*, recognized as the most important voice of British nonconformity. Nicoll was not a political threat, but Northcliffe clearly frightened Lloyd George because of his wealth, power and megalomania. It was no accident that the new Premier looked around for a way of occupying Northcliffe outside Europe, especially when Northcliffe, who controlled not only *The Times* but also a very high proportion of London's newspaper sales, started to rake Lloyd George with hostile articles in 1917. The explanation was simple enough: Northcliffe was a passionate supporter of the admirals and the generals. Lloyd George was sceptical about both groups. Interestingly, Lloyd George chose to send Northcliffe to the United States in June 1917 as head of a British War Mission, charged with the task of coordinating (so as to eliminate overlap) the various purchasing programmes of the many British purchasing commissions active in America on behalf of various UK departments of state.

The Prime Minister admitted to another journalist, C. P. Scott, editor of the *Manchester Guardian*, that as far as Northcliffe was concerned, 'It was essential to get rid of him. He had become so "jumpy" as to be really a public danger and it was necessary to "harness" him in order to find occupation for his superfluous energies'.[2] Lloyd George had inherited the public stature, and potential glamour of the Asquithian premiership, but not its full powers. He was surrounded by powerful political barons who, apart from Bonar Law, were not of comparable stature to himself, but who had to be handled with care. Bonar Law was extraordinarily tactful and indeed strengthened Lloyd George's exercise of his predominant share of prime ministerial authority by ensuring that it was exercised within prudent limits. He was even as an administrator an admirable com-plement to the Welshman, for though the latter had been Chancellor of the Exchequer in both peace and war, and politically a very significant one, he had never been other than disconcertingly incompetent on the purely practical side. Of course, his own image-creation and polishing machine always preached the message that Lloyd George as Chancellor had been God's gift to the finances of the UK. It was not true. He was downright lucky that the Great War made the provisions of the 1914 budget irrelevant, and he did not compensate for the fiasco of the April 1914 budget by a firm handling of the early problems of war finance. On the contrary, instead of trying to control inflation by adequate increases in

---

[1] David Dutton, *Austen Chamberlain: Gentleman in politics* (Ross Anderson Publications, London 1985), pp. 134–5.

[2] Kathleen Burk *Britain, America and the Sinews of War, 1914–18* (Allen and Unwin, London 1985), pp. 139–40.

direct taxation, he stoked it by increasing indirect taxes on the staples of the poorer classes: beer, tobacco, tea and sugar. Having helped raise the cost of living, he then devised a virtual formula for currency inflation by relying on the sale of Treasury bills to cover the bulk of additional war costs. He was anxious to attract foreign funds into this market and, with high interest rates, did so but the bulk of the bills were bought by UK banks which, by so increasing their reserves, could expand their loans at lucrative rates.[1] By 1916 it was an irredeemable fiscal mess, and Bonar Law was the last man to shift an adequate weight of taxation onto the wealthier groups who were doing distinctly well out of the prevailing high interest rates, but at least he was competent with, nay uncannily comfortable with, the most complex sets of figures, so Lloyd George could leave the book-keeping to him, as well as the House of Commons.

For the next twenty years of his life, Lloyd George lived in large measure off his reputation as 'the man who won the War', which he was not. The phrase was a crazy one for two reasons. One is the deep ambiguity which by 1916 surrounded the whole concept of knock-out victory. France was an even more extreme example of this than the UK. It had been unusually passive in the face of events in August 1914; had entered the Great War, which was fought mainly on its own soil in the west, with a large measure of national unity; and had followed the UK pattern of placing the legislature on hold to the point where no government fell as a result of an adverse vote in the Chamber of Deputies before 1917. Yet the decision endorsed by this consensus, to go on fighting until outright victory, proved by 1917 so costly as to call in doubt the goals which it was supposed to achieve. There was the terrible bloodletting in the European nation least able to bear it. A quarter of the accumulated wealth of France, and most of its foreign investments, were consumed between 1914 and 1918. The Third Republic was permanently fiscally undermined.[2] The UK was not of course subject to some of the more obvious constraints upon French policy-makers. There were only two rational war aims for the British. One was to prevent the elimination of France as a Great Power. This necessarily involved the complete restoration of Belgian independence. The other was permanently to cripple the German naval and colonial challenge. Beyond that, there were no set British interests, least of all the elimination of Germany as a Great Power in Europe. The idea of a totally victorious Russia, for example, was appalling. Bad enough in Europe, it would have also meant that, all over the globe, Westminster would face tensions with a militaristic, unstable and stupid Tsarist regime.

Hence the very sensible initial British strategy of serving primarily as the banker and arsenal of the Allies, as well as their main naval force. It was designed to ensure that when peace negotiations came along, the Westminster government would be strong enough to impose terms on 'friendly' as well as hostile combatants. Yet by the latter part of 1916, this scenario had become totally unreal. British independence was rapidly vanishing into a bottomless pit of financial dependence on the United

---

[1] French *British Strategy and War Aims*, p. 90.

[2] D. Stevenson *French war aims against Germany 1914–1919* (Clarendon Press, Oxford 1982), conclusion, pp. 209–10.

States of America. Long before 1916, McKenna and the Treasury had lost control over the spending departments, and especially of the Ministry of Munitions, where Lloyd George displayed boundless optimism about the ability of the Westminster Government to raise credit in America. The firm of J. P. Morgan and Co. were employed to raise the huge sums needed by the United Kingdom if it were to continue with its vast and increasing level of purchases of American machine tools, raw materials, manufactured goods and foodstuffs. To make matters worse, the UK had mercenaries rather than continental allies, the French alone excepted. After September 1915, the UK guaranteed the American purchases of the Italians and Russians, and after May 1916 even the proud French needed similar support. By late 1916, over 40 per cent of UK overseas purchases were in the United States. The Foreign Office called together an interdepartmental committee at the end of September to assess the degree to which the British war effort had become dependent on America. The conclusions reached were alarming. By the end of October, Reginald McKenna was telling the Cabinet about 'Our Financial Position in America'. He warned his colleagues that:

> We ought never to be so placed that only a public issue in America within a fortnight stands between us and insolvency. Yet we are quickly drifting in this direction.
> If things go on as at present, I venture to say with certainty that by next June or earlier the President of the American Republic will be in a position, if he wishes, to dictate his own terms to us.[1]

Things did so go on. There were political differences between America and the UK. In December 1916, an angry President Wilson in effect encouraged a run on sterling so serious as to nearly wreck it as an international currency. To support the value of the pound, J. P. Morgan's bank had to increase purchases of it from $150 million in the quarter ending September 1916, to $350 million in the quarter ending December 1916. Lloyd George became Premier in the middle of the crisis. His policies guaranteed that the long-term trend towards dependency would accelerate, though day-to-day relations were improved by better management structures and above all by America's entry into the war on the Allied side in April 1917. Nevertheless, if the United Kingdom had embarked on war in large measure to secure its own long-term future as an independent Great Power, the drive for total mobilization of its resources in pursuit of a knock-out victory, of which Lloyd George had been a leading advocate, had, by the time he became Premier, gone far to undermine the original primary war aim.

Nor was this the only area in which events were beyond the new Premier's control. Even more striking was his inability profoundly to influence the one area of policy which, more than any other, he passionately wanted to control: the conduct of the war. He came to power with grave and justified doubts in his mind about the use which the admirals and generals had made of the enormous degree of independent authority which they had been allowed in the early years of the conflict. This was a European-wide phenomenon. Germany, Austria-Hungary and Russia

---

[1] Cited in Robert J. Scally *The Origins of the Lloyd George Coalition: The politics of Social-Imperialism, 1900–1918* (Princeton University Press, Princeton, NJ 1975), p. 344.

were military monarchies anyway, but even in France and the United Kingdom, there was widespread willingness, partly rooted in pre-war cults of 'the expert', to give the military reinforced authority in exchange for their technical capacity to deliver victory. In fact, the generals and admirals lacked any such capacity. Yet the French General Staff, whose suicidal creed of the all-out attack had crippled the early French war effort, and whose subsequent offensives had by 1917 driven the French Army to (well-justified) mutiny, was the effective executive power in France until well into 1917.[1]

The British equivalent development had, for a time, reduced Asquith's Government to a supply department for Lord Kitchener. Even the steps taken to allow for Kitchener's demonstrated administrative incapacity, such as the installing of 'Wully' Robertson as Chief of the Imperial General Staff, had reinforced rather than weakened the grip of the military 'expert'. Robertson was the Government's sole strategic adviser, and the only person authorized to send strategic instructions to generals, or to move their armies. As A. J. P. Taylor shrewdly pointed out, 'Wully' in his heyday was possessed of freedom of action only fractionally less extensive than that of his French opposite number, General Joffre, and much greater than was ever enjoyed by Ludendorff on the German side.[2] In the UK, Secretaries of State for War existed to feed Mars, not to control him.

And this was the situation which Lloyd George faced on his accession to power in late 1916. After splitting the Liberal Party, he could not survive without Unionist support, so the slightest tendency to backtrack on a policy of total commitment to absolute victory would have seen him out on his ear. He could at most hope to influence means, not ends. Even that was difficult enough. The leading generals were all elaborately plugged into the political game, partly through the social network provided by the British Establishment, and partly through direct links with the politicians. Haig carefully cultivated an intimate relationship with George V which enabled him to access the old-boy network from somewhere near its social and sartorial apex. Probably more significant in real terms was the existence of two political pressure groups: the Unionist Business (later War) Committee and its much smaller right-wing Liberal equivalent. The Unionist War Committee was at one stage reputed to have the allegiance of 150 MPs. It had been Carson's chosen vehicle when he resigned from the first coalition in order to hound Asquith out of office, and it was suffused with that deeply unintelligent faith in admirals and generals which characterized the Unionists and right-wing Liberals, from Austen Chamberlain and Carson downwards. Bonar Law shared his party's tendency to leave the strategic management of the war to the professional warriors, but he did not share their instinctive deference to the military. There was no topic on which Haig and Robertson were more stridently insistent than the need to concentrate all available forces on what they saw as the only decisive area: the Western Front. George V, whose political views were those of one of the

---

[1] John Gooch *Armies in Europe* (Routledge and Kegan Paul, London 1980), Chap. 6: 'The First World War'.

[2] A. J. P. Taylor *The First World War: An illustrated history* (Penguin edition, London 1966), p. 103.

more aimiable and least intelligent members of the Unionist War Committee, was shaken to discover that, with his usual glum insight, Bonar Law could see the case for the rival 'Easterner' point of view, believing privately '. . . that Robertson and the soldiers were all wrong, with the result that we have lost Serbia, Roumania, and very likely Greece.'[1]

In the ferocious guerrilla warfare between Lloyd George and the generals between 1916 and 1918, the Premier scored only marginal victories. His biggest one, which came close to shaking his Government, was to manoeuvre Robertson into resignation in 1917, but Robertson was replaced as Chief of the Imperial General Staff by Sir Henry Wilson, the ultimate military intriguer. Haig, whom Lloyd George hated, proved irremovable as C-in-C of the BEF. After the appalling casualties on the Somme in 1916, the Prime Minister was deeply unhappy about the massive offensive which Haig was anxious to launch in the late summer of 1917 in Flanders. Haig's arguments included the need to distract German attention from the very serious mutinies which had broken out in the French Army, though it has to be said that the French troops involved always insisted they would man the trenches and resist any German attack. The idea that an ablutions detail from the Pomeranian Grenadiers could have marched through the French defences is nonsense. What the long-suffering French infantry demanded in the aftermath of General Nivelle's unsuccessful, and much-hyped offensive, the last in a long sequence of bloody failures, was not an end to the war but rather no more patently stupid offensives.[2] This was not a point emphasized by Haig, of course. He received massive support from the First Sea Lord in the difficult task of selling his offensive to the Cabinet Committee which Lloyd George had set up specifically to stop it. Out of the blue, Admiral Jellicoe dropped a monumentally alarmist memorandum saying that if the British Army did not seize the German submarine bases on the Flemish coast, the UK would be knocked out of the war by shortage of shipping. Neither event occurred, but the offensive which eventually ground to a halt in the mud and blood of Passchendaele did, 500,000 British casualties later.

Purely in retrospect, Haig worked out a theory that Passchendaele was part of a long-term campaign of attrition which effectively 'demoralized' the German Army. Now, using this kind of argument, a case can be made for Haig, though the scale of scholarship and ingenuity needed to lever him into the antechamber of the hall of the 'Great Captains' of history is somewhat misplaced.[3] Lloyd George was right to recall bitterly that what Haig sold so ebulliently to the Cabinet Committee was not attrition, but decisive victory. He started the Passchendaele offensive confident of a breakthrough; he continued it expecting daily the disintegration of the demoralized Germans; and he ended it fighting savagely for a muddy ridge which would not have been relevant but for his initial offensive. The 'demoralized' German Army on 24 October 1917, in the latter stages of the

[1] Blake *The unknown Prime Minister*, p. 358.
[2] Marc Ferro (trans. Nicole Stone) *The Great War 1914–1918* (Routledge and Kegan Paul, London 1973), pp. 181–4.
[3] John Terraine *The Western Front 1914–1918* (Hutchison, London, 1964), pp. 182–93.

Battle of Passchendaele, supplied the six divisions which spearheaded the combined German-Austro-Hungarian offensive in Italy; at the great combat of Caporetto it inflicted a massive defeat on the Italians, capturing 250,000 prisoners and 3,000 guns, as well as making substantial gains of strategic territory. In Haig Lloyd George had to live with a soldier who simply never admitted to himself, or anyone else, that any criticism of his handling of the BEF in France, from start to finish, was possible.[1].

In so far as Lloyd George had any major influence over the conduct of operations, other than by starving Haig of reinforcements in 1918, it was in the naval field. Even there, it has been exaggerated and over-dramatized, needless to say, first and foremost by Lloyd George himself in his *War Memoirs*. The campaign of unrestricted submarine warfare which the Germans began on the first day of February 1917 did indeed pose an acute problem for a UK dependent on imported food, especially in the aftermath of poor American and Canadian harvests in 1916, which compelled heavy reliance on Australian grain imported over long, exposed ocean routes. The Admiralty, under the leadership of First Lord Admiral Jellicoe obstinately clung to a 'hunt'n'hit' policy against submarines, which proved about as efficient against that elusive foe as it does on a typist's keyboard. Convoy, the traditional, indeed the only effective answer (since submarines had no choice but to come towards their escorted prey), was something the higher leadership of the Royal Navy had set their face against. By early April, food shortages were acute; stringent rationing was unavoidable; and shipping losses unacceptable.

However, junior officers of the Royal Navy, to whom the Premier, with his usual cheerful contempt for the decencies, spoke behind their superiors' backs, were of a different mind. They knew that coal convoys to French ports were working admirably, that the Grand Fleet habitually moved in convoy, and that change had to come. So did the Secretary to the Cabinet and Committee of Imperial Defence, Sir Maurice Hankey, who had revived the policy of convoy ten days before what Lloyd George later saw as his own decisive intervention on 30 April. Three days before that, even the Lords of the Admiralty had authorized an experimental convoy which sailed from Gibraltar in early May without loss, proving that merchantmen, despite what admirals said about them, could keep station in convoy. The Premier's formal descent on the Admiralty confirmed a vital development, and gave the self-satisfied Sea Lords a shaking from which the generals might have benefited, but it was not all-important.[2]

So what did Lloyd George do as a war premier, apart from hardly attend the Commons, and wrestle unsuccessfully with British generals? Vast amounts of his time and energy were expended on interminable inter-Allied conferences. At these, very senior UK representation was essential. Lloyd George very much took control of this aspect of government work, and he approached it in a constructive spirit. He tried to encourage the Italians after the Caporetto débâcle. He tried to persuade the Americans

[1] Gerard J. De Groot *Douglas Haig 1861–1928* (Unwin Hyman, London 1988).

[2] Gooch *Armies in Europe*, 174–75, provides a more up-to-date summary than Robert Rhodes James *The British Revolution: British politics 1880–1939* (University pbk edn, Methuen, London 1978), pp. 369–70.

to increase the pace of their contribution to the Allied war effort in 1918. At innumerable meetings with the French, he genuinely tried to create some sort of unified Anglo-French command structure, all the more enthusiastically because he saw in such a structure a means of doing down Robertson and Haig. It cannot honestly be said that much emerged from all this well-publicized activity. Even a real measure of military co-ordination on the Western Front came only in the face of the supreme German offensive of 1918, and then only because the British and American generals were willing to grant to the French General Foch limited but significant authority as Commander-in-Chief of the Allied Armies in France.

All the conferring enabled Lloyd George to build up his image as a 'statesman'. In this he had, on the whole, the support of the press barons such as Lords Riddell, Rothermere and Northcliffe, with whom he spent a lot of time. They also did their best to sell him as a 'man of the people', with very positive coverage of his visits to the BEF and numerous pictures of the Premier empathizing with plucky, grinning British Tommies. It was not as straightforward a game as the press lords tended to assume, and before the collapse of Imperial Germany occurred, Lloyd George's grip on wider British public opinion was probably pretty fragile. His own image was one of the Premier's major obsessions. A key member of his personal entourage was 'Bronco Bill', otherwise known as Sir William Sutherland, Political Secretary to the Prime Minister. Deeply ambiguous in more than one respect, Sutherland manipulated the press by selective feeding, tacit censorship and positive disinformation, though of course the attempted manipulation could be two-way, as the proprietors all had egos of princely proportions.

Hanging on to power was an exercise which brought out the ruthless street fighter in Lloyd George as surely as it had roused the stubborn cunning of Asquith. In May 1918, Asquith had tried to take advantage of press revelations by General Sir Frederick Maurice (a recent head of Military Intelligence), to the effect that Lloyd George and Bonar Law had deliberately lied about their policy of keeping Haig short of reinforcements, to move in effect a vote of censure on the Government. Though it does seem that there was substance to what Maurice said or implied, Lloyd George put on one of his rare virtuoso performances in the Commons, pinned the badge of disloyalty and lack of patriotism on the Asquithian Liberals (who never forgave him) and secured a thumping majority. When the editor of the *Daily Chronicle*, Robert Donald, made the mistake later in the year of hiring General Maurice as his military correspondent, to add edge to an already very critical view of the Government, Lloyd George hit back savagely. In a couple of days at the beginning of October, he arranged for a pro-Government syndicate headed by the Liberal businessman and MP, Sir Henry Dalziel, to buy out the paper for £2,000,000; sack Donald summarily; and switch the paper's editorial policy to one of deep admiration for Lloyd George.[1]

Inevitably, after 1916, Lloyd George found himself presiding over an

[1] Kenneth Morgan *Lloyd George* (Weidenfeld and Nicolson, London 1974), p. 107 and pp. 115–6.

expanded structure of bureaucratic government in the UK. Given the strength of the political drive for all-out commitment to waging war, with the concommitant need for compulsion and regulation, this development was unavoidable. Conservative Unionists were in the forefront of these tendencies, though usually with a mental reservation to the effect that much of this extension of state activity was 'for the duration only'. Since the agreed division of sovereignty left parliamentary, party and Exchequer matters to Bonar Law, Lloyd George had the time to relate to this vastly enlarged administrative labyrinth; to play with the huge amounts of patronage it made available to him; and to invent techniques and organizations which would enable him to exercise more than just nominal oversight. Here, more than anywhere else, there have been charges of 'dictatorial' behaviour. Though high office undoubtedly increased Lloyd George's natural conceit, and developed his tendency to use a dictatorial manner under certain circumstances, the charge of institutionalized dictatorship rings very hollow.

He did strengthen the office of prime minister by accelerating the process, which had already gone quite far under Asquith, whereby the Cabinet ceased to be a political committee, becoming instead the focus of a complex administrative structure largely controlled by the premier. Sir Maurice Hankey, who had been seconded from military service to run a secretariat for the Committee of Imperial Defence, quite naturally evolved into the man who ran a new Cabinet secretariat which duly became the Cabinet Office. Hankey had served Asquith loyally, but 'his manifest loyalty to the office of Prime Minister rather than the man enabled him to move easily into Lloyd George's confidence after the change of government'. That change was not only marked by the creation of the War Cabinet, but also by new departments such as the Ministries of Food, Shipping, and Labour; the Department of National Service; and the Air Board. From the start, the Premier controlled the agenda and, of course, in theory, the personnel of the War Cabinet. In practice, Hankey and his minions heaped so much work on the War Cabinet that it just could not cope with everything. Increasingly, decisions were taken by standing committees; ad hoc committees set up by Lloyd George, and by no means confined to War Cabinet members; or even latterly abroad by inter-Allied bodies such as the Supreme War Council set up at Versailles in November 1917. A large number of decisions were simply taken informally by Lloyd George. The reasons for this were practical rather than machiavellian.

Notoriously, Lloyd George also established the Garden Suburb, a personal secretariat whose name derived from its housing in temporary huts in St James's Park. This has been seen as a sinister clique of social imperialists whose pre-war ideological formation had made them avowed enemies of democracy and exponents of a dictatorial, corporatist state. There were such people around, though hardly in the Garden Suburb. The outstanding example was Alfred, Viscount Milner, a former South African proconsul, leading Unionist foe of the Asquith governments and arch-imperialist. A great bureaucrat, Milner rightly denounced the Westminster system for having brought the UK to the verge of bloody dissolution in 1914. Less defensibly, he was devoted to 'the Empire' without being prepared to ask hard questions as to what that term meant. Utterly unsympathetic to the political game Lloyd George played with such zest, he was nevertheless brought by Lloyd George into the War Cabinet. Something of an 'Easterner' in strategic matters due to his imperial viewpoint, he replaced Lord Derby as War Secretary late in the war when Lloyd George finally managed to move the latter, an ardent supporter of the generals, into the Paris Embassy. Milner was genuinely grateful to the little Welshman, who alone had given him an opportunity to serve in high office during a major crisis. Lloyd George used him, not he Lloyd George.[1]

The Garden Suburb did contain disciples of Milner such as Philip Kerr, later Lord Lothian. He had served Milner in South Africa in that group of young aides known as 'Milner's Kindergarten'. They all developed a deep reverence for their chief and indeed in books and articles in later life they puffed his reputation to ridiculous heights. Kerr was a wealthy, deeply earnest young man, originally Roman Catholic, latterly a devout Christian Scientist. Though not a keen party man, he was a Liberal in politics. In 1926 and 1927, he was often at Lloyd George's Surrey house, working on the Liberal Industrial Inquiry Committee. He had been closely involved with the group of advocates of closer Imperial unity who ran the *Round Table* magazine; indeed, he edited it at one point. Ideally, he hoped for a single Imperial Navy giving weight to a united Imperial foreign policy. Long before 1914, the utter impracticality of such aims had become clear. At a special Defence Conference in 1909, Canada and Australia had announced their decision to build their own navies, and Sir Wilfred Laurier, the Canadian Premier, had in 1910 stated publicly that Canada would not necessarily support the UK in a major war. The Imperial Conference held in London in 1911 had made it clear that Westminster was as unenthusiastic about sharing responsibility for UK foreign policy with the Dominions as Canada was about accepting any such responsibility. Kerr was an unsuccessful idealist, typical of a permanent, serious minority within the British Establishment which worries about its amoral aimlessness and offers successive 'missions' to the peoples of the UK ranging from imperial unity, to Moral Rearmament in the 1930s to ardent Europeanism in the late twentieth century. None of these vague imperatives are meant to be subject to critical analysis. Indeed, the demand for uncritical commitment behind these *de haut en bas* prescriptions implicitly rules out the idea that what the peoples of the UK might reasonably set as their first objective is a more meaningfully democratic and more participative form of government. Kerr never fought an election in his life.[2]

In the Garden Suburb, Kerr did little more than gather information which helped enhance to quality of political decision-taking by keeping Lloyd George better informed and giving him access to information filtered through minds other than those of established civil servants. It is significant that the two members of the Garden Suburb who urgently expected to parlay their influence over the Premier into concrete political results were unhappy men. David Davies wanted to see radical new approaches to the war by the generals. This was more than the entire War Cabinet could

[1] A. M. Gollin *Proconsul in politics: a study of Lord Milner in opposition and in power* (Anthony Blond, London 1964).

[2] J. R. M. Butler *Lord Lothian (Philip Kerr) 1882–1940* (Macmillan, London 1960).

achieve and Davies resigned. Waldorf Astor, owner of *The Observer*, was more persistent, but no more successful in his ambition to nationalize (and of course restrict) the liquor trade. The Garden Suburb suffered from confusion with disreputable figures like 'Bronco-Bill' Sutherland. He could be found peddling baronetcies in West-End clubs when not, as in May 1917, altering a statement issued by Christopher Addison, Lloyd George's former Parliamentary Secretary, and the Amalgamated Society of Engineers, to give the quite false impression that Lloyd George had single-handedly solved an engineering strike. The Suburb necessarily liaised with the press, but it did not indulge in this sort of skulduggery. Nor did it leave much of a heritage when it dissolved at the end of the war. It had only very partially implemented plans which would have made its members liaison officers between the Premier and the administrative departments. Few members of the Garden Suburb seem to have regretted its passing.[1]

Lloyd George was an incorrigible wheeler-dealer occupying the main executive position in a Government which was democratic only in the sense that it was confident that if it could win a decisive victory, it could manipulate public opinion, at a time of its own choosing, into endorsing its grip on power. It was dominated by a Unionist Party which had decisively lost three consecutive pre-war elections. Its grip on the Westminster Parliament was in theory not very reliable, but in practice that body verged on the moribund as a political institution (as distinct from a legislative facility for Government), and its rare spasm of vitality, such as the Maurice debate, usually proved containable. Over significant parts of the United Kingdom of Great Britain and Ireland, the Lloyd George Government was poisonously unpopular, but until late in the day it remained crassly unaware of the depths of hostility it faced.

In Ireland, after the collapse of the near-settlement mediated by Lloyd George in 1916, Westminster had no policy, and less interest. It did have the wit to exclude Ireland from the Conscription Act of 1916, but its deepest wish was also its silliest: that the Irish problem would solve itself. It therefore waited hopefully for the outcome of an Irish Convention which met in July 1917, chaired by Sir Horace Plunkett, and which turned out to be hopeless, not least because it could carry with it neither of the only two viable political forces in the country: Sinn Féin and the Ulster Unionists. Survivors of the 1916 rising, such as the only surviving Republican commandant, Eamon de Valera, started winning by-elections in what had been safe Home Rule seats. By late 1917, De Valera headed both a strengthened Sinn Féin political structure and its military wing, the revived Irish Volunteers. Westminster did nothing, despite the fact that Sinn Féin's policies guaranteed that there could be no agreed settlement. After American entry into the war, paralysis could be excused by the need not to offend American opinion, though in the end allowing events to slide created a far worse situation in Anglo-American terms.

Then came the inspissated folly of a new piece of legislation which empowered the Government to extend conscription to Ireland. This was a Lloyd George masterpiece: too clever by half. By linking conscription with

[1] John Turner *Lloyd George's Secretariat* (Cambridge University Press, Cambridge 1980).

the grant of Home Rule, he hoped to finagle the Ulster Unionists into swallowing Home Rule, whilst he 'wangled' (a favourite verb with Miss Stevenson) the Nationalists into an acceptance of conscription. Neither were half as stupid as he thought. Far more than the Easter Rising, the 1918 conscription crisis led Catholic Ireland to declare political independence. The Roman Catholic Church declared resistance to conscription a duty. The Home Rulers left the Palace of Westminster. Sinn Féin was able to seize almost total control of its community's political life. Bonar Law had always thought the proposed extension of conscription unwise. Even Carson deemed it counter-productive. Conscription was not in the end extended to Ireland but, by early 1919, Westminster faced a rival legislature and executive of the Irish Republic in being. To divide the Lloyd George premiership between triumphant war years and post-war anti-climax is nonsense. Lloyd George reaped what he sowed during the period 1916–18, though care has to be taken to identify the areas in which he had effective powers of decision; the areas in which men like some of the generals could and did go on taking decisions of which he disapproved; and the largest area of all, which was the one in which he was carried along by the inherent impetus of the forces to which he had, by 1916, committed himself.

Sir Arthur Salter, who spoke with the experience of a man who had been a civil servant and who later became an MP and a junior minister in the early stages of the Second World War, was absolutely clear that Lloyd George knew the fearsome price to be paid if he alienated the Civil Service. As a result he was:

> . . . anxious to avoid as far as possible incurring the bitter hostility of the established public services and had no desire to attempt any change which would permanently transform their character.[1]

If Asquith in his heyday had presided over a Cabinet which was the central decision-taking group in Westminster politics, Lloyd George and Bonar Law presided over a much looser central group of decision-takers, whose core was no doubt the War Cabinet, but which in practice stretched far beyond it, and which included men who were civil servants rather than professional politicians, as well as businessmen and co-opted individuals, who in extreme cases might be British only by the widest extension of that elastic term. The situation, under the unique stresses of the Great War, prefigured developments later in the twentieth century, including a tendency for the precise balance of power between the elements of this only partially publicly-acknowledged political élite to be somewhat fluid.

The Treasury began its resistable but relentless rise to disproportionate political power. Its sense of divine right was well-established by 1914, feeding on the fact that it took all of those who passed at the top of the Civil Service examinations between 1906 and 1913. Its arrogance, known to the rest of the Civil Service as 'Treasury manners', was equally mature, but the parameters of its authority were driven out steadily between 1914 and 1919 as it permanently enhanced its grip on issues of external finance

---

[1] Arthur Salter *Personality in politics: studies of contemporary statesmen* (Faber and Faber, London 1947), p. 46.

and the rate of exchange for the pound, and as it rapidly reasserted after the end of hostilities its normal control of public expenditure and an extended grip over the Civil Service. By 1924, it had the benefit of a standing rule that no item involving finance should be discussed by the Cabinet or by any of its committees until it had first been discussed with the Treasury.[1]

Effectively, the decision-taking élite was secure from democratic control. It was heavily dependent on social and political deference, built up over centuries of integration and propaganda in order to secure acquiescence in the assertion of state power. Its own solidarity behind the war policies of Lloyd George and Bonar Law was partly the product of a sacrifice of sons so appalling as to render criticism of the policies which had led to that sacrifice unendurable. After all, traditionally the British Establishment was careful of its comparatively small social élite. Edward VII, during the Boer War, felt obliged to warn the aristocracy about over-exposure in a combat which saw an Earl of Airlie killed in action, and the young 'Bend Or', second Duke of Westminster, the most fabulously wealthy subject in England, dashing around in a cavalry regiment (by the First World War, he had taken to being equally dashing in armoured cars). King Edward was emphatic to a noble subject:

> Enough men of your class have gone already to show your devotion; more than are really needed for the purposes of war. Wait a little. If matters go badly, it will be time enough for you to depart.[2]

But the Great War was different, partly because it was originally expected to be short, there was a rush of the sons of the élite to secure early commissions. It then settled down into a bloody slog in which officer casualties were disproportionately high.

Asquith lost his son, Raymond. Bonar Law lost two sons. The fact that both men showed no bitterness after the war towards Germany was truly impressive, and compared well with the mentalities displayed by most English and Scottish, and nearly all Irish politicians, for whom bitterness was a stock commodity. Nevertheless, the acquiescence of large populations in wartime sacrifice was crucially dependent on the apocalyptic preaching of the Protestant churches, that this was not a war, but a crusade. Every Anglican newspaper, with the saving exception of the *Challenge* edited by William Temple, preached the theme that, '. . . This is the holiest war in history, and every soldier of the Allies who strikes a blow in it performs a religious duty.'[3] Nor were the Scottish churches far behind in their enthusiasm. The local press referred quite unselfconsciously to the 'rousing recruiting sermons' of the Minister of the First Charge of the Parish Kirk of the Holy Trinity in St Andrews, who himself lost a son in the Great War. What is true is that, as the Church of Scotland Commission

---

[1] Kathleen Burk 'The Treasury: from impotence to power', in *idem* ed., *War and the State: the transformation of British government, 1914–19* (George Allen and Unwin, London 1982), pp. 84–107.

[2] Michael Harrison *Lord of London, a biography of the Second Duke of Westminster* (W. H. Allen, London 1966), p. 74.

[3] Albert Martin *The last crusade: the Church of England in the First World War* (Duke University Press, Durham, NC. 1974), p. 142.

on the War made clear in 1918, the kirk's apocalyptic vision included not only combat, but church reunion, and social reconstruction in the post-war era which included not just better housing, desperately needed though that was, but also radical industrial reforms allowing a participative role for workers and consumers.[1] In short, the Westminster leadership was riding on forces it only half-understood and on expectations it only very partially intended to satisfy, if at all. Only in Catholic Ireland was it exposed to the wet smack of reality when the local church did not discourage young men who in 1918 preferred self-defence to submission to the mud, the carnage and the brutal discipline underpinned by a revival of summary military executions which characterized service in the British Army in Flanders.[2]

The reaction of Lloyd George and most of his colleagues to this phenomenon was simply anger. Much the same was true of their response to the other significant group which proved resistant to heightened social control: the Labour Movement. The Lloyd George who had made his name as a social reformer believed in state relief for the casualties of society, of whom there were plenty under pre-1914 Liberal governments, when working-class living standards were usually falling. From 1915, Lloyd George was anxious to associate Labour leaders with his policies, especially dilution of skilled labour. However, he always held the threat of industrial conscription over workers. He used compulsory arbitration under the Munitions Act of 1915 as part of a policy of trying to hold wages down, whilst being much less willing to act against soaring prices and profits. He had to make tactical concessions, especially when skilled workers held a key role in war supply. From about four million in 1914, trade-unionists increased to 6.5 million by 1918, but it was the business class which was successfully confirming its permanent alliance with government by serving in the administrative structures of the war economy and impressing the Premier with the virtues of the self-made entrepreneur.[3]

Yet the Government lurched into 1918 with no very clear notion as to how to win the war. It had been fortunate in that the collapse of Russia in 1917 had been more than counterbalanced by the entry into the war of the United States of America. The Americans had a massive economic interest in the Allied cause, but it had required two stimulants supplied by Germany to bring America to the point of declaring war in April. One was the German decision to embark on unrestricted submarine warfare, which at one point did nearly bring Britain to its knees. The other was the lunatic German ploy of offering Mexico an offensive alliance against the United States. The 'Zimmerman telegram' which embodied this absurdity was decoded by the British and passed to the Americans. Nevertheless, with the UK economy well beyond the bearable limits of effort, politicians were seriously discussing the campaigns of 1920. Perceptive critics such as H. W.

---

[1] Stewart J. Brown 'The social vision of Scottish Presbyterianism and the Union of 1929', *Scottish Church History Records* (XXIV, 1990), p. 85.

[2] Anthony Babbington *For the sake of example: capital courts martial 1914–20* (Leo Cooper, London 1983).

[3] Chris Wrigley *David Lloyd George and the British Labour Movement: peace and war* (Harvester Press, Hassocks, Sussex 1976).

Massingham, editor of the radical *Nation*, could see the paradoxical nature of the situation, which helps explain why that newspaper was in 1917 briefly banned from circulation abroad. The occasion of the ban was the paper's advocacy of a negotiated peace, very much along the lines of Lord Lansdowne's proposal, but its columns were carrying mordant critiques of Government positions on other issues. It was, for example, well aware that under the Defence of the Realm Act passed at the beginning of the war, a war which in 1917 appeared to have no likely end, the traditional liberties of the subject, for which people were told they were fighting, were almost entirely subordinated to the convenience of executive government. It even commented naughtily on the fact that the British Empire confused foreigners by being one for the purposes of rhetoric, but five (the UK, Canada, Australia, New Zealand and South Africa) for the purposes of dividing-up the war loot.[1]

In the spring of 1918 the twin directors of the German war effort, Hindenburg and Ludendorff, finally took Robertson and Haig's advice to heart, concentrated every available man and gun for an offensive on the 'only front that really mattered'—the Western Front—and promptly lost the war when their 'knock-out' blow failed to prove decisive. Thereafter, a combination of 'Westerner' and 'Easterner' strategies proved feasible. As the German line on the Western Front slowly retreated under costly pressure from Haig and his French and American allies, the large Allied forces imprisoned in Salonika finally surged forward under their French commander, Franchet d'Esperey, knocking Bulgaria out of the war and totally destabilizing an Austria-Hungary whom the Germans could no longer reinforce. Further, the combined effects of blockade and the criminal neglect of agriculture by their leaders fatally sapped German civilian morale. That victory would be followed by an election in which the Government tried to turn a military breakthrough into a political one was a certainty. The gambit was central to the thinking of a high proportion of the political leadership In the case of the Unionists, the ideological linkage between war and the recovery of political power had deep pre-war roots. Yet they had originally envisaged a war-time election.

The precise timing of the event was a matter of some controversy. Lloyd George had a vested interest in committing the other parties in the Coalition Government to an election under his leadership, if only to consolidate his precarious personal ascendancy. The passing of legislation early in 1918 which greatly broadened the electorate by introducing universal male suffrage and extended the franchise to women over thirty provided a standing excuse for the holding of an election, and by the summer of 1918, with the Northcliffe press baying in sympathy, Lloyd George was pressing his more reluctant allies for one. The day after Germany asked for an armistice, the Unionist and Liberal sections of the Government agreed to fight an election under Lloyd George. Two days later, on 14 November, the Labour Party decided to leave the Coalition and fight as a distinct party. In September 1918, Lloyd George had discussed the prospect of an election with his friend the newspaper proprietor Lord Riddell, who

---

[1] *1920 Dips into the Near Future by Lucian* (Headley Bros., London 1918). These are *Nation* articles from the last quarter of 1917, slightly amended.

stressed to the Premier, 'the necessity for re-establishing the authority of Parliament in the country'.[1] It was a significant remark, but probably the last consideration in the Prime Minister's mind. The so-called 'Coupon Election' of December 1918 was based on an arrangement broadly sketched out between Freddie Guest, the Chief Government Liberal Whip, and the Unionist whips, as early as July. According to it, the leaders of the Coalition agreed to endorse a mutually-agreed slate of candidates (identified basically by their support of the Government in the previous eighteen months). By the time of the election, Lloyd George's prestige was such that he had no difficulty in securing Unionist agreement to support 150 Lloyd George Liberal candidates. Outside Wales, supporters of Asquith controlled most Liberal Associations in the constituencies, so the Lloyd George Liberals were exceptionally dependant on the letter of endorsement, or 'coupon', which they received from Lloyd George and Bonar Law. Despite the resentment of the Unionist party managers against what they saw as an excessively generous concession in an election they were confident of winning, only a handful of constituencies saw local Unionists refuse to bow to Unionist Central Office pressure to stand down before an endorsed Liberal candidate.

The campaign itself turned into little more than an endorsement of Lloyd George's image. Whilst it was being fought in November, Northcliffe made it clear that he had reversed his previous position with respect to Lloyd George. From a strong supporter, he had become a rabid critic. The reason appears to have been personal spleen. Northcliffe was addicted to the standard press baron temptation to stray across the line separating formidable but acceptable influence over the policy-making élite, to a direct attempt to usurp direct power from that élite, which was not acceptable. When it became clear that Northcliffe's egomania demanded a leading role on the British side at the forthcoming Peace Conference, the Premier told him to go to hell. The result was that, as well as harrassing the Prime Minister for alleged 'softness' towards Germany, Northcliffe in his papers actually made some perfectly valid criticisms of a more than usually meaningless electoral process. Voting 'for Lloyd George', though it has been seen even by modern historians as a great radical gesture, was, as Northcliffe pointed out, largely a leap in the dark unless the Premier spelled out the future structure of his Cabinet. Whatever the little Welshman said, and however generous the electoral deal he cut with Bonar Law, he and his crew of rootless supporters were likely to be massively outnumbered by conservative Unionists. Lloyd George might say he opposed political reaction, but reactionary Unionists were not likely to be far to seek.[2]

The election was, in many ways, an example of seat-of-the-pants flying by the Government. Nobody could truly tell what would happen, least of all Lloyd George. The addition of a vast additional block of female voters, for example, drove the Premier to encourage sympathetic ex-Suffragette speakers like Christabel Pankhurst. He even came up with a lady who was

[1] Entry for 22 September 1917 in *The Riddell diaries 1908–1923*, ed. J. M. McEwen (Athlone Press, London 1986), p. 237.
[2] Reginald Pound and Geoffrey Harmsworth *Northcliffe* (Cassell, London 1959), pp. 676–93.

Welsh, an ardent Lloyd George Liberal, and an eisteddfod bard. In practice, female persons voted much like male persons and the only female elected, from about the most patriarchal part of the British Isles as it happened, did not take her seat, for she was the Countess Markiewicz, a Sinn Féiner. Even after the campaigning was over, the Premier was vague in the extreme about the likely outcome. His Unionist allies were confident of a Coalition majority of over 200. He himself thought a majority of 100 was a safe bet, and was prepared to be very happy with anything over 120 but, as he said, 'The real difficulty comes from the popularity of the Government. No one opposes and candidates are pretending support who mean murder'.[1]

Though party identities were so fudged as to make precision impossible, the result was shatteringly clear. The Coalition did not have so much a large majority as a ridiculous one, with over 520 MPs, 473 of them with the coupon. On the Opposition benches sat 59 Labour MPs and a mere 29 Independent Liberals, mostly Squiffites (i.e. supporters of 'Squiffy' Asquith) but some, in theory, supporters of the Government.

This election is traditionally depicted as a dramatic event. It was so only in terms of its results. The campaign in most parts of the UK was positively dull. Despite the fact that the electorate had nearly tripled to over 21 million, the turnout was only 58.9 per cent, far lower than in any previous twentieth-century election. The results grossly misrepresented opinion in the UK as a whole. Despite a majority of over 400, the Coalition actually received a minority (on one count 47.6 per cent) of votes cast. Ireland was an even more interesting case. There, the Sinn Féin party, committed to republican independence, won seventy-three seats, reducing the old Home Rule Party to a mere six, and facing a somewhat strengthened Irish Unionist group of twenty-six MPs. Sinn Féin seized control of Irish political life, but on a clear minority of Irish votes cast, and greatly assisted by unopposed returns in 26 constituencies where, even in 1918, it was already becoming physically dangerous to stand against Sinn Féin. A shoot-out between the Unionist-dominated Coalition and the Sinn Féiners was quite inevitable, but at a deeper level they represented a very similar phenomenon: the seizure of political initiative within a community or group of communities (in the case of the Coalition) by a well-organized minority exploiting a hopelessly divided opposition and the fact that such a situation under the UK voting system invariably produced results unrepresentative to the point of the crooked.[2]

To Lloyd George, the function of the election had not been to re-establish the authority of the Westminster Parliament. In fact, it fatally wounded it over a large area of the United Kingdom of Great Britain and Ireland. What

[1] Lloyd George to Megan Lloyd George, 13 December 1918, printed in *Lloyd George Family Letters 1885–1936*, ed. Kenneth O. Morgan (Oxford University Press, London 1973), pp. 188–9.
[2] Precise figures are difficult to establish because of the vagueness of party allegiance, but the main source, used and slightly modified here, is David Butler and Jennie Freeman *British Political Facts 1900–1967* (2nd edn, pbk, Macmillan, London 1968), p. 141. By far the best succinct comment on the ambiguities behind Sinn Féin victories in Ireland is J. C. Beckett *The Making of Modern Ireland 1603–1923* (pbk edn, Faber and Faber, London 1969), p. 445.

the Welshman needed at Westminster was a parliament so constituted as to solidify his authority over the other members of the political élite. In a sense, he did achieve that, though at a price, which he cheerfully paid. Hankey remarked at the time of the election on the Premier's lust for power and dictatorial manner. Although privately well aware of the folly and danger of both proposals, Lloyd George shouted for the extradition and trial of the former German Emperor, and eventually also for unlimited reparations from the defeated Germans. The Coalition would have won the election anyway. Dutch good sense in refusing the extradition of the Kaiser saved the Allies from themselves, but the quite impractical reparations commitment was a demon which the Premier had helped conjure up, and from which all his evasive disingenuity could not enable him to escape.

'The Goat', as his Unionist partners privately called him in an evocative summary of their mixture of contempt, fear and phallic envy, moved to cash in on his military and electoral successes and to do it on the stage of Versailles. There, as one of the Allied 'Big Three', alongside President Woodrow Wilson of America, and Georges Clemenceau, Prime Minister of France, he could enjoy publicity and forge an image such as even he had never enjoyed. It was like money in the bank: he could, and to some extent did, live off it for the rest of his life. Though large parts of the Government, including much of the Foreign Office, moved over to Paris for the peace conference, Lloyd George really did dominate the British input into what he seems to have seen as a sort of World Eisteddfod, with himself as star performer. Not much wonder that he stubbornly resisted heavy pressure from the British Establishment to include Asquith in the delegation. He was not going to hand a future rival a chance to polish his competing image as a 'statesman'. The Foreign Secretary, himself a former premier, posed no such threat. Arthur Balfour was at his most cynical and idle at Versailles. Tough, clever and with a refreshingly modern mind when he was interested enough to use it, Balfour had always been amused by the strivings of less fortunate mortals to reach positions into which he floated on the currents of privilege. In Paris he was, as Curzon, his successor as Foreign Secretary, indignantly pointed out, scandalously unaware of what was going on in his own field. Musical soirées and tennis matches were pleasanter and more civilized. There was little point in overworking when one had retained a lower middle-class Welsh solicitor, who seemed to suffer from political St Vitus Dance, to do that sort of thing.[1]

When Lloyd George returned triumphant from Versailles, after combining with Clemenceau to overpower the humane vision of the vulnerable Woodrow Wilson, he stood on a pinnacle, but he was still tethered to the Unionists. No longer were they the party of repeated electoral failure. Now they were deeply confident. 'The Goat' was capering high. His tether was longer, as his mounting insolence, remarked on by J. M. Keynes and many others, showed. However, if the tether was longer, it was also much thicker.

[1] A. Lentin *Lloyd George, Woodrow Wilson and the Guilt of Germany* (Leicester University Press, 1984).

5

Too Little, Too Late:
The Reaction Against the Excessive Concentration of Power 1919–23

I lunched with Bonar today. He cheered me up as usual by telling me I looked very much older than he did and as to the political situation it was so bad as to be quite irretrievable. I don't like the outlook and as I am not clear what to do I am worried and unhappy.
> David Lloyd George to his wife Margaret, 6 September 1922

At no time . . . had a baronial attempt to compel the king to reform his ways and those of his servants had more than a temporary success. What was needed was a new king.
> K. B. McFarlane, from his 1964 Raleigh Lecture to the British Academy on 'The Wars of the Roses'.

Between the end of 1916 and October 1922 what most distinguished the political regime at Westminster and Whitehall was that it was based on power-sharing. Nothing was normally more anathema to a twentieth-century UK government. It is no accident that power-sharing was implemented only during the First and Second World Wars, and that when at any other time the government started talking about the virtues of power-sharing in any specific part of the UK this was a thinly-veiled indication that it hoped in the medium term to get rid of that region. UK politicians had of course to accept that the policy-making élite included elements other than themselves, such as bureaucrats, or foreign governments capable of influencing the behaviour of the UK, not to mention the formidable complex of financial interests concentrated in London and known as 'the City'. This did not unduly worry the professional politicians. They were predominantly conservative men who saw these influences as normally conservative in impact. The role of the City, provided it did not stretch out directly for the levers of power, was perfectly acceptable as a necessary reflection of the sort of social order which the majority of politicians were anxious to uphold: one in which, in Lord Riddell's characteristically blunt words, 'Money is Power'. However, flexibility stopped short at the electorate, and professional politicians were deeply enamoured of the technique which had tamed and marginalized that potentially dangerous and importunate beast. Party was the palladium of the politician. Organized mass parties capable of polarizing the electorate to the point where many voters experienced physical revulsion at the thought of voting for any other than 'their' party, were a wonderful invention. They enabled a party supported by a minority of votes cast in a General Election (always an even smaller proportion of these entitled to vote) to seize absolute control of both political decision (in so far as professional politicians took such decisions), and of political patronage. Indeed, the hierarchy within a well-whipped party enable a very tiny minority of the leadership of a parliamentary party itself resting on a minority vote, effectively to monopolize most of the politicians' input into major decisions.

Yet many Unionists had been shaken to the marrow between 1906 and 1916 by the realization that God had not given them an absolute monopoly of the benefits of this system. Liberals had used and abused it, latterly propped up by Irish Home Rulers. The latter, though they had to be treated and were treated as a ruling party with respect to patronage in Catholic Ireland, possessed the great virtue of not seriously challenging the Liberal Party monopoly, which was largely the premier's monopoly, of top political patronage at Westminster. By definition, Home Rule MPs did not want seats in the UK Cabinet. Asquith therefore preserved his powers, albeit latterly by a system of wheels, gears and levers. Nevertheless, even so opportunistic a Unionist as F. E. Smith, Lord Birkenhead, carried well into the war years a psyche scarred by memories of bondage in Egypt under the lash of pharaohs Campbell-Bannerman and Asquith. The result of this was a willingness to contemplate fundamental re-structuring of UK political mechanisms which he was later to prefer to forget.

For example, in 1917 he was a strong advocate of proportional representation during the debate on the Representation of the People Bill which had emerged from an all-party Speaker's Conference in 1916. Best remembered for its endorsement of womens' suffrage, this conference had also recommended the use of proportional representation, at least in some of the larger cities, where electoral results invariably lead to massive under-representation of large groups of voters. Edwin Montagu, then a Treasury minister, fiercely opposed the idea, arguing it would lead to weak government, and would have reduced the Liberal 'landslide' of 1906 to a mere thirty-eight of a majority. Smith jumped on this admission that the claim of the Liberals after 1906 to pass anything they pleased was less than convincing. Though Attorney-General at the time, F. E. returned to the fray at the report stage, arguing that if Swedish peasants could understand and work proportional representation, the English could at least give it a try. He was voted down both times, by only eight in the first case. An adverse majority of 22 the second time may well have reflected MPs' instinctive aversion to the principal supporting argument deployed by Smith in the first debate when he said:

> . . . I say to those who heretofore in this House have defended the cause of stability, and who think themselves concerned in the future to establish and maintain the centre of gravity of the State; your one chance of salvation is to

establish an exact equipoise in the State between the strength of the constituencies and the strength of the House of Commons . . .'[1]

Apart from the dead weight of unintelligent conservatism, he faced in his
audience too many men shrewd enough to realize that their own public
position, and access to power and privilege, hinged precisely on ensuring
that such a matching be never allowed to occur. This was particularly true
of the significant group of party loyalists with little electoral charisma or
appeal of their own, and no capacity whatever to appeal across party lines.

As late as 1919, Unionists were committed to significant measures to
modify the political structures which had proven so inadequate and
dangerous by 1914. The reform of the House of Lords is another example.
Though they would happily have gone on using their power cynically to
manipulate a purely hereditary house with the powers it had possessed
before 1911, they had been deeply shaken by the way in which, in the last
analysis, the hereditary peers had backed down in 1911, leaving the UK
with a totally unbalanced structure of government. As Austen Chamberlain
insisted, the truth was that:

> (1) the country wouldn't restore the old powers to the old House, and (2)
> that, even if they could, the old House wasn't strong enough to wield them.[2]

The Unionists therefore knew full well that it would be essential to modify
the hereditary principle if they were to restore any power to the upper
chamber. Their intentions were of course conservative, but that did not
mean that their criticisms of the existing situation were invalid. On the
contrary, they were shrewd. To a Premier who had his Cabinet behind
him and the usual whipped majority in the Commons, there was ultimately
no political check on any issue below the level of a threat of armed
rebellion, which was one reason why such threats had become a regular
feature of UK politics, most recently in 1919 in the shape of the threat
which had stopped the attempt to apply conscription to Ireland. On the
other hand, circumstances were changing rapidly. After the 1918 election,
it was the Unionists who were grossly over-represented, in terms of their
percentage of votes cast, in the House of Commons. With due allowance
made for MPs who had run as Conservatives without the coupon, they
had a majority over all other parties. Nevertheless, they still felt strongly
about the second-chamber issue. They insisted in 1918 that its reform be
part of the Coalition manifesto. To a man like Lloyd George this was not
a sympathetic issue. It was not just the amiable Miss Stevenson who found
supreme political power aphrodisiac: her lover was himself deeply excited
by the arbitrary exercise of unbridled power.

It is too facile to dismiss the constitutional issue as a mere 'diehard'
hobby horse, by definition 'unprogressive', and to rejoice that 'a cause
dear to the hearts of Unionists peers, was safely shelved and given a

---

[1] Cited in Birkenhead, *F. E.* p. 323. The role of F. E. Smith in the 1917 debates is here
conveniently summarized on pp. 322–3.

[2] Austen Chamberlain to Mrs Joseph Chamberlain, 23 October 1911, printed in Sir
Austen Chamberlain *Politics from Inside: An epistolary chronicle 1906–1914* (Cassell,
London 1936), pp. 364–5.

suitably low place in the Coalition's manifesto'.[1] Without some willingness to reconstruct some sort of constitution, which almost certainly would require the use of techniques such as regional representation and voting by proportional representation, both of which had featured in most of the various schemes mooted for the reform of the Lords, neither the unity of the United Kingdom nor the protection of its inhabitants from alarming concentrations of personal power were causes with much future.

Many Unionists, like Lord Selborne, had been committed for years to an overall reconstruction of the government of the United Kingdom on federal lines. The stimulus had of course been the pre-war Irish crisis, but the impetus of the idea of more general devolution was sufficient to secure the convening of a conference on the subject under the Speaker of the House of Commons in 1919. Federal devolution made no appeal to the the triumphant Lloyd George of 1918, as he made clear to a deputation of peers and MPs who lobbied him on behalf of federal devolution in that year. If implemented, it was bound to massively reduce the power of the prime minister, so the little Welshman played his English card. It was an ace if the Government did not want to take the lead, for it consisted of the argument that there was no positive demand for devolution from the bulk of UK voters: 'here is a population of 34,000,000 out of 45,000,000, and unless you have got a substantial majority of the English representatives in favour of it, it is idle to attempt it.'[2] The conference could reach no agreed conclusion. By 1920 it was clear the issue was running into the political sands.

It was simply not true that there was little support for a form of federal devolution outwith a minority of Westminster politicians. Scottish Liberals had taken Asquith's vague assurances at face value that the Irish Home Rule Bill was only the start to a more extensive review of UK government. A Scottish Home Rule Bill proposed by Sir Henry Cowan received a second reading in 1913. The rising political forces in Scotland in the shape of the Scottish Trade Union Council and the Labour Party were, if anything, even more militantly in favour of some form of devolution. The Scottish Council of the Labour Party passed resolutions in favour of Home Rule at every annual conference after its formation in 1915 up to 1923. In 1920, the Scottish Executive set up a committee to work with the Parliamentary Labour Party and the National Executive of the Labour Party, with a view to framing a Scottish Home Rule Bill, which was presented unsuccessfully by George Buchanan in 1924. The trade unions were even more positive. When STUC representatives met the Prime Minister and Secretary of State for Scotland in 1918 and 1919, Home Rule was at the top of the agenda. That probably did the cause (endorsed unanimously or with large majorities by the STUC every year between 1914 and 1923), little good, for Lloyd George was out to rally all other forces against the challenge of Labour. As Home Rule became identified with new political forces in Scotland, older ones denounced it as a plot by Bolsheviks or Papists or both. A 1922 correspondent in the *Glasgow Evening Citizen* wrote, in what was to be by the late

---

[1] Kenneth O. Morgan *Consensus and Disunity: the Lloyd George Coalition Government 1918–1922* (Clarendon Press, Oxford 1979), p. 35.
[2] Cited in Vernon Bogdanor *Devolution* (Oxford University Press, Oxford 1979), p. 37.

twentieth century a fairly typical style for political commentary in the UK press that: 'Those who advocate Home Rule are principally Socialists, Communists and Irish, whose aim is to establish Russian rule in Scotland.'[1]

This perceptive person need not have worried. Federal devolution would have implied a major, irreversible extension of power-sharing. Almost from the start, the Coalition government set out to reduce the degree of power-sharing characteristic of wartime decision-making. The military were, with poetic justice, amongst the first to go, their exit chute oiled with peerages and payments. Once down it, they were never likely to be able to claw their way back up again, for their political power had been dependent on the existence of a frustrated, power hungry Unionist Party which had used them as sticks to beat Liberals, and had then developed during much of the Great War a knee-jerking deference towards their supposed expertise. By 1919, disillusionment had set in, and in any case Bonar Law had never been much of a party to the illusion. The paladins did not go quietly. First Sea Lord Admiral Sir David Beatty had settled for a viscountcy. Haig rejected one indignantly (even Field Marshal French had one, he pointed out). He wanted an earldom; £250,000 of grant (the Government was thinking of £100,000); and, to his great credit, concessions from the Government which would ensure more realistic pensions for disabled soldiers. Haig's threat of a public refusal to accept any honours brought Lloyd George to a more generous provision for the disabled. He held Haig at the £100,000 he had initially suggested, but also had to grit his teeth and hand out an earldom.[2]

However, Haig's last political victory had repercussions. Beatty went up to an earldom by a natural process of currency inflation. Honours and cash grants were lavished on generals, admirals, airmen and even on the Secretary of the War Cabinet (at Lloyd George's insistence), but when Admiral 'Rosy' Wemyss, First Sea Lord in succession to Jellicoe, opened his newspaper, he found that his name was conspicuously absent from the War Honours. He promptly sent in his resignation, sparking off yet another crisis of embarrassment which culminated in his retiring to the South of France to the Villa Monbrillant, but only after being gazetted Baron Wester-Wemyss. Of his farewell dinner in the House of Commons, his wife remarked acidly that it was one 'from which the Prime Minister had the grace to excuse himself.'[3]

Sir Henry Wilson, perhaps the most compulsive intriguer amongst all the generals, looked as if he would last longer than the others as a player of the political game. Though a Southern Unionist, he secured an Ulster Unionist seat in the Commons, only to be permanently retired by being brutally murdered in London by two fellow-Irishmen. The professional politicians had had enough. They did not at all enjoy being on the receiving end of the combination of arrogance, presumption, deviousness and power which they so often dealt out to others, and with Winston Churchill as

[1] Cited in Michael Keating and David Bleiman *Labour and Scottish Nationalism* (Macmillan, London 1979), p. 62.

[2] De Groot *Douglas Haig*, pp. 396–8.

[3] Lady Wester Wemyss *The Life and Letters of Lord Wester Wemyss* (Eyre and Spottiswoode, London 1935), p. 451.

Premier during most of the Second World War, the lesson was well-remembered. In any case, there was no comparison between the desperate Unionist Party of 1914, which had been the generals' route into the heart of decision-making politics, and the almost ridiculously ascendant Conservative Party of 1939. If anything, the pendulum was to swing too far the other way after 1940.

If the departure of the warrior-kings was at times a messy process, it was still pretty automatic. The extrusion of Labour from the power-sharing élite was trickier. It required all the undoubted talents of Lloyd George in the fields of prevarication and the unctuous doublecross. There was never the slightest intention amongst the Coalition leaders that Labour should retain the significant but subordinate bargaining power within the Government which it had been granted due to the exigencies of war. In manipulating public opinion for electoral purposes, this did pose a problem. The Coalition sold itself, by definition, as a sort of sacred union, a coming-together of all 'patriotic' forces. Lloyd George had already broken with the ablest Labour leader, Arthur Henderson, a loyal member of the Government since 1915, over the International Socialist Congress on War Aims held in Stockholm in 1917. The details do not matter, though Henderson's resignation did. Even more important was the impression made when it became known that Henderson had been kept standing outside the door 'on the mat', while the Cabinet, of which he was a member, debated his future. As Henderson's in many ways conservative colleague Philip Snowden put it in an article in *Labour Leader*:

> This incident shows plainly that while Mr Henderson was in the Cabinet he was never of it, and that the Prime Minister regarded him as useful only for the purpose of deluding democracy into the belief that it was exercising an influence upon the policy of the Government.[1]

It was only part of the story, but fair comment as far as it went, and mild compared with the dishonest and venomous abuse Lloyd George had publicly lavished on Henderson.

After 1918, the Coalition's preferred strategy was to have a collection of tame 'patriotic labour' MPs in the shop window, serving much the same function as tailors' dummies. They performed the same task as the odd Protestant Nationalist so assiduously advertised by both Home Rulers and Sinn Féin. Like them, they tended to have a sticky relationship with the host body, even if they were, for their own reasons, anxious to make a success of the relationship, and like them were pathetically unrepresentative of their own community. In the 1918 election, under the resounding title of the National Democratic Party, ten such MPs came in on the coattails of the Coalition, as well as four former Labour MPs expelled from the party for remaining in the Coalition. Two of the latter were kept in office after 1918. All began to look like stooges as events unrolled. Every single National Democratic MP was beaten by a Labour Party candidate in 1922. Two of the ex-Labour MPs chose not to face the electorate again. One lost in 1922, the other in 1923. They were a failure as fig-leaves go, and their private reality was often more sad than sorry. Bonar Law in effect

[1] Cited in James *The British Revolution*, pp. 376–7.

subsidized some. What can be said in mitigation of the behaviour of the one or two who ended up in this position is that they were not the only contemporary Labour leaders happy to sell out surreptitiously to the bitterest foes of the working classes. Ben Tillett, the great Victorian dockers' leader, a founder of the Labour Party, went the same way. He used the Great War to secure election to the commons as a 'moderate and patriotic' Labour man. His arrival as an MP, ominously, was reported to be 'rather popular' in that citadel of Toryism, the Carlton Club. Paraded around back areas of the war zone in Flanders, with maximum publicity, to encourage support for the war, his post-war career was an unsavoury mixture of trying to keep a Labour Party and trade union career going, while privately wheeling and dealing with the Tories. By 1923, he was asking them for money. He still hoped to tear-jerk his way into senior trade union jobs on a sympathy vote, but eventually exhausted the patience even of his old comrades. He seems to have ended up a Tory pensioner, given to denouncing the effects of cynicism and corruption to Moral Rearmament gatherings. He should have known.[1]

That the post-war Coalition Government was a great 'lost opportunity' for a radical reconstruction of society was a myth assiduously propagated by contemporary intellectuals such as George Bernard Shaw and the Christian Socialist scholar R. H. Tawney, not to mention modern historians. Though Lloyd George clearly did not know what size of ransom conservative forces would have to pay in exchange for restoring the substance of the pre-war order, and might in his own unprincipled way have been prepared to pay a much bigger one than his Unionist colleagues proved willing to swallow, there was never any serious question of the Government not following the conservative path demanded by business interests.

The Premier had, towards the end of the 1918 election campaign, deliberately broken with the Labour Party by launching what was, even by his standards, a dishonest demagogic onslaught on the Labour leadership as an 'extreme pacifist, Bolshevist group'. He had the impudence to name his 'Bolsheviks'. They were Ramsay MacDonald, Philip Snowden and Robert Smillie. On top of his breach with Arthur Henderson, this was too much. MacDonald, who lost his seat in 1918, was particularly bitter, for he knew that Lloyd George was consciously lying. Before the war, MacDonald's willingness to 'cooperate' with government by defusing potentially embarrassing Labour criticism from within had verged on the dishonest. His opposition to the First World War had given him a wholly spurious reputation for radicalism, but it was a position tortuously reached and held with genuine moderation, of which Lloyd George was well aware, for MacDonald had talked to him intimately about his position.

It is true that 1919 saw a great deal of unrest which naturally frightened the more conservative members of the ruling élite like Lord Curzon and the Unionist politician Walter Long. Inflation had bitten deeply into the real value of wages, and demobilization of the vast conscript army of the United Kingdom was not particularly well handled. On top of all that there was turmoil in Ireland, capped by the far grimmer reality of the Russian Revolution, which had finally provided a concrete identity for the spectre

[1] Jonathan Schneer *Ben Tillett: portrait of a Labour leader* (Croom Helm, London 1982).

of social upheaval which had always haunted the minds of the privileged and the wealthy. Phased demobilization, though accelerated by a series of mutinies by bored and frustrated troops, ensured that the labour market was not flooded, so substantial concessions had to be made by employers in many industries on wages and hours. On top of the eight-hour day, employers faced strikes in the police force and mutinies in the army. The traditional coercive apparatus available for use against strikes seemed for a time unreliable. Lloyd George himself may have at one point felt that the nationalization of the mines was a possibility. Nationalization of the rail system was even more widely supported. There was indeed a good case for it, since the railways were, up to a point, natural monopolies which had operated under extensive state regulation for decades.

Yet the Commons was dominated by a crushing conservative Unionist majority. Though not wildly different from previous houses in social composition, it was seen at the time, and has been seen since, as selfish in tone and reactionary compared to general public opinion. There was no way such a body was going to accept measures opposed by the bulk of the business community. A good example is the proposal for a capital levy on the vast fortunes made by some businessmen out of the war. Because so large a proportion of war expenditure had been financed by high-interest loans rather than direct taxation (itself a technique catering admirably to the wealthy), the UK emerged from the Great War with a heavy burden of debt-servicing charges, which in 1920, 1921 and 1922 absorbed 34, 31 and 36 per cent of peacetime revenue respectively. There were two possible approaches to the problem. One was for a capital levy on the wartime increases in fortunes over £10,000: a conscription of capital for national service akin to that conscription of labour for which most capitalists had called so stridently between 1917 and 1919 it had the open support, not just of the more radical elements in the legislature, but of people like Bonar Law and conservative Asquithian Liberals like Herbert Samuel. Lloyd George was strongly for this policy until June 1920 when, to the dismay of his Coalition Liberal colleagues, he turned against it. By a combination of delaying tactics and increasingly bitter opposition, the Unionists managed to rule out a levy on war-wealth, a forced loan or a more general capital levy. Austen Chamberlain, as Chancellor of the Exchequer, relentlessly pounded the bass drum of the rich: the need to preserve 'business confidence'. He stressed the discouragement to investment such a step implied, though of course he was to contemplate with equanimity the wage cuts and cuts in services which were the alternative, and which undoubtedly impoverished the consumer market which was the real seed-bed of innovative investment in the interwar UK.

The dismantling of the controlled wartime economy was just a question of time. The workers' militancy was contained by a policy of temporary wage increases, and by royal commissions and conferences, always favourite government devices for wasting time. The National Industrial Conference was duly set up and then duly ignored by Lloyd George. The Sankey Commission on the coal industry had a more complex and protracted history, but came to little more in the end, not least because the employers' association, the Mining Association of Great Britain, rapidly grasped the scale of leverage which a memorial against mine nationalization signed by

305 MPs gave them. The Government knew that when the post-war boom ran out there would be massive pressure from employers for reduction of wages. That, as much as the smouldering dispute with the miners, lay behind the eventual passage in October 1920 of the Emergency Powers Act which replaced the wartime Defence of the Realm Regulations. The Labour Party at Westminster was not at all sympathetic to arguments that an inequitable voting system could be compensated for by direct industrial action. After its successes in 1918, it suffered from euphoria, and the delusion that it might soon be in power itself. At a deeper level, its leadership was more interested in office than power. Nor were they unaware that the inequities of the voting system might in the long run work for them, at least against Liberals. Thus, when the miners finally stumbled, isolated, into a long and bitter strike on 'Black Friday', 15 April 1921, abandoned not only by the parliamentary Labour Party, but also by their two allies in the so-called 'Triple Alliance', the railwaymen and the transport workers, it was not a prepared government plot, but nor was it in any way an accident.[1]

By 1921, it was in fact becoming rather difficult to see what difference the Premier made to the price of green cheese. His selling of the pass to his Unionist allies on every major domestic issue was becoming blatantly obvious. It was rooted in two factors. One was his lust for office. He was interested in little else, indeed outside politics he was rather a bore. Though tired by 1919, he only offered resignation when it would underline the desire of his Cabinet colleagues to keep him. The other factor was his lack of a real party base. There is no doubt that his natural instinct was to offer a firm but constructive response to the challenge from the Left, but he had too few counters on the board in the Commons to have his way. The Coalition Liberals, or 'Coaly Libs', were far from being merely a stage army for Lloyd George, but they were a curious and indistinct party in the sense that their constituency organizations were few and far between, and many of them hoped for eventual reunification with the Asquithian Liberals, who had in any case kept control of most of the old Liberal organization. Coaly Lib parliamentary whips were never clear to whom they should send their whip. Worse still, Coaly Libs fared dismally in by-elections, Unionists candidates put up by the Coalition being much more successful. Fusion with the Unionists into a new party led by Lloyd George was not a concept viewed with enthusiasm by most Unionists. It could hardly have made a great deal of difference to policy, given the ascendancy of the Unionists, but by 1920 both Churchill and Birkenhead were calling, if not bellowing, for it. Lloyd George and Churchill privately tried to bully their Coaly Lib colleagues in the Government, only to find that these ministers were alienated, partly by the bullying and partly by the violence of the Lloyd George–Churchill swing to the right in policy. By crudely banging his anti-Bolshevik drum, the Premier on 18 March 1920 produced a similar effect on his Liberal MPs.[2] Fusion died. So did the Coaly Libs, but nothing became them so much as their demise.

---

[1] Chris Wrigley *Lloyd George and the Challenge of Labour: the post-war coalition 1918–1922* (Harvester Wheatsheaf, London 1990).
[2] Morgan *Consensus and Disunity*, p. 184–6.

It has been shrewdly said that 'there was surely something, not dictatorial, but distinctly *presidential* about Lloyd George's regime'.[1] The description, however, is not wholly satisfactory. It is a comparison with the American presidency, which operates in a checked and balanced system, with separation of powers. Lloyd George did not. He would have revelled in the unbridled authority which an obedient party majority in the Commons would have given him. The snag was that he did not have it. As Bonar Law's health began to fail, and that close ally seemed to fade out of politics, the Premier compensated for his political captivity with wilder and wilder abuses of his monarchical position in the system. He had always enjoyed treating his Foreign Secretary, George Nathaniel Curzon, like dirt. Despite his abilities and workaholism, that noble lord's combination of snobbery, arrogance and mean-minded insecurity, simply invited abuse. It did not occur to Lloyd George that even an English worm could turn. Longer and longer absences abroad, combined with unpredictable and disruptive intrusions into home administration, did not endear the Premier to those trying to run the UK. By the latter part of 1921, his eccentric working hours (an abuse later carried to offensive lengths by Churchill in the Second World War) were capped by eccentric workplaces such as the telephoneless Gairloch, in the Western Highlands, where he was vacationing, or the Inverness Town Hall, to which he summoned the Cabinet.

That Lloyd George was by nature a 'centrist' politician is clear enough, but one by one his 'centrist' policies were sacrificed to his Unionist allies. For none of those policies was the Premier prepared to go to the stake. To some extent, an economic boom sustained Government popularity with broad segments of opinion which before the war had been Liberal in loyalty or which after 1918 might have been expected to rally to the Labour Party. There was inevitably a rather difficult period of transition between war and peace when more workers were released from the forces and munitions work than could immediately be absorbed by civilian work, but the state provided support for a significant period. A high proportion of the new women entrants into the wartime paid workforce appear to have withdrawn into more traditional domestic roles. By the spring of 1919, a boom had set in which ran into 1920. Much of it was generated by post-war re-stocking and reconstruction. It was hardly surprising that it turned into a sharp depression after the spring of 1920. Between 1920 and 1922, the UK paid the price of economic and political instability in its export markets; gross over-development of capacity in certain heavy engineering and coarse textile sectors due to war demand; and above all a high costs due to higher real wages in traditional industries.

There was never serious doubt amongst the policy-makers that in the long run wages would have to come down. Labour had been extruded from central decision-making. The 1920–2 slump helped to soften up organized labour and make any effective resistance to a reassertion of the primacy of the business community in economic policy definition impractical. There was still a spectrum of possible responses within the Coalition to the slump. A committee headed by the Premier's Liberal colleague Commander Hilton-Young was urging him as late as October 1921 that though

[1] Martin Pugh *Lloyd George* (Longman, London 1988), p. 121.

wage adjustment (i.e. reduction) was inevitable, so was unemployment relief. It also argued that state action could encourage exports, and that 'means be found by which State assistance could enable works to be undertaken which otherwise would not be done at the present time'. Against this, the Treasury urged in a memorandum on deflation in 1921 a line much more acceptable to most Unionists, defining the problem as 'while giving the minimum assistance necessary to prevent starvation to do as little as possible to create permanent unemployment by maintaining uneconomic prices.'[1]

There was little doubt as to which way the Welsh cat would jump. Lloyd George had already ruthlessly dumped his most vigorous radical colleague, Christopher Addison, first from the Ministry of Health and then from the Government. Admittedly, Addison's subsidies to housing had been extravagant, but he was sacrificed primarily as a scapegoat for the social programmes so disliked by Unionists. The appointment in August 1921 of the Geddes Committee to recommend expenditure cuts shook some politicians like Churchill because of the way it appeared to transfer executive authority from the Cabinet to five businessmen, four of them Scots as it happened: the shipping magnates Lord Inchcape and Sir Joseph Maclay; the railway barons Lord Faringdon and Sir Guy Granet; and their Chairman, Sir Eric Geddes. In fact, the committee was a device to ensure the ascendancy of Unionist policies. It was guaranteed to recommend the rich man's response, not so much to the slump as to any situation which enabled the wealthy to assert successfully their class interest—low taxation through savage cuts in state expenditure, especially on social programmes for the less privileged. Not much wonder that Lloyd George was for a quick election early in 1922 before the Geddes Committee reported. Significantly, it was the Unionist Party which stopped him dead in his tracks.

Relations between Lloyd George and Conservative Central Office were never good. The Premier's capacity to relate well to his Unionist colleagues was concentrated on a tiny clique of leading figures: Bonar Law and Balfour, Austen Chamberlain and Birkenhead. In the constituencies, there were too many unreconstructed Tories who recalled the Welshman's radical past, and saw no cause to alter their fixed dislike of him. Central Office balanced between Westminster and the constituencies, with a leadership which neatly encapsulated the social balance within the élite which controlled, funded and publicized the party. The Edinburgh brewer, banker and railway director, Sir George Younger, was Chairman (1916–1923). Close behind him came Sir Robert Sanders, an archetypal English squire, and Sir Malcolm Fraser, a newspaper owner. There were inevitable squabbles over seat allocation at elections, not to mention the despair of Central Office at the feebleness of Coaly Lib constituency structures, and its alarm at the decay of Unionist structures in constituencies where no Unionist candidate ran, but basically it saw less and less reason for sharing power with Lloyd George. Fusion Central Office did back as a means of

---

[1] The two memoranda are cited in S. Howson, 'Slump and Unemployment' in *The Economic History of Britain since 1700, Vol. 2: 1860 to the 1970s*, eds. Roderick Floud and Donald McCloskey (Cambridge University Press pbk edn, Cambridge 1981), pp. 275–6.

eating Coaly Libs. The proposal for an early election in 1922 it killed, for fear of it giving a new lease of life to the Coalition. Younger knew that many of his prospective candidates would simply refuse to endorse the Coalition. He himself wanted it dead.[1]

Having compelled Lloyd George to rule as a Conservative Prime Minister, his Unionist allies could by 1922 argue convincingly that he was an extremely bad one, and they were of course not unaware that he might be used as a scapegoat for the manifest failure of the Coalition to live up to its 'land fit for heroes', and its initial power-sharing rhetoric. Their criticisms were no less valid for being by interested parties on the right. The unmitigated shambles of the Premier's Irish activities (policy is too flattering a term) is a good example. Bizarrely, the squalid end in 1922 of a squalid business has been hailed by admirers of Lloyd George as a glorious triumph.[2] Contemporaries knew better. At the time when he had so catastrophically threatened to impose conscription on Ireland, Lloyd George had been intoxicated by the delusion that he was Abraham Lincoln come again, to the point of talking about putting anyone resisting his will against a wall and shooting them. In 1919, a year of crucial importance in Ireland, the Westminster Government ignored the place, most of the time, even more than usual. It preferred to concentrate on Europe, a theme of gratifying grandeur. Instead of sensible attention, it gave Ireland proconsular government under Lord French. Field Marshal Lord French was the first and last Lord Lieutenant to wield decisive authority over the whole Dublin administration. By the time he was deprived of real power by administrative reforms in May 1920, he had presided over a steady slide into chaos.

Sinn Féin had unmistakably seized the political leadership of Catholic, Nationalist Ireland in the 1918 election. It was a political party with little control over its military wing, the Irish Republican Army, which by 1920 was busy trying to dismantle the mechanism of the Union state by assassinating its administrative officials (it narrowly failed, to its own considerable advantage, to kill French); the members of the two police forces (the Royal Irish Constabulary and the Dublin Metropolitan Police); and officers and men of the British Army. The majority of its victims were Irish, and the kill rate was negligible compared with the sort of annual homicide figures which any major city in the United States was by the later twentieth century simply taking for granted. The trouble in Ireland was significant mainly because it underlined the political and military bankruptcy of the Westminster Government. There was really no alternative to recognizing rather than proscribing Sinn Féin as a political body, nor to waging effective counter-insurgency war against the IRA. Though it was asking too much of any Irish politician to expect him to face the consequences of his programme, the IRA quite clearly embodied two impractical demands. One was for the coercion of Ulster. That had been shown to be impossible before 1914. The other was for the instant recognition of an independent

[1] D. D. Cuthbert 'Lloyd George and the Conservative Central Office, 1918–22' in A. J. P. Taylor, ed. *Lloyd George: Twelve essays* (Hamish Hamilton, London 1971), pp. 165–187.
[2] Notably in A. J. P. Taylor's celebrated 1961 Leslie Stephen Lecture, *Lloyd George: Rise and fall* (Cambridge University Press, Cambridge 1961), p. 33.

Irish Republic. Since any Westminster premier conceding that would fall, there was no limit to the resistance to be expected. The IRA understood Westminster as little as it they.

Sensible advice, such as the need for a far better intelligence service, tended either to be ignored by French and his Westminster political masters, or drowned by their facile optimism about the use of 'scientific' methods, like tanks, seaplanes and airships against the IRA. Against such imbecility, the Inspector General of the RIC, General Sir Joseph Byrne, set some sensible suggestions. He urged the futility of banning a political philosophy like Sinn Feín. He also opposed the creation of ill-disciplined para-military police units like the Black and Tans and the Auxiliaries (or Auxis) on the grounds their activities would be counter-productive. Byrne wanted disciplined, small army units dispersed over the country to assist the RIC. Such good sense could have only one outcome: he was superseded in 1920, though latterly he enjoyed the solace of a series of colonial governorships.[1] The Government of Ireland Act of 1920 was scarcely a masterstroke, for incipient opponents like Birkenhead were persuaded to swallow it on the grounds that Sinn Feín would not, but it was at least the beginning of the end of total drift. It set up two Home Rule parliaments in Belfast and Dublin, with a Council of Ireland as a link. The Belfast one did become operative under Ulster Unionist control. The other provisions remained inoperative. Eventually mutual exhaustion produced negotiation between the London Government and representatives of Sinn Feín late in 1921.

Since the resulting agreement (the 1922 Anglo-Irish Treaty) was the occasion for a civil war within the new Irish Free State, which it set up, it has always been regarded as contentious in that part of the world. Considerable energy was, in the 1930s, invested in building up the minutiae of the negotiations into a moral drama for the UK market, mainly by Frank Pakenham, the future Lord Longford, whose _Ordeal by Peace_, published in 1935, was, in its author's mind, part of a campaign to assist his hero, Eamon De Valera, a Republican foe of the Treaty in 1922 and now in power in Dublin. Pakenham, scion of a Conservative Southern Irish landed house, had experienced a Pauline conversion to De Valera's interpretation of Irish Nationalism in 1932. Further conversions, to socialism, and then to Roman Catholicism followed in the next five years. Pakenham was anxious to influence English opinion against the survival of Northern Ireland in the long run, and in favour of De Valera's reinterpretation of the Anglo-Irish relationship in the short run. Yet, the more interesting fact is that the original idea for the book seems to have come out of the Birkenhead circle.[2] Having identified himself with the negotiations and 1922 Treaty, Birkenhead was almost at once anxious to mythologize the negotiations.

They were, in fact, totally unsurprising. Both sides entered them in bad faith, intending to break on issues discreditable to the other side. Both, for

---

[1] Eunan O'Halpin _The Decline of the Union: British Government in Ireland 1892–1920_ (Gill and Macmillan, Dublin 1987), pp. 191–2 and 194–6.

[2] Frank Pakenham _Peace by Ordeal: An account, from first-hand sources, of the negotiation and signature of the Anglo-Irish Treaty 1921_ (Jonathan Cape, London 1935). For the Birkenhead connection, see Frank Pakenham, Earl of Longford _The Grain of Wheat_ (Collins, London 1974), pp. 234–5.

different reasons, were exhausted. The Coalition was at the end of its political, and the IRA near the end of its military tether. Both threatened renewed violence throughout. Nothing else would have secured the reasonable side of their objectives, or persuaded the other side to drop the impossible side of theirs. Force was the one language Westminster and the IRA both understood. The outcome was much the same as had already been approached twice—once before 1914 and once during the war— because it was the only feasible outcome. If the Sinn Feín representatives counted on a promised Boundary Commission making Northern Ireland non-viable, they were foiled in 1925 by the facts of political life, not by Lloyd George's ill-will. By the end of the negotiations, he would happily have thrown the Ulster Unionists to the wolves with the same cynical ruthlessness with which he sold the Southern Unionists down the river.

Failure decisively to crush the IRA before the inevitable grant of Home Rule to the 26 counties exacted a heavy price in both Ireland and the British Isles. It institutionalized in Dublin a political tradition whose crackpot linguistic revival theories were on a par with its historical mythology. The fact that political intolerance allied to a careful cultivation of bitterness, reinforced by assassination, had proved so profitable boded ill for the future. The British Army showed conspicuously little ability to adapt to guerrilla warfare during the conflict, but the Government was ultimately responsible for the disastrous failure to achieve unity of command, a logical military policy, or indeed any consistent policy or grip at all. Even after the Scots bureaucrat Sir John Anderson had reformed the legendary inefficiencies of the Irish administration centred on Dublin Castle in the spring of 1920, the Union administration continued along the line it had been following for 40-odd years: insufficient coercion to achieve results, but enough to manufacture widespread resentment. The campaign had been a disaster; the Treaty was a sell-out, with a face-saving clause for Lloyd George in the shape of a mandatory oath of allegiance to a sovereign whom both he and Bonar Law had treated as a nonentity.[1] The Unionist Party had lost its central ideological identity. It was understandably sour, and correctly sceptical of the rhetoric in which Birkenhead in particular tried to wrap up a fiasco.

Arguably, Ireland was simply and extreme case of an underlying shift in the social balance which was general throughout the British Isles. The old all-purpose supranational aristocratic governing class, rooted in landownership, plunged into final decline. In Ireland, it had been being dismantled for decades, mainly by Unionist administrations. Politicians like Arthur Balfour's brother Gerald swore blind that their Land Bills facilitating tenant purchase would clear the way for the Irish aristocracy once again to play an active role in Irish political life based on goodwill and 'influence'. Southern Unionists knew this for the drivel it was, but they had no positive alternative. In Ireland, some eleven million acres had changed hands under UK legislation, helped by £100,000,000 of taxpayers' money. In Wales, Scotland and England, private enterprise went far to produce similar results. In Wales, land sales gathered momentum between 1910 and 1914.

---

[1] Charles Townshend *The British Campaign in Ireland 1919–1921: The development of political and military policies* (Oxford University Press, Oxford 1975).

After a wartime pause, improved rentals and values produced a huge surge of sales after 1919. The pattern in England and Scotland was much the same. Though 1921–2 marked the beginning of a new agricultural depression in Great Britain, sales only stagnated in the mid-1920s and were to pick up again in the 1930s, though never on quite the scale seen immediately after the Great War. In England, the bulk of sales were to sitting tenants, and by 1924 the impact was such that Edward Wood could say in the House of Commons that he saw, '. . . a silent revolution in progress . . . We are, unless I mistake it, witnessing in England the gradual disappearance of the old landed classes.'[1]

Their heirs, as the new political ascendancy, were undoubtedly the business classes. By the 1880s, business fortunes had overtaken landed ones as the greatest accumulations of wealth in the UK. About the same time, the (discreetly veiled) sale of peerages to businessmen began. The core group of wealth-holders in UK society in the late nineteenth and early twentieth centuries were a conservative group concentrated in the fields of finance and commerce rather than manufacturing. Given these characteristics, it is hardly surprising that these people were concentrated in London and its neighbourhood.[2] One corollary of this fact was that provincial élites, such as those of Scotland or Northern Ireland contained a higher proportion of manufacturing-based wealth. The Great War saw the making of mushroom fortunes on a scale which required the establishment of new public (i.e. private) schools like Stowe[3] to process the offspring of the expanding class of affluent businessmen into the accent and style of their aristocratic predecessors. Much activity by the social aspiring centred round that supreme status-symbol, the horse, and a finishing course at Oxford or Cambridge also helped. Enough continuity of style was established to ensure that, outside Belfast and Dublin, the assinine bray of those whose voices betrayed the conviction that they were born to command remained much as it always had been.

Such people took it for granted that the government existed primarily to serve their own interests. This did not mean that government did not need to do anything, but it did mean that it should not waste effort and money on activities serving anyone else's interests. Education and welfare on a public basis clearly ranked as waste. The by-election triumphs of the Anti-Waste League sponsored by Lord Rothermere were one of the factors which hounded Lloyd George towards the Geddes Committee. In a by-election in the Abbey division of Westminster in August 1921, a 'Constitutional and Independent Conservative Anti-Waste' brigadier fought a lieutenant sponsored by the Anti-Waste League, and an 'Independent Liberal and Anti-Waste' mere civilian. Discipline was upheld. The brigadier won. The public had the good sense to be turned off. The poll was low,

[1] David Cannadine *The Decline and Fall of the British Aristocracy* (Yale University Press, New Haven, CT 1990), p. 111.

[2] W. D. Rubinstein *Men of Property* (Rutgers University Press, New Brunswick, NJ 1981).

[3] David Niven's account of Stowe is one of the more believable bits of his frequently misleading memoirs: *The Moon's a Balloon: Reminiscences by David Niven* (Hamish Hamilton, London 1971).

but the by-election did show the depths to which a mischievious press-baron could reduce politics, at least temporarily.[1]

Honours were a different story. There press barons and politicians were the sole beneficiaries of a system of handouts for the undeserving rich. Others usually had to pay. They also had to be reputable, and patient, and pay in approved ways, be those party funds or royal-supported charities. By 1922, there was widespread disquiet in the Unionist ranks about the way Lloyd George was using and abusing the honours system. Parts of it were simply forms of encouragement for comparatively humble people, but even here the Premier had carried matters to extremes. He had invented the Order of the British Empire (OBE: there were sundry irreverent alternative versions of the meaning of the acronym) in 1917 and shovelled out membership with such gusto that by 1922 there were 22,000 of them. It is hardly surprising that the Empire remained a fog of ambiguity when Lloyd George found the mystique of its name so handy. Knighthoods, baronetcies, and peerages he sold. He needed money for political purposes and newly-rich businessmen had it. Undoubtedly, the scale of his creations and his willingness to ennoble convicted criminals whose crimes ranged from fraud, to food-hoarding and trading with the enemy were threatening to undermine the minimum of acquiescence from the public without which the system could not survive.

There was an element of humbug in Unionist complaints. Tories had been selling peerages since the end of the previous century. Conservative Central Office resented the fact that the Premier's minions poached customers for honours from it. Under Bonar Law, the Unionists pocketed their share of the racket which earned for post-war London the label of the city of dreadful knights. Above all, the Unionists believed money should be power, so their Welsh ally naturally gathered for his political fund the money which rich men paid him for Ruritanian baubles; the institutionalized snobbery which their wives often relished; and, less defensibly, for access to the House of Lords. Yet there was something deeply corrupt about the frantic extremism with which Lloyd George drove the system. He had to agree to a Royal Commission which eventually spawned the 1925 Honours (Prevention of Abuses) Act. By 1925 Lloyd George was out of power. His erstwhile allies, now unabashed Conservatives again, had never intended to stop the sale of honours—merely to put it back on a basis of prudence and discretion. When the most notorious super-tout, Maundy Gregory, fled abroad in 1933 to avoid legal proceedings which might have washed too much dirty linen in public, we now know that he was subsidized by the Conservative Party to stay there.[2]

It was however in the field of foreign affairs that the Lloyd George regime finally pushed its luck too hard. Fully to grasp why this was so, it is essential to understand how the inner core of government came to be constituted after the retiral of Bonar Law in May 1921 from office, though

[1] Morgan *Consensus and Disunity*, p. 245.
[2] Gerald Macmillan *Honours for Sale: The strange story of Maundy Gregory* (The Richards Press, London 1954). The strange story of how Gregory's career as a remittance man was funded by Sir Julian Khan, who had to be paid off with a barony by Stanley Baldwin, of all men, is in Cannadine *Decline and Fall*, pp. 323–4.

not of course from the Commons. Lloyd George was without question the kingpin. His crucially important link with the Unionist Party was its new leader, Austen Chamberlain, a man passionately convinced of the need for the Coalition as a barrier against Socialism. Not the brightest of politicians, he was never likely to be truly intimate with the Premier. Intimacy increasingly came to be confined to an inner court of two: Winston Churchill and Lord Birkenhead. Churchill had been brought back into the Government at the end of the war as Minister of Munitions. From there he moved to the War Ministry and then became Colonial Secretary. Oddly enough, Lloyd George could and did always in the last analysis dominate Churchill, despite the fact that Churchill was a courageous man, and the Premier a coward, as frightened of zeppelin raids in the First World War as he was to be of bombers in the Second. Churchill was too disliked by the Unionists to be a threat to Lloyd George. Birkenhead, the Lord Chancellor, though a good legal mind, was equally unthreatening politically. A peer, often drunk, always rude to more people than he could afford to offend, he knew that his future in the inner circle of power depended on the survival of Lloyd George as Premier. So small an inner court was not to be seen again in the UK until the reign of Ted Heath in the 1970s, when the very different personalities of William Whitelaw and Lord Carrington filled the roles of Churchill and Birkenhead. In 1922, the ruling trio did not effectively control the majority party of which two—Churchill and Lloyd George—were not members. Naturally, they focussed their attention on areas of international policy where they could exert executive initiative.

The result in Churchill's case was something of a disaster, for the Russian Revolution of 1917 seemed literally to unhinge his never very sound judgement. To the end of his life, his grasp of social reality as it existed for over 90 per cent even of Englishmen was virtually zero. His own life was both privileged and highly unusual. He could, under the influence of Lloyd George, see the poor as objects of his own heroic condescension, pity and succour, just as he could congratulate himself on his heroic magnanimity in allowing groups like the Boers or Sinn Feín to escape from effective control by Westminster; but he was driven to near frenzy by the threat implicit in the events of 1917 that there might be mutiny in the ranks of the core of deferential toilers and conscripts who had to be there to generate the power and influence which was the launching-pad for his own brilliant career. Exploiting the presence of British troops sent to Russia to secure communications and prop up an eastern front, he was determined to intervene massively in the Russian civil war on behalf of the 'Whites' to crush the 'Reds'. Lloyd George warned him that the UK was war-weary, and that intervention would merely enable the Bolsheviks to appeal to nationalist sentiment. The Premier had hoped that on the Allied Supreme War Council, President Wilson of America would snub Churchill's zeal for an Allied plan for intervention. In fact, Woodrow Wilson, badgered for intervention by the French and British, and provoked by the behaviour of the Bolsheviks which combined most of the anti-social tendencies of Tsarist Russia with a messianic belligerence all of their own, failed to stop Churchill.[1] The

[1] George F. Kennan *Soviet-American Relations, 1917–1920, Vol. II: The decision to intervene* (Princeton University Press, Princeton, NJ 1958).

British Labour Movement was enraged. The conservative forces at the opposite end of the spectrum, though of course fulminatingly anti-Bolshevik, shied away from the cost of intervention. Austen Chamberlain, who was Chancellor of the Exchequer during the two years, 1919–20, when intervention shambled towards manifest failure, was a bitter critic of what he rightly saw as a wilful and futile waste of assets needed at home.[1]

Nor was Russia the only scene of such Churchillian over-commitment. Despite the defeat at Gallipoli and the Indian Army's rout in Mesopotamia, the collapse of the Ottoman Empire at the end of the war under the success-ive hammer blows of Field Marshal Allenby's offensives had opened a wide vista for British aggrandizement, and an even wider one for British meddling in the Middle East. At the outbreak of war, a British protectorate had been proclaimed over Egypt, and a puppet sultan of suitably tame disposition installed in place of the pro-Turkish reigning monarch, who was declared deposed. Vague promises of liberation and self-government held out to Arabs during the war, to encourage revolt against Turkish overlordship, did not go unnoticed by Egyptians, but Churchill publicly referred to Egypt as an integral part of the British Empire, ensuring that when he went there as Colonial Secretary in 1921, he was received by stone-throwing mobs. By 1920, the United Kingdom held mandates from the new League of Nations over Palestine and Iraq. In Palestine, from which Transjordan was separated in 1920, the British were committed by the Balfour Declaration of 1917 to the establishment of 'a national home' for Jews. Nobody was quite clear what this meant, but any fool could see it meant trouble in an Arab land. In Iraq, there had been a rebellion, requiring 40,000 British troops at a cost of £30,000,000 per annum to main-tain control. Early in 1921, Churchill, who doubled up as Air Minister, made arrangements for low-profile, low-cost policing by the Royal Air Force in the Middle East, thereby cutting troop costs and pleasing an RAF which needed work and had polished its counter-insurgency techniques against the 'Mad' Mullah in British Somaliland in 1920. Nevertheless, public opinion was justifiably sceptical of the whole involvement.

Lloyd George himself had difficulty keeping control of Churchill. His own strategy for political survival hinged largely on cutting a figure as an 'international statesman'. He loved the publicity and deference of inter-national conferences. By 1922, his score of conferences was well into the twenties, and his strategy clear. Domestically he was a Unionist prisoner, but in personal diplomacy, with a bullyable Foreign Secretary like Curzon in the background, he hoped to emerge as the arbitrator and pacifier of Europe. It was a good example of the *folie de grandeur* to which a discon-certing proportion of twentieth-century UK premiers were to succumb in the latter stages of their reigns. At Genoa in 1922, Lloyd George tried to achieve a general settlement, based on the readmission of Germany and Russia to the comity of nations and on a substantial easing of what he well knew to be the unreasonable reparations demands he had supported in 1919. As Curzon acidly remarked, Genoa was a platform for the Premier to play on, complete with an audience of 600 journalists. Northcliffe, who was to die mad in 1922, was by this time denouncing Lloyd George in

[1] Dutton *Austen Chamberlain*, pp. 159–60.

all his papers, but Joe Garvin, editor of *The Observer*, was leading the counter-attack. The greatest exponent of overwriting on a gargantuan scale of his day, Garvin usually focussed on his arch-hero, Joseph Chamberlain, whose multi-volume biography he predictably failed to finish. At Genoa in 1922, he was installed in an apartment a few yards from the conference hall, and had made arrangements to have preferential access to the tele-graphic service, which he proceeded to choke with his fantastically long telegrams.[1] Alas France, in the person of Raymond Poincaré, proved intransigent. The Russians and Germans cocked a snook at the Concert of Europe by signing a secret economic pact, which rapidly ceased to be secret. The conference was a flop.

The Premier's policy towards Turkey was very much the straw which broke the came's back. Even Churchill thought that Lloyd George's enthusiasm for Greece, and his backing of Greek claims to Turkish terri-tories in Asia Minor, were extreme and irresponsible. A resurgent Turkey under Kemal Pasha was no easy prey for Greek imperialism, and it kept vainly but very reasonably trying to get across the message, unfortunately mainly through the tarnished agency of Major-General Townshend of Kut fame who had become an MP in 1920,[2] that it wanted good relations with the UK. Lloyd George's interventions in the complex situation were nearly all disastrous. A Greek offensive which he tacitly encouraged in 1921 failed. In August of that year, he successfully agitated for the lifting of an arms embargo on the combatants—and the Turks promptly secured large amounts of arms, especially from the French, who actively opposed British policy in Asia Minor. In August 1922, the Premier made a pro-Greek speech so violent as to provoke a pre-emptive Kemalist offensive which took and sacked the city of Smyrna, and ended with a dangerous confrontation with British troops guarding the Dardanelles at Chanak and Ismid.[3] Fortunately, the British commander was sensible, and Kemal had no desire for war when he knew diplomacy would give him all he wanted in the area.

Yet the Coalition Government contrived to give universal offence by its response to the crisis, which was to issue a belligerent warning to Kemal whilst trying to whip up public support in the UK and the Dominions. There was widespread suspicion that Lloyd George, Birkenhead and Chur-chill were willing to risk a war to try to enhance their shaky political position. They certainly hoped for a snap election on the back of the Chanak affair. Their handling of Canadian, South African, Newfoundland, Australian and New Zealand opinion, though wholly consistent with their arrogance towards the British people who lived in the UK, was distructively inept. Without a flicker of consultation, they called for support from Dominion public opinion, to which they appealed directly, to the rage of the several Dominion administrations. What fragile Imperial unity had been built up since the creation of an Imperial War Cabinet in 1917 disinte-grated. Only New Zealand and Newfoundland replied positively. Unworried, the Cabinet (with only the obscure Stanley Baldwin dissenting)

---

[1] David Ayerst *Garvin of the Observer* (Croom Helm, London 1985), pp. 195–9.
[2] Ronald Miller *Kut: The death of an army* (Secker and Warburg, London 1969), p. 288.
[3] A. E. Montgomery 'Lloyd George and the Greek question, 1918–22' in A. J. P. Taylor, ed. *Lloyd George: Twelve essays* (Hamish Hamilton, London 1971), pp. 257–284.

decided for a snap election. It was Austen Chamberlain's attempt to crush Unionist resistance to this which triggered the famous Carlton Club meeting at which the Unionist Party repudiated the Coalition.

In one sense, the episode was unpredictable. Baldwin went determined to oppose what he saw as an evil clique, but expecting to lose. Bonar Law had published in the press on 7 October a famous letter which, if supporting firmness in the ongoing confrontation at Chanak, indicated deep disquiet about the whole direction of the policy which had led to that confrontation. It contained the eminently realistic statement that: 'We cannot alone act as the policemen of the world. The financial and social condition of this country makes that impossible.' Nevertheless, it was some time later that he seems to have decided to emerge from retirement and offer himself as the only other possible prime minister. None of this proves that the Coalition had much staying power left in it. It was mortally wounded. Its unpopularity with the bulk of the public was matched by its unpopularity with most of the press barons. If the Cabinet, Curzon excepted, was with Lloyd George, the Unionist Junior ministers and undersecretarys of state, not to mention the backbenchers, were against the Coalition. They were mutinying as much against Austen Chamberlain as anyone. His 'gentleman in politics' image owed more to his monocle, orchid buttonhole and frozen 'Champagne Charlie' smile for the cameras, than to reality. He was in fact lazy, vain, tiresome, not very bright (Baldwin thought him 'silly') and condescendingly arrogant. The Unionist party was on the verge of splitting. To hold it together, Bonar Law overthrew the already shaky throne of David, with whom fell his two distrusted familiars —the outrageous and drunken Birkenhead and the reckless chancer Churchill. Their pompous Lord Chamberlain was swept aside by the mutiny of the lesser barons.

At another level, it was all about the ability of a minority party to seize and use power. With Catholic Ireland out of the game, and the Liberals hopelessly divided, the Conservative Party could re-emerge from the Unionist chrysalis to spread old rather than new wings. With Lloyd George as an ideal scapegoat, the question was how big the Tory majority would be. Outside the best-informed circles, there was even doubt as to that majority. Inside, the guesses ran from the 25 of Bonar Law and Younger to the more accurate 75 of Whickham Steed, editor of *The Times*. There was no doubt what that majority would be used for if obtained. J. C. C. Davidson, Bonar Law's former private secretary, who had become an MP in 1920, had laid down a rough programme for a re-established 'great Conservative Party' in a letter to his chief in January 1922. It was almost entirely negative. 'Honest Government' meant ditching the Lloyd George–Churchill–Birkenhead trio. 'Drastic Economy' meant as little social expenditure as possible. 'No Adventures abroad or at home' was merely a repetition of the first two themes, and 'National Security' was the usual Conservative stress on exaggerated and ambiguous patriotism, with the usual tacit reservation that Conservatives were likely to be keener on talking about it than on paying for it.[1] Even nominal power-sharing was out. Government was to be run for the benefit of those backing a single party.

---

[1] The phrases cited are from J. C. C. Davidson to Bonar Law, printed in Blake *The Unknown Prime Minister*, p. 437.

Lloyd George resigned as soon as he heard of the Carlton Club vote. Bonar Law would not accept office until elected leader of what still misleadingly called itself the Unionist Party. Democratic punctilio this was not. Bonar Law meant to rule on a minority vote from the electorate. Party solidarity was the rock on which he had to base his reign. He was genuinely reluctant to serve and, even after winning the election, did not claim the new Government was necessarily better than its predecessor. What he did claim was that it was a healthy change and a reminder that nobody had the right to be premier for life. The election campaign was predictably dull and formless. There were no opinion polls. Party structures were so confused and loose that the election has been described more like a bundle of by-elections than a national event, but this goes too far. Calculations on a UK basis were central to Conservative strategy. Many politicians were keeping options open against the possibility of an indeterminate result. In practice, Bonar Law campaigned well and parried wild lunges from Churchill and Birkenhead in particular so deftly as to expose the fatuity of the claim that ex-Coalition ministers had a monopoly of brains. With 38.5 per cent of the votes cast, the Tories won 55.8 per cent of the seats, a total of 343 MPs.[1] That was all that mattered. As long as the Conservative Party held together, the other parties—and the 61.5 per cent of those who had voted and who had cast their ballot for them—could not hope seriously to influence the Government.

Not that the other parties offered any discernible alternative, with the very partial exception of the Labour Party. Lloyd George pulled his punches to keep open the possibility of a new coalition with the Conservatives. Asquith had no new ideas whatsoever. All he really offered was Asquith. Apart from self-esteem, his main motivating force was personal hatred of Lloyd George and other 'renegades' like Churchill and Edwin Montagu, over whose defeats in 1922 he made no bones about gloating. The Liberals remained hopelessly divided. Labour, though its share of the vote rose to 29.4 per cent, which was much the same as that of the combined Liberal factions, secured 142 seats to the 116 of the Liberals, and advanced to the barren honour of being the official Opposition. It elected, narrowly, a new leader in Ramsay MacDonald, who returned to the Commons in 1922. A few political simpletons like Austen Chamberlain really did think that Labour represented an appalling threat. Publicly nearly all Conservatives regularly denounced the Labour Party as the harbinger of a Bolshevik revolution. Privately, their leaders, with the odd exception like Austen Chamberlain, were unworried. Dealings with trades union leaders and Labour Party leaders between 1918 and 1921 had left them with the clear impression that they were all paper tigers and that some were buyable.[2]

Having rejected protection as impractical and a threat to party unity, Bonar Law could confidently count, if he lived, on four or five years of

---

[1] Michael Kinnear *The Fall of Lloyd George: The political crisis of 1922*. (Macmillan, London 1973) provides the best survey of the election as it appeared at the time to all but the Conservative leadership, on which he is not so perceptive.

[2] Maurice Cowling *The impact of Labour 1920–1924: The beginning of modern British politics* (Cambridge University Press, Cambridge 1971), pp. 423–44.

office. He was unlikely to be tripped up by an unexpected crisis, as he had virtually no policies, except that of reducing taxation. Historians have invented historic roles for him. It would be wiser to accept his own definition of his role: not being Lloyd George. This was a Premier dedicated to reducing the powers of the prime minister. Therein lies his true historic significance.

'Brilliant' had been the adjective which the inner élite of the Coalition habitually applied to one another. It implied that most other people were, at best, clodhoppers. When Birkenhead went up to Dundee in December 1922 to speak on behalf of his friend Churchill, in an election Churchill was to lose, he stooped to levels of mud-slinging and appeals to crude chauvinism which left so bad an impression of this 'brilliant statesman', that even Clementine, Winston's wife, acidly dismissed Birkenhead as drunk, the speech as counter-productive. An audience which included some of the poorest industrial workers in Scotland was reduced to embarrassed silence by this gilded bug which had flitted in from the metropolis, to sting and stink.[1] Bonar Law deliberately dismantled this offensive court culture. With it went the wilder extremes of bribery and corruption in connection with honours. When Rothermere demanded an earldom for himself and a place in the Government for his son as the price of support from his newspapers, Bonar Law literally refused to countenance him, and seriously thought of making the episode public.

Curzon had the management of foreign affairs returned to him, which enabled him to display his real talent as a negotiator in an intricate Middle Eastern settlement negotiated at Lausanne. Faced with French intransigence on reparations and determination to occupy the Ruhr, Bonar Law simply left Paris for home. He was not prepared to waste more time. Ironically, his determination to make the premier once again primarily a chairman of a committee of departmental ministers had the effect of making him the unwilling participant in what he regarded as a foolish settlement of the problem of the £900,000,000 war debt owed by the UK to the USA. It had been incurred mainly for munitions, of which a great part had gone to countries like France and Italy, for use by their forces. The UK's European allies owed her four times the UK's debts to America, and Arthur Balfour had in 1922 made it clear that the two problems were effectively linked: if the European countries would repay their debts to the UK to the tune of £900,000,000, the balance would be cancelled. Bonar Law shared Balfour's view and made this clear in public before the departure in January 1923 for America of his new Chancellor of the Exchequer, Stanley Baldwin, and the Governor of the Bank of England, Montagu Norman, to discuss the debt question with the US government. That curious pair were not authorized to make an independent settlement, but they did, and then publicized it.

It was a dismal performance by which they accepted tough American terms on interest rates, and undertook to shoulder an annual interest and sinking-fund charge of £40,000,000 (which was 4 per cent of the current budget, scheduled to continue for 60 years) with absolutely no linkage

[1] Tony Paterson *A seat for life: The story of Winston S. Churchill when he was Liberal Member of Parliament for Dundee from 1908–1922* (David Winter, Dundee 1980), pp. 237–9.

with European debt repayment. So angry was Bonar Law that he seriously thought of retiring in protest, but since the rest of the Cabinet were unanimously in favour of a bargain which, though a bad one, reinforced the hegemony of 'sound' monetarism, he swallowed his objections. Cancer of the throat, not exasperation at his colleagues' stupidity, was to remove him from power in May 1923 and kill him a few months later.[1]

Resignation over the debt settlement would have destroyed the Government, probably to the advantage of Lloyd George and his cronies, so Bonar Law was in a weak position. Nevertheless, his eventual acquiescence was in line with his general attempt to lower the prime minister's profile. It did not mean that he was a weak chairman of Cabinet: quite the reverse was the case. It did mean that he refused to have national issues like unemployment dramatized round his own personality. He directed deputations from the unemployed to the appropriate departmental minister: the Minister of Labour. Of course, he did this with all the more firmness because he had no intentions of doing anything for them anyway. Both before and after the First World War, he had insisted that the Unionist Party had a positive commitment to social reform. It was simply not true by 1922. Even his own undoubted technical interest in the housing problem found expression in regrets that nothing could possibly be done.[2]

Of identity and belief Bonar Law had only a little left by the end. He was unpretentious. He chose to represent the Central Glasgow constituency where he had made his early career. He did not believe that a British people should be forcibly expelled from a British jurisdiction under which they wanted to remain. Government, he thought, should be minimal: of the rich, for the rich and (by and large) by the rich, but not provocative in style. He did come very close to deciding to close down the Cabinet Office which far more than the Garden Suburb, embodied the aggressive bureaucratization of prime ministerial power. Though pre-war practices such as a cabinet without a secretary, agenda or records could clearly not survive, an attack on the Cabinet Office would have been a real counter-revolution. It survived, as did the great surge of Treasury power under Sir Warren Fisher, very much a Lloyd George protegée, in 1919–20, when three Treasury Circulars established the Permanent Secretary to the Treasury as Permanent Head of the Civil Service; gave the Treasury power to draw up regulations for all departments; and extended the premier's patronage grip by requiring the consent of the prime minister for the appointment or removal of permanent secretaries, their deputies, principal finance and establishment officers in all departments.[3]

The premiership was in fact too valuable an instrument for people like Treasury mandarins, who sought power without responsibility, or the wealthy backers of a minority-based party anxious to rule without making positive concessions to a hostile majority of voters. Like Prussian *junkers* in the eighteenth-century heyday of that little Great Power, they were all for 'our king, absolute as long as he does what we want'. Bonar Law was,

[1] Blake *The unknown Prime Minister*, Chaps. XXIX and XXX.
[2] H. A. Taylor *The strange case of Andrew Bonar Law* (Stanley Paul, London n.d.), pp. 248–9.
[3] Peter Hennessy *Whitehall* (Fontana Press, pbk edn, London 1990), pp. 70–3, and 297.

in his negative way, more radical than his party. That party had moaned and groaned about the 'dictatorial' style of Lloyd George. Politically, they had first emasculated him, and then dumped him. The fate of his nearest analogue in another still unmistakably British political culture—Australia —suggests that these events were virtually preordained, however uncertain the specific timing. 'Billy' Hughes of Australia held the premiership during the war as the hard-liner who could split the Labour Party and rule with support from conservative elements. After a ferocious defence of Australian interests, as he saw them, at the Peace Conference, he was by 1922 widely accused of 'dictatorship' and forced to resign in favour of the conservative businessman Stanley Melbourne Bruce in February 1923.[1] The Tories were not opposed to the prime ministerial absolute monarchy. The trouble was that Lloyd George was not their king. In his 200-day reign, Bonar Law altered the style rather than the substance of his office. Arguably the style had to be changed, not least because as Lloyd George himself was stressing by the latter part of 1922, the Conservatives had 'three-fifths of the members' while supported by 'not half the votes'.[2]

[1] Marjorie Barnard *A history of Australia* (Angus and Robertson, Sydney 1962), pp. 526–7.
[2] Riddell *Diaries*, entry for 18 November 1922, p. 382.

6

In safe hands:
Baldwin and his fussy alter-ego 1923–5

Mr Stanley Baldwin . . . is much liked by all shades of political opinion in the House of Commons, and has the complete confidence of the City and the Commercial world generally
from J. T. Davidson's memo for George V, 1923

I am never sure whether the P. M. is thinking at all or simply wool-gathering. Here in his rural home one feels the old England of the villages is getting a bit of its own back for once in the person of Stanley Baldwin.
Thomas Jones, *Whitehall Diary*, entry for 25 November 1923

Mr MacDonald said he 'wanted to lay down one simple proposition with regard to the unemployed . . . It was this. In a society, as it was organised today, the spiritual things of life were absolutely subordinated to the material things of life.' . . . Surely the opponent of Sir John Rolleston and Mr Broadhurst can say something more businesslike than this . . .
Leicester Evening News, December 1904

The 1922 political revolution headed, however reluctantly, by Bonar Law, had been designed to change the spirit and style of the United Kingdom's central power structures rather than their substance. In the classic sense of revolution—the return of a great cycle of political development to a previous position of rest—it was indeed committed to rolling back certain trends, perceived as unhealthy, most of which had had the effect of increasing the capacity of the prime minister's office for imposing initiatives on the political nation. Logically, this rolling back implied the dismantling of certain developments in the central bureaucracy, but by the time of Bonar Law's resignation this was simply no longer on the political agenda. Equally logical would have been the re-installation of features of the political process which impeded executive initiative. In the shape of plans to restore some of the recently lost powers of the upper chamber, that option survived the eclipse of Bonar Law, though not in the best of political health. What the succession struggle did reveal was the enduring power of the office of prime minister, because it remained the key to what politicians could control in the rest of the political game. Nobody should have been more conscious of this than the man most widely tipped to succeed Bonar Law, George Nathaniel Curzon, Marquess Curzon of Kedleston, the Foreign Secretary. Of course Curzon was an obsessively ambitious and competitive man who instinctively reached out for the next rung on any social or political ladder. He had importuned Lloyd George for his marquisate; fumed over delay and then when it was granted he privately bitched that:

> Even radical newspapers, ordinarily none too friendly, actually complained that I had not received a Dukedom, in order to lend distinction to a somewhat tarnished order.[1]

This was a little hard on the poor but honest dukes, but premiers were more potent than the peers they manufactured. When, in 1903, Curzon had let it be known that he had accepted an extension of his term as Viceroy of India, he had received an anguished remonstrance from his friend Sir Schomberg McDonnell. The latter was a voice from the very heart of the British Establishment, for he was the liaison man between the royal family and the Westminster Government. He must have been well aware of the extreme difficulty involved in offering George Nathaniel Curzon sensible advice, especially when Curzon's ego was even more inflated than usual as the result of the flattery, pomp and deference surrounding his viceregal throne. McDonnell had therefore tried to convey his message in informal, literally racy, language, saying to Curzon:

> Of what use is it for you to go back when the situation demands you here? You have got to train now (I lapse again into racing slang) for P.M. When you win the race you will dictate the policy of the Empire—India included —but you won't win it if you remain away much longer.[2]

McDonnell oversimplified the situation in every way, but he was accurate in the extreme in ranking the premiership above all other prizes in the Westminster system, indeed as being in a different category to all the other prizes. Now, 20 years later, Curzon could virtually taste success. He was not the only one to anticipate his own triumph. Normally, he was semi-estranged, and nearly always physically separated from his second wife Grace, the former Mrs Alfred Duggan, a wealthy American widow whose money was essential for Curzon's extravagant lifestyle. Much of that money was tied up in the Argentine, where her first husband's estate had been situated. As her relationship with Curzon (who had ditched the novelist Elinor Glynn after a passionate affair to marry her) soured, her handouts to him had become more erratic, her absences longer and longer. However, whilst in Paris, Grace picked up rumours about Bonar Law's terminal illness, and she phoned her spouse not only to tell him the news, but also to inform him that she meant to be with him in his hour of triumph. The pair retired to Curzon's telephoneless house at Montacute for the Whit weekend, emerging on the Tuesday in response to a brief telegram from Lord Stamfordham, Secretary to George V, which simply

---

[1] Cited in Leonard Mosley *Curzon: The End of an Epoch* (Longman, London 1960), p. 213.

[2] Cited in *ibid.*, pp. 109–10.

summoned Curzon to London. Despite raging toothache, which she strove to conceal by wearing a veil, Grace Curzon managed to give a passable if totally bogus performance as the devoted and attentive wife of the great man in the course of what amounted to a triumphal progress into town. If Curzon was agog with dreams of power, Grace must have been equally excited. As spoiled a brat as he, though without his application and high intelligence, it was the social pre-eminence associated with his expected elevation which she intended to exploit.

Cruel was their disappointment. Stamfordham visited them in Carlton House Terrace to say that George V had asked Stanley Baldwin to form a government. Curzon was thereafter always convinced he had been cheated out of the premiership by a conspiracy of personal enemies. He had plenty of those, but there was more to it than that. The official explanation offered by the King—that with the Labour Party as the biggest opposition group and virtually unrepresented in the Lords, a premier in the Commons was essential—was probably one of the less pressing reasons for the decision. After all, 1922 had seen a dramatic revolt against perceived abuse of the premier's powers by a premier deeply distrusted for his own character and those of his intimates. Curzon was regarded by almost everyone as an unbalanced character, often ridiculous, at his worst odious. When he died in 1925, David Lindsay, Earl of Crawford and Balcarres, a former Unionist chief Whip, confided to his journal:

> . . . we have watched the gradual and effective growth of a gigantic myth, namely that George Curzon was a great man. . . . I never knew a man less loved by his colleagues and more hated by his subordinates, never a man so bereft of conscience, of charity, or of gratitude. On the other hand the combination of power, of industry, and of ambition with a mean personality is almost without parallel.[1]

Too many central figures in the Establishment thought like that for Curzon to have a chance. Bonar Law declined to offer any opinion to the King, but one reason seems to have been his desire to avoid responsibility if Curzon should perchance succeed: at least he could not be blamed for re-commending him. Then there was the other powerful consideration that Curzon had made it clear he would as soon as he succeeded reach out to incorporate the 'Old Gang' of Austen Chamberlain, Lord Birkenhead and Winston Churchill into the Conservative Party and Government. This would have spelled the end of hopes for more swift advancement for Stanley Baldwin, who had spoken strongly against the Coalition at the Carlton Club in 1922, and Neville Chamberlain. The latter, after being sacked by Lloyd George as Director of National Service in wartime, had recovered to be Postmaster General under Bonar Law. Then he progressed to Minister of Health in February 1922 when the previous occupant of that post failed to make his expected return to the Commons via a by-election. When Reginald McKenna, the former Liberal Chancellor, accepted an offer of the Exchequer from Baldwin later in 1923, but could not find a seat, a similar logic was to propel Neville Chamberlain into the Exchequer.

[1] Entry for 28 March 1925 in *The Crawford Papers: The Journals of David Lindsay Twenty-seventh Earl of Crawford and Tenth Earl of Balcarres (1871–1940). During the Years 1892 to 1940*, ed. John Vincent (Manchester University Press, Manchester 1984), pp. 506–7.

Several of the architects of the 1922 upheaval in the Unionist ranks were strategically placed directly or indirectly to influence the thinking of the King. That the monarch should be so pivotal was not surprising. A great deal of the executive initiative possible for a UK government was based on the usurpation of previously royal powers and prerogatives by the executive in general and the premier in particular. When a premier demitted office without leaving the majority party in the Commons with a recognized leader (a very likely occurrence if the premier was being forced into resignation by a crisis in his health), then the King was bound to resume at least a few of his powers to fill the vacuum. Since a sensible monarch knew that this window in time was likely to be brief and he would soon return to his normal role of a powerless public-relations officer, he used his discretion only after consultation with party elders and always in such a way as to attempt to avoid any continuing controversy involving the Crown. J. C. C. Davidson, who had been Parliamentary Private Secretary to Baldwin in 1921–2, and then to Bonar Law in 1922–3, and who wrote the most important memorandum on the succession submitted to George V, was Conservative MP for Hemel Hempstead. He was typical of the foot soldiers who had carried Bonar Law into power in 1922. His family was Scots–Argentinian, and much of his private fortune remained invested in Argentina, but he was a thoroughly Anglicized product of Westminster School and Pembroke College, Cambridge, who went on to be a notable Chairman of the Conservative Party. Men like Davidson were likely to see the possibility that Austen Chamberlain might be before long run by Birkenhead and Churchill as an alternative premier to a Curzon somewhat isolated in the Lords, and probably even more isolated from necessary support by ballooning arrogance and offensive rudeness.

On the other hand, the *coup de grâce* to Curzon's hopes had been administered by his old Coalition colleague Arthur Balfour, with characteristic elegance. When consulted by George V, he did not dwell on Curzon's personality. He urbanely expounded practical difficulties if a peer were to be prime minister, citing the considerable problems which had afflicted his own uncle, the Marquis of Salisbury, when placed in a similar position (and which, it must be said, had restricted his tenure of the premiership to a mere 13 to 14 years *in toto*). The famous exchange with an excited lady enquirer was nearer the truth. On returning to a house-party after seeing the King, Balfour was asked, 'And will dear George get the Premiership?' He replied, 'No, dear George will not.'

The British Establishment had been prepared to go to great lengths to stop an immoral scamp like Birkenhead from becoming Chancellor of the University of Oxford. Curzon had been acceptable as Chancellor of Oxford, but not as Prime Minister[1]. George V reached a decision highly acceptable, if surprising. Before doing so, he checked if Baldwin accepted the need eventually to reunite with the dissident Conservatives. Baldwin did accept the need; but there was no need for haste. Curzon, for all his pomposity, had resigned for the last time, and unwillingly at that, as Viceroy of India in 1905. He needed the prestige and income derived from office. He became Baldwin's very competent hired hand at the Foreign Office after a mini-

[1] *Ibid.*, pp. 507–8.

mum of persuasion. The 'Old Gang', now reunited with Lord Beaverbrook in a 'brilliant' mutual-admiration society, sulked. Birkenhead, as usual, was making mischief. In his legal capacity, he helped hand down judgements which made the Government's life difficult, particularly with respect to attempts to expel Irishmen known to be actively supporting the war-effort of the Irish Republican Army against the new Free State. The situation was ridiculous and a product of the massive confusion in nationality law and legal rights which Birkenhead had done more than most to create by his ardent backing of the 1922 Irish 'settlement'. The Westminster Government had in the end to pay £50,000 compensation to IRA militants transferred to internment in the Free State.

However, public opinion was rightly against Birkenhead in the UK, and the operation was cheap at £50,000, as William Bridgeman, the Home Secretary, said.[1] The dissident ex-Coalition Tories could also run unofficial candidates against Central Office candidates, but this form of wrecking, though spectacular when it split the Tory vote, had a limited life to it. The dissidents were led by a clique of high-spending adventurers who needed the backing of conservative and wealthy people to survive. They were not likely to find wealthy sponsors for gambits which might permit Labour candidates to win Tory seats. The great bulk of Establishment opinion was rapidly thrown against any rocking of the boat. The process which made Stanley Baldwin Premier was not democratic, but then nor was much of UK political procedures. This particular procedure had the great virtue of being both manipulable by representative party figures, and swift and private. It spared the ruling party the embarrassment and divisions of a contested election. The Tories remained quite happy with it until the 1960s, when a demitting premier, Harold Macmillan, was widely perceived to be manipulating it himself in order to control his own succession. George V, who was far less politically naïve than many assumed, was anxious to bury the whole business in oblivion until it lost political relevance. When, after Curzon's death, Grace Curzon told the king she was thinking of writing her memoirs, the royal response was instant: 'Lady Curzon, don't do that yet. It is sure to stir up controversy. Wait for twenty-five years'.[2] She waited thirty.

There was no reason why Baldwin's first administration should not have jogged on for at least three years. He had a working majority. He stressed his affection for Bonar Law, and in many ways his Government looked like a further stage in the normalization of the Bonar Law regime. Because of the reluctance of prominent Conservatives to abandon the Coalition, that Government had certain unmistakably temporary features—such as the fact that four out of five Secretaries of State were peers. This was not a social counter-revolution by the archetypally middle-class Bonar Law, simply a demonstration to the conceited grandees of the Coalition that the country could be run just as well, if not better, without them. By the

---

[1] 1923 memo by William Bridgeman printed in *The Modernization of Conservative Politics: The Diaries and Letters of William Bridgeman 1904–1935* ed. Philip Williamson (The Historians' Press, London 1988), pp. 164–6.

[2] The Marchioness Curzon of Kedleston *Reminiscences* (Hutchinson, London 1955), p. 250.

time Baldwin came to power, that message was getting through. Nor was Baldwin slow to establish a grip on the administrative and party machines which were the real keys to effective government. Bonar Law had fiercely distrusted the Cabinet Secretariat, but Baldwin rapidly established close and friendly relations with the Welsh Deputy Secretary to the Cabinet, Tom Jones. The Secretary to the Cabinet, Sir Maurice Hankey, whose term of office was to outrun Baldwin's political life, for it ended only in 1938, was too closely associated with Lloyd George to move into an intimate working relationship with a Premier whose obsessive dislike of 'the Goat' extended to defacing his image on postcards in scrap books. In his Olympian way, Sir Maurice was loyal. Top Civil Service mandarins were quick to become close to Baldwin. Sir Warren Fisher, Head of the Civil Service, was a regular dinner guest from the summer of 1923 and Horace Wilson, who headed the Ministry of Labour which was clearly in the front line of political action, was another figure with whom Baldwin established early and close relations.

Baldwin also moved decisively to set his stamp on the Conservative Party. He was in many ways a more attractive, certainly a vastly more approachable personality than Bonar Law, and unlike him, was genuinely committed to governing in a way which healed rather than exacerbated the wounds inflicted on the body politic by class antagonisms. Yet he never doubted for a moment that the instrument of power was his own political party. He brought in one of his closest friends, Eyres Monsell, as Chief Whip. It was a very Baldwinish appointment. Reluctantly agreeing to do the job for a year, Monsell did it for a decade, making shrewd use of the newly-institutionalized reminder of party power, the 1922 Committee, and totally reorganizing the Whips Office.[1] Towards the end of Baldwin's career the historian Arthur Bryant published a somewhat gushing work which he had the honesty to call a tribute to rather than a biography of Stanley Baldwin. He made the point that one of the factors which helped the relatively unknown Baldwin to project his personality in 1923 rapidly onto the widest stage was the marvellously evocative image which came across in his photographs in the big daily newspapers. Used to politicians like the Chamberlains, Churchill, or indeed the Labour leader Ramsay MacDonald, who deliberately tried to project a aura of sartorial elegance and dashing style, the public was delighted to find in Baldwin a prime minister denounced at some length in the pages of *The Tailor and Cutter*. If some are born baggy, some achieve bagginess and some have bagginess thrust upon them, Baldwin was born baggy. Bryant was also correct to argue that part of the appeal of Baldwin's image lay in the impression it created that 'Here was a politician who was scarcely a politician at all'.[2] There the image was entirely misleading. Baldwin was a politician to his fingertips.

He was also that unusual phenomenon a politician who broadly meant what he said. Like Henry Pelham, coming to power in the wake of the Walpole ascendancy in the eighteenth century, Baldwin was a decent

---

[1] Keith Middlemas and John Barnes *Baldwin: A Biography* (Weidenfeld and Nicolson, London 1969), p. 177.

[2] Arthur Bryant *Stanley Baldwin: A Tribute* (Hamish Hamilton, London 1937), pp. 100–1.

Anglican gentleman acutely conscious of the need to cleanse what he saw as the Augean stables of attitudes surviving from the Coalition era. Lloyd George in the latter stages of his reign had hardly bothered to go near the House of Commons. Baldwin treated it as a club, not because he wanted to make it a dynamic part of government—quite the reverse—but because it enabled him to stay in touch with the rank and file of his ruling Tory Party whilst also providing him with a platform from which he could launch his campaign to conciliate and incorporate the Labour Party into a broad political consensus capable of securing acquiescence to, if not positive endorsement of, existing social and political structures. Baldwin did not believe in interfering in the internal management of departments of state which he had entrusted to Cabinet colleagues any more than he believed in compulsively reading of newspapers or of the contents of official red boxes. He preferred to retain his sanity and think about broad issues. This did not make him a weak leader.

Indeed his first major move was one of quite astonishing boldness about which controversy has ever since raged, and which underlined the formidable capacity of his office of prime minister for seizing initiatives and setting agendas. The extraordinary aspect of Baldwin's behaviour was the initiative he chose. He had come to office unexpectedly, with a commitment to honesty and plain dealing, and an image which was concomitant, in that it stressed his plain English, indeed his Worcestershire roots. Now Baldwin's image, though latterly much hyped by the Conservative Party, was never fraudulent. It was always over-simplified and partial. He really did enjoy puffing his pipe whilst leaning over a gate and scratching a pig, but he actually came from a wealthy West Midlands ironmaster's family (admittedly fallen on hardish times financially), which had distinguished literary connections by no means confined to his cousin, Rudyard Kipling. He spoke fluent French, passable German and could read Russian. His long-standing custom was to spend a couple of months a year holidaying on the Continent. Compared with a later premier like Edward Heath, with his wooden French and limited grasp of French and German realities, Baldwin might have described himself, in Heathian terms, as a Better European. In fact, for public purposes, he played down his cosmopolitan side. That he was well-acquainted not only with France but also with Switzerland and Northern Italy, and had gained his knowledge of Vienna by travelling to it via Berlin, Dresden, Munich and Salzburg, was something he never stressed. In office, he carefully disguised his considerable knowledge of foreign languages. Baldwin was a clever, complex man who on the public stage pretended to be a slightly slow-witted and simple one. As a result, historians have tended to have difficulty with him. They have known for some time that his declared priorities on entering office were European. He told Tom Jones in late May 1928 that:

> We can't wait for emigration and Empire development. We live by our export trade. We can't afford to let Europe go to pieces with all the serious economic consequences.[1]

Then, at some point in the autumn of 1923, Baldwin decided to adopt

---

[1] Cited in Middlemas and Barnes *Baldwin*, p. 180.

protection in the form of a general tariff (though he excluded wheat and meat eventually) as the main Conservative policy and to hold an election in November to secure a mandate for that policy, on the grounds that the Government was still bound by a pledge against protection given by Bonar Law in the previous year. It all underlined the extent to which Baldwin saw his Government as Bonar Law's continuing, and it led to electoral disaster, the more extraordinary as it is clear that most people had forgotten all about Bonar Law's pledge.

The fact that Baldwin was able to carry his party with him in this radical and utterly unexpected initiative is a tribute to both his personality and his office. Saved from pomposity by his sense of fun, and from megalomania by a mystical high Anglican faith, Baldwin had from the start been well aware of the dignity and power of the premiership. He said and meant that prayers were more appropriate than congratulations for anyone achieving that office, but shortly after achieving it he had written to his confidante, Phyllis Broome, that he now held 'the biggest job in the world and if I fail I shall share the fate of many a better man than I.' He added, characteristically, that 'one may do something before one cracks up.'[1] The problem of why he chose to take this particular protectionist initiative so soon after becoming Prime Minister has haunted historians ever since. Baldwin himself in retrospect produced several explanations or rationalizations, none of which quite seems to fit contemporary facts.

The idea that Lloyd George was thinking of going protectionist and that, by adopting such a policy first, Baldwin 'dished the Goat' and thereby guaranteed the long-term future of the Tory Party by attracting its alienated Coalitionist rump, led as it was by Austen Chamberlain, is just too neat. Even more improbable is the view that Baldwin had calculated that it was worth losing an election to achieve these long-term aims. It is inherently more convincing to embrace the hypothesis that he did what he did because he thought it was the right thing to do, and that he assumed he would get away with it. Apart from an underlying conviction that Bonar Law's government had no policy, and that this was indefensible, Baldwin seems to have been motivated by two factors. One was despair at the slow rate of economic stabilization and reconstruction in Europe, and the other was a profound unease about the problem of long-term structural unemployment in the United Kingdom.

It was a commonplace in the higher circles of British government that the reparations provisions of the Treaty of Versailles were basically impractical. Furthermore, it did not require vast analytical acumen to see that the only way the Germans could possibly pay the huge levels of reparations which the French would have liked to screw out of them was by a massive increase in their exports, and that such a development could only make life more difficult for the ailing export-oriented economy of the UK. Thus, the Franco-Belgian military occupation of the Rhineland in January 1923 was regarded by the Westminster Government as neither likely to solve the reparations problem, nor helpful in the unavoidable long-term task of restoring Germany as a cooperative trading partner. French attempts to destabilize the German Weimar Republic by artificially-stimulated

---

[1] Cited in *ibid.*, p. 169.

separatist movements, especially in the Rhineland, were seen as positively hurtful to the latter objective. Baldwin as Premier did not dream of intervening directly in foreign relations. That was the job of his Foreign Secretary, Curzon, but Baldwin was acutely aware of the paralysis of pro-duction, monetary chaos, and artificial distortion of trading patterns which the Franco-Belgian action was producing. He was also well aware of the intransigence of the French Premier, Poincaré, for in September 1923, he had had long conversations with him in Paris on his way back from vaca-tion at Aix-les-Bains, and concluded that Poincaré had no plan to solve the problems his actions had conjured up.[1]

When Baldwin moved towards an open advocacy of a general tariff shortly afterwards, he understandably caused the small minority of enthusiasts for Imperial economic unity as a prelude to closer political unity within the British Empire to feel euphoric. In particular, Leopold Amery, currently at the Admiralty, was surprised and delighted, though there is no reason to doubt Baldwin's later insistence that he was not seriously influenced by Amery in taking his decision. If the relationship between rhetoric and reality in the Westminster system of politics was often very slender, the most extreme example of this fact lay in the Imperial field. There was an ideological cluster of ideas and formulae and prejudices about the British Empire which politicians found too useful as a manipulative device when dealing with their constituents to be willing to ditch it. Nor were politicians the only ones so to behave. Businessmen found it so convenient that it was difficult for the UK consumer to buy a packet of cigarettes, a bar of soap, or a packet of biscuits without a high likelihood of being reminded of the idea of empire. The Tory Party had tried, by no means always successfully, to monopolize this rhetoric since the days of Disraeli,[2] but men who exercised real power at the heart of the Establish-ment were expected to be able to distinguish between the rhetoric and the messy reality. Amery, like other products of Lord Milner's 'Kindergarten' of bright young men in early twentieth-century South Africa, never quite could. Those who knew him best were clear that there was a streak of unbalanced enthusiasm of an irrational kind close to the core of his per-sonality.

The British Empire to which Leo Amery gave a long lifetime's devotion was already by 1923 a notably incoherent phenomenon. It fell into several categories of which the self-governing dominions such a Canada, Australia and New Zealand were effectively independent states allied to the UK but on a fluctuating basis. The Indian Empire was a category of its own. Once the mighty, autocratically-governed continental power-base which had lifted the United Kingdom of Great Britain and Ireland to superpower status, it was by 1923 a massive strategic liability which the Westminster Government could neither govern in any very dynamic fashion, nor easily extricate themselves from. By repudiating the ruthless tactics which in 1919 had led General Dyer to disperse an unarmed if illegal assembly at Amritsar

---

[1] Anne Orde *Great Britain and International Security 1920–1926* (Royal Historical Society, London 1978), p. 54.

[2] John M. MacKenzie *Propaganda and Empire: The Manipulation of British Opinion 1880–1960* (Manchester University Press, Manchester 1984).

in the Punjab by rifle-fire which killed 379 people, the British Government had made abundantly clear its lack of will to rule indefinitely. Yet independence for India, even behind the diaphanous veil of 'Dominion Status', was not an acceptable immediate political possibility in Westminster. The dependent colonial empire fell into two main sections. One was the detritus of previous phases of overseas economic imperialism, of this the scattered imperial slums in the British West Indies were a good example. The other was a vast collection of territories, mainly African, acquired in the late nineteenth century almost entirely for the negative purpose of keeping them out of the hands of other European powers. They were of very limited economic value; their colonial governments were minimal because self-funded by minute local revenues; and since the UK and its colonial dependencies were run on a basically free-trade system, they by no means traded exclusively with the imperial power. Malaya, which was the only truly wealthy British colonial possession, produced 53 per cent of the world's rubber and 55.6 per cent of its tin. Of the latter product, only ten per cent of Malayan production went to the UK, which continued for commercial reasons to buy non-Malayan rubber on a significant scale. For similar reasons, the UK did not monopolize the output of the highly strategic Trinidad oil industry.[1]

The fact that when he became Premier Baldwin was conspicuously ignorant of this mass of ambiguity, strategic over-commitment and insoluble dilemmas was probably on balance an advantage. It cleared his mind of much irrelevance. There had been since the end of the war low-level pressure for preferential treatment for Dominion exports to the UK, and this was something which could up to a point be catered for under the Byzantine provisions of the Safeguarding of Industries Act of 1921, a measure designed to protect a very few 'key' industries vital for defence purposes, and to provide a wider measure of protection against 'dumping', a concept both narrowly and obscurely defined in the legislation. The Treasury was unenthusiastic about the whole concept. It was positively hostile to expenditure on assisted emigration to the Dominions, and even more hostile to proposals for any sort of Imperial economic development fund. The Empire Settlement Act of 1922 therefore represented a triumph for Leo Amery, though the Treasury kept its funding down to £3 million per annum instead of the £5 million Amery had hoped for, and that leading Treasury Knight, Sir Oscar Niemayer, referred to Amery as the 'Mad Mullah Minister', after the Islamic gentleman who had proved so tiresome to the British Army in Somaliland. Baldwin, as his cited remarks to Tom Jones showed, did not believe that Imperial migration was a serious substitute for European recovery.

When he lurched into an election on behalf of a protectionist policy, he appeared to be defining that policy as he went along. This may have been a deliberate cultivation of ambiguity. He needed all the support he could muster. His speeches were garnished with appropriately elevating references to the development of the Empire. An Imperial Economic Conference was sitting in October and November 1923. Yet by excluding the possibility

[1] Correlli Barnett *The Collapse of British Power* (Alan Sutton pbk edn, Gloucester 1984), pp. 75–6.

of duties on basic foodstuffs, he excluded the only products of significance to Canada, Australia, New Zealand, South Africa and, for that matter, the farmers of the UK.[1] Imperial rhetoric may have been like the large Union Jacks which tended to cover the tables from behind which Baldwin was wont to deliver his public orations: i.e. part of the decoration designed to enhance the gravity and acceptability of the speeches. What Baldwin actually offered in 1923 was a system of industrial protection for the United Kingdom of Great Britain and Northern Ireland.

Apart from despair at the slowness of European reconstruction, there is no doubt that unemployment was the single most important factor influencing Baldwin's judgement. The immediate aftermath of war had seen a vigorous economic boom based on restocking; the replacement of assets destroyed in war; pent-up consumer frustration finally released; and not least the relative prostration of the industrial economies of several former export rivals. After midsummer 1920, however, a decline in employment set in which by the end of the year, accelerated by stoppages of work due to industrial disputes in the vital coal industry, had become a full recession in many trades. By 1921, a full-blown slump was devastating the employment market. A bitter coal strike which lasted three months from April 1921 made a bad situation worse, and the slump really only bottomed out in the latter part of 1921. By 1922, 'monetary Slump was over, but employment was still, according to pre-war standards, extremely bad.'[2]

As Premier, Baldwin was facing what the leading analyst of unemployment in the period has called 'The Doldrums', a period from 1923 through 1925 when the economy was gently recovering and when, by pre-war experience, unemployment should have been relatively low, but when in fact the Government was faced with the problem of 'the intractable million' of unemployed. Nor were forward prospects encouraging for British exports. War-expanded industries naturally had to shrink. Industrialization in Japan and India threatened the future of the UK's heavily export-oriented textile industries. Coal exports were affected by foreign competition and technical developments such as hydro-electricity. With international recovery, the price of agricultural products, especially European ones, fell so low that UK agriculture suffered acutely, and it was simply not necessary to export as much as had been needed before the war to secure the huge proportion of the UK's food supply which was imported.[3] Another factor of which Baldwin was acutely conscious was that the position of the export trades in 1923 was artificially and temporarily buoyed by the appalling economic consequences of the Franco-Belgian occupation of the Rhineland, and of the policies followed by the German Chancellor, Wilhelm Cuno, to meet it with 'passive resistance'. The mark collapsed, industrial production plummeted, and raging inflation radically destabilized the shaky foundations of the Weimar Republic, encouraging working-class militancy, middle-class alienation and upper-class disloyalty

[1] Ian M. Drummond *Imperial Economic Policy 1917–1939: Studies in expansion and protection* (George Allen and Unwin, pbk edn, London 1974), pp. 26–7.
[2] A. C. Pigou *Aspects of British Economic History 1918–1925* (Macmillan, London 1947), p. 40.
[3] *Ibid.*, Parts II and III.

to republican institutions. By August 1923, a new Chancellor, Gustav Stresemann, was beginning patiently to lead Germany back from the brink of chaos.[1]

Baldwin was no systematic economic theorist. Given the limited degree of contact with reality characteristic of most highly-developed systems of economic thought, this was no great disadvantage. It did enable him intuitively to move towards the position that the neoclassical dogmas adopted and reiterated to legitimize a successful nineteenth-century export economy were simply inappropriate when the UK needed, because of changes in the terms of trade, to export far less than before to secure essential food and raw materials. Free trade had become a preservative of the pathological, a sort of ideological formaldehyde, particularly appreciated by that great majority of UK managers whose solution to most problems was to cut wages. Dundee, which had long been the seat of Winston Churchill, one of the most vocal of free traders, was an interesting example. It had an overdeveloped, dominant jute industry which was in long-term decline. Wages were so low that the only new products with a future in the Dundee market were products like margarine, which were even cheaper substitutes for old staples.[2]

Though Baldwin spent so much time talking about the values of an older rural England, his policies were aimed at a contemporary industrial one. Land settlement, in the shape of breaking up large estates into small farms in Great Britain, or subsidizing surplus population to go out to farm in Canada was not something he saw as a serious solution to the contemporary economic malaise. There was a head of pressure for land seizure by small farmers, but it tended to be concentrated in the parts of the British Isles which had not experienced 'modernization' as the early twentieth century understood that term (i.e. the creation of a plural society based on urbanization and industrialization). For example, much of the Irish Republican Army's activities in Munster and Connaught between 1918 and 1922 look suspiciously like thinly disguised land raiding, locally organized by groups which shared Nationalist slogans with their nominal commanders in Dublin, but who otherwise paid little heed to them. Localized tensions compounded of a partial suspension of land purchase schemes; a stoppage of emigration in wartime; and additional pressure due to demobilization may explain more than the ideology of Nationalism itself. Certainly, in areas without such tensions there was no lack of potential Nationalist heroes, just a lack of demand for their services.[3] It was no accident that it was in the Hebrides that the other contemporary example of widespread land raiding occurred. In the absence of towns and industry, it was by seizing land that returned ex-servicemen secured the economic base which saw many of them through the bitter years of the Great

[1] A. J. Nicholls *Weimar and the Rise of Hitler* (Macmillan, 3rd edn, London 1991), chap. 7.

[2] B. P. Lenman, C. Lythe, and E. Gauldie *Dundee and its Textile Industry 1850–1914* (Abertay Historical Society, Publication No. 14, Dundee 1969); Bruce P. Lenman and Kathleen Donaldson 'Partners' Incomes, Investment and Diversification in the Scottish Linen Area 1850–1921', *Business History*, (XIII, 1971), pp. 1–8.

[3] Charles Townshend 'Modernisation and Nationalism: Perspectives in Recent Irish History', *History* (66, 1981), 241–3.

Depression. Their use of violence was sub-homicidal, but land raiding in the Hebrides persisted into the mid-1920s, fuelled by, among other memories, recollections of the promises of postwar access to land which politicians had made so recklessly to encourage wartime recruiting.[1]

Lloyd George never quite shook off the rural North Welsh bias which made him take land reform and settlement more seriously than its essentially peripheral appeal to the bulk of the urban population merited. When he began to try to recreate some of the impetus of his own old radicalism, a central part of the endeavour was an enquiry into the land question, begun in 1923 and completed in 1925. The result was a 'Green Book', *Land and the Nation*, which proposed that the state should become the ultimate landlord, with responsibilities for rural development. These proposals outraged wealthy conservative Liberals like Sir Alfred Mond, who were to find Baldwin's departure from the shibboleth of free trade in the long run more palatable. Baldwin's decision to hold an election 'for narrow partisan purposes' on that issue, when he had a majority capable of seeing him through four years has been described, by a shrewd and distinguished biographer of Lloyd George as 'a shameless abuse of prime ministerial power',[2] but this is perhaps a shade too much the view of Baldwin's political opponents. Viewed from a more detached point of view, the decision to hold an election on tariffs was indeed an astonishing display of prime ministerial power, but eccentric rather than outrageous, and even then behind the eccentricity lay genuine conviction that here was the only positive policy which could possibly be adopted by Government in order to check unemployment and alter the highly predictable slow downwards drift, in relative terms, of the UK industrial economy. Besides, Baldwin expected to win a majority, not of votes cast, as Lloyd George was quick to point out, but of seats. The Unionist Central Office's official estimates of the likely results gave him a majority of between 87 and 95. He was in fact to end up in a minority of almost exactly 95. We know from the diary of Tom Jones that the sharp swing against the Tories came as a great shock to Baldwin and his closer associates.[3]

It was an era when the electorate had undergone, and was to undergo, rapid change with the progressive enfranchisement of women. Opinion sampling by means of polls was not a technique used as it was to be later in the century as the principal determinant of the decision to call an election. Baldwin, as usual, operated on instinct, and it failed him, as results in the shape of 257 Conservative MPs, 158 Liberal and 191 Labour showed. Though the Tories won 18 seats, they lost 40 to Labour and no less than 67 to the Liberals. One of Baldwin's harshest critics was later to say:

> It would be hard to imagine a stupider decision. No sane person . . . would have dreamed of confronting them with an election on the fiscal issue without taking some little time to put the Protectionist case before them again. Nobody outside a lunatic asylum (or the Unionist Central Office) would have

[1] Leah Leneman *Fit for Heroes?: Land settlement in Scotland after World War I* (Aberdeen University Press, Aberdeen 1989), Chap. 2.

[2] Pugh, *Lloyd George*, p. 162.

[3] Thomas Jones *Whitehall Diary. Vol I: 1916–1925*, ed. Keith Middlemas (Oxford University Press, London 1969), entries for 4, 6 and 7 December 1923, pp. 257–9.

given the disunited Liberals and Socialists so heaven-sent an opportunity to combine against the Government.[1]

This criticism was unfair in that it entirely eliminated the question of conviction, of which Baldwin had plenty, but as a summary of the tactical disadvantages of opting for protection, it could hardly be bettered. Asquith had lost his Fife seat in 1918, but his Squiffite remnant was kept distinct as a group in the Commons under the leadership of Sir Donald Maclean, handpicked by Asquith as devoid of the qualities which might establish him as a rival. By 1920, Asquith was back as MP for another Scottish constituency, Paisley. He was even more devoid of positive ideas than he had been in 1918, but his hostility to Lloyd George was undimmed. The threat to free trade enabled the ranks of the Liberals to come together in 1923—slightly unconvincingly to those who watched Lloyd George and his National Liberals accept Asquith as Leader, and embrace the Squiffites —but effectively for electoral purposes. Lloyd George even made £100,000 available from his notorious political fund to help field 457 Liberal candidates.

The Labour Party was every bit as dogmatically committed to free trade as the Liberals, fighting the election with a manifesto which said that:

> Tariffs are not a remedy for unemployment. They are an impediment to the free interchange of goods and services . . . They foster a spirit of profiteering, materialism and selfishness, poison the life of nations, lead to corruption in
> politics, promote trusts and monopolies, and impoverish the people.

As Philip Snowden, himself a fanatical free trader, later pointed out with pride, it was an election fought on the sole issue of protection which was the prelude to Labour's entry into office.[2] It was also the last election which saw Winston Churchill fight as a Liberal. He lost a rowdy election in West Leicester in which he manfully rebutted taunts about the Dardanelles campaign with the reply that he did not regret a good idea, only its failure. His victorious Labour opponent, F. W. Pethick-Lawrence, recalled that when the result was announced, Churchill approached him to say, 'Well, anyhow it is a victory for free trade.'[3]

Though the 1980s were to see extremely contentious policies pushed through by a Conservative government based on a surprisingly small percentage of the votes cast, their ability to do this was rooted in the hopelessly divided nature of the opposition groups. Baldwin in 1923 showed both the power of prime ministerial initiative and its limits because his contentious policy united the opposition, even if in defence of negation. He lost that whipped majority which both Bonar Law and he knew was the essential bedrock of Tory government.

As it happened, no other party gained a majority, and despite predictable hysteria in the City of London at the prospect of 'Socialist' government,

[1] Cited in A. W. Baldwin *My Father: The True Story* (George Allen and Unwin, London 1955), p. 125.

[2] Philip Viscount Snowden *An Autobiography. Vol. II: 1919–1934* (Ivor Nicholson and Watson, London 1934), pp. 591–2, where the appropriate section of the manifesto is cited.

[3] Martin Gilbert *Winston S. Churchill. Vol V: 1922–1939* (William Heinemann, London 1976), pp. 16–20.

most professional Conservative politicians were well aware that the situation was comfortably in hand. Asquithian Liberals differed from Conservatives only in the sense that they were, if anything, more conservative. That was why they were for no change in tariff policy. As for the Labour Party, Neville Chamberlain 'was clear on all grounds that Labour should be given office'. He added, 'it would be too weak to do much harm, but not too weak to get discredited'.[1] Asquith may originally have hoped to vote out Labour with Conservative support, and then vote out the Tories with Labour assistance, before assuming office himself as the great 'moderate' compromise. The perils of office were such that the Labour leadership had considered whether it was worth assuming office whilst in a small minority in the Commons and a ridiculous minority in the Lords. In an article in the *Morning Post* in the early part of 1923, Philip Snowden had contemplated the prospect of office as the largest party in the Commons, but with no majority. He concluded, with impeccable logic:

> A situation like that would be full of embarrassment for the Labour Party.
> It would provide no test of what a Labour Government with a Parliamentary
> majority would do . . . It would probably so discredit the party that the day
> when it would become the majority would be indefinitely postponed.

He went on to argue that a coalition with the Liberals would be even worse, and that the best tactics would be to force a Liberal-Conservative coalition and oppose it strongly. Yet in December 1923, when the situation Snowden had considered arose, the Labour Party could not prevent Asquith from forcing the card of office on it. Even though Asquith made no secret of his view that it would be difficult to find 'safer conditions' for the experiment of a Labour government, refusal to shoulder responsibility would clearly harm the party electorally. Its leader, Ramsay MacDonald, also pointed out to his colleagues that if they shunned office, and the Liberals replaced the Tories, the latter would become the official Opposition, ousting Labour from a position gained only in 1922, and which was an important source of prestige and publicity.

Ramsay MacDonald clearly wanted to accept office from the start. Whether he would inherit the full patronage powers of the premiership as shaped by Liberal and Tory regimes was less clear. It would have been more in accord with the party's tradition if there had been some system of election of the Cabinet by the entire body of Labour MPs. The party's leading Fabian Socialist, Sidney Webb, lectured MPs and trade union executives on the paramount importance of allowing MacDonald total discretion. As no structure for an elective process existed, Webb's views were quickly accepted. Arguably, the Labour Party thereby doomed itself to long-term futility, for MacDonald's power over it became immense, and when he emerged from self-imposed purdah in his native Lossiemouth with his Cabinet formed, it contained a crucially important appointment which more or less guaranteed policy paralysis. Of course, like other premiers, MacDonald had to take advice when forming a cabinet, and to make allowances for the personal preferences and political clout of prospective colleagues. His sustained and increasingly bizarre attempts to exclude

---

[1] Cited in Middlemas and Barnes *Baldwin*, p. 251.

Arthur Henderson, one of the few Labour men with previous ministerial experience (during the war), proved impractical and Henderson emerged as Home Secretary.[1] It was however the appointment of Philip Snowden as Chancellor of the Exchequer which was crucial. A former Excise clerk, lonely, crippled and sour in public manner, Snowden was not even personally friendly with MacDonald. He had supported J. R. Clynes against MacDonald for the leadership, arguing that MacDonald, behind a handsome front, was devious and given to compromising with the enemy. MacDonald would whisper to friends that Snowden was little more than a thinly-disguised Liberal. Both men were to be congratulated on their perceptiveness, but their innate conservatism made them tend to agree on major policy decisions, however much they disliked one another personally.

Beatrice Webb, Sidney's wife, predicted the likely consequences of Snowden with brutal frankness. She thought it would have been far wiser to have J. R. Clynes as Chancellor with the fiscally radical Penthick-Lawrence as Financial Secretary and a powerful Cabinet Committee, to help prepare a budget which was as much a political as an economic exercise. Snowden she denounced as 'chicken-hearted', as an Asquithian cheese-parer who would oppose all expenditure. He had already, she knew, demurred at proposals for public works to relieve unemployment: 'Where was the money to come from?, he asked, with a Treasury Clerk's intonation.'[2]

It was true that MacDonald's policy of demonstrating that Labour was fit to rule by a policy of studied 'moderation' had much to be said for it. Office was a valuable opportunity, even without a working majority, for Labour to acquire 'hands-on' experience of the administrative machine, both for the sake of future effectiveness, and to deprive their political opponents of the damaging charge that Labour simply did not know how to run a government. On the other hand, George V must have known he was handing MacDonald a poisoned chalice when he invited him to form a government. J. C. C. Davidson, who as Chancellor of the Duchy of Lancaster under Baldwin, had a chance to become well-acquainted with King George was emphatic that:

> The atmosphere at Court was definitely conservative. The King was a marvellous man and it was remarkable how he hid from the world that he was an absolutely dyed-in-the-wool conservative . . . He was very right-wing and he knew where his friends really lay, and that the Conservative Party was the King's Party . . . But he managed to persuade the Labour Party that he was entirely neutral. That must have required a very great deal of self-discipline.[3]

So the refusal of MacDonald to put his foot down about the Court's insistence that Labour cabinet ministers dress up in Gilbertian flummery, braid and feathers (when contemporary evening dress would have been a breath of dignity and sanity), augured ill for the future of the Government. That

[1] Colin Cross *Philip Snowden* (Barrie and Rockliffe, London 1966), pp. 192–6.
[2] *Beatrice Webb's Diaries 1912–1924*, ed. Margaret I. Cole (Longman, Green and Co., London 1952), entry for 12 December 1923, pp. 255–6.
[3] *Davidson's Memoirs*, pp. 177–8.

his own vanity was tickled by the fine figure he cut in fancy dress might not matter much, but his self-deception about the positive friendliness of King George was dangerously naïve.

If there was a disconcerting enthusiasm in MacDonald's coming to terms with the social side of the British Establishment, the meeting of Philip Snowden and the Treasury mandarins led by Sir Warren Fisher was a marriage of kindred souls, as Winston Churchill was to point out in his book on *Great Contemporaries*. The mandarins might have feared that a Labour Chancellor would challenge some of their most cherished principles. Indeed, he should have, for those principles had been carefully crafted into an intellectual system designed to make any breach of established patterns of government virtually impossible, and by implication to safeguard the social order which had generated that pattern of government. Snowden was more Treasury-minded than the Treasury. It was a situation only parallelled in the late 1960s when Foreign Office mandarins developed a similar affection for another Labour minister, George Brown, and for similar reasons.

MacDonald doubled up as Prime Minister and Foreign Secretary, which was not unreasonable, though very arduous. The new Premier was a well-travelled, well-informed and cosmopolitan man. He was also, like Lloyd George, capable of working out that association with foreign dignitaries at international conferences gave instant publicity, usually favourable, and enabled a politician to claim to be a statesman, the most overused word in the business apart from brilliant (which Stanley Baldwin said always reminded him of the word 'brilliantine', a greasy cosmetic). He was also lucky in that the European situation was ripe for some constructive developments, especially in the long Franco-German confrontation in the Rhineland over reparations, where the French had worked out they could not achieve their more extreme aims, and the Germans had grasped they would have to pay something.

Ramsay MacDonald's talents for tact and patient negotiation helped him to have a tolerable relationship with Poincaré, but after that hard-liner was replaced by Herriot, it proved possible to implement a plan for reparations within Germany's capacity, in exchange for an end to military occupation and attempts to break up the country, as worked out by an expert committee under the American General Dawes. Vague commitments by MacDonald to the new international body, the League of Nations, went down well, as did a carefully-publicized personal appearance at the League of Nations Assembly in Geneva. A perfectly sensible attempt to restore trading relations with Soviet Russia proved less happy politically. It began with official recognition of Soviet Russia, then moved, through difficult negotiations, to a proposed package: a commercial treaty, followed by a partial settlement of Russian debts, and a guaranteed loan to Russia. It was an invitation to political opponents to beat the anti-Bolshevik drum, which they did, led by an angry Lloyd George who reckoned the Tories would have to follow his lead and that it was not to his long-term advantage for a purely Labour government to succeed.[1]

[1] W. N. Medlicott *British Foreign Policy since Versailles 1919–1963* (Methuen, 2nd edn, pbk, London 1968), pp. 53–8.

By late 1923, the Government's days were obviously numbered. Domestically, it had achieved very little, and nothing at all on the unemployment front. MacDonald and Snowden were between them a massive force for inertia, and in any case the radicalism behind the first Labour government was much less formidable than contemporary conservative critics allowed. They continually harped on what was to become a standard conservative theme of the twentieth century: that a 'moderate' Labour leadership masked control of the party and the government by 'extremists'. In fact, these wolves in sheep's clothing as often as not turn out to be sheep in wolves' clothing when subjected to historical scrutiny. MacDonald was often thought to owe his election to the leadership of his party to a group of 'extremist' MPs known collectively as Red Clydeside. MacDonald certainly owed a lot to support from Scots Labour MPs. They identified with a fellow-Scot who as late as February 1921 was being slandered into defeat at a Woolwich by-election by such malodorous players of the patriot game as Horatio Bottomley, but Red Clydeside as such was not particularly for MacDonald. Its best-known members such as Jimmy Maxton and Davey Kirkwood were extrovert tactical incompetents who achieved nothing. Baldwin and Churchill soon regarded them with patronizing affection. It was the Roman Catholic businessman John Wheatley who in his 1924 Housing Act made the only significant legislative contribution to domestic affairs to emerge from either Red Clydeside or the first Labour government. Much the most important of the interwar acts offering subsidies to local authorities to build houses, it established a constructive and effective partnership between the state and private firms, as well as between central and local government. The houses built were beyond the means of the poorest, but Wheatley's legislation did enable some progress to be made even in the very worst centres of urban deprivation and overcrowding.[1]

The demise of the Government was a messy business in which MacDonald mishandled situations which were not very damaging in such a way as to make them look worse than they were. One example was the granting of a baronetcy to an old and wealthy friend who had made available to the new Premier a Daimler car and the income from £40,000 of securities to uphold his lifestyle. The friend was more than worth a baronetcy as a philanthropist, but the ineptitude of the affair was staggering, and damaging when revealed. The Conservatives also made hay with the suspension of the prosecution of a Communist editor, John Campbell, for publishing a piece appealing to the British Army not to shoot down 'the workers'. The decision to prosecute was a silly one, drawing attention to an irrelevance. Political influence on the decision to prosecute in such cases was not only unavoidable but had been commonplace under Conservative administrations. Nevertheless, once again MacDonald's reluctance to shoulder responsibility proved disastrous. Much more significant was the Government's decision not to accept a lifeline in the shape of a select committee offered by Asquith, but to go for bust. The Tories voted for

---

[1] Iain McLean *The Legend of Red Clydeside* (John Donald, Edinburgh 1983). For the impact of Wheatley's act in the poorest major city in Great Britain, *vide* Bruce Lenman and W. D. Carroll 'Council Housing in Dundee', *Town Planning Review* (43, 1972), pp. 275–85.

Asquith's proposal, which the Government opposed. Defeated, Mac-Donald used one of the most formidable and personal of a premier's powers. The Cabinet on the night of the Government's defeat 'took note of the Prime Minister's intention to see the King at 10 a.m. on the following morning' to ask for a dissolution. Lloyd George had, at the time of the formation of the Labour Government, expressed shrewd doubts whether it would try to do anything constructive, and he always made it clear that he was profoundly contemptuous of MacDonald, whom he saw as an indecisive, vain and fussy version of Stanley Baldwin. Over the dissolution, which George V granted on the grounds that no other party 'could form a Government that could last', MacDonald was very decisive. George V told MacDonald privately 'that he granted the election with great reluctance', but, in fact, he must have known that the Tories were likely to win it.[1] Equally, MacDonald knew, if only from by-election results, that an election at that time was bound to be disastrous for the Liberals. Deep down, King and Premier were less unhappy than they pretended. It was to be the 1970s before a Conservative premier actually threatened dissenting members of his own party with a punitive dissolution if they failed to support him over Common Market entry, but the precedents as to the highly personal nature of a dissolution request had been long established by then. In the last analysis, a twentieth-century UK premier who could not endure a given situation at Westminster could always abolish that particular parliament by dissolution, provided he was prepared to accept the political consequences.

If Ramsay MacDonald did much to fasten the classic pattern of prime-ministerial power on the Labour Party during his first brief tenure of office, Stanley Baldwin contrived, paradoxically, to reinforce the roots of that power within the Conservative Party during his short period in opposition. This was a remarkable performance, for the Conservatives had reason to be resentful at the authority which had plunged them into an unnecessary and unsuccessful election. Backbenchers were profoundly unamused. The majority of them had had to find their own election expenses, to the tune of £1,000, which in the money of the period was not insignificant. The Executive of the 1922 Committee had seen four of its members defeated, and survivors expressed concern about their own reduced majorities. Understandably, the 1922 Committee called for 'regular Party meetings under the chairmanship of the Leader . . . at which, from time to time, an indication would be given to the rank and file of the general Policy of the Party'. The sting lay in the tail: 'and an opportunity afforded to members to raise any questions or points that seemed to them of importance.' The leadership stonewalled. Baldwin expressed sympathy, but said such meetings would simply spawn leaks to the press. Austen Chamberlain, characteristically, agreed with Baldwin about the need for secrecy; said such meetings would breed schisms; and patronizingly told his audience that more experience would teach them the need to trust their leaders. That was rich from a leadership whose sudden dive for protection had left the

---

[1] The quotations are from Ramsay MacDonald's diary for the period which is extensively cited in David Marquand *Ramsay MacDonald* (Jonathan Cape, London 1977), pp. 377–8.

committed free traders in the Conservative Party in an impossible position. The 1922 Committee failed to obtain any real participation in policy formulation, though even the Whips Office had to accept it as an institutionalized consumer council for Tory MPs.[1]

The Lancashire Tories also raised very fundamental issues, led by the pomp and circumstance of Lord Derby, and managed in sometimes uneasy cooperation with him by Sir Archibald Salvidge, the long-standing boss of the Tory machine in Liverpool. They had lost five Manchester and two Liverpool seats to the Liberals after an election in which they had been in a state of utter confusion over protection. Derby flirted with an abortive conspiracy to dump Baldwin. That proved quite impractical: the way Baldwin had lost his election had enabled the former Coalitionist Tories, most of whom, like Austen Chamberlain, were ardent protectionists, to rally to him. However, at a Manchester meeting of Lancashire Conservatives, Salvidge on 9 February 1924 had moved and carried a motion which demanded some element of participation by local organizations in the formulation of central party policy. By February, the National Association was voicing similar demands, with the suggestion that what was needed was some sort of liaison committee between it and the leadership. The latter was utterly unenthusiastic about the proposed power-sharing. Party government to them implied the control of the party by the Westminster leadership of the parliamentary party.

In the event, Baldwin was able to preserve that principle with only cosmetic concessions to backbenchers and party activists. He defused the internal party crisis by abandoning the protectionist policy whose consequences had made his critics militant. This he could do sincerely and openly, for he believed in consensus government, and he was perfectly prepared to admit that the election had proved that there was no consensus for protection. He then settled down to what he could be fairly sure would be a short spell in opposition during which he contrived to have the best of both worlds. On the front bench, whence he seldom attacked the Government with any violence, and in the smoking room, where he was affable to Labour and Conservative MPs alike, he exuded moderation and benignity. Meanwhile, other Conservatives were taking advantage of Commons procedures, especially on committees where the minority Government had no majority. They systematically crucified those few Labour ministers who wanted to do anything by making sure that their legislation made extremely slow or no progress. Wheatley was the great exception.

The Conservatives, free of the burdens of office and sobered by defeat, were in a mood to accept a measure of internal reorganization, which Baldwin used to set the stamp of his own personality on the party machine. Nobody really blamed the organization for the defeat, but the Principal Agent, Admiral Sir Reginald Hall, was the one sacrificial victim offered up, all the more easily because he had contrived to lose his own seat at the election. 'Blinker' Hall had been a very distinguished Director of Naval Intelligence. He was not a success as Principal Agent. He was an early case of the insane levels of paranoia which were to distinguish the senior ranks

[1] Philip Goodhart with Ursula Branston *The 1922: The Story of the Conservative Backbenchers' Parliamentary Committee* (Macmillan, London 1973), pp. 22–31.

of the UK's security forces in the late twentieth century. To him, there was no difference between the Labour Party and Bolshevism, and Ramsay MacDonald he was sure was the mere tip of a Communist iceberg. Hall was replaced by the infinitely more conciliatory Herbert Blain, a business efficiency expert. Contacts with the Security Service MI5 were however maintained by the recruitment from it of Joseph Ball to handle Tory propaganda work. The best agents were moved to marginal constituencies where the electoral decision lay. In general, the mere existence of a Labour Government stimulated that local grass-roots Conservatism with which Baldwin was always careful to be identified. It also frightened Liberal voters into the Tory camp.

The scale of the Conservative victory in the October 1924 election probably surprised Baldwin. There were 412 Tory MPs to 151 Labour and a mere 41 Liberals. Unopposed, and therefore free to roam, Baldwin had been a dominant figure in the campaign. He was also the only party leader to make relaxed, masterful use of the new medium of radio. He even had a coherent set of policies, including quite extensive housing and social proposals. That his campaign benefitted from a typical *Daily Mail* Red scare stunt in the shape of the so-called Zinoviev Letter, purporting to reveal a widespread Communist campaign of subversion, was in many ways an irrelevance. Baldwin thought the letter genuine. We now know it to have been a forgery produced in Poland and planted by a gullible MI5 both on the Foreign Office and, via Conservative Central Office, on the *Daily Mail*. The letter was a passable summary of the wilder fantasies of the Moscow regime. The Tories, it is clear in retrospect, were sure of a comfortable majority without it. As it was, the Conservative share of votes cast, at just under 47 per cent, probably represented, when allowances are made for thinly disguised Conservative candidates like Winston Churchill (who was returned at Epping as a 'Constitutionalist'), and uncontested seats, the equivalent of support by well over 50 per cent of the voters.[1]

Baldwin had finally put the pieces of the jigsaw puzzle together. Since the enormous surge in the power of the premier dating from the Parliament Act of 1911, that office had become a paradoxical one. It was potent, but distrusted. Both Asquith and Lloyd George had difficulty legitimizing their authority. In both cases, it had rested on unstable, indeed self-destructive coalitions. Bonar Law had seized power from a narrow, single-party base supported by so small a proportion of the electorate as to render restraint and caution mandatory. Throwing caution to the winds, Baldwin had lost office. Now he regained it, his premiership solidly buttressed by a united party machine, of which he was the shrewd unchallenged boss, and by widespread public support. The Labour Party could not have been more helpful. Its rhetoric rallied the middle classes to the Conservatives whilst its passivity in office enabled the Tory leaders to contemplate the demise of the Liberals with equanimity. Incapable of power, Labour might expect spasms of office in a two-party system, and behind the vanity and vacuous preaching of Ramsay MacDonald now lay a positive passion for the gratifying splendours of the office of prime minister.

---

[1] John Ramsden *A History of the Conservative Party. Volume 3: The Age of Balfour and Baldwin 1902–1940* (Longman, London 1978), pp. 188–206.

7

Baldwin's progress via the steps of the guillotine to political heaven 1924–31

Son of St Louis, ascend to Heaven.

Priest to Louis XVI on the scaffold

It takes three British bricklayers to do the work of one French bricklayer. But then it takes three British Ministers to do the work of one French Minister. When there is a change of Government in France eighteen new Ministers replace eighteen old Ministers. With us sixty Ministers replace the outgoing sixty Ministers. Yet France has a more centralized Government, and her colonial, foreign, and defence problems are very much the same as ours.

Lord Rothermere to Winston S. Churchill, 12 February 1925

If God succeeds in making Ramsay do Baldwin's economy for him and pull the TUC for that policy as well, I really shall believe in a personal Deity—with one motto 'this is my beloved son Stanley'.

Walter Elliot, 20 August 1931

The scale of the Conservative victory in 1924 was massive. It ranks with such decisive triumphs as the Liberal victory of 1906 and the Labour victory of 1945. Baldwin had a majority of over 200, and though the Labour Party had gained a million votes (partly by running 90 more candidates than in the previous election), they had come back with fewer MPs. The decisive collapse had been that of the Liberals, from 151 to only 40. They had only been reunited by the issue on which Baldwin had chosen to fight the 1923 election. Now that he had publicly abandoned any commitment to the introduction of protectionism, they had lost any convincing reason for existing, and their wealthier supporters were bitterly hostile to the efforts of Lloyd George to provide Liberalism with a new, radical and relevant platform. From the point of view of the Government, it was a very satisfactory Opposition. Of course, though it was as powerless as any Westminster opposition facing a massive government majority, there was always the possibility that the electorate might become so disenchanted and disgruntled over a period of years that Labour might creep into office on a minority basis after a general election. This was scarcely an alarming prospect, as there was already plenty of evidence to suggest that a Labour government in office rather than power provided the Conservative Party with a vacation and an opportunity to sort itself out, whilst Labour self-destructed in less than half the term of a Parliament. The Liberals, though gratifyingly moribund and hopelessly divided, were still there as an ulti-mate safeguard, syphoning off protest votes into a party which, its Lloyd George wing always excepted, the Tories had good reason to assume would do their work for them.

When, for example, the Conservative Party was seeking from 1927 to establish a substantial endowment for its new adult education establish-ment, the Bonar Law Memorial College at Ashridge, it received big donations, covertly, from wealthy Liberals. The second Earl of Inchcape, a hereditary shipping magnate, called on Baldwin with a brown paper parcel containing a large sum in untraceable bearer bonds. His lordship's unwonted modesty derived from the fact that he was currently a member of the Liberal Council. Stanley Baldwin sent him off to see J. C. C. David-son, who arranged for the money to go into the Ashridge endowment. Davidson subsequently remarked, with great truth, that 'That was an example of where a lot of support for the new Toryism came from—old Liberals; he wouldn't have given one penny for Lloyd George'. Davidson went on to cite Lord Cowdray as another nominal Liberal who followed a similar path.[1] The then Lord Cowdray was a civil engineer and another example of a man whose fortune had been based on the great age of British overseas entrepreneurship and investment before 1914.[2]

By and large, a significant and very powerful element in the moneyed groups which provided the financial backing for the interwar Tory Party, and whose sons often occupied its parliamentary seats, was not only living off the fruits of late Victorian UK industry, but also in the mental world created to meet the needs of the late Victorian entrepreneur and investor. Many of the paradigms built into that world-view were outdated by the 1920s, but in a crassly simplified form they still possessed the virtue of telling the wealthy that what they wanted was right, not just for them, but for everyone, from Welsh coal miner to Mexican peasant, to Lascar deckhand. There were only three basic principles, apart from the mainten-ance of law and order (i.e. the existing social order): sound money; as low taxation as possible; and, if there was economic distress, a restoration of international competitiveness by cutting costs. This last point was a transparent code for cutting wages and the labour force.

The first Earl of Inchcape, James Lyle Mackay had been a free-trader and Liberal, who believed in minimal government. He served on the Geddes Economy Committee and the Indian Retrenchment Committee of 1922–23 before crossing to the Conservative benches in the House of Lords in 1926. His relentless, tunnel-vision passion for economy roused widespread support among Tories, to the point where Baldwin by 1925 was a prisoner of this negative cheeseparing mentality. Baldwin's victory in 1924 had been

[1] Davidson *Memoirs*, pp. 291–2.
[2] Colin M. MacLachlan and Jaime E. Rodriguez O *The Forging of the Cosmic Race: A reinterpretation of colonial Mexico* (University of California Press, Berkeley 1980), pp. 334–7.

based on ditching the only positive programme his party was prepared to embrace, and so the Premier himself felt freed of responsibility: he had offered the country an alternative, and it had been rejected. Retrenchment was as much an evasion of problems as a solution. Bad management was never mentioned, but much UK management was poor. Inchcape's sale of 2.5 million ex-German tons of largely obsolete German shipping to his fellow shipowners, for example, was not the triumph Inchcape saw it as. They had already thrown away an alarming proportion of their reserves in reckless speculation in the 1919–20 boom, compounded by devices like issuing bonus shares and watering capital, so as to massively increase their liabilities. They would have done better to commission modern ships, or not spend their money at all.[1]

There was, therefore, a paradoxical quality to Baldwin's position. On the one hand, he was the beneficiary of a crucially important build-up of prime ministerial power between the Parliament Act of 1911 and his own electoral victory in 1924. Between these two events, there had been the great increase in the capabilities of the office due to the political heritage and bureaucratic innovations of Lloyd George. Bonar Law had pruned rather than uprooted this growth, and both he and Baldwin had firmly linked the office of premier to the office of Leader of the Conservative Party, a party for which Baldwin's conciliatory style had helped to win an unusually wide degree of positive support, and an even wider measure of acquiescence in its rule. If Lloyd George tended to plebiscitary elective dictatorship, Bonar Law and Baldwin were in effect personal monarchs, serving, far from slavishly but nevertheless serving, the interests embedded in their party's structure and personnel. The political loaves and fishes which went with electoral success, and to which no Geddes ever dared take an axe, naturally reinforced Baldwin's authority. Austen Chamberlain found him as courteous and pleasant as ever, but 'a good deal changed and stiffened by his victory'. He added that when it came to forming his Government, Baldwin was 'not inclined to accept advice or suggestions unless they chimed with his own ideas.'

On the other hand, Baldwin was ultimately controlled by the negative nature of the views held by the bulk of his own supporters. It is too facile to blame the lack of positive policies on the domestic front between 1924 and 1929 on the somewhat elderly nature of the Government, and the indolence of Baldwin. It was bred into the very bones of regular Tories and those new Tories who had been Asquithian Liberals. They did not want to do anything, as Baldwin, in his own way a great party boss, knew full well. The partial exception to this was the one which proved the rule, for it was Baldwin's closest colleague, Neville Chamberlain, who was the heir of that Radical Liberal Unionist tradition which had since 1886 been perhaps the most constructive strand in the politics of the British Isles.

Baldwin used the Premier's prerogative to hire ministers with remarkable freedom, and little consultation. The raft of peers which had helped carry

[1] The *DNB* has a good entry for the first Earl of Inchcape, while H. J. Dyos and D. H. Aldcroft *British Transport: An Economic Survey from the Seventeenth Century to the Twentieth* (Penguin Books pbk edn, London 1974), pp. 309–310, has a devastating critique of the mismanagement of UK shipping after 1919.

Bonar Law and Baldwin through the period when the ex-Coalitionist Tory grandees were boycotting the Government was unceremoniously sunk. Lords Balfour, Devonshire, Derby and Peel were offered neither warning nor explanation. Sir Robert Horne, who wanted the Chancellorship of the Exchequer, and angrily refused the Ministry of Labour, then was reduced to 'a state of dementia' when Baldwin floated the story that Horne's business commitments precluded any acceptance of office. Though Baldwin had offered as a reason for keeping Horne out of the Exchequer the fact that the City of London viewed him with modified rapture, this upwardly mobile son of the manse from Stirlingshire was able to find subsequent solace in lucrative directorships. Birkenhead scraped into office, the India Office to be precise, as a personal favour to Austen Chamberlain whose installation in the Foreign Office confirmed the reintegration of the alienated Coalitionist element in the party. Even so, Chamberlain had been careful not to demand the Foreign Office, and this was wise, for Horne was an example of the fact that Baldwin was liable to assert himself by refusing direct requests.

The Head of the Civil Service, Sir Warren Fisher, does not appear to have fully grasped this, for he had lobbied Austen Chamberlain, appealing to him to take the Exchequer so as to act as a check on Baldwin's tendency to unorthodoxy, especially under the influence of men like Leopold Amery, J. C. C. Davidson and Philip Lloyd-Greame (later Cunliffe-Lister, and later still, Lord Swinton). Fisher regarded all of these men as 'unsound'. Though his own machinations proved pointless, they underline the highly politicized nature of the top civil servants, and the way in which the Establishment tried instinctively to control the prime ministerial monarchy, with its disturbing range of powers, not only by using the Conservative Party (seen as an integral part of normal governance, which is what it was) to choose a safe incumbent, but also by surrounding that incumbent by impeccably orthodox colleagues through whom alone the Premier could function. Baldwin underlined the limitations of this approach by unexpectedly appointing Winston Churchill Chancellor of the Exchequer. Admittedly, it was an appointment which in retrospect has struck historians as odder than it seemed to contemporaries.

Many Tories resented Churchill's return to their fold on the perfectly reasonable grounds that he had abandoned the Conservative Party when it entered a phase of being unable to win elections and give him office, and he was now ditching the Liberal Party for similar reasons. He was, however, a great figure, and he had at the election effectively reboarded the Tory ship on which, if not given office, even Austen Chamberlain warned Baldwin he would lead a mutiny within six months, if only to force himself on the leadership by sheer nuisance value. Baldwin certainly did not see Churchill as first choice for the job. He offered the Exchequer to Neville Chamberlain. The latter moved the Premier deeply by refusing it for the more junior position of Minister of Health, on the grounds that he felt he could be a great Minister of Health, but only a run-of-the-mill Chancellor of the Exchequer.[1] Churchill, who would notoriously have

---

[1] David Dilks *Neville Chamberlain. Vol. I: Pioneering and Reform, 1869–1929* (Cambridge University Press, Cambridge 1984), pp. 398–401.

snatched gratefully at the Chancellorship of the Duchy of Lancaster, a supernumerary post if ever there was one, found himself to his astonishment at the Exchequer. When Curzon died in 1925, Baldwin brought in A. J. Balfour as Lord President to complete a pair of appointments which, though they reinforced the unity of the Conservative Party, had little else to be said for them. The egotism of Churchill, the cynicism of Balfour, and the irresponsibility of both were to leave behind a baleful heritage for the United Kingdom in the 1930s.

All that was blessedly hidden in the future as the Government settled down in office in 1925, a year which in many ways was the peak of Baldwin's achievement. He later had to cope with the aftermath of his own political triumph in the shape of the despair and frustration of the organized working class when they realized that they had been effectively excluded from any participation whatsoever in the formulation of government policy, at a time when mounting economic distress made that policy crucially important to them. In a deep sense, Ramsay MacDonald and his colleagues in office had really taken that decision by refusing to cooperate with the Lloyd George Liberals in a policy of reform. At a time when there is evidence that Lloyd George would have been prepared to support the nationalization of electricity and the railways, though not of coal mines, MacDonald's attitude was a clear choice of the perks of office over the realities of power, but the rage of the articulate working class naturally focussed on his Tory successors in office.[1] It was true that at the highest levels of trade union leadership there had been profound disillusionment with the style of Labour government in 1924. One of the few genuine gestures of cooperation had come from J. R. Clynes, the Home Secretary, who had passed on to the Trade Union Council secret intelligence to help the TUC in its endless battle to exclude members of the Communist Party of Great Britain from union office. However, TUC leaders were indignant when Shaw, the Minister of Labour, stopped the well-established custom of civil servants showing proposed Bills to the TUC when they affected labour, and holding confidential consultation. MacDonald and Arthur Henderson fiercely defended Shaw to the point of trotting out the phrase about the 'sovereignty of Parliament' which had, since the eighteenth century, been the stock in trade of Westminster politicians anxious to exclude British peoples from meaningful participation in their own governance.

The trade unions were in fact beginning discreetly to distance themselves from the Labour Party by 1925, realizing that a Labour government in a minority would almost certainly end up courting Liberal and Conservative support by snubbing its own major supporting interests. Some of the more perceptive union leaders, like Ernest Bevin, tried to commit the Labour Party to the eminently sensible policy of never accepting office again when in a minority, but he could not even secure majority support for this view at the TUC Annual Congress.[2] Baldwin may, in his instinctive way, have sensed the way the wind was blowing. He must have been aware that as

[1] Chris Cook 'A Stranger Death of Liberal England', in Taylor (ed.), *Lloyd George: Twelve Essays*, p. 312.

[2] Keith Middlemas *Politics in Industrial Society: The Experience of the British System since 1911* (André Deutsch, London 1979), pp. 187–9.

unemployment relentlessly rose, labour militancy in general was falling, despite the existence of one or two intractable problems. He was certainly anxious to make it clear that he would not use the huge Tory majority for purely partisan ends, and he showed this in another astonishing display of a premier's authority when he persuaded first the Cabinet and then his party in the Commons to drop a controversial proposal by a Scots Conservative, one Macquisten. It was designed to change the political levy used by trade unions to fund the Labour Party from an 'opting-out' to an 'opting-in' basis. About a quarter of union members did in fact go through the written procedure needed to be exempt from the levy. Arguably, it was unfair on the substantial number of union members voting Tory, and the Macquisten Bill was therefore popular at all levels of the Conservative Party. The effect of inertia alone, if its provisions were enforced, was guaranteed to slash Labour's funding. Baldwin appealed to his party to make a real sacrifice as a gesture of goodwill, and abandon this proposal. In March 1925, his eloquence carried the day, and Baldwin to a pinnacle of leadership he never reached again.

That speech ended in the famous words, 'Give peace in our time, O Lord'. It was ironic, therefore, that Baldwin's next major crisis was a general strike, though there is much to be said for the view that it was the outcome of a chapter of accidents. The trade union movement had been on the defensive since the grim winter of 1920–21, when unemployment had doubled, reaching over two million by the summer of 1922. Skilled workers like the miners and engineers had been forced to accept significant cuts in wages. Union membership fell by nearly a third between 1921 and 1924. The time bomb at the heart of the industrial scene remained the confrontation between two exceptionally stubborn groups, both of which thought in terms of total victory or total disaster: the coal miners and the coal owners. The General Council of the TUC found itself saddled with the task of negotiating on behalf of miners whom it could not control and whom it deemed unreasonable, while the Government ended up in a not dissimilar situation *vis à vis* the employers, whom Baldwin thought 'stupid and discourteous', and whom the Government could not coerce into reasonable behaviour.

Even Churchill criticized the owners, though he rightly argued that there were too many miners at a time when UK coal was not competitively priced against resurgent Continental European rivals in international markets. The TUC was anxious for compromise and willing, in the end, to grasp at the various schemes produced under the aegis of Herbert Samuel, a former Liberal Cabinet Minister. They amounted to a national wage body patently designed to arbitrate lower wages, in exchange for Government backing for re-organization in the shape of amalgamation and closing of pits; better working conditions; and the nationalization of coal royalties. As the TUC called out layer after layer of unionized workers, its aim was not to usurp political authority, but to pull the Government into the negotiations. The owners' demand for longer hours necessarily required Government involvement, since it went against existing statutory limits. Working-class solidarity was remarkable, but the TUC was involved in a game it had no wish to play and knew it must lose. Government had most local authorities, the police, the military and its own long-prepared emergency organization at its disposal, plus overwhelming support from the middle classes. Road transportation had developed to the point where striking railway workers could no longer paralyse the country. The TUC called off the strike at the first decent opportunity and the unions resumed their conservative policy of accommodation and acceptance of reduced circumstances. By 1928, the Mond-Turner talks, organized by Sir Arthur Mond of Imperial Chemical Industries and Ben Turner, a textile trade union leader, symbolized the search for constructive cooperation, in the last analysis, on the owners' terms. Mond persuaded other industrialists to talk aimiably if indecisively with Turner and younger union leaders such as Ernest Bevin and Walter Citrine.[1]

Baldwin had handled the general strike with confidence. He painted it as a struggle to defend 'the Constitution', that curiously evasive animal which defied definition and lived quietly in a top hat until it suited a political conjuror to produce it, but privately he was well aware that the situation was essentially a mess and a political dead-end for the Labour Party. He was greatly encouraged by the fact that the leaders of that party quite sincerely repudiated the challenge to parliamentary authority implicit in the strike. MacDonald specifically denounced the concept of the general strike. In office, he had regarded any significant strike as 'disloyal'. Deference to politicians in office ranked high on his list of virtues, to the point where Baldwin quite seriously explored the possibility of a joint statement by himself and MacDonald against the general strike. The collapse of the strike made the idea unnecessary. J. H. Thomas was another leading Labour Party figure who, in May 1926 in the Commons, had spelled out his view that in a straight political battle between the TUC and the Government, the latter simply had to win, though he summed up the real objectives of the TUC in saying to the Government:

> You force the coalowners to give us some terms never mind what they are, however bad they are. Let us have something to go upon.[2]

It is hardly surprising that with this sort of background Baldwin firmly controlled those of his colleagues whose instinct was to make a bad situation worse. Neville Chamberlain was one such: his paternalism's other side was always a harsh discipline for those who dared challenge his paternal authority. Churchill was another, due to his instinctive self-dramatization. Baldwin astutely marginalized him by placing him in charge of the Government's information and propaganda paper, the *British Gazette*, where he could rave and rumble subject to discreet censorship by J. C. C. Davidson, but to no great effect. Given the massive display of police, and special constable power; frequent baton charges; free use of powers of arrest under the Emergency Regulations; and conspicuous flexing of military muscle, including armoured cars and artillery, it was clear enough who would win if push came to shove.

It was in the aftermath of the general strike that the Premier's stature

---

[1] John Stevenson 'The United Kingdom' in Stephen Salter and John Stevenson eds. *The Working Class and Politics in Europe and America 1929–1945*, (Longman, pbk edn, London 1990), pp. 129–131.

[2] Cited in Ralph Miliband *Parliamentary Socialism: A Study in the Politics of Labour* (Merlin Press, London 1961), p. 134.

began to shrink. The miners, the original cause of the crisis, were left isolated fighting hopelessly for six months until driven back with not just longer hours, but also lower wages and district, not national, agreements. The owners won a total victory; secured the repeal of the Seven Hours Act and the introduction of an Eight Hours Act to extend the working day; and accepted none of the steps towards closure, amalgamation, restriction of recruitment and modernization which might have begun the obviously necessary task of creating a smaller, more efficient industry. His biographers have demonstrated that Baldwin tried very hard indeed to secure a more constructive final settlement of the coal dispute before retiring, a weary man, to Aix-les-Bains for his summer vacation in 1926.[1] He left Churchill in charge of Government dealings with the dispute, and such was the allure of a well-publicized settlement that there was now fear in Tory circles that Winston would break ranks to pull off the coup. It was impossible. The miners were as mulish as the owners, and the owners knew that they had the gut sympathy of a now triumphant Tory Party. Besides the owners had a combination of parliamentary and extra-parliamentary clout, carefully coordinated by their mouthpiece in the Commons and the press, Austin Hopkinson, which guaranteed success. He was independent MP for Mossley, 1918–29, and 1931–45 and in 1926, he was writing in the columns of the *English Review* that it was the policy of the owners to make life so miserable for 'interfering politicians' that they would 'think twice before they meddle with the basic industries of the country'. From men reliant on legal, police and military support, and who assumed that legislation they needed would be forthcoming, this was priceless. To crown it all, Hopkinson lobbied Baldwin at a crucial point. In any system which concentrates power of initiative in an individual, politics tends to become the politics of access. It mattered that Hopkinson 'had got at him'.[2]

With enemies like Ramsay MacDonald and J. H. Thomas, Baldwin hardly needed friends. Yet Baldwin had to live with his friends and allies in the political party which was his instrument of power. To retain his throne, he had to cut with the grain of the business-dominated, negative, conservative consensus which was becoming the norm in the English-speaking North Atlantic world of the mid-1920s. After all, 1923–28 was the era of President Calvin Coolidge, that puritan in Babylon, whose political career took off when, as Governor of Massachusetts, he responded to a police strike with the sentence: 'There is no right to strike against the public safety by any-body, anywhere, at any time.' Succeeding the egregiously inadequate President Warren Gamaliel Harding, Coolidge had had to clean up the Republican Party act so as to remove those entrepreneurial appointees of his predecessor who had preached self-help whilst helping themselves to large parts of the public domain. This he did sufficiently successfully to declare with his usual straight face that 'the business of America is business'. Even more significant, perhaps, was author Bruce Barton, whose book *The Man Nobody Knows*, sold nearly a million copies to Americans

[1] Middlemas and Barnes *Baldwin*, chap. 16.
[2] Robert Boothby *Boothby: Recollections of a Rebel* (Hutchinson, London 1978), pp. 40–4.

anxious to know an entrepreneurial Jesus Christ who selected 'twelve men from the bottom ranks of business and forged them into an organisation that conquered the world.'[1]

More telling still is the way in which developments in the new Irish Free State (established in 1922) ran along institutional and political lines very much akin to Mr Baldwin's UK. This was remarkable because within Sinn Féin and therefore amongst those who drafted the Free State constitution, the predominant cast of mind was anxious to break with such 'British' precedents as party government. Sinn Féin had been lucky in late 1921 in dealing with a small group of powerful opportunists at Westminster, such as Lloyd George, Birkenhead and Churchill, who were prepared to cut and run from Ireland with only minimal emotional camouflage. However, many IRA gunmen, used to killing people who represented a different political option, were unlikely to swallow what were to them utterly unpalatable features of the Anglo-Irish treaty of 1922 at the behest of a new civilian regime in Dublin. They secured the adherence of Eamon de Valera, the best natural politician to emerge from the post-1916 turmoil, though one whose usually sure judgement became decidedly ragged between 1919 and 1922. From the resulting civil war in 1922–23 emerged the first regime in Ireland since 1800 with the support, the means and the will to govern effectively.

Its new constitution was full of populist features. The legislature had in theory the right to choose 'extern ministers' who would be directly responsible to it and no part of the cabinet-type Executive Council, whose President was clearly not meant to be just another UK-type prime minister. There were also referendum and direct initiative provisos which sought to remove the legislative monopoly from politicians. The need for an executive strong enough to put Republican prisoners against a wall and shoot them, plus the political polarization and party formation encouraged by such measures rapidly moved the entire structure towards the Westminster model with a President of the Executive Council who was Premier, with a Cabinet, and a whipped party in the lower house which was his power-base. The Senate, to some extent a sop to the tiny former Unionist minority, was not unlike the House of Lords, in that it had little real power. Apart from proportional representation by single transferable vote, all the non-Westminster features became moribund.

If anything, the Free State was 60 years ahead of the UK in giving the central authority (in the shape of the Minister of Local Government) power to override county authorities by dissolving them and replacing them for up to three years by appointed Commissioners.[2] That proviso was an indication of just how effectively the traditions and prejudices of the central bureaucracy in Whitehall had taken root in Dublin. If Westminster had obdurately refused certain concessions, it had thrown piecemeal sops to Cerberus on such a scale that by 1921 the Irish central bureaucracy and courts were dominated by Nationalists and Catholics.[3] The traditions of

---

[1] Alistair Cook *Alistair Cook's America* (British Broadcasting Corporation, London 1973), pp. 316 and 324–5.

[2] Lyons *Ireland since the Famine*, pp. 473–84.

[3] Lawrence W. McBride *The Greening of Dublin Castle: The Transformation of Bureaucratic and Judicial Personnel in Ireland, 1892–1922* (Catholic University of America Press, Washington D. C. 1991).

Union bureaucracy were therefore within the Nationalist defences by 1922. Thereafter the whole drive, summed up in the Ministers and Secretaries Act of 1924, was towards sweeping away the tentative attempts of the later Union regime to create administrative structures somewhat adapted to Irish realities, in favour of the closest possible parallel with Whitehall. C. J. Gregg, an Irishman who was a friend of Cosgrove, was loaned from the London Board of Inland Revenue, and he more than anyone else shaped the new system.

All three regimes in the British Isles in the 1920s were committed to broadly similar policies of free trade, low taxation and minimal state interference with the economy. That was one reason why, until de Valera converted the Irish Free State in the 1930s from one of the least to one of the most protectionist of states, the existence of a land boundary in the British Isles was largely an economic irrelevance.[1] Politicians lived by dramatizing cultural, religious, class and regional tensions, trying to extract from them balances of power acceptable to themselves and their supporters. It needed the Great Crash of 1929 on Wall Street to render it conceivable that they should seriously lay hands on the economy. Before then, their societies did not keep people like prime ministers for such a purpose.

Neville Chamberlain, who had entered the House of Commons in 1918 in his fiftieth year, was the only minister in Baldwin's government of 1924–9 with a consistent record of achievement on the domestic front. Between 1924 and 1929, he steered as many as 21 Bills through the House of Commons. Admittedly, many were of very minor importance, but it was obviously this relentless record of work in an otherwise somnolent administration which confirmed in Chamberlain, a man with no very successful record heretofore in either politics or business, an unshakeable sense of superiority and mastery. The Tory Party needed him to put some discipline and motivation into them, and his brisk paternalism offered the public a firm, well-meaning, controlling hand. Here seems to have lain the genesis of that combination of headmaster and bad-tempered nanny which he brought to full flower as premier.

Admittedly, his first piece of legislation of substance, the Widows, Orphans and Old Age Contributory Pensions Bill of 1925 was a major development, achieved in cooperation with Churchill, who made financial provision for it in his budget. As well as having an infinite capacity for re-inventing himself, Churchill had an endearing knack of re-inventing his father. When he wrote Randolph's biography, he was a member of Campbell-Bannerman's Liberal government who had recently been a Tory MP, so Randolph in the final pages was a Liberal manqué, held in the Tory ranks only by an exquisite sense of honour. Now that he was one of the three most powerful men in Baldwin's second Government, Winston persuaded himself that this mighty Conservative majority might be the base for that constructive Radical Toryism which had ever been his father's chief aim. In fact, that egotistical chancer's principles had been as non-

[1] J. J. Lee *Ireland 1912–1985: Politics and Society* (Cambridge University Press, Cambridge 1989), pp. 105–11; D. S. Johnson 'The Northern Ireland Economy, 1914–39' in *An Economic History of Ulster, 1820–1940*, eds. Líam Kennedy and Phillip Ollerenshaw (Manchester University Press, Manchester 1985), pp. 188–90.

existent as F. E. Smith's and his radicalism hot air, but his son revered him even as he subconsciously used him to justify funding a significant step forward in social security. Everyone insured under National Health Insurance was now covered not just against sickness and unemployment, but also for a pension for insured workers and their wives at age 65. Widows' pensions, and allowances for dependent children and orphans were also provided. There was no measure to match it until Chamberlain's equally important Local Government Act of 1929 which transferred the functions of poor law boards of guardians to counties and county boroughs. As a former mayor of Birmingham, Chamberlain believed in local government. Churchill was bent on derating agricultural land and industrial premises (as an indirect subsidy which was a substitute for tariffs), leaving counties dependent on the regressive and inadequate system of domestic rates for revenue. Block grants from the Treasury repaired the deficiency, and though there were controls on high-spending local authorities, the system was not designed with the positive hostility to local government characteristic of Conservative administrations of the 1980s. Nevertheless, it increased dependency on central funding to an alarming degree.[1]

These and other measures in effect increased the fire insurance taken out by the politicians against social desperation and unrest. Spending on social services rose from £101 million in 1913 to £596 million in 1938, or an increase from 4.1 to 11.3 per cent of Gross National Product. By the late 1920s, there was an income transfer of £200–£250 million a year from the prosperous, mostly to the very poor with incomes under £125 per annum. The poor only paid three-quarters of the cost of the social services they enjoyed. Between 1920 and 1931, the real value of unemployment benefit rose nearly two-and-a-half times. Cuts in 1931 set it back, but to roughly the lowest subsistence wages of the employed of 1914.[2] The unemployed were as little a threat to political stability as women between the ages of 21 and 30, who were finally given the vote in 1928.

Politics became a very dull business by 1925, when the Lord Chief Justice was forecasting that 'the Government might stay in for twenty years if it avoided two questions, viz. protection and the House of Lords.' Year after year, the diaries of that stalwart Tory MP Sir Robert Sanders (later Lord Bayford) record the dullness of the parliamentary scene, and Sanders was a man of such automatic honesty that he was one of the few Conservative MPs to refer to the Labour Party by its name instead of referring archly to 'the Socialist Party'. By Sunday 18 March 1928, he was recording:

> Never has a session been so dull and dead as this one has been so far. Already the House has twice been counted out.[3]

Even the Trade Disputes Act of 1927, though fiercely resented by Labour, and the principal legislative consequence of the general strike, was singularly unimportant in many ways. It ruled a general strike illegal: another

---

[1] L. C. B. Seaman *Post Victorian Britain 1902–1951* (Methuen, pbk edn, London), pp. 182–4.

[2] Stevenson, *art cit.*, p. 141.

[3] *Real Old Tory Politics: The Political Diaries of Sir Robert Sanders, Lord Bayford, 1910–35*, ed. John Ramsden (The Historians' Press, London 1984), pp. 219, 225, 231 and 238.

one was remotely unlikely, but if widely supported it could hardly be handled by trying to jail five million people. Equally, the assault on the political levy which it embodied was no more than Macquisten had asked for, and Baldwin improbably contrived to postpone. In so far as there was any liveliness in the political scene, it was provided by the jockeying for the succession to Baldwin, and the chief protagonist was Winston Churchill.

His own wife, in the spring of 1924, had seen Winston as an automatic rival to Baldwin if readmitted to the Tory Party, saying:

> . . . the minute you become a Conservative his Leadership is endangered—both by you and F.E. whom you would bring back with you as a possible Leader.[1]

She was wrong about F. E. Smith, whose drinking had reached the point where he had become an unthinkable contender for supreme office. So bad was it that he had reached the point of privately speaking the truth to his fellow-politicians, as he did when drunk during a party at the home of the millionaire political host, Philip Sassoon, on 30 October 1924, the day after the election. Churchill said that he was waiting to see what he was offered before he decided if he was prepared to accept office under Baldwin. F.E. roared out that, on the contrary, Churchill had been frantic for office for two years, would descend to any trick to get it, and would jump at anything he was offered. Baldwin's informant added:

> After that there was general mud-slinging, but my informant was very much struck by the outward deference paid to you and their acceptance of you as dispenser of patronage.[2]

Though he accepted office, F.E.'s health and finances were both shaky. Like most of the rest of the political élite, he revelled in the secretive nature of policy formation, but he needed the money which could be derived from the marketing of political memoirs under his fancy title of Earl of Birkenhead. Eventually he wrote them. Dictated in the evenings in a deeply bored voice, with a cigar in one hand, a whisky in the other, they were sad and uninformative stuff. The problem of his occasional articles in the press, which by their nature tended to be less bland, plagued the second Baldwin Government from the start. He had to be discreetly bribed with £5,000 a year from Conservative Party funds (the equivalent of the Lord Chancellor's pension which he was foregoing by being Secretary of State for India), to give up the habit.[3] His day was done.

Churchill's, on the other hand, appeared to be dawning after Baldwin's bizarre decision rocketed him to near the top of the political tree. Circumstances were exceptionally favourable. Churchill had always adhered to the free-trade imperialism of the mid-Victorian era. It was a measure of the depth of his conservatism. Now, even Baldwin had renounced protectionism. For Churchill, ambition and conviction could go hand in hand. Though capable of prime-ministerial initiatives, as over protection or the

[1] Clementine to Winston S. Churchill, 19 April 1924, printed in Martin Gilbert *Winston S. Churchill. Volume V: Companion Part 1 Documents: The Exchequer Years 1922–29* (Heinemann, London 1979), p. 147.

[2] Sir William Tyrrell to Stanley Baldwin, 1 November 1924, *ibid.*, p. 229.

[3] Davidson *Memoirs*, pp. 276–7.

Maquisten Bill, Baldwin believed in Cabinet government. Colleagues were given great freedom within their areas of responsibility. Churchill both used and abused this. He was enough of a realist to make some concessions to the protectionist instincts of the party he had just rejoined. He accepted a Safeguarding of Industries Act under which perhaps half a dozen industries might be given some protection against 'unfair' foreign competition, though it was no easy matter to define 'unfair'. Beyond that, he could assume general free trade, and he moved swiftly to master the intricacies of Exchequer business, and indeed to tighten the already formidable Treasury control.

He was soon urging Sir Warren Fisher to take steps to deprive spending departments, as far as possible, of flexibility in their presentation of accounts.[1] Later in life, it suited Churchill to suggest that he did not really understand what he was doing as Chancellor, for his record in the office was a damning indictment of his later messianic image, but in fact he knew very well. He had vast administrative experience, including big spending departments like the Admiralty. He was prodigiously hard-working and quick-witted. Very great technical facility indeed was needed to put up the performance which he clearly hoped would make him the next premier. He never really liked Baldwin, but he was grateful to him for his job, and he needed him. In the medium term, he now needed to cultivate the support of the Conservative power élite, of which the City of London was a central pillar.

That fact goes far to explain his decision to return to the gold standard, with sterling at its pre-war parity of $4.86 US dollars to the pound sterling, in 1925. That decision was highly controversial at the time. It was generally believed that in real terms it over-valued the pound by some ten per cent. The Federation of British Industries was a representative body for manufacturers which in its early days often had difficulty reaching any sort of consensus. In 1924, it issued an unequivocal warning against the implications of an over-valued pound, which were severe deflation to reduce wages and prices to the level needed to restore competitiveness to British exports. The Labour Party had predictably little to say on the subject. Critics of the policy from further left were instantly discounted as subversive extremists, but the power-wielders were clearly far from unanimous. If there was little disposition to oppose the gold standard on principle, there was much disquiet about the timing of the decision and the level chosen. It was most famously expressed in the Cambridge economist J. M. Keynes' writings, eventually collected under the irresistibly funny title of *The Economic Consequences of Mr Churchill*. Though an intellectual gadfly rather than a power in his own right, Keynes in the 1920s often expressed views which had widespread support in influential ciricles. His criticism of the insoluble transfer problems for the UK in any attempt to extract limitless reparations from Germany had become widely accepted in Government circles.

It has been demonstrated that the decisive advice came from a narrow section of the City, dominated by those interested primarily in international

---

[1] Winston S. Churchill to Sir Warren Fisher, 16 November 1924, printed in Gilbert, ed. *Documents: The Exchequer Years*, pp. 246–7.

finance, who were represented by the Bank of England under its autocratic chairman, Montagu Norman, and supported to the hilt by scarcely less autocratic Treasury mandarins.[1] They could argue that the UK decision would accelerate a stabilization of international currencies without which trade and therefore employment could not recover. In practice, when France and Belgium went back on the gold standard in the next year, they deliberately undervalued their currencies for competitive advantage. Lord Cunliffe, whose official Committee on Currency and Finance had started the drive for the gold standard at pre-war parity, had been sacked by the wartime Chancellor Bonar Law when, as Governor of the Bank of England, he arrogantly challenged Government power. It was a pity that Bonar Law's gesture was never repeated.

Norman was out of the Cunliffe stable, but Churchill was no weakling, and he knew that there were powerful arguments against the policies Norman was advocating. Reginald McKenna, to whom Baldwin had offered the Exchequer in 1922 (but for whom a safe City seat could, significantly, not be found), was to articulate many of them later in a series of speeches as Chairman of the Midland Bank. McKenna, as a wartime Chancellor, had worked with Keynes, and had established a very close social relationship with him.[2] Nevertheless, even McKenna, at the point of decision, thought political factors would make Churchill go on gold at the 1913 par. Keynes was unrealistic in blaming the experts solely. They were divided. What mattered in the overlapping social, business, bureaucratic and political élite which generated policy was the strategic position of the banking group. The élite was a centralized, metropolitan one, and for any politician anxious to achieve leadership of its overtly political structure—the Tory Party—a reputation for 'soundness' in the City was invaluable.

It was also imperative for a Chancellor with leadership ambitions to cut direct taxes. Technically, this was not easy in 1925, but to show where his heart lay Churchill cut income tax by sixpence in the pound, thus reducing it to four shillings in the pound or 20 per cent. He promptly took back with the left hand what he gave with the right by imposing indirect taxes. Luck ceased to attend him for the next couple of years when industrial turmoil, allied to massive American debt repayment charges, left no margins for tax reduction. Indeed, there was a feeling in orthodox circles that taxation ought to be increased, but Churchill contrived in his third budget of April 1927 to raise £35–40 million of additional income without increasing major taxes. It was to some extent a series of conjuring tricks covered by verbal fireworks. Several of the expedients verged on the dishonest, and his juggling with payment schedules with existing taxes was a means of increasing taxation without admitting he was doing so.[3]

---

[1] Notably in Sidney Pollard *The Gold Standard and Employment Policies between the Wars* (Methuen pbk edn, London 1970), which offers selections from the relevant literature prefaced by an incisive introduction.

[2] The social intimacy between the McKennas, the Asquiths and Keynes comes out in R. F. Harrod *The Life of John Maynard Keynes* (Macmillan, London 1966), pp. 210–1.

[3] There is a convenient summary of Churchill's Exchequer years in Pelling *Winston Churchill*, chap. 15.

It was from 1927 that he bombarded Baldwin with plans for a 'large new constructive measure' which he claimed would enable the Government to seize the political initiative and dominate the public mind. Churchill had appointed as his parliamentary private secretary Robert Boothby, the well-connected young Tory MP for East Aberdeenshire (he was a nephew of Lord Cunliffe, the banker), and through him he came in contact with Harold Macmillan, the 'progressive' Conservative MP for Stockton-on-Tees, one of the most industrially depressed areas of north-east England. Both younger men were odd examples of Tories who would have fitted far more comfortably into the activist and egocentric atmosphere of a Lloyd George regime. Macmillan appears to have been the origin of the derating scheme which eventually removed rates entirely from agricultural land, and left industry with an obligation to pay only a quarter of normal rates. Macmillan was unofficially allowed great influence over the details of the scheme, partly to help overcome the resistance of Neville Chamberlain who, to his credit, was appalled by the implications for local government of simply removing both its economic base and any incentive to the business classes to take it seriously. The Treasury, through its principal spokesman on this subject, Alfred Hurst, took a radically different viewpoint, favouring the least power possible for local government on the grounds that:

> Experience in connection with Parliament would seem to shew that true economy can only be achieved by an administrative machine like the Treasury, well removed and carefully protected from electoral influences.[1]

The argument that industrialists would retain obligations and interest as residential ratepayers was even in the 1920s wearing thin due to the automobile and the joint stock company. Chamberlain added that industry would continue stridently to demand expensive facilities and services from local governments to which it would contribute little. Macmillan, for all his subsequent image as a caring, progressive MP in a heartless era, remarked cynically: 'Moreover, if the fat kine are taken away, the lean kine will have nothing left to devour but their own proletarian hides.'[2] Pharoah Macmillan of the 1950s and early 1960s was there in embryo in the 1920s. A more immediate danger was the way Churchill set about finding the surplus to fund derating.

A new fuel tax was at least straightforward, but his campaign for massive cuts in the armed forces, which began as soon as he became Chancellor, was all the more disturbing because his experience of service departments allowed him to bring to it the technical trickiness which was the hallmark of his Exchequer years. Defence was the obvious area in which to look for savings. In August 1919, the Cabinet had laid down the notorious 'Ten Year Rule', which said that service estimates should be based 'on the assumption that the British Empire would not be engaged in any great war during the next ten years'. Churchill as Chancellor knew full well that the rule gave the Treasury a permanent whiphand over the service depart-

---

[1] Cited in Gilbert *Winston S. Churchill. Volume V: 1922–1939* (Heinemann, London 1976), pp. 254–5.
[2] Memorandum by Harold Macmillan of 11 December 1927, cited in *ibid.*, p. 259.

ments, so by late 1924 he was pressing for its extension or renewal. By 1928, he had secured the self-perpetuating version of the rule which said that at any given date 'for purposes of framing estimates', in the absence of a formal decision to the contrary, it should be assumed that there would be no major war for ten years. The Royal Navy was the main sufferer from this relentless economy drive and would have suffered even more had not the First Lord of the Admiralty, W. C. Bridgeman, been prepared to go to the brink of what would have been for Baldwin a politically damaging resignation to force Churchill to modify his more extreme demands. Nevertheless, right up to 1928–29, Churchill maintained a ferocious pressure, often at a highly technical level.

Anti-aircraft defences on Royal Navy ships, for example, were alarmingly deficient, but the Admiralty had even at this late date to show great resolution to protect the production of new eight-barrel close-range AA weapons, and in 1928 Bridgeman wrote angrily to Churchill about 'the present Tendency of the Treasury to try to put off indefinitely even the most inevitable naval expenditure, vaguely imagining that we could redeem our position by a great intensive effort at some future date.'[1] The Army and Royal Air Force declined even more sharply in terms of their European significance. The RAF justified its existence mainly as a cheap imperial gendarmerie, bombing the villages of recalcitrant tribesmen. The British Army, apart from providing the ultimate sanction behind civil power in the UK, was also primarily an imperial police force. Having abandoned conscription, it had to spend the bulk of its funds on its relatively expensive volunteer manpower. It never spent more than £2 million in any one year on new equipment. Once a pioneer of mechanized war, its expenditure parameters guaranteed that, in the long run, it was likely to lag where it had led.[2]

Baldwin loyally backed Churchill, as he did his Foreign Secretary, Austen Chamberlain. By the end of Churchill's run at the Treasury, its senior mandarins, despite their zeal for economy, sat uncomfortably to his combination of political expediency, creative accounting and convenient optimism about future revenue yields. In Austen Chamberlain, the Foreign Office had the 'soundest' of lords and masters, yet he was fated to preside over trends which, combined with Churchill's disarmament drive, left the UK in a disturbingly fragile international position.

He played a key role in the drawing up of the 1925 Locarno Pact which confirmed and guaranteed existing western European frontiers. The most francophile member of the Government, Chamberlain, was happy to give an unequivocal commitment to the defence of the French Rhine frontier, but not any commitment to the defence of the new eastern European frontiers. The Polish corridor between East Germany and Pomerania he specifically ruled not worth the bones of a British grenadier. It was a defensible position, if reconciliation and cooperation with a democratic Germany could be achieved. Despite good personal relations between Chamberlain and his French and German counterparts, Briand and Strese-

---

[1] Cited in Stephen Roskill *Naval Policy Between the Wars. I: The Period of Anglo-American Antagonism 1919–1929*, p. 561.
[2] Taylor *English History 1914–1948*, footnote p. 232.

mann, trust proved elusive. Down to the final agreement on reparations under the American-inspired Young Plan of 1929, absence of consensus and grudging concessions dominated European diplomacy.[1]

Unfortunately, the UK's wider global position was marked by a widening gap between commitments and capacity. Attempts to use the League of Nations to provide an ongoing framework for Anglo-American cooperation aborted when America refused to join the League. Apart from providing a cover for the sub-imperialism of South Africa and Australia, the League mandate system for ex-German colonies had been designed to pull a USA which was a League member into association with, and sympathy for, imperial problems.[2] Instead, Westminster faced the danger of a naval race with an isolationist and intermittently anglophobic America. The Washington conference of 1921–22 at which the UK accepted parity in capital ships with the USA, and conceded regional supremacy to Japan in the Pacific by agreeing to a 5:5:3 battleship ratio between these powers, probably represented no surrender by either London or Washington of anything likely to be built by regimes dominated by tax-cutting conservative influences. However, the simultaneous abandonment, under heavy American pressure, of the Anglo-Japanese alliance which had served the UK so well in the Far East was the first step along a path of sustained appeasement.

It was a policy endorsed by the highest bureaucratic and political levels in the UK. Sir William Tyrrell, Permanent Under-Secretary at the Foreign Office, was not only very much in harmony with Chamberlain, but also so close to Baldwin as to spend at least one weekend a month socializing with him. His successor in 1928, Ronald Lindsay, shared his views, and like other senior Foreign Office men was married to an American.[3] The Imperial Conference which met in London in 1921 showed that Australia and New Zealand, understandably, were anxious the Anglo-Japanese treaty be renewed. The Canadian Prime Minister, Arthur Meighen, who had already come under heavy American pressure to make sure it was not renewed, was extremely vocal against the treaty. He also made it clear that Canada would contribute not a penny to the common defence of the Empire.[4] The UK Foreign Office was for pleasing Americans at almost any cost, and so the alliance went. Typically British compromises were emerging which secured for the UK the worst of all possible worlds. Canada, which spent virtually nothing on defence, regarded itself as entitled to considerable influence over vital UK policy decisions, though also entitled angrily to repudiate any UK attempt to interfere in Canadian policy-making. The Americans, offered concession after concession to their views and prejudices on the Japanese alliance, Ireland, war debt repayments and naval strengths, regarded all these as no more than their due and moved on to their next set of demands. A weakened UK did not even have the

[1] John Jacobson *Locarno Diplomacy: Germany and the West 1925–1929* (Princeton University Press, Princeton, NJ 1972).

[2] This important conclusion can be found in Peter J. Yearwood 'Great Britain and the Repartition of Africa, 1914–19', *The Journal of Imperial and Commonwealth History* (17, 1990), pp. 316–41.

[3] B. J. C. McKercher *The Second Baldwin Government and the United States, 1924–1929* (Cambridge University Press, Cambridge 1984), p. 22.

[4] Roskill *Naval Policy Between the Wars. I*, pp 292–9.

advantage of a virtual alliance with the USA. By 1927, the Americans were pressing London for the extension of parity to cruisers, of which the Admiralty was convinced (rightly) that the UK had more need than America, because of the global sprawl of its commercial and political interest, as well as for a major surrender of traditional claims by the Royal Navy for control of neutral shipping during a war. Churchill by this time sensed preparations for a sell-out by the Foreign Office on all these issues. Though denounced at the time as 'die-hard', the analysis he embraced was eminently sane. It was not really consistent with his behaviour as Chancellor, but then consistency was, for him, the weakness of lesser men.

The Foreign Office believed in unconditional surrender to aroused American opinion. It argued that a war-crippled Britain was helpless before:

> . . . a State twenty-five times as large, five times as wealthy, three times as populous, twice as ambitious, almost invulnerable, and at least our equal in prosperity, vital energy, technical equipment and industrial science.[1]

The cynical adage which became popular towards the end of the twentieth century—that if the Home Office looked after interests at home, the Foreign Office safeguarded the interests of foreigners—had some substance a good deal earlier. Churchill and Amery argued in vain that, faced by the usual arrogant American assertion of self-interest thinly disguised as cosmic benevolence, the correct strategy was to stall indefinitely. The French went one better. Reluctant late adherents to the capital ship limitation agreements, they eventually simply refused to give way to the Americans on cruisers.

The French knew who they were. By 1926, the inhabitants of the United Kingdom knew they were British, and that they were members of the British Commonwealth and Empire, but the definition of the latter phenomenon was as ambiguous as the meaning of the term 'British' was vague. A. J. Balfour, who as Premier had indulged in scholastic disputations in public with himself as to what his policy might be, was just the man to make it vaguer. At the 1923 Imperial Conference, Meighen's successor as Prime Minister of Canada, Mackenzie King, had effectively struck down the last chance for serious military and diplomatic coordination and cooperation between the UK and the Dominions. Yet the UK was still stuck with a global web of commitment. It would have been vastly saner to deal on a bilateral basis with Australia and New Zealand within a formal military pact like the future North Atlantic Treaty Organization, and let Canada go where it chose, but no such nettle-grasping occurred. By 1926, the presence of Mackenzie King, the hard-liner Afrikaner white-supremacist Herzog from South Africa and representatives of the Irish Free State ensured that the Commonwealth had become worse than a nothing. It had become a shadow theatre where states whose citizens, too mean or poor to pay for a real foreign policy backed by diplomats and armed services, could pretend to have one by twisting the Westminster lion's tail, secure in the knowledge that the beast never bit back.[2]

---

[1] Foreign Office memorandum of 1928 cited in McKercher, *op. cit.*, p. 174.
[2] Barnett *The Collapse of British Power*, chap. 4.

Even the acerbic Correlli Barnett, the first historian to grasp just how disastrous the appeasement of Mackenzie King was, believed that 'In 1920 Canada had, with British consent, appointed her own minister in Washington.' Not so: Canada announced in 1920, with considerable publicity, that it was asserting the right to appoint its own minister in Washington. Canada did not allocate funds for the post, and there was no Canadian ambassador in Washington until 1927.[1] By the time of the Imperial Conference of 1926, the presence of representatives of the Irish Free State, a state which basically did not want to belong to the Commonwealth, guaranteed that vacuity and fudge would be the keynote. The much—redrafted Balfour Report on 'Inter-Imperial Relations' produced a mellifluous piece of verbal juggling defining the 'position and mutual relation' of Commonwealth members:

> They are autonomous Communities within the British Empire, equal in status, in no way subordinate one to another in any aspect of their domestic or external affairs, though united by a common allegiance to the Crown, and freely associated as members of the British Commonwealth of Nations[2]

The Balfour Committee then went on the say that a benighted foreigner might think such a formula designed to make mutual interference impossible rather than cooperation easy. The foreigner would have been right. Though the Free State Navy was hardly capable of activities beyond fishery protection, it did show in 1939 that it could convey the body of the poet William Yeats from France to Ireland. The Royal Canadian Navy, with four destroyers for two oceans in 1935 was an equally formidable force, especially when compared with the regular army of 3,600 men and the Royal Canadian Air Force of 1934, with its one modern military aircraft, which it did not own but had borrowed from the Royal Air Force. In such company the UK had, by 1929, drifted into a position of appalling vulnerability.

Baldwin had presided over the process with equanimity. In the absence of strong initiative from the Premier, policy formation was departmental. Churchill could dominate Treasury initiatives, but not block Foreign Office initiatives of which he disapproved. Chamberlain's decision to remain in the Ministry of Health underlined his confidence in the freedom of initiative he was likely to enjoy there. Policy emerged from complex and usually secretive dealings between top politicians, the Civil Service mandarinate, business and banking pressure groups, and foreign governments. The Dominions, for their size, were a privileged sub-category of countries with exceptional ease of access to the Westminster ruling groups. In all of this, the great bulk of Conservative MPs, who provided the essential validating majority, hardly mattered. They could define the parameters of the possible by mutinying against proposals which threatened their own interest or those represented in their constituency associations, but given the

[1] *Ibid.*, p. 196.
[2] From 'The Report of the Inter-Imperial Relations Committee, Imperial Conference, 1926, Section 1: 'The Status of Great Britain and the dominions', printed in *Speeches and Documents on the British Dominions 1918–1931: From Self-Government to National Sovereignty*, ed Arthur B. Keith (Oxford University Press, London 1932), p. 161.

pervasive conservatism of the policy-makers, this was a rare conjuncture indeed.

Baldwin's defeat in the election which he called in the spring of 1929 came as a great shock to him. He had expected to win by a small majority, mainly on his record. In practice, it had little current appeal. The trio of Churchill, Boothby and Macmillan, which had launched the derating scheme, had grossly exaggerated both its economic and its political impact. Many Conservatives disliked it, as they did the final instalment of votes for women, and changes in local government. The Government looked tired, but Baldwin finally ducked any pre-election reshuffling of the Cabinet as likely to generate resentment. His own personality was still widely admired, as his reception on campaign showed. On the other hand, his Home Secretary, the puritanical William Joynson-Hicks, had tactlessly drawn attention to the ugly side of the political system by embarking on a crusade against vice in London using (to their limits) powers conveyed by the Defence of the Realm Acts. Churchill's attempt during the campaign to generate a Bolshevik scare was grotesque, and while the snores of the Government echoed through the land, the Tories went down to defeat behind a poster showing Baldwin's portrait, under the slogan 'Safety First'.

He had been unlucky. The Conservatives sank to 261 seats, while Labour rose to 287, and the Liberals, despite an exceptional effort, reaped only 59 seats. Yet again, the electoral system had grossly misrepresented the way votes had been cast. The Conservatives, with 8.66 million votes, had outstripped Labour's 8.36, and the Liberals, with nearly 5.31 million had secured a contemptible return for the volume of their support. Lloyd George had secured control of that party in 1926, and had pumped into it not only money from his notorious fund, but also ideas on a spectacular scale. Buoyed by good run of by-election results, the Liberals poured out literature promising a decisive assault on the unemployment problem through a scheme of public works designed greatly to enhance the economic infrastructure. Liberal publications such as *We Can Conquer Unemployment* helped keep the issue of the recalcitrant million of unemployed alive, and did contribute to Baldwin's defeat. At the general election, there were 29 Liberal gains from the Conservatives, to two losses, while the Liberals lost 17 seats to Labour against two gains. All three major parties had fought over 500 seats.[1] It was a great reassurance to the Conservatives and Labour that the electoral system could render nugatory a truly massive revolt against their respective brands of immobilism.

Inevitably, the Conservative Party showed considerable disgruntlement with Baldwin's leadership. In defeat, its right wing, sitting for the safer southern English seats, tended to survive better than more moderate elements. Its agricultural lobby became clamant for protection whilst Baldwin remained conscious of the need not to alienate the northern and urban interests which had to be regained to provide a Conservative majority. Depressed by defeat, moody, and often absent from the Commons, Baldwin was reluctant to mount vigorous attacks on the new Labour Government which was kept in office by Liberal votes. As long as Labour's party

[1] Roy Douglas *History of the Liberal Party 1895–1970* (Sidgwick and Jackson, pbk edn, London 1971), pp. 198–207.

discipline held, and the Liberals could not be persuaded to abandon their support for the Government, the Conservatives were wasting their time at Westminster. From 1929 until 1931, they not unreasonably concentrated on internal struggles, and Baldwin came close to losing his grip in his party. Though it has been suggested that the Conservative Party's squabbles carried with them a real threat of disintegration and that any premature move on its part towards protection might have exposed it in a snap election to further losses to the free-trading Labour and Liberal parties, neither contention is very convincing. Another election within a year would have been unusual and perceived as pure opportunism. In any case, by the spring of 1930, by-elections were registering swings against the Government which persisted and rapidly rose to 9 per cent in several cases. Over 40 per cent of Labour seats in 1929 were held on minority votes after three-cornered struggles.[1] MacDonald was not the man to risk so vulnerable a position. Tories could afford to squabble, indeed had to, for they were settling the policies of the next administration likely to hold both office and power.

Twice Baldwin came close to resignation as leader. By 1930, he was being hounded by the two most egregious of the press lords: Beaverbrook and Rothermere. The former had embarked, complete with candidates at by-elections, on an Empire Free Trade campaign. Apart from the utter unreality of its proposed objective, which was unattainable and, if attained, would have destroyed UK agriculture, the campaign was politically preposterous in another way. With characteristic modesty, Beaverbrook acceded to Rothermere's suggestion that Beaverbrook should assume the leadership of the Tory Party: Rothermere's political ineptitude enabled Baldwin to retain his leadership and escape from confrontations behind the phrase borrowed from Kipling about the press lords seeking power without responsibility: the prerogative of the harlot. The Conservative agent who said, 'Bang goes the harlot vote', was a realist. So was Baldwin. He never objected to press barons who were generally supportive of the Conservative leadership. The Berry family, headed by Lords Camrose (proprietor of the *Daily Telegraph*) and Kemsley, were examples of this. It was the unpredictability of Beaverbrook and Rothermere he found offensive, and their lack of respect for established political leadership. Nevertheless, the Tory party was a machine for enabling wielders of social and economic power to coalesce and, subject to the limits of the possible as defined by the political leadership, control the political agenda. Beaverbrook and Rothermere were by wealth and power natural members of a ruling social coalition and Baldwin accepted that fact. Behind the defiant words, he searched for an acceptable deal with them. At the height of the struggle, Baldwin had to throw his old friend J. C. C. Davidson to the wolves. He was replaced as Chairman of the Conservative Party by Neville Chamberlain, who had little to do as Chairman, but much to do seeking, in vain, accommodation with the press lords.

Old-fashioned Conservatives like Lord Derby, who was by October 1930

---

[1] John Stevenson and Chris Cook *The Slump* (Quartet Books, pbk edn, London 1979), pp. 94–8.

privately urging Baldwin to resign, simply wanted to pay less taxes, and complained bitterly that,

> You had four years of Office . . . there was practically no economy and . . . money was spent with a lavish hand in an attempt to outbid the Socialists.[1]

His lordship, whom nobody could accuse of having a lean and hungry look, was all for tightening every belt but his own. Ousting Baldwin, however, hinged, as Derby said, on electoral victory under Baldwin's leadership being 'very problematical'. By the time Baldwin finally struck a stable deal with Beaverbrook in March 1931, this was not so. Baldwin had ridden out the storm. In particular, economic and political circumstances now enabled him to offer commitment to 'emergency' protection on a sufficient scale to allow Beaverbrook to back down from confrontation with some self-respect.

The Labour Government, which contained few new faces compared with that of 1924, had largely fulfilled the forecast of Beatrice Webb, whose husband, Sidney, was Colonial Secretary in the new administration. Beatrice noted in her diary in July 1929:

> In home affairs, I doubt the zeal of the P. M. and Snowden and the capacity and courage of Thomas, Greenwood and Margaret Bondfield. In foreign affairs it may be that this Cabinet is vastly superior to the last.[2]

It was a comprehensive demolition of the Labour Cabinet in which Snowden was Chancellor; J. H. Thomas, Lord Privy Seal; Greenwood Minister of Health and Bondfield, Minister of Labour; but not an unfair one. Margaret Bondfield was the first woman to reach the Cabinet. Other positive achievements on the domestic front proved few. The Premier, anxious for short-term success, and cheered by what turned out to be a temporary fall in unemployment in the summer of 1929, placed the bulk of his effort into foreign affairs. The Foreign Secretary Arthur Henderson he neither liked nor trusted. Henderson's Parliamentary Under-Secretary, Hugh Dalton, had the grace to be deeply disliked by Snowden and J. H. Thomas as well as MacDonald. The Government was under pressure from the Liberals for electoral reform, but the Liberals rightly feared another election, and Hugh Dalton summed up the situation when he said in his diary: 'And we shall hold the Liberals for a long while, I hope, on the string of electoral reform enquiry'.[3] That they did.

In the field of foreign policy, the new Government saw itself as radical and far more committed to international reconciliation, disarmament and a strong League of Nations than its predecessor. Resumption of diplomatic relations with Soviet Russia, leading to a doubling of the admittedly small volume of UK exports to the Soviets (who enjoyed a very positive balance of payments with the UK) was a breakthrough, but much of the rest of the

---

[1] Lord Derby to Mr Stanley Baldwin, 28 October 1930, cited in Randolph S. Churchill *Lord Derby 'King of Lancashire'* (Heinemann, London 1959), pp. 583–5.

[2] Entry for 26 July 1929 in *Beatrice Webb's Diaries 1924–1932*, ed. Margaret Cole (Longman, London 1956), p. 208.

[3] Entry for Sunday 3 to Monday 5 August, in *The Political Diary of Hugh Dalton 1918–40, 1945–60*, ed. Ben Pimlott (Jonathan Cape, and the London School of Economics and Political Science, London 1986), p. 63.

programme was simply a logical projection of existing trends. MacDonald reserved Anglo-American relations for his own special attention. When no American invitation was forthcoming, he invited himself for a well-publicized visit to Washington; this was the prelude to the London naval conference of 1930 at which the Foreign Office policy of accepting American demands for equality of cruisers at the dangerous level of 50 ships was triumphant. Japan, the other party to the agreement, demanded parity and reluctantly settled for a 70 per cent figure which sealed her Pacific ascendancy. A Hague conference accelerated the withdrawal of British and French troops from the Rhineland. Characteristically, Snowden nearly wrecked the conference by arguing fiercely over a comparatively small sum in reparations and received for his pains that most dubious of accolades for a Labour Chancellor: freedom of the City of London. On India, the Government continued unswervingly to work for agreements between the major Indian interests which would enable India to move faster towards that Dominion status which it had been publicly offered by the reigning Viceroy, Edward Wood, Lord Irwin. The latter was the intimate friend and nominee of Baldwin, who strongly supported the Labour regime's Indian policy. It was, after all, an accelerated version of his own. A Round Table conference in London showed how difficult progress was in the face of the differences between the British, the Hindus, the Moslems and the Indian princes. Baldwin had his own price to pay: by the spring of 1930, Churchill and the imperialist right of the Tory party were at open war with him over his bipartisan Indian policy. In general, however, MacDonald at first derived personal and party advantage from his foreign policy activities. As Lionel Robbins, a young economics professor whose sharp mind could produce endless arguments for total inactivity on the part of the Government, told his patron, Hugh Dalton, Labour:

> . . . are the most popular government since the war, chiefly due to the Prime Minister's flying about in service aeroplanes, and Snowden standing up to the foreigners.[1]

Most of the second Labour Government's work for the League of Nations and disarmament was rendered futile by the political consequences of the global economic slump which by 1931 had reached calamitous proportions, but it was the domestic impact of that slump which swept away a non-doing Labour government. Even before it assumed power in 1929, it had become clear that the traditional staple export industries of the UK were in deep trouble. Never having had the frenetic boom of 1920s America, the UK was at first relatively unaffected by the Great Crash on Wall Street. Between 1927 and 1929, employment was at a high level for the interwar era, but that still left an official unemployment rate of 9–10 per cent. This unemployment was heavily concentrated by industry and region. By 1929, a quarter of all coal miners and iron and steel workers were jobless. Nearly half the cotton workers were unemployed, as were a third of shipyard workers. Regions with a tradition of such export staples like Northern Ireland, Central Scotland, South Wales and Tyneside suffered acutely. By

[1] *Ibid.*, p. 63, entry for Saturday 10 – Monday 19 August.

comparison, the south-east of England, where new consumer industries developed, did well. Then from the summer of 1929 what Ramsay Mac-Donald christened an 'economic blizzard' swept over the land. By August 1932, 23 per cent of the insured population was unemployed. The figure stayed above 20 per cent for two years, which meant over two million jobless. Allowing for the uninsured and unregistered, true unemployment may have been over three million in 1931 and three and three-quarter million when it peaked in September 1932.[1]

MacDonald and Snowden simply had no positive responses to the problem. The Premier was much happier swanning around international conferences, like the Imperial Conference of 1930, where he could make speeches exuding vague good will, and where like as not difficult issues or choices would be fudged or ignored, and the disgruntled appeased with words. There was a story current in Labour circles in 1930 that he had told an able Labour candidate that the gravity of the unemployment problem was being exaggerated compared with conferences which 'will live in history'. Whether true or not, it shows the impression he made on his own. It has been argued convincingly that there was no way Labour in office could produce a policy alternative to the relentless deflation which was the Tory answer to the crisis.[2] Though unenthusiastic about the return to the gold standard, Labour accepted it, like the other parties. Abandoning it was politically difficult, and would have required a protective tariff to make internal reflation and devaluation workable. Snowden became apoplectic at the mere mention of protection. Government controlled so small a proportion of the economy that stimulating it by public works would have required an expansion in state activity which the social, political and bureaucratic élites would just not have tolerated from Labour. Not that Labour was likely to try. Sir Oswald Mosley, a wealthy outsider who as a Labour MP played a brutal Punch to MacDonald's dithering Judy, produced proposals for planned trade, reflation and state-directed investment. Rejected at every level of the party, he had been driven to found the tiny New Party by February 1931. As Lloyd George unkindly pointed out, the Government was exceptionally under the thumb of its senior civil servants, and Sir John Anderson, the pompous but able Permanent Under-Secretary at the Home Office, turned his great mind to the subject of public works in June 1930 seven weeks later; concluded, to his own ineffable satisfaction (and MacDonald's), that nothing could be done about unemployment.[3] The other Labour Party in power in the Commonwealth was the Australian one. It deflated, even bringing in the UK Treasury's Sir Otto Niemeyer to advise them how to do it.

The Government was heading for defeat, first in the Commons, where conservative Liberals and Tories were about to unite to unhorse them, and then at the polls, as by-elections showed. Its commitment to electoral

[1] S. Pollard. *The Development of the British Economy 1914–1950* (Edward Arnold, London 1962), p. 243; Stevenson and Cook, *Slump*, p. 55.

[2] Ross McKibbin 'The Economic Policy of the Second Labour Government 1929–1931', *Past and Present* (68, 1975), pp. 95–123.

[3] Robert Skidelsky *Politicians and the Slump: The Labour Government of 1929–31* (Macmillan, London 1987), pp. 215–7.

reform was shallow. In any case, the Conservative majority in the Lords could delay any such measure past the life-expectancy of the Government. Lloyd George was no lifebelt, more a piece of driftwood bobbing as much towards the Tories as Labour. Baldwin had no reason to compromise. At the price of a rightward swing to a policy of protection, minimal expenditure, and no constructive social legislation, he had kept control of the Tory Party. As a relieved Neville Chamberlain, now the heir apparent, had said, by concessions on specific issues the leadership had preserved the principle 'that decisions on policy are made by the Leader, after taking such advice as he chooses.'[1] When, therefore, the Government found itself unable to swallow the recommendations of the May Committee on Economy, which it had, with characteristic ineptitude, inflicted on itself, the political logic would have been its replacement by a Conservative-Liberal coalition which would have had to effect cuts in the salaries of all state employees, and in an unemployment benefit system which was, by international standards, generous. American bankers demanded cuts in unemployment benefit as a condition for a crucial loan. The Trades Union Congress applied its own powerful pressures against this demand. The Cabinet split. Both the TUC and the bankers were applying extra-parliamentary pressure, but that was standard practice. Bankers could be pretty peremptory with Tory administrations, though they naturally laid their cudgel across the hindquarters of the sacred cow of parliamentary sovereignty with redoubled zest when coercing Labour.

Farce was turned into tragedy for Labour by the intervention of George V, who persuaded MacDonald not to resign, but to serve as the nominal head of a National Government, with an emergency remit to effect economies, balance the budget and save the gold standard. Instead of doing his job as party leader, which was to quit office in the way calculated to keep impending electoral damage to a minimum, MacDonald emerged, looking very pleased with himself, still Premier, with a Cabinet of nine: four Conservatives led by an unenthusiastic Baldwin, two Liberals and three members of the old Cabinet (a high proportion of MacDonald's surviving Labour supporters). Snowden and J. H. Thomas, who had at one stage held special responsibility for measures against unemployment, were both by this time deeply unpopular with much of the Labour Party. The third Labour member of MacDonald's new Cabinet, Lord Sankey, being a law officer, was a less contentious figure. In retrospect, the Labour Party was to denounce the initiative taken by George V as 'unconstitutional'. This was not so. Anything was constitutional that a politician could get away with within a framework which guaranteed that general elections would eventually recur. George V was a minor but cunning Conservative politician in a crucial position. Nobody understood better than he the susceptibility of MacDonald to astute flattery. This waffling Scotsman was arguably the most dispensable man in England, but King George told him he was indispensable. There was nothing a National Government proposed to do which a Conservative-Liberal alliance would not have done, but the predominant Conservative element, which was almost bound to win a

[1] Stuart Ball *Baldwin and the Conservative Party: The Crisis of 1928–31* (Yale University Press, New Haven and London 1988), p. 107.

clear majority at the impending election, would undoubtedly have suffered in the medium term from the unpopularity of its measures. Whilst howling at the Labour Government for economy, Conservatives had been very reluctant to spell out specific economies.[1]

The political appeal of rigorous 'monetarist' policies was irresistible, but there was a good deal of pragmatic doubt amongst the more open-minded economists about their efficacy, and the TUC had shown, in opposing deflationary cuts, that it could argue its own interest with a fluency at least equal to that of the bankers. The National Government, in fact, failed miserably in its avowed objectives, despite an emergency budget of cuts and increased taxation from Snowden. The flight of capital from the UK continued, accelerated by news of a refusal in September 1931 of duty by men of the Atlantic Fleet at Invergordon in the Cromarty Firth anchorage, as a protest against cuts in pay.

Mishandled by the Board of Admiralty, this brief episode shook confidence enough to drive the UK off the gold standard. None of the dire effects predicted followed. Exports benefited.[2] Nor did party warfare die down. Rid of its paralytic former leadership, the parliamentary Labour Party, now led by Arthur Henderson, was much more united in opposition to the cuts than it had been under the burden of office.

Baldwin had taken the non-departmental office of Lord President of the Council in the new Cabinet. It hardly accorded with the realities of power, which were better reflected in his occupancy of the Downing Street house usually given to the Chancellor of the Exchequer. He liked its comfort and from it he said, 'I could always keep by eye on my Prime Minister.'[3] Like his keeper, MacDonald had repeatedly said the National Government was purely temporary. Baldwin looked forward to the freedom on tariffs which a Conservative election victory would give him. However, Conservative opinion from the 1922 Committee to the shadow cabinet rapidly grasped the lethal power of a snap electoral appeal based on the National label. Improbably, Churchill and Amery combined to write to Baldwin demanding tariffs and an early election. MacDonald was unhappy about it, but moving to accept the idea even before the Labour Party expelled him. He had already formulated a plan to destroy that party's new leadership by offering Henderson a peerage. It was refused.[4] Objections by free-trade Liberals to a dissolution because of Tory tariff plans were finally fudged over with the notorious appeal for a 'doctor's mandate'. In October 1931, Baldwin led his party out on campaign, with the Liberals, apart from a

---

[1] Apart from the work cited above, there are two articles by Stuart Ball which are essential: 'The Conservative Party and the Formation of the National Government: August 1931', *The Historical Journal* (29, 1986), pp. 159–82; and 'Failure of an Opposition? The Conservative Party in Parliament 1929–31', *Parliamentary History: A Yearbook, Volume 5, 1986* (Allan Sutton, Gloucester 1986), pp. 83–98.

[2] Kenneth Edwards *The Mutiny at Invergordon* (Putnam, London 1937), copes with unpalatable reality by ascribing the episode to 'Bolshevik' influences, and 'hooligans'. More realistic analyses are David Divine *Mutiny at Invergordon* (MacDonald, London 1970), and Alan Ereira *The Invergordon Mutiny* (Routledge and Kegan Paul, London 1981).

[3] Middlemas and Barnes *Baldwin*, p. 640.

[4] Marquand *Ramsay MacDonald*, pp. 644 and 663.

tiny group of intransigents around Lloyd George, tied to his cause, and a former Labour premier working hard to confuse and divide the enemy. From the steps of the guillotine, Baldwin had progressed, mainly buoyed by the simple faith that something would turn up, to the gates of a politician's heaven.

8

Overkill and aftermath:
From Baldwin to elective dictatorship without elections 1931–40

We have been brought low by Socialist misgovernment. We seek to restore our ancient strength and fame by National Government. The larger the majority, the better the chance for all . . .

   The formation of a strong National Government stands between us and the further de-valuation and possible collapse of the £ sterling. If this were to happen our money might become almost trash; and everybody's savings, salaries, wages, pensions or Insurance benefits would buy half or even a tenth of what they buy now . . .
Winston S. Churchill: To the Electors of the Epping Division of Essex, 20 October 1931

Neville Chamberlain was, in fact, among Prime Ministers, more than usually resolute, authoritarian and strong-willed. He acquired a dominance over his Cabinet, and over Parliament, which had been scarcely approached in the interval between Gladstone and Lloyd George. His Ministers were the instruments of his personal policy, his supporters were disciplined with excessive severity.
From Arthur Salter *Personality in Politics: Studies of Contemporary Statesmen* (Faber and Faber, London 1947), p. 67.

Apart from Amery, Baldwin had been the last of the Conservative leaders to abandon the idea of fighting the next election as a straight Tory, with an unequivocal pro-tariff platform. It was significant that latterly he faced a shadow cabinet and a 1922 Committee which were both unanimous for an appeal to the country on a National ticket, with MacDonald as prospective premier. Patriotic emotion explained some of this, but not the unanimity. Electoral advantage was an obvious attraction of the proposal. The more crudely unscrupulous Conservatives, like Beaverbrook, had been pressing for a snap election almost from the moment the National Government was formed. Beaverbrook was hoping that part of the preparation for the election would be the ditching of committed free traders in the National camp, such as Snowden and the group of Liberal MPs led by Sir Herbert Samuel.[1] A second group of Liberals led by Sir John Simon posed no problems. Indistinguishable from Conservatives on most other issues, they had made it clear that they were also prepared to abandon free trade. Great was Simon's reward for his flexibility: a string of glittering offices included the Foreign Secretaryship (1931–5); the Home Secretaryship (1935–7); the Chancellorship of the Exchequer (1937–40); and the Lord Chancellorship (1940–5). It was however in their handling of Snowden and the Samuelite Liberals that Baldwin and Chamberlain displayed profound political professionalism.

The Samuelites did not want an election. Like everyone else, they could see that the real winners behind the National banner would be serried ranks of Tory MPs, nearly all determined to bring in tariffs. In terms of numbers and their enduring political base in the country, the Samuelites were almost as unimportant as Snowden. In terms of electoral artistry, they, like him, were the keys to obliterative victory. The endless hours spent reaching the meaningless compromise embodied in the phrases 'a doctor's mandate' and 'a free hand' were as much a tribute to the political intelligence of Baldwin and Chamberlain as they were a sad commentary on the lack of acuity of Snowden and Samuel, though it has to be added that the judgement of the latter two may have been clouded by subconscious fear of the future. Outside the National Government, their electoral prospects were poor.

The British Establishment undoubtedly smelled blood, in the sense that it saw that with the help of a combination of fear and patriotic hype, a National Government appeal could just about wipe out serious opposition to basically Conservative rule. Nobody was more aware of this than George V. Through the elegant prose of the ghostwriter, the views of his son and heir on a father he found stuffy emerge with the ring of truth. The future Edward VIII protested that there was nothing simple about the lifestyle of George V. That monarch was widely regarded as a simple man, and much given to stressing to politicians, especially Labour ones, his own ordinariness, but of course he lived like the multi-millionaire he was. Nothing was excessively ostentatious in his private life. Everything, from his fine hammer-action shotguns by Purdey, to his cigarette cases by Fabergé, the Russian imperial jeweller, was just perfect, and the same standards of food and wine obtained at his shooting lunches at Sandringham as at Buckingham Palace.[2] Having launched the National Government on its first, remarkably unsuccessful, short spell of office, he was fanatically determined to see it trample all opposition underfoot at an election.

Like Baldwin, he grasped the electoral significance of Ramsay Mac-Donald, and wrestled with his hypersensitive personality. A mixture of cajoling and firmness was the key. MacDonald was assured of his indispensability, and brusquely informed that he simply had to secure an agreed electoral formula, for his resignation would not be accepted. The trouble was that, though he could be vacuous about many things, MacDonald's

[1] Middlemas and Barnes *Baldwin*, pp. 639–48.
[2] *A King's Story: The Memoirs of H.R.H. The Duke of Windsor K.G.* (Reprint Society edn London 1953), p. 174.

thin skin made him highly perceptive about his own position, and how anomalous that position would be if he became a National Labour premier almost entirely dependent on Conservative MPs. After the election was over, he wailed:

> It has turned out all too well . . . The Conservative Head Office pretended to do what it never did and indeed played a shady game. It saw its advantage and took it, and unfortunately the size of the victory has weakened me. Once again I record that no honest man should trust in too gentlemanly a way the Conservative wirepullers.[1]

Nobody had contributed more to the election result than himself, unless possibly Snowden. Like most politicians of a generation trained to platform rhetoric, MacDonald had never coped well with radio. Yet in the 1931 election campaign, his more-in-sorrow-than-in anger denunciation of his own party came across brilliantly and movingly on radio. So did his faith in a genuinely National consensus (a faith all the more sincere as it confirmed his pivotal position). His own return in Seaham, a Durham mining constituency, was a personal triumph. Baldwin exuded moderation during the campaign and made few personal attacks on Labour opponents. He hardly needed to. Snowden made an enormous impact with his venomous denunciations of his former colleagues. Their programme he described, preposterously, as 'Bolshevism run mad', and he moved swiftly to endorse the highly dishonest scare first launched by Walter Runicman, a Simonite Liberal candidate, to the effect that the savings of the poor in Post Office Savings Bank accounts were about to be squandered and rendered valueless by the last Labour Government. As warped in mind as in body, Snowden could not forgive people who committed the sin against the Holy Ghost of disagreeing with him. In this he differed very little from, say, a Treasury mandarin, but whereas the latter instinctively sought to outmanoeuvre his opponent, Snowden instinctively sought to pulverize him.

George V was quite clear that, as he told Sir Maurice Hankey in gossip after a Privy Council: 'I want the National Government to get every vote possible.'[2] He not only ordered Hankey (a Liberal) to vote for it, but also instructed members of his private household to vote for it. There is no reason to think that the monarch's canvassing seriously strengthened what had become a massive electoral swing against Labour. Alarmists like Churchill who had been ringing the tocsin against Lenin's surrogate, Ramsay MacDonald, in election after election, suddenly found that under MacDonald's leadership, their paranoid style was securing a strong electoral response. Of course, it was exaggerated by the electoral system, but it was still impressive. 471 Conservative MPs were returned as against a mere 52 Labour. There were 35 National or Simonite Liberals, 33 Samuelite Liberals, and four members of the Lloyd George family group. The largely phantom National Labour Party returned twelve members. The Tories won 202 seats, mostly from Labour, which lost 215 seats, 182 to Conservatives. The Labour leadership was annihilated. Arthur Henderson, the new leader, went down to defeat among twelve former members of the Labour Cabinet, as

---

[1] Cited in Marquand *Ramsay MacDonald*, p. 671.
[2] Stephen Roskill *Hankey Man of Secrets: Volume II. 1919–1931* (Collins, London 1972), p. 569.

did 21 former junior ministers. One former member of the Cabinet, George Lansbury, survived as did two former junior ministers, Clement Attlee and Stafford Cripps, each by the narrow margin of about 500 votes. The Labour Party had been decisively, and in the foreseeable future irreversibly, rubbished.

Its popular vote was higher than in any previous election apart from 1929. Because of the number of seats it had won by a whisker in that year, Labour was very likely to lose a fair number of seats, particularly after a spell in office led by MacDonald and Snowden, but a fall in votes from 8,370,417 in 1929 (37.1% of all votes cast) to 6,649,630 (30.8%) hardly justified the loss of four out of five Labour seats, and electoral disaster in every region, including some English and Scottish constituencies which were strongly working class in composition. Conservatives created a retrospective legend whereby in constituency after constituency the unemployed had selflessly responded to the National Government appeal by voting for a cut in their own benefits. It was all nonsense. The Labour vote, statistically, held up well in predominantly working class areas, and especially in areas of heavy unemployment. Only in the unique case of Seaham is there any sign of working class defection from Labour on a large scale. What dished Labour was a united front against it, combined with the electoral system and the power of the Premier to secure a snap dissolution from an accommodating sovereign. The scale and hysteria of press hostility, cutting for once with the gain of the electorate, undoubtedly heightened the débâcle. Municipal elections held in November 1931 immediately after the general election enabled the non-Labour parties to benefit doubly from the situation and drive Labour almost as decisively out of positions of influence in local as in central politics.[1]

It is fashionable to point out that the new Government was not just a Conservative front. For example, despite a huge Commons Tory majority and 55 per cent of votes cast, there were only eleven Tories out of twenty Cabinet members. This was however misleading. MacDonald summed the situation up shrewdly when in July 1934 he moaned: 'This is nae my ain hoose, I ken by the biggin' o't'.[2] The National Government palace was 'biggit', or built, in a strange fashion. There was, indeed, a presence chamber in it, where MacDonald sat enthroned under a canopy of state, but like many early modern sovereigns, his job was largely the symbolic one of encouraging acquiescence amongst the subjects. The corridors of power did not run towards him. They largely terminated in the antechamber wherein sat, placidly puffing his briar pipe, the mayor of the palace: Baldwin. When the Conservative Party really wanted something, like tariffs, it insisted on having its way, regardless of its partners' views.

There was a price to be paid, of course, but the Tories were prepared to pay it. Their victory or a National ticket had been deeply ambiguous. Formed to save the gold standard, the Government, which had then abandoned it (something no Labour Government would have dared contemplate), had campaigned behind wild allegations of monetary disaster if they were not returned. Appealing for unity, the National ticket had none

[1] Stevenson and Cook *The Slump*, pp. 102–15.
[2] Cited in Marquand *Ramsay MacDonald*, p. 678.

except against Labour, for the Conservatives campaigned for a tariff, the Samuelites strongly against it, and National Labour, led by the Prince of Imprecision, announced it would have to think about the question, after the election. After the election, Snowden, who had ceased to be an MP, became a peer and Lord Privy Seal, a post with few duties but which carried a seat in the Cabinet. In terms of public perception of the National character of the Government, he was probably more important than the Liberals. Their vote had fallen from over 5.3 million in 1929 to 1.4 million in 1931, and only ten of the 72 Liberals elected had faced a Conservative opponent. They were vitally dependent on Tory forbearance. By January 1932, Snowden and the Samuelite members of the Cabinet were on the verge of resignation in the face of tariff proposals they detested. In the autobiography he published in 1934, Snowden claimed that when he and his allies had tried to talk the issue over with MacDonald:

> The Prime Minister, as usual was discursive and incoherent, and when we left the meeting we asked each other what he had said and where he stood, but none of us could give the answers to these questions.[1]

A more than usually absurd compromise to the effect that Cabinet ministers might 'agree to differ' held Snowden and the Samuelites until it became clear after the Ottawa Commonwealth economic conference in August 1932 that the Westminster Government was committed to permanent tariffs with a system of Imperial preference. Snowden, Herbert Samuel and Archibald Sinclair resigned. Snowden genuinely felt as strongly about free trade as he did about the fiscal crisis of 1929. He was shocked to find that the Conservatives, who had been so attentive to him when he could help destroy the Labour Party, simply did not want to know about his new anguish. In the few years left to him, his bitterness focussed on Ramsay MacDonald, whose reputation he blasted with acid tongue and biting pen. George V, who remained most anxious to keep MacDonald in office, was furious at Snowden's assault on so useful a symbol, to the point in 1933 of formally rebuking Snowden.[2] By 1933, MacDonald was an exhausted old man, increasingly incoherent in the House of Commons.

That he should have been by then enshrined in Labour Party fantasy as the arch-traitor who had long prepared the foul betrayal of 1931 was ironic. It was a convenient fantasy, sparing what was left of the parliamentary party the need to face the truth: they had been victims of a very British coup, triggered by George V and pushed through by Tory rankers, with Baldwin and MacDonald tagging reluctantly behind. The nature of both the premiership and the electoral system were crucial to the whole business. Few Labour MPs wished seriously to re-examine either. MacDonald's misfortune was that, though he resigned as premier in 1935, he knew he had become in functional terms an ex-premier in 1931. Being ex-sovereigns, such creatures tended to be an embarrassment to others and themselves, if they had no source of identity and status other than the tenure of supreme power. The aristocratic and philosophical A. J. Balfour could regard his later career as part of an interesting innings in a fascinating

---

[1] Snowden *Autobiography* Volume Two, p. 1007.
[2] Cross *Snowden*, p. 333.

game. Rosebery, a millionaire with highly-developed sporting and cultural interests, was no more of an embarrassment in public life after his spell as prime minister than he had been during it. Asquith was, however, a distinct embarrassment by the 1920s. Even those, like the Tory Earl of Crawford, who deprecated attacks upon the former premier, had to grant that: 'Squiff of course is a bit of a reactionary and shows small sympathy for artisan aspirations for a "good life".'[1] His groping sexual career had always lacked the panache which characterized that of Lloyd George, but R. B. Haldane was right to express amazement that a school of sycophants, ably encouraged after his death by his daughter, Lady Violet Bonham Carter, managed to turn him into a saviour figure betrayed by the Welsh Judas, Lloyd George. The latter was a tragically frustrated figure after 1922. Unlike Asquith, he did reach out for new ideas, and his sales-resistance to Establishment bandwagons was impressive, but like Asquith, he never seems to have grasped how utterly peripheral to the significant political élite he had become.[2] If he was not a significant politician, he was nobody.

MacDonald was fortunate in the immense tact and respect shown to him by Baldwin, but it was basically cruel to expose his senility in the office of prime minister as late as 1935. After he had resigned that office, and been resoundingly repudiated by the Seaham electors in 1935, his retention as Lord President was grotesque, and the way he was shoe-horned in for an utterly inappropriate Scottish Universities seat by massive Tory machine pressure was squalid.[3] Baldwin used his non-Conservative colleagues partly as an electoral talisman, and partly as a device to confirm his ascendancy in intra-party policy disputes, which were, after all, the only policy disputes outside the higher realms of the bureaucracy which really mattered. The Labour opposition was in parliamentary terms a joke. The Communist Party of Great Britain was a minor political convenience to Conservative propaganda. Stalin's Russia was a bigger Tory asset. The bold and creative mind of Oswald Mosley was rapidly marginalized. The press barons thoughtfully arranged a systematic boycott of any coverage for his New Party. When despair and vaulting ambition drove him into setting up the British Union of Fascists, his activities simply alienated the political class and the police, who saw him as a rival order-enforcement and decision-taking entrepreneur. His constructive economic ideas, which enabled him to attract progressive Conservatives and some of the more dynamic Labour MPs quite late in his trajectory towards fascism were rapidly swamped in the public mind by his lurch into anti-semitism and his association with Hitler and Mussolini.

It is by no means clear that the violent attacks on his meetings and processions in London were provoked by their tone. Up to 1937, there had only been one conviction for insulting language out of hundreds of meetings in the East End. Rather is it clear that by passing the Public Order Act (1936), the Government preferred to appease the often highly-organized

[1] Entry for 13 June 1923, *Crawford Papers*, ed. Vincent, p. 485.
[2] Stephen Koss 'Asquith Versus Lloyd George: The Last Phase and Beyond' in Sked and Cook. eds. *Crisis and Controversy*, pp. 66–89.
[3] L. MacNeill Weir *The Tragedy of Ramsay MacDonald* (Secker and Warburg, London 1938), Chap. 64 gives an acidic but factual account of 'The University By-Election'.

and violent attacks on those meetings by banning both political processions and political uniforms. The judiciary, increasingly no friend to the traditional liberties of an Englishman, cooperated by means of a series of executive-friendly decisions in the 1930s which, by extending police right of search and entry and power to ban meetings, gave the Government sweeping power to stop the spread of views it disliked. Subjects in the UK had no fundamental rights. By the 1930s, it was clear that freedom of speech, if challenged, would be upheld only if it suited the executive to uphold it.[1]

That made Conservative criticism the only dangerous criticism of Government. Had Baldwin won an election as a straight Conservative in 1930, the Cabinet would have had to have included men who were bitterly opposed to the direction in which he wanted to go. Churchill, in retrospect, placed his finger on the dismissal of his friend George Lloyd as British High Commissioner in Egypt by the incoming Labour Government in the summer of 1929 as the start of a mortal struggle with Baldwin:

> Here began my differences with Mr Baldwin . . . My idea was that the Conservative Opposition should strongly confront the Labour Government on all great imperial and national issues.[2]

However, Austen Chamberlain and the Foreign Office mandarinate had disliked Lloyd's abrasive confrontations with Egyptian nationalists to the point of being poised to remove him before the election. As a result, Baldwin refused to support Churchill who reported angrily after the debate that: 'Our Party had been damped down as much as possible by the Whips, and of course we are much hampered by our own past.'[3] Churchill's denunciation of Foreign Office officials was deemed bad taste, since it breached the mythology of an impartial Civil Service, and many Conservatives saw his activism in opposition as a conscious bid to seize leadership from Baldwin.

It was probably a combination of opportunism and conviction, as his sustained offensive against concessions to nationalists in India showed. Churchill was both ambitious and racist. Like the Victorian he was, he believed in self-government, but for white communities. He opposed the bipartisan approach which Baldwin preferred and allied with the 'die-hard' India Defence League. When along with all the other ardent imperialists of stature, he was excluded from the National Government, he went into opposition to its liberal Indian policy. Despite bitter criticisms (from Lloyd in the Lords and Churchill in the Commons), the second and third sessions of the round table conference in London inaugurated by Labour were held under National Government auspices, with participation by the Indian princes, the Indian National Congress, and the Muslim League. Eventually, the Government of India Act of 1935 laid down an intricate federal structure for India which pleased nobody and never became operative, but if stillborn at the centre it cleared the way for the implementation of

---

[1] Robert Skidelsky *Oswald Mosley* (Macmillan, pbk edn London 1975), pp. 256 and 415–21.
[2] 'Recollections', printed in Gilbert *Churchill. Volume V: Companion Part 2 Documents: The Wilderness Years 1929–1935* (Heinemann, London 1981), p. 25.
[3] Winston S. Churchill to Lord Camrose, 28 July 1929, printed in *ibid.*, pp. 26–7.

responsible government at provincial level in India in 1937, and psychologically it undermined what little chance there was of an imperialist backlash in the UK. Churchill lost partly because of suspicions about his motives and doubts about his judgement. The antics of his son Randolph, who clearly did hope to ride to fame and fortune on the Indian issue by appealing to hard-line Conservative imperialist instincts, did not help. Against his father's will he fought a by-election in February 1935 as an Independent Conservative, polling well enough to let Labour win against a split Conservative vote. Though even Government ministers admitted that only a fraction of the huge Conservative majority in the Commons were enthusiastic about the Indian policies dear to Baldwin, the idea of splitting their party and undermining their domestic hegemony appalled most Tory MPs and their constituency supporters.

Henry Ludwig Mond, Lord Melchett, former Liberal MP, latish convert to Toryism, and leading figure in Imperial Chemical Industries, has some claim to be the most reliable weather-vane in the ranks of the wealth-holders. As early as November 1934, he wrote to Churchill, saying that though he was himself a member of the India Defence League, it was not worth splitting the Conservative Party, and possibly admitting Socialists to office, for the sake of India.[1] That mentality goes far to explain why, despite sustained and heroic efforts, Churchill failed to swing the National Association of Conservative constituency associations against Baldwin. In the Commons, Baldwin was probably always much less worried about his Indian legislation than Sir Samuel Hoare, Secretary of State for India, who was on the receiving end of Churchill's repeated attacks. Churchill wanted to break up the National Government, which he depicted as a pinkish betrayal of Toryism led by 'a Socialist', which was his unlikely term for MacDonald. Unfortunately for him, something like 150 Conservative MPs after 1931 were significantly dependent on the National label to secure former Liberal or Labour votes and their own return. When to this was added the payroll vote of office holders, and the general power of the party machine to reward friends and punish enemies, Baldwin's grip was unlikely to weaken. Liberal intentions, as under Asquith, were being used to justify an extraordinary extension of executive power.

Churchill understood what he was up against. He was supported by Rothermere's papers, but the BBC, under Sir John Reith, stonily recognized the almost Stalinist party hierarchy which controlled the legislature. When Churchill wanted to broadcast on India in 1931, he was enraged to find that Reith had decided 'to refer my request to the Whips'. As Churchill later fumed, it was the power of the whips which enabled the executive to ram through Indian legislation supported positively by only a handful of MPs in the vast Conservative majority.[2] By 1935, an exhausted Churchill

---

[1] Lord Melchett to Winston S. Churchill, 22 November 1934, printed in *ibid.*, pp. 930–3.

[2] Winston S. Churchill to Sir John Reith, 2 March 1931; and 'Winston S. Churchill: draft press statement'. 11 April 1933 printed in *ibid.*, pp. 287–8 and p. 571. The fact that the letter to Reith was not sent, and that the strongest expression in the press statement —'despite the tremendous pressure exerted by the Whips'—was excised before release, gives us an insight into Churchill's genuine opinion, as distinct from what he dared say in public.

had accepted the unpalatable facts and was trying to ingratiate himself with Baldwin. At the height of his offensive against the National Government, Churchill's fantastic energy had enabled him also to be adding another volume to his successful *The World Crisis*, whilst he dictated a multi-volume biography of his ancestor, John, Duke of Marlborough. By 1935, his drinking was approaching F. E. Smith proportions. The House of Commons merited the contempt he felt for it, but his infrequent and petulant performances there did not endear him to MPs. He looked washed up and finished.

Baldwin never deviated from the position he had reached in opposition after 1929, nor did the Conservative Party. Tariffs apart, there was never to be another positive social programme from it. Neville Chamberlain was the only minister who had any sustained legislative achievement to his credit, and by 1935 he was complaining that he was tired of carrying the Government on his back.[1] Baldwin's great achievement, after taking over as premier in May 1935, was to arrange an electoral victory so sweeping as to hold a great part of the 1931 windfall and thereby to confirm the 'practical derogation' of parliamentary sovereignty which had been a creeping reality long before 1931, but which had been greatly accelerated by the events of that year. Well before 1940, when the process accelerated again, the Westminster parliament had lost all power to initiate policy or legislation. 'Private members' bills' were a well-publicized fig-leaf dealing with matters peripheral to power. The gap between reality and public perception widened. As late as 1977, a survey suggested that nearly half of secondary school leavers believed that all important political decisions were taken in the Commons. For many decades almost no such decisions had been taken there.[2] Executive dominance meant that ministers and bureaucrats, and indeed foreign governments which could influence them, formed the prime policy-making community in the UK. Full prime-ministerial power could only be wielded by someone in control of a whipped, single-party majority, even if, as in the case of Baldwin latterly, control was paradoxically upheld by keeping that majority in an equivocal coalition.

Baldwin was probably genuinely worried by the furious reaction of public opinion to the new national assistance rates for the unemployed introduced by the central Unemployment Assistance Board set up by Neville Chamberlain's Unemployment Act of 1934. The proposed new rates, especially in distressed areas, were often below those paid by the old local public assistance committees. The Bonar Law implicit compact was being decisively breached in the sense that an administration heavily backed by the rich appeared to be behaving provocatively towards the poor. By 1935, the Government had backed down, ordering a supposedly independent Board to maintain the rates. Its other problems were relatively trivial. It had lost a few by-elections, but then after 1931 it was bound to lose a few. There was a great deal of sniping at the Government in the Conservative press for 'staleness' and 'indecisiveness' (i.e. for not being conservative enough) but at a general election the proprietors could be relied upon to rally to the National Government. The independent Liberals

---

[1] Ramsden *History of the Conservative Party: The Age of Balfour and Baldwin*, p. 331.
[2] Middlemas *Politics in Industrial Society*, p. 307–9.

were divided; their constituency structures were derelict; and funding was pitiful. The Labour Party was only a very little better. It was desperately short of money. Early in October 1935, its annual conference deposed George Lansbury, who had led it since the 1931 disaster. An honourable Christian Socialist and convinced pacifist, Lansbury was troubled in mind and body and out of date in the world of 1935. He was replaced by the uncharismatic stopgap, Clement Attlee, and within a fortnight Baldwin had called an election. Already there had been a sustained propaganda campaign by the Conservatives in 1934–5. Now their well-funded campaign rolled forward, making skilful use of radio and the new medium of film, as well as the usual concentrated press barrage. Their earlier fears of losing an election, though grossly exaggerated, had served a purpose. All dominant machines run scared. Even Mayor Richard J. Daley of Chicago, perhaps the greatest of machine politicians, in a then overwhelmingly Democratic city, always ran 'the Machine' scared in his heyday in the 1950s and 1960s.[1] Starting scared in 1934, the Tory masters of the National Government ended triumphant in November 1935.

Labour leaders did not expect victory. Significantly, the Stock Exchange remained buoyant throughout, expecting, as *The Times* said, 'a good majority for the National Government'. There was no return to the political pluralism of 1929: 435 National candidates were returned, 388 of them Conservatives. Of 180 opposition MPs, Labour had 154. It benefitted from a UK-wide swing to it of 9.4 per cent; it was not enough to be significant. With a majority of 255, Baldwin did not need again to repeat his policy reversal of 1934–35.[2]

Underpinning his triumph was economic recovery, expressed in falling unemployment and rising real wages. Not having had the hectic boom of the 1920s which had occurred in countries like the USA and Germany (economies linked by heavy American lending to Germany), the UK was inherently less vulnerable to the depths of the consequent crash. Leaving the gold standard spared the country the worst extremes of rigorous deflation, and tariffs probably helped marginally to insulate its economy from the wilder swings of the international economy. The Imperial preference which was a hereditary trust to Neville Chamberlain, a fanatical faith to Leo Amery, proved difficult to set up at Ottawa and limited in scope and results. Over large parts of the strictly dependent British Empire, such as many of the African colonies, international agreements already in existence made it impossible for Westminster to introduce Imperial preference, but then the economic weight of such colonies was slight. India had achieved tariff autonomy with the setting up of a Tariff Board in New Delhi in 1923. Nevertheless, industrial depression in the UK and plummeting primary product prices for Canadian wheat farmers, New Zealand dairy farmers, and Australian wool producers (who saw wool prices fall by 50 per cent between 1928 and 1931), did make it possible to create a network of hard-won preferential agreements. In 1929, UK imports from the

---

[1] Mike Royko *Boss: Mayor Richard J. Daley of Chicago* (Granada, Paladin pbk edn, 1972), p. 73.
[2] Tom Stannage *Baldwin Thwarts the Opposition: The British General Election of 1935* (Croom Helm, London, 1980).

Empire-Commonwealth were 29.4 per cent of total imports. By 1936, the figure was 39.1 per cent. Some of this increase would have occurred in any case.[1] Canada remained determined to keep privileged access to the American market as well as the UK one. Australian wool also needed world markets. The Ottawa agreements angered the Americans and Japanese, despite their limitations, and after 1936, Australia incurred a costly six-month trade war with Japan.[2]

It was however the relative buoyancy of the UK domestic economy which ultimately underpinned what by 1937 was no more than a thinly-veiled Conservative ascendancy. After the slow growth rates of 1913–29, the economic crises of 1929–32 had further retarded development, though income and consumption held up well compared with other lands, even when in the third quarter of 1932 the number of unemployed rose to nearly three million or 22.7 per cent of the insured labour force. Exports fell by a third. By 1933, a recovery was clearly gathering strength. Devaluation helped export industries, but the strongest surge was in such domestic sectors as construction, transportation, electricity, and services, including entertainment. Investment and exports picked up in 1934. By 1937, continued recovery had increased real income by 19 per cent since 1932; domestic gross output by over 25 per cent; industrial production by almost 46 per cent; gross investment by 47 per cent; and exports by 28.4 per cent. At the peak of the boom in the third quarter of 1937, there were still 1.4 million unemployed, or 9.1 per cent of the insured workforce. 1937–8 saw a definite if mild recession, but by 1939 the economy was swinging upwards, assisted by then by rearmament orders.[3]

Most of the new prosperity was however concentrated in the Midlands and the south-east corner of England, especially London. The northern and western parts of the UK, whose industrial complexes tended to be dominated by old export staples like coal, iron, shipbuilding and textiles, suffered disproportionately. Their low income levels discouraged the new consumer industries from siting manufacturing facilities in them. In the multinational UK, whole nations like the Scots and the Welsh, and proud regions with a sharp sense of identity like the north-east of England or Northern Ireland, suffered from much higher unemployment, lower living standards and far less investment, than the fortunate parts of England. Between 1923 and 1936, more than a million people relocated in the south of England. What is striking is how little regional discontent shook the ability of the London-based Government to command allegiance.

Northern Ireland was an extreme case. Of all the regions of the UK, only Wales had a worse unemployment record. The three Northern Irish staples —agriculture, shipbuilding and linen—all faced immense structural problems over which they could exert little control, for they were all heavily export-oriented, the latter two to global markets. Between 1923 and 1930,

[1] Nicholas Mansergh *The Commonwealth Experience* (Frederick A. Praeger, New York 1969), pp. 243–6.
[2] Stuart Macintyre *The Oxford History of Australia. Volume 4: 1901–1942, The Succeeding Age* (Oxford University Press, Melbourne 1986), pp. 289–90.
[3] Derek H. Aldcroft *The British Economy between the Wars* (Philip Allan, pbk edn, Oxford 1983).

an average of 19 per cent of the Northern Ireland insured workforce was out of work. Between 1931 and 1939, the figure rose to 27 per cent. Yet the province's performance in relative terms was not as bad as it looked. Only four out of the ten major UK regions generated a higher proportion of new jobs between 1923 and 1937. The province's proportion of UK industrial production fell between 1924 and 1935, but large parts of the north of England experienced greater relative industrial decline. Given its sectarianized social and political structure and a tradition of violence, it is unsurprising that there were riots in working-class areas of Belfast in the 1930s. In 1932, there was an encouraging phenomenon: a non-sectarian riot when the Catholic Falls district and the Protestant Shankhill rioted together against a ban by the Northern Ireland Minister of Home Affairs on a demonstration by the unemployed. In 1935, however, the city reverted to type with three weeks of rioting between the Falls and Shankhill, costing twelve lives. In fact, these were utterly abnormal events. Apart from the years 1922 and 1935, there were very few political murders in inter-war Ulster. Between 1922 and 1955, the total homicide rate in Northern Ireland was proportionately half that of England and Wales. Baldwin firmly refused to intervene in 1935 on the grounds that order in the province was the responsibility of its own administration at Stormont, outside Belfast.[1]

That decision probably kept down the risk of escalation in communal violence. Certainly the brutal inter-community slayings of the 1970s were fuelled by the uncertainty following massive Westminster intervention in the province in 1969. By and large, the creeping attack by Westminster on local government autonomy in Great Britain itself did not reach proportions which encouraged any serious backlash in the inter-war period. There were, for example, stirrings of Scottish nationalism, closely connected with a Scottish literary renaissance of some stature. However, the connection with a literary world remarkable for alcoholism, sexual and political ambiguity, and rampant eccentricity did not make for meaningful, effective politics, let alone forward-looking policies. In 1929, an observer commented, fairly, that the most visible contemporary Scottish nationalists either harked back to 'a Jacobite restoration' or wanted to restore the Auld Alliance with France and turn the clock back to before the Reformation. With the formation of the Scottish National Party in 1934, as the result of a merger of pre-existing groups, an element of sanity began to emerge, but the political impact of Scottish Nationalism before 1939 was zero.[2]

In practice, Baldwin had more trouble with his nominal sovereign than with his peripheral subjects during his final spell in supreme office. The whole protracted and messy business of the abdication of Edward VIII, who succeeded George V in January 1936, and abdicated in December to marry a twice-divorced American, Wallis Simpson, has been seen as 'a great irrelevance', distracting attention from the real problems looming in

---

[1] Ian Budge and Cornelius O'Leary *Belfast: Approach to Crisis: A Study of Belfast Politics, 1613–1970* (Macmillan, London 1973), p. 151; *An Economic History of Ulster, 1820–1940*, eds. Liam Kennedy and Philip Ollerenshaw (Manchester University Press, Manchester 1985), Chap. 6.

[2] Murray G. H. Pittock *The Invention of Scotland: The Stuart Myth and the Scottish Identity, 1638 to the Present* (Routledge and Kegan Paul, London 1991), pp. 146–8.

foreign affairs. In fact, the monarchy, as the widespread response to George V's Silver Jubilee in 1935 had shown, was a formidable instrument for creating loyalty and securing allegiance. Its technical authority remained very considerable, and was regularly and conveniently used by prime ministers to validate executive initiative. There remained always the problem of ensuring that it was thoroughly subordinated to the politicians' convenience. Ultimately this was an insoluble problem. All the Dominions had the same system. Mackenzie King had had a fierce clash with Governor-General Lord Byng in 1926 when King, a minority Premier after the Canadian federal election of 1925, in effect demanded that Byng surrender all discretion over granting a dissolution to King. Byng rightly refused. Having tried secretly and unsuccessfully to persuade Westminster to pressure Byng into yielding, King then, with a characteristic mixture of self-righteousness and dishonesty, fought the next election on the theme of resistance to 'British interference'.

Edward VIII was shallow, self-indulgent and mildly unconventional. His politics, ironically, were those of a Baldwin Conservative, in so far as he had political thoughts. The wilder smears which were retrospectively manufactured to blight his reputation and that of Mrs Simpson may be dismissed for the rubbish they are. He was not a Nazi spy who hoped to recover his throne as Hitler's puppet. She was not a former Russian spy who learned her sexual techniques in a Hong Kong brothel, let alone the mistress of Ribbentrop, Hitler's ambassador in London in 1936–8.[1] He was however determined to marry in such a way as to create severe problems for both the Government and the leaders of the Church of England. It is interesting that the first attempt to propel Baldwin into outright confrontation with Edward VIII seems to have originated in the higher echelons of the Civil Service.[2] Baldwin was genuinely reluctant. Had Edward simply sat tight, there would have been little the Government could have done. When the besotted monarch decided to demand a morganatic marriage, which would have made Mrs Simpson his wife, but not the Queen, he placed himself at the mercy of the politicians, for that option required legislation.

One or two politicians broke ranks and rallied to the monarch. They included a few young Labour figures like Michael Foot, and (discreetly) Hugh Dalton, but the most spectacular examples were Churchill and Beaverbrook. Churchill was motivated by quixotic chivalry and residual resentment at Baldwin. Beaverbrook did what he did, and in his own words, 'To bugger Baldwin!',[3] whom he hated and whom he accused (fairly) of deviousness and (unfairly) of systematically plotting the monarch's downfall.[4] Baldwin's success in marginalizing his opponents,

---

[1] Out of the disproportionately vast literature devoted to this subject, Philip Ziegler's *King Edward VIII: The Official Biography* (Collins, London 1990) is sensible. The 'Black Legend' is well represented by Charles Higham *Wallis. Secret Lives of the Duchess of Windsor* (Sidgwick and Jackson, London 1988), and Michael Bloch *The Duke of Windsor's War* (Weidenfeld and Nicholson, London 1982) is a salutary antidote.

[2] Middlemas and Barnes *Baldwin*, pp. 987–8.

[3] Quoted in Ziegler *King Edward VIII*, p. 314.

[4] Beaverbrook's version of events and attack on Baldwin can be studied in *The Abdication of King Edward VIII by Lord Beaverbrook*, ed. A. J. P. Taylor (Hamish Hamilton, London 1966).

shepherding Edward VIII into voluntary abdication and exile; and replacing him with his earnest if not very bright brother Albert, who was duly crowned as George VI, preserved the existing power-structure in church and state in the UK and avoided any agonizing reassessment of Commonwealth relations. For that, as much as anything, Baldwin was heaped with adulation when he duly retired, as Earl Baldwin of Bewdley, in May 1937. Arguably all of these politically sensitive areas would have benefited from the compulsory re-thinking precipitated by an unacceptable royal marriage. The coronation confirmed the quasi-liturgical fudge surrounding the UK-Dominions link, but one earnest Conservative author had to admit in 1938 that '. . . there remained and still remains, some uncertainty as to what that link really is.' He added, plaintively, that:

> Numbers of people have been starting since last year to try and find it. At Ashridge, there have been courses to study what Great Britain really stands for. Groups in London and elsewhere, have been meeting to see how far a common basis can be found.[1]

The succession of Neville Chamberlain as Prime Minister was therefore triply ironic. Baldwin, who had devoted his life to burying elective dictatorship, handed over to Chamberlain a potentially very extreme one. Monarch, legislature, law and the subjects in the UK were all now firmly subordinated to the will of an executive headed by the premier who was leader of both the Conservative Party and the National Government. Chamberlain had been less than loyal, as Baldwin knew, during Baldwin's post-1929 troubles, but the new Premier took for granted his personal ascendancy over his party. Secondly, a political culture deeply rooted in ambiguity and obfuscation (both of which increased the executive's room for manoeuvre) was now headed by a limited but notably clear mind. Thirdly, at a time when official propaganda relentlessly stressed 'parliamentary government', parliament had never been less significant. The Prime Minister was no great parliamentarian. His natural habitat and power-bases were Whitehall and Central Office. State and party *apparatchiks* were his acolytes.

Chamberlain came to power with a justified sense of his own power of work, and a dangerous sense of self-righteousness, saying to his sister Hilda that:

> It has come to me without my raising a finger to obtain it, because there is no-one else and perhaps because I have not made enemies by looking after myself rather than the common cause.[2]

It was a somewhat over-simple view. He was indeed the inevitable successor by 1937. Though 67 years of age, he was robust and capable of sustained application. In reaction to the doziness of Baldwin's later regime, he insisted that his ministers draw up their legislative proposals with a view to welding them into a two-year programme, and also with a view to working out what might appropriately be held in reserve for an election

---

[1] William Teeling *Why Britain Prospers* (The Right Book Club, London 1938), pp. 190–1.

[2] Neville to Hilda Chamberlain, 30 May 1937, printed in Iain Macleod *Neville Chamberlain* (Frederick Muller, London 1961), p. 199.

manifesto in 1939 or 1940. True to his Liberal Unionist faith, Chamberlain was, in matters domestic, a conscious improver and reformer. His Cabinet, which he changed very little between 1937 and 1939, contained plenty of experienced administrative talent in the shape of Lord Swinton, his Secretary of State for Air, Hore-Belisha at the War Office; Kingsley Wood at Health; and Malcolm MacDonald in the Dominions and Colonials Secretaryships. There was an inner group of senior ministers whose counsel he heeded: Sam Hoare, Home Secretary; Sir John Simon at the Exchequer; and Halifax, Lord President, and, after Eden's resignation in 1938, Foreign Secretary. Nevertheless, the Cabinet received a very firm lead from the Prime Minister. Because of political realities, consolidation and rationalization rather than innovation were the keynotes. There was a comprehensive Factories Act. An Insurance Act extended pension-provision to non-manual workers on a voluntary basis. Housing legislation focussed on slum clearance. There was a start made to the modernization of criminal law, and we know that the Premier looked forward to further tidying up of local government structures, as well as more control over urban and industrial sprawl. He did see the passing of a Physical Training and Recreation Act which was innovative as well as looking back to the 'national efficiency' obsessions of the pre-1914 era. The most radical of the Chamberlain administration's achievements was the passage, over stiff opposition in the Lords, of a Coal Act nationalizing mining royalties and allowing compulsory amalgamation of firms into more viable units.[1] That was the exception proving the rule, Because it was the Labour Party which was swept from office and split by the repercussions of the Great Crash, there was no irresistible pressure for more extensive or innovative state action to cope with the economic crisis. Apart from devaluation and tariffs, the Government's main policy was cheap money. By June 1932, bank rate, aided by a set of natural pressures, had fallen 2 per cent, where it remained for years. There was never likely to be a version of the American New Deal in the UK. In the USA in 1932, the conservative Republican businessman, President Hoover, was buried at the polls by the Democratic professional politician, Franklin D. Roosevelt. The latter was astute enough to commit himself to a welter of experimental innovation only after he assumed power. Activism was essential to hold his electoral coalition together especially in the face of critics on the populist left like Governor Huey Long of Louisiana, and renewed recession after 1937, but the political architects of the New Deal remained functional illiterates in economics.[2]

The nearest approach to a New Deal in the British Isles was the regime of De Valera in Dublin from 1932. That Catholic Irish version of Mr Gladstone had emerged from prison in 1923; ditched his Sinn Féin associates whilst keeping their rhetoric; and shuffled into the Dáil in 1927 in good

---

[1] Apart from Macleod, *op. cit*, chap. 12, there is a survey of Chamberlain's domestic record as Premier in Keith Feiling *The Life of Neville Chamberlain* (Macmillan, London 1946), chap. XXI.

[2] Anthony J. Badger 'Huey Long and the New Deal' and Stephen W. Baskerville 'Cutting loose from prejudice: economists and the Great Depression' in Stephen Baskerville and Ralph Willett, eds. *Nothing Else to Fear: New Perspectives on America in the Thirties* (Manchester University Press, Manchester 1935), pp. 64–103 and 258–84 resp.

time to learn the tricks of the parliamentary trade and then reap the benefits of the ultra-conservative Cosgrove regime's embarrassment in the face of an unprecedented slump. De Valera's party Fianna Fáil, with 44.5 per cent of the 1932 Free State vote, could have expected a clear majority under UK rules, but proportional representation ensured that it needed the support of the small Labour Party to govern. Basically, the social structure of the Free State in 1932 was fiercely conservative, sectarian and provincial, both in country and in town.[1] De Valera was almost devoid of economic under-standing. It was politics which fuelled the interventionist programme of his new regime. Taxes, civil servants, tariffs, pensions and unemployment assistance provisions all expanded. Tariffs and arguments over repayment of land purchase loans triggered a damaging economic war with the UK which De Valera was lucky to escape from in 1938 when Chamberlain decided, literally, that De Valera like Hitler needed to be appeased by generous terms. Much of this made no economic sense at all. It did not matter. Broadly, these policies gave comfort, psychological and fiscal, to those who voted for De Valera and their price was paid for disproportion-ately by those who did not.[2]

Chamberlain presided over an administration which had, thanks to George V, avoided the traumatic defeats of Hoover and Cosgrove. Pro-vided employment and income trends were in the right direction, the National Government could hardly fail to win general elections. It had enormous freedom of manoeuvre in policy and could choose the time of elections. Stupidity alone could doom it. Stupid Chamberlain was not. Nor was he charismatic. Despite an affectionate family life, he projected an icy public persona. He said, with great honesty after seeing himself on film, that his corvine appearance and bloodless voice were not appealing. Bald-win warned him about talking to opponents as if they were dirt. Neverthe-less, he was the chosen chief political executive to the Tory Party and the propertied and business classes which ultimately funded and dominated it. Like Bonar Law and Baldwin, Chamberlain had himself been a business-man, but politics were becoming, for those ambitious for power, a full-time job. Diversification in patterns of wealth-holding gave the majority of Con-servative and National Liberal MPs substantial business interests. Mergers had created corporations so complex as to rule out the idea of their senior executives finding time for the House of Commons, though they often accepted peerages. Business influences permeated the Government to the point where policy seriously affecting any industry would invariably by worked out in association with its proprietors.[3] Barring external crises, which of course proved decisive, Chamberlain would no doubt have arranged to win another comfortable majority in 1939 or 1940. His cushion of seats was huge. His personality was off-putting, but he would have been packaged and marketed by a well-funded, increasingly sophisticated

[1] Conrad M. Arensberg and Solon T. Kimball *Family and Community in Ireland* (2nd edn, Harvard University Press, Cambridge, MA 1968).

[2] K. Theodore Hoppen *Ireland since 1800: conflict and conformity* (Longman, pbk edn, London 1989), pp. 211–6.

[3] John Turner 'The Politics of Business' in J. Turner, ed. *Businessmen and Politics: Studies of Business Activity in British Politics, 1900–1945* (Heinemann, London 1984), pp. 16–8.

publicity machine. It is even clear enough how it would have been done. His interest in fishing and entomology was being stressed, no doubt to build him up as a rural ruminant philosopher of the Baldwin school. During his brief hour of triumph after the Munich agreement, the predictable phrases emerged. Chamberlain was a 'typical home-loving Englishman', but one who 'wears the livery of the great with equal ease'.[1] A press which could turn an empty-headed little man like Edward, Prince of Wales into a Prince Charming was capable of almost anything.

In the event, it was not to be. Foreign policy and war undermined the foundations of Chamberlain's power. His misfortune was to grapple with an international situation which was uncontrollable from a domestic power-base which was only too well controlled. Secrecy levels rose sharply shortly after the formation of the National Government. To secure a crushing electoral victory in 1931, the Establishment, from George V down, had been willing in effect to shoot another sacred cow: Cabinet secrecy. It was extremely damaging to the Labour Party to allow J. H. Thomas to reveal how deeply split the Labour Cabinet had been over the proposed cuts in unemployment assistance. Maurice Hankey, supreme guardian of Cabinet secrets, was rather shocked at this cavalier approach. He had already had his troubles with ex-Coalition grandees like Lloyd George and Churchill, who had taken official papers with them when they left office, and who used them partly to skew historical perception by writing memoirs which justified their own actions, and partly as a source of income to sustain their life-style. In theory, once a politician reached the Cabinet, he was sworn of the Privy Council, which oath bound him not to divulge state secrets without the express approval of the sovereign. Since that approval depended on the 'advice' of the premier, the logic of this typical misuse of royal authority would have been a veto on political memoirs exercised by the premier. After 1934, the Government actually embarked on a campaign to recover all Cabinet papers in private hands. 62 living former ministers simply obeyed, despite the very shaky legal basis of the campaign. Of nine who refused, all but one were ex-Coalition or Labour. Churchill and Lloyd George were gallantly to the fore in refusal. They were too eminent fish to fry. Sprats could however be singed as a warning, using the Official Secrets Act. Compton Mackenzie, writer, Scottish nationalist and associate of the Secret Service, was so dealt with for a book of memoirs resented by his former associates amongst the secret policemen. His anger at having to plead guilty at heavy cost in fine, court costs and, above all, legal fees came out in his bitter 1939 allegation:

> . . . that the tendency of our democratic rulers moves steadily towards repression, and the Official Secrets Act is a convenient weapon for tyranny . . .[2]

It was fair comment. The arrogance which lay behind Chamberlain's public

[1] *Vide* the captions on the photographs of Mr and Mrs Chamberlain in *Europe's Fight for Freedom: A Record and Review of the Origins, Progress and Personalities of the World Crisis 1938*, ed. Sir John Hammerton (The Amalgamated Press Ltd., London n.d.), pp. 28–9.

[2] Cited in John F. Naylor *A Man and an Institution: Sir Maurice Hankey, the Cabinet Secretariat and the Custody of Cabinet Secrecy* (Cambridge University Press, Cambridge 1984), p. 211.

manner pervaded the policy-making élite whose real policy debates, as distinct from the largely irrelevant hot air of parliamentary or hustings pronouncements, were kept very private indeed. In this secrecy, the élite revelled. It made one of their favourite arguments a self-fulfilling prophecy. Critics were ill-informed. Indeed they were. How could they be anything else? Significantly, the serious alternative options in crisis after crisis were available only to a small inner circle. That was even true of the first major foreign policy crisis of the 1930s, when Japan seized control of Manchuria in 1931, and set up the puppet state of Manchukuo. The American Secretary of State, Henry L. Stimson, was big on moral disapproval and contrived to give the impression later that if the UK had stood firmer, the US would have done more. Even the notably uninformative memoirs of the then Foreign Secretary, Sir John Simon, are at pains to indicate that nothing was further from the truth.[1] Behind a public display of League of Nations activism in organizing general non-recognition of Manchukuo, the Government was paralysed between different schools of thought. The Treasury hankered, rather sensibly, after some restoration of Anglo-Japanese understanding. The Foreign Office vetoed this because it would annoy the US. It had no solution for the Japanese who stormed out of the League of Nations. Banking interests led by Montagu Norman and his close associate Sir Charles Addis (who had come to the Bank of England from long service with the Hongkong and Shanghai Bank) favoured League action against Japan. They still hankered after a re-establishment of British financial dominance in China against the competition of both America and Japan. The Foreign Office opposed them.[2]

The gap between rational policy calculation and public posture had provoked a desperately embarrassing episode in 1935 when the National Government had secured itself against erosion of its majority by campaigning at the election on a strong League of Nations, collective security ticket, and then turned to realpolitik during Mussolini's much-denounced invasions of Abyssinia. After joining in economic sanctions, but jibbing at including fuel oil, the Government approved a deal cut by its new Foreign Secretary, Sir Samuel Hoare, with his French opposite number, Pierre Laval, and Mussolini. Under it, Abyssinia was to be partitioned, leaving an Amharic Coptic core independent and transferring the predominantly Muslim lowlands to Italy. It was, in many ways, a sensible proposal, yet it was repudiated, not because of a barrage of letters from an enraged public (comparatively few reached MPs), but because members of the Cabinet, a significant number of Conservative MPs and other key Establishment figures like the Archbishops of York and Canterbury, said they found it intolerable. The politicians regarded the U-turn from recent election pledges as obnoxious and a threat to their credibility. Hoare was made the fall-guy. The League was finished. Abyssinia fell unexpectedly fast, and

[1] *Retrospect: The Memoirs of the Rt. Hon. Viscount Simon* (Hutchinson, London 1952), pp. 188–92.

[2] George C. Peden *British Rearmament and the Treasury 1932–39* (Scottish Academic Press, Edinburgh, 1979), p. 110; Roberta A. Dayer *Finance and Empire: Sir Charles Addis 1861–1945* (Macmillan, London 1988), p. 235.

Neville Chamberlain endorsed the subsequent abandonment of sanctions as the only sane course.[1]

Hitler had come to power in 1933. He reoccupied the previously demilitarized Rhineland during the Abyssinian War. By 1937, Neville Chamberlain faced the full threat of the triple challenge facing a globally over-extended United Kingdom whose power in no way matched its commitments. In the Far East, Imperial Japan, lurching into all-out war against China, was clearly dangerous and unpredictable. Mussolini's Fascist Italy, much admired by many conservatives in all parts of the British Isles, was an erratic threat to the crucially important Mediterranean communication lines to the directly dependent British Empire. Finally, there was the looming menace of Nazi Germany which the Government as early as 1935 recognized in private, if not in public, as ultimately the most serious potential enemy. Churchill's Ten Year Rule had been allowed quietly to lapse in early 1932. Contrary to subsequent slanders, Baldwin fought the 1935 election of a firm commitment to moderate but significant rearmament. Chamberlain was notably clear in 1935 on the need for rearmament, but his early weeks as Premier brought an emphatic reminder that the powers of his office only worked when cutting with the grain of social and economic power embodied in his own party. As Baldwin's Chancellor, he had devised a National Defence Contribution designed both to reconcile rearmament and sound finance, and to tax most heavily those firms which profited most from expenditure of taxpayers' money on rearmament. It was to be a percentage of the increase of profits from a base calculated between 1934 and 1936. What reporters called 'Tory industrialists' waxed indignant at once with a litany starting with socialism and brigandage, which would no doubt have gone on to atheism, Bolshevism and free love had not Chamberlain withdrawn his original proposal under pressure from backbench Tory MPs. Chamberlain thought the industrialists' reaction hysterical, which is what it was. Nevertheless, five days after becoming Premier he withdrew the scheme. A modified version based on a flat percentage of profits was later passed, but as it enabled manufacturers to calculate the tax in advance and build it into the price, it lacked the distinguishing feature of the original plan.[2]

The Government was in fact completely dependent on cooperation from businessmen to mount any effective rearmament drive. It had virtually no productive capacity itself. The Air Ministry had no factories. Royal dockyards existed, but were geared primarily to repair work. There were only three Royal Ordnance Factories before 1936. The Civil Service had no members with experience of large-scale armaments production, though it has to be said that due to the run-down of defence, few businessmen had such experience either. Yet business and the Government were politically integrated. Lord Weir, an industrialist whose attitude to Labour administrations had been confrontational, served as principal contact man between

---

[1] Daniel Waley *British Public Opinion and the Abyssinian War 1935–36* (Maurice Temple Smith, London 1975).

[2] Robert Paul Shay, Jr. *British Rearmament in the Thirties: Politics and Profits* (Princeton University Press, Princeton NJ 1977), pp. 147–55.

industry and the Government after 1933.[1] There was therefore no question of the state taking draconian powers to coordinate and accelerate the rearmament drive. Nor was Chamberlain's administration, or any other conceivable administration based on a Tory majority, likely to violate the Treasury orthodoxy that rearmament must not be pushed to the point where soaring state expenditure stoked inflation, created a massive negative balance of payments, and led to a collapse of the economy. Without a viable economy, there could by definition be no sustained war-making capacity. Chamberlain had that orthodoxy bred into his bones. If anything, Treasury influence was on the increase in the late 1930s. When Hankey retired in 1938, Sir Warren Fisher, Permanent Secretary of the Treasury and Head of the Civil Service, took the initiative which ensured that, as Secretary of the Cabinet, Edward Bridges succeeded Hankey. The core of Hankey's empire of influence thus went to a Treasury official. His secretaryship of the Committee of Imperial Defence went to H. L. ('Pug') Ismay, who had been his deputy, and who shared his professional service background.

It is quite clear that the Treasury did not exercise a neutral financial control over rearmament. No control could be wholly neutral, and the Treasury had never tried to be neutral, though it tried hard and successfully to conceal that fact. For example, it had always detested the expense of the Singapore naval base, to which Westminster had committed itself in the early 1920s, as a reassurance to Australia and New Zealand, and an implicit check to Japan. The Treasury seized the opportunity offered by Labour administrations to add its weight to successful pressure to suspend work on the base. By the late 1930s, the base had become an imperative necessity, but it has to be said that Treasury influence was as powerful as ever, and on the whole sensible. The squabbling armed services were forced into financial self-restraint and rational prioritization. It even proved possible to inject an element of rationality into the plans of the Royal Air Force.

That service was fanatically attached to doctrines of the primacy of strategic bombing strongly articulated by its founding father, Lord Trenchard. It had established effective control over the Fleet Air Arm in 1924, with baneful effects on Royal Navy appreciation of, and development of, naval aviation. To the Air Marshals, every plane and pilot with the navy reduced resources for strategic bombing. Only in 1937, did Chamberlain finally firmly endorse the sensible plan supported by Sir Samuel Hoare, who had been both Secretary for Air and First Lord of the Admiralty, that the shipboard Fleet Air Arm become a part of the Royal Navy, whilst control of the shore-based Coastal Command remain with the RAF.[2] That was a minor triumph for common sense compared with the success of Sir Thomas Inskip, appointed Minister for the Co-ordination of Defence in 1936, and the Treasury in forcing the RAF after 1937 to give reluctant priority to fighter squadrons at a time when it was hell-bent on even more, hideously

---

[1] George Peden 'Arms, Government and Businessmen, 1935–1945' in Turner, ed. *Businessmen and Politics*, pp. 130–45.

[2] Stephen Roskill *Naval Policy Between the Wars II: The Period of Reluctant Rearmament 1930–1939* (Collins, London 1976), Chap. XIII.

expensive, emphasis on bombers. There is no reason to think that changes in administrative structure, such as the appointment of a Minister of Defence, would have made much difference. A Ministry of Supply with drastic powers over industry was only acceptable if war was thought inevitable, which is why Chamberlain sacked Inskip in January 1939 and replaced him with Lord Chatfield when Inskip announced his support for a Ministry of Supply. Inskip had to go if Chamberlain was to keep control of the Cabinet and foreign policy.[1]

Chamberlain had told Lady Astor, immediately after his succession to Baldwin, that:

> . . . He meant to be his own Foreign Minister and also to take an active hand in coordinating ministerial policy generally, in contrast with Stanley Baldwin.[2]

He did indeed mean it. Critics like Churchill, who on the basis of somewhat alarmist estimates of the pace of German rearmament, especially in the air, were thundering out demands for much faster rearmament and confrontation in foreign policy were hopelessly at odds with both the logic and the prejudices of a massively ascendant Establishment. They were unlikely to succeed. It was all very well complaining about 'the PM's dictatorship in the Cabinet', as did Oliver Harvey, Private Secretary to Anthony Eden at the Foreign Office until Eden's resignation in February 1938, and then to his successor, Lord Halifax.[3] Any prime minister who was firmly in the saddle could opt for that style of leadership, if he so chose. As long as he was not threatening his party with imminent electoral disaster, or violently assaulting the interests of the bulk of its supporters, politicians were unlikely to stop him in the medium term. Churchill was gambling, more or less openly, on war, which would compel a radical reconstruction of the Cabinet, and waft him into high office. That did not make him patient. Though he had remarkable literary and real artistic talents, not to mention passable and well-publicized bricklaying ones, he was a perfect product of the Westminster system. Life was about office and wielding power. His celebrated 'black dog' manic depressions were products of the political frustration of being out of office. His son Randolph had raged at the exclusion of his father—'the greatest statesman of his time'—from office in 1935. Winston had hopes in 1937.[4] They were unrealistic.

Chamberlain's basic contention that the strategic position of the British Empire-Commonwealth was so vulnerable that any commitment of the UK to a major European war would probably lead to total disaster was correct.

[1] Shay *op. cit.*, supplemented by Peden, *British Rearmament*, and Gustav Schmidt *The Politics and Economics of Appeasement: British Foreign Policy in the 1930s* (Berg, Leamington Spa 1981), provides a very full overview of the effective politics of rearmament.

[2] Reported in Thomas Jones to Abraham Flexner, 30 May 1937, printed in Thomas Jones *A Diary with Letters 1931–1950* (Oxford University Press, London 1954), pp. 349–50.

[3] Entry for 12 October 1938, recording a conversation with Miss Marjorie Maxse, Chief Organisation Officer, Conservative Central Office, in *The Diplomatic Diaries of Oliver Harvey 1937–1940*, ed. John Harvey (Collins, London 1970), p. 213.

[4] Paul Addison 'Patriotism under Pressure: Lord Rothermere and British Foreign Policy' in Gillian Peele and Chris Cook, eds. *The Politics of Reappraisal 1918–1939* (Macmillan, London 1975).

He rearmed as fast as any ruling politician could and rightly focussed on the sea and air defences of the UK. To add a Continental-scale army spelled state bankruptcy within a very few years. It was very desirable to come to terms with one of the three great predatory powers and even strategically-placed critics of Chamberlain, like Sir Robert Vansittart, Permanent Under-Secretary at the Foreign Office, were appeasers. The difference was that the flamboyant Vansittart had preserved the strident anti-Germanism of the pre-1914 Foreign Office. The power he wanted to appease was Italy. Faced with the Government's increasing zeal for an approach to Germany, he leaked information to critics like Churchill. In retrospect, he deemed Churchill 'an embarrassing ally'. Winston's idea of subtle intrigue was to stride into Vansittart's office in broad daylight.[1] It was understandable when Chamberlain kicked 'Van' upstairs to powerless eminence as Chief Diplomatic Adviser in January 1938. Given the violence of the man's views and personality, it was inevitable that the Premier should lean on advice from another part of the Civil Service. Hence the increasing prominence of Sir Horace Wilson, technically the Government's chief industrial adviser, an expert on negotiation and conciliation, who provided advice and support which did not run clean contrary to Government policy, and who rose to be Head of the Civil Service.

There was nothing particularly sinister about the increasing prominence of senior civil servants in what were clearly policy-moulding positions. In reality, they had always been part of the policy-making élite. A good example of this was Sir John Anderson, the enormously able and insufferably pompous Scots meritocrat whom Chamberlain brought into the Cabinet in 1938 as Lord Privy Seal with special responsibility for civil defence against air attack. He had moved irresistibly upwards through the Colonial Office, Dublin Castle, and the Home Office, to be an effective Governor of Bengal in the troubled years 1932–37. A right-wing Conservative, he rejoiced in the opportunity which the National Government offered him not to face up to this fact about himself becoming, in 1938, a National backbench MP, and being rewarded with the sort of lucrative hand of directorships which sound chaps in the City could make available to distinguished and sound chaps in the Commons. His entry into the Cabinet involved considerable financial sacrifice.[2]

After Chamberlain's fall from power, a mythology was rapidly manufactured and sold to an enthusiastic public market which was looking for scapegoats for political and military failure. Its first great document was *Guilty Men*, published in 1940 by three outstanding Beaverbrook journalists: Peter Howard, Michael Foot and Frank Owen. Howard described the book as 'splenetic'. Though Beaverbrook himself disliked its attack on men still in the Government, the authors were apt pupils of their employer. *Guilty Men* was a triumph of crass over-simplification, concentrating not on policy formation or political structures, but on an alleged 'criminal' failure to rearm due to a handful of 'guilty men' in high places.[3] This

[1] *The Mist Procession: The Autobiography of Lord Vansittart* (Hutchinson, London 1958), p. 497.

[2] John W. Wheeler-Bennett *John Anderson Viscount Waverley* (Macmillan, London 1962).

[3] 'Cato' *Guilty Men* (Victory Books No. 1, Victor Gollancz Ltd., London 1940); Anne Wolridge Gordon *Peter Howard Life and Letters* (Hodder and Stoughton, pbk edn, London 1970), p. 141.

particular emphasis finally achieved classic form in Winston Churchill's first volume of his Second World War memoirs, *The Gathering Storm*, written with highly privileged access to official record in the underemployed state to which electoral defeat in 1945 had reduced him. As ever in such circumstances, he turned his enormous energy to controlling and manipulating the record of his own achievement. The book exaggerated the coherence of the group of 'anti-appeasers' who had gained office in his wartime coalition, and plugged the theme of inadequate rearmament due to rejection of Churchill's clarion call to arm faster. Thus in November 1937, he depicted Anthony Eden, the Chamberlain's Foreign Secretary, as moving towards resignation 'increasingly concerned about our slow rearmament'.[1]

In fact the men who from within the Government opposed Chamberlain were not a particularly cohesive band. Anthony Eden, serious, highly-strung and privately deeply unhappy, did not much like the lazy and amatory First Lord of the Admiralty Duff Cooper. They resigned from office for different reasons. Eden was inclined to be less hard on Germany, but violently resented all concessions to Italy. He found prime-ministerial prerogative difficult to swallow, being enraged when Chamberlain dismissed out of hand an approach from President Roosevelt for a world conference to discuss all outstanding problems. This was the unrealistic hot air Chamberlain thought it was, but his response prepared the way for Eden's break with the Government over proposed talks with Mussolini.

Duff Cooper resigned later over a much more dramatic issue. In March 1938, Nazi Germany had engulfed Austria. The Sudeten German minority in Czechoslovakia provided the excuse for the next surge of Nazi expansionism, and Chamberlain and his new Foreign Secretary, Lord Halifax, a former Viceroy of India (as Lord Irwin), offered mediation. They were acutely aware of advice from their service advisers that the UK would be incapable of waging a major war before 1939. Cooper, First Lord of the Admiralty, eventually agreed to the transfer of Sudeten areas after a plebiscite. Chamberlain had bought time by sending the Lord President Walter Runciman on a mission of enquiry to Czechoslovakia, and had then made two dramatic personal visits to Hitler which set up the transfer. What Cooper could not stomach was Hitler's insistence on immediate German occupation of Sudeten areas, which was, in the end, conceded to him by the Munich agreement of September 1938.[2]

Chamberlain's personal diplomacy reflected one of the deepest instincts amongst the Whitehall power élite: however bad the situation, it will be better if I have more of a grip on it. His perilous flights to see Hitler at Berchtesgaden and Bad Godesberg at an advanced age were arguably totally undesirable because they were motivated by a desire to be involved in order to avert war. Even the Foreign Office had been at a loss after the fall of Austria. Its policy preference for British resistance to Germany had never been very practical. It now seemed physically impossible to go to

---

[1] Winston S. Churchill *The Second World War. Volume I: The Gathering Storm* (Cassell, London 1948), p. 225.

[2] John Charmley *Chamberlain and the Lost Peace* (Hodder and Stoughton, London 1989), Chaps 5–6; John Charmley *Duff Cooper* (Macmillan, pbk edn, London 1987), Chaps. 14–5.

the aid of Czechoslovakia. Anti-appeasers appeared to be as much at a loss as appeasers were as the fleet was mobilized and trenches dug in London parks. Even allowing for the exaggerated contemporary view of the likely effects of air raids, it was all rather futile. The brutal reality was that there was everything to be said for a war, and no great need for British involvement of any kind. The Czechs had a powerful army, strong defences and a will to fight. The first shots would technically have activated the Franco-Czech alliance (to the distress of the French politicians who begged Chamberlain to pressure the Czechs into yielding). Czechoslovakia did not need to win a war. It just needed to fight effectively for a long enough period (weeks rather than months) to trigger intervention by emboldened enemies of Nazi Germany, or more likely, the removal of Hitler by his generals. Chamberlain was ruthless with his friends the Czechs, whose will he broke by isolation and menace, and supinely helpful to enemies.

That was standard practice for a Westminster regime. The inhabitants of the United Kingdom were, for example, being subjected to the most unscrupulous manipulation of their perception of reality. In 1937, Chamberlain inherited a well-developed system whereby the contemporary media could be used to disseminate an official view, or indeed blot out an offending reality. The astonishing boycott in the UK press of any news on the Edward VIII-Wallis Simpson affair, which was headline news in America for months before it was allowed to break in London, had been a chilling precedent. It was all based on networking and solidarity among a power élite which ranged from Baldwin to the press barons. By 1936, the radio was potentially a potent rival to the press, but the British Broadcasting Corporation was entirely dependent on state funding, and quite tame. Between 1937 and 1939, press sycophancy towards Chamberlain's foreign policy was simply incredible and, with the rarest of exceptions, wish-fulfillment was substituted for rational analysis. Early surveys of opinion by polling in 1938 seem to show that there was little positive enthusiasm left for Chamberlain's foreign policy. Chamberlain fell for his own propaganda much more readily than his people did. Through such devices as tame Lobby correspondents with privileged access to off-record briefing, he had fed his interpretations of developments into the newspaper columns, and then believed them. As early as February 1938, there appears to have been a grassroots majority less gullible than he.[1]

The trouble was that his grip on the Conservative Party, the only effective political structure, appeared unshakeable. The Duchess of Atholl, who had been selected and elected a Conservative MP in the mistaken belief that she would be a safe nominal woman, resigned her Kinross and West Perthshire seat to force a by-election as a mini-plebiscite against Munich in December 1938. She lost. There were long-term reasons, like her articulate opposition to the Nationalist insurgents led by General Franco in the long, festering and opinion-polarizing Spanish Civil War of 1936–38. She feared the impact of Italian and German intervention of Franco's side on the strategic position of the British Empire, but her position alienated a power-

[1] Richard Cockett *Twilight of Truth: Chamberlain, Appeasement and the Manipulation of the Press* (Weidenfeld and Nicolson, London 1989).

ful very pro-Franco Roman Catholic element among Perthshire Tories. Her criticism of Chamberlain added enough Protestant enemies to deselect her as Tory candidate and Central Office poured resources into the by-election to ensure her defeat. One of her supporters, Shiela Grant-Duff, had published a Penguin Special which stressed both the ability of and need for the Czechs to fight. Ironically, 'Kitty' Atholl and she were among the few with the guts to see the potential benefits of a war in central Europe. Politically, neither was ever heard of again.[1]

Chamberlain's grip on his party remained unshaken. There were rebels but they were few. Apart from lightweights like Duff Cooper, they included rising young men who had failed to rise like Bob Boothby and Harold Macmillan, and the odd figure of substance like Eden. The latter avoided Churchill and made repeated signals to the Premier that he would like another job. The crumbling of the Munich settlement as Hitler occupied what was left of Czechoslovakia in March 1939 made no real difference. Italy occupied Albania in April 1939. With the failure of Anglo-Soviet negotiations that summer, Chamberlain was spared an alliance deeply repugnant to his basic instincts, but the consequent Nazi-Soviet pact left eastern Europe beyond Westminster's reach. The necessary steps to accelerate rearmament, such as overriding the Treasury's defined limit for 'safe' borrowing; introducing conscription to establish the basis of a mass army which had hitherto been impossible; and erecting a Ministry of Supply, were all taken. The guarantees to Poland and Romania which were the prelude to the declaration of war against Germany by France and the United Kingdom on 3 September were psychologically satisfying but military madness.

Halifax, the 'holy fox' who was Chamberlain's most formidable associate and Foreign Secretary, justified the Munich agreement as necessary to bring both the Commonwealth and the UK united into war.[2] Certainly, the 1932 Statute of Westminster registered the moonbeam nature to which Commonwealth links had been reduced by the pressure of Herzog and Mackenzie King and the cynical acquiescence of Balfour. Yet the 1937 Imperial Conference had shown that Dominion leaders were only too ready to try to exert strong pro-appeasement influence on UK foreign policy.[3] Arguably, appeasement was only rational if those selected for the treat-

[1] Stuart Ball 'The Politics of Appeasement: The Fall of the Duchess of Atholl and the Kinross and West Perth By-election, December 1938' *The Scottish Historical Review*, (LXIX, 1990), pp. 49–83; Duchess of Atholl *Searchlight on Spain* (Penguin Special, London 1938), where the dust jacket (on a paperback) refers to 'International Implications', and 'Effect on British imperial strategy'. Less happily, it also calls the author 'one of the most prominent of English women politicians'. She was very British, but just how hard this is on a Ramsay of Bamff married to a Gaelic-speaking Murray of Atholl may be gathered from S. J. Hetherington *Katharine Atholl 1874–1960: Against the Tide* (Aberdeen University Press, Aberdeen 1989). Chapter 19 of this work covers the by-election.

[2] The Earl of Birkenhead *Halifax: The Life of Lord Halifax* (Hamish Hamilton, London 1965), pp. 425–6.

[3] Denis Judd *Balfour and the British Empire: A Study in Imperial Evolution 1874–1932* (Macmillan, London 1968), Part 5: H. Blair Neatby *William Lyon Mackenzie King 1924–1932: The Lonely Heights* (Methuen, London 1963); D. C. Watt *Personalities and Policies: Studies in the Formulation of British Foreign Policy in the Twentieth Century* (Longman, London 1965), Part III. 'The Impact of the Commonwealth'.

ment were handled very toughly indeed, and made aware of the UK's determination to use power to protect its major interests. Limited concessions would then be received with gratitude. Dominion pressures were for general spinelessness. They exacerbated the disastrous trend which Chamberlain's egotism had set in motion, whereby appeasement was seen as an end in itself, and concessions which merely whetted appetites as triumphs of negotiation. Halifax was disingenuous when he later defended Munich as a way of gaining time. His Prime Minister saw it as a confirmation of his role as a strong ruler whom Providence had marked out to curb jingoist excess at home whilst cutting essential deals with foreign rulers, even at the price of concessions which a less firmly bridled public might well have shied at.

Though there was no coherent policy for waging, let along winning the war, there was no serious opposition to it. The Government was slightly broadened, with Churchill as First Lord of the Admiralty becoming a major figure in the War Cabinet, and Eden becoming a rather disgruntled Dominions Secretary outside the War Cabinet. Poland fell. Mass air-raids on London failed to materialize. In January 1940, during the deceptive lull of the 'Phoney War', Chamberlain pushed Leslie Hore-Belisha (Jewish and disliked by generals) out of the War Office in favour of the more acceptable Oliver Stanley. When Hore-Belisha jibbed at the consolation prize of the Board of Trade, Chamberlain was shocked, saying, 'You are an ambitious man. You surely do not want to go out into the wilderness'.[1] He went, and never came back.

Potency and office were inseparable, and Churchill held major office. Conservative MPs grumbled about Chamberlain's inability to harness the trade unions to a war effort which appeared to have no immediate goal. Hence, perhaps, the Anglo-French desire to find something to do as long as it was not a direct offensive against Germany. One upshot of this was the complex of proposals ranging from mining Norwegian territorial waters to blocking iron ore shipments to Germany; to invading Norway; violating Sweden; and fighting with the Finns against the Russians in the currently-raging 'Winter War'. Altogether, these ideas 'defy rational analysis'. Churchill was only partially responsible for them, but he was an enthusiast for some sort of northern campaign, and a difficult, unhelpful colleague for the two other service ministers in the débacle which followed when the Germans launched a pre-emptive invasion of Norway. The campaign has not unfairly been seen as a Churchillian disaster. Ironically, it was Chamberlain who lost support on the Conservative benches in the parliamentary debate on the defeat. Yet he still had a clear majority. Prizing him from the premiership was said to be as difficult as wrenching a limpet off a corpse, and the launching of a general German offensive in the west at first moved him to stay on. Its success would have finished him anyway. His illusions that Nazi Germany would crumble from internal tensions collapsed. Sir Howard Kingsley Wood was a close enough colleague to persuade him to go. Calculation, not destiny, determined the succession.

---

[1] Conversation between Chamberlain and Hore-Belisha, Thursday 4 January 1940, recorded in *The Private Papers of Hore-Belisha*, ed. R. J. Minney (Collins, London 1960), pp. 269–70.

Both Wood and Chamberlain preferred Churchill to the only Conservative alternative, Halifax. Chamberlain thought Churchill less of a barrier to a resumption of power by himself after the war. Wood urged Churchill to remain silent if asked to serve under Halifax. Labour's willingness to serve under Churchill set the seal. An unsuccessful despotism had been tempered by a palace coup.[1]

[1] Kevin Jeffreys 'May 1940: The Downfall of Neville Chamberlain', in *Parliamentary History* (10, 1991), pp. 363–78. The phrase about the Finnish expedition is A. J. P. Taylor's in *English History 1914–45*, p. 469.

9

From supreme warlord to headmaster 1940–51

The PM talked a lot. Pouring out another glass of brandy, and eying us all benevolently, he said that these Planners, on whose deliberations so much depended, could not afford to have more than one glass of brandy; but it was different for him who had only to take the responsibility. It was curious but in this war he had had no success but had received nothing but praise, whereas in the last war he had done several things which he thought were good and had got nothing but abuse for them.

From entry for 31 August 1940 in John Colville *The Fringes of Power: Downing Street Diaries 1939–1955*.

Philip Jordan tells me that Attlee says the enthusiasm of his meetings today far exceeds that of 1945. I think this is because Attlee himself has increased so much in repute and popularity. He says that Attlee expects to get back with a majority of 60. The Labour Whips say, 'If we have a majority of 80, we shall sleep comfortably; if we have a majority of 60, we shall have to take sleeping draughts; if we have a majority of 40, we shall all be dead in two years.'

From entry for 13 February 1950, in Harold Nicolson *Diaries and Letters 1945–1962*.

Churchill had reached supreme power within the framework of the existing party system. As Lloyd George shrewdly pointed out at the time, the Coalition Government over which he presided was essentially a coalition of parties and their nominees. In his post-war memoirs, Churchill made no bones about this. The Government at the time contained 'between sixty and seventy Ministers of the Crown'. Of course, at the highest level, the Premier made the final choice, after duly weighing his personal preferences, political expediency and the perceived capacities of possible appointees. Even Churchill however said that he had:

. . . to attach due weight to the wishes of the party leaders as to who among their followers shall have the offices allotted to the party. By this principal I was mainly governed. If any who deserved better were left out on the advice of their party authorities . . . I can only express regret.[1]

This meant that the Conservative grip on the majority of offices remained a strong one. Churchill made it clear that in purely parliamentary terms he did not need the Labour Party. What he and most intelligent Conservatives wanted was the active cooperation of the trade unions, as embodied in their outstanding leaders like Ernest Bevin and Walter Citrine. The Labour Party presence in the Coalition was a means to that end. In addition, it was an important symbol of the unique status of the prime minister, and a necessary one, for Neville Chamberlain retained the leadership of the Conservative Party and the vociferous support of most of its MPs. Churchill was not a party boss. His small inner War Cabinet therefore balanced two Labour leaders in Clement Attlee, Lord Privy Seal, and Arthur Greenwood, Minister without Portfolio, against Neville Chamberlain, Lord President of the Council, and Lord Halifax, Foreign Secretary.

Churchill was no doubt happy as the fifth figure in an otherwise evenly-balanced War Cabinet, though Chamberlain was commendably loyal and cooperative. It was however the assumption of the title of Minister of Defence by Churchill which really indicated the thrust of his ambitions. He was later to cite approvingly Napoleon's adage that constitutions should be short and obscure, as they must be to pose no problems for a dictatorial will. Apart from the fact that the Chiefs of Staff Committee would be under the supervision and direction of the new Ministry of Defence, nobody knew what the powers of that ministry were. In effect, they were what Churchill chose to make of them for, as he said:

> As this Minister was also the Prime Minister, he had all the rights inherent in that office, including very wide powers of selection and removal of all professional and political personages.[2]

The new Prime Minister meant from the start, to assume sweeping powers over the war effort. Home affairs were of vastly less interest to him. There is no reason to doubt his account of the utter confidence in his own powers with which he took the helm, or of the amazing psychological and physical resilience with which this 65 year-old man shouldered the burdens of supreme office. He had always wanted that office, preferably before he was 40, and if destiny had not given him it by then, it had reserved it for a time dominated by the only subjects in which he had any true remaining interest: war and diplomacy. He could always put together a speech on domestic issues full of vague Whiggish phrases about progress, but he had no positive proposals left in him. He needed someone to run the home front, and that job was handled, with characteristic efficiency, by Neville Chamberlain, who was rather proud of the fact that the Labour men who now worked with him found him not the odious opponent they had known, but a cordial, progressive colleague.

The disposition of senior posts was made in strict accordance with the weight which participating parties carried in the Commons. The result was

---

[1] Winston S. Churchill *The Second World War Volume II: Their Finest Hour* (Cassell, London, rev. edn, 1950), p. 11.
[2] *Ibid.*, p. 15.

15 Conservative ministers to four Labour and one Liberal. Predictably, the Liberals were unhappy about this, and particularly unhappy that their leader, Sir Archibald Sinclair, was outside the War Cabinet. If anything, Churchill had a soft spot for the Liberals, and especially for Sinclair, who had fought under his command in the First World War, and supported demands for rearmament in the 1930s. Sinclair was made Secretary of State for Air. At first there were remarkably few changes. The really big catch from Labour, from the Prime Minister's point of view, was Ernest Bevin, who, after receiving the blessing of the Transport and General Workers Union (which he had created), accepted the portfolio of Minister of Labour and National Service. Some of Churchill's cronies naturally moved into office, most notably the unpredictable Beaverbrook, who became Minister for Aircraft Production in time to produce a timely surge in fighter production in the crucial summer of 1940, though by means which do not bear close examination. If persisted in, they would have led to disaster.[1] The 'anti-appeasers' were not over-rewarded. Eden took the War Office, Duff Cooper only the Ministry of Information.

There was no backlash against Sir Horace Wilson. Despite being denounced by name in *Guilty Men*, he continued as Head of the Civil Service until retirement in 1942. Churchill had secured a good deal of his ammunition for his criticism of Chamberlain's policies before 1939 by discreet leaks from sympathetic members of the bureaucracy. He was accustomed to senior bureaucrats participating in policy formulation and the highest levels of administration. Under his aegis, the public acknowledgement of this reality reached unprecedented heights. In 1942, a former Permanent Under-Secretary, Sir James Grigg, was appointed to the post of Secretary of State for War. Even allowing for the effective downgrading of the three service ministers by the ascendancy of a masterful Minister of Defence, the appointment of a career civil servant to a post hitherto always filled by a politician was remarkable. Yet it was little remarked upon. Sir John Anderson had, it is true, become a backbench MP and company director after his spell as Governor of Bengal, but in spirit and manner he could no more cease to be a civil servant than a cat could stop mousing. In November 1938, he was appointed Lord Privy Seal, with special responsibility for precautions against air attack, or civil defence as it became known. At the outbreak of war, he became Home Secretary with the additional office of Minister of Home Security, though not with membership of Chamberlain's War Cabinet. In that position, he was retained by Churchill in 1940. Sir Warren Fisher wrote to Anderson in September 1939 expressing indignation that Anderson, whom with bureaucratic solidarity he described as the ablest man in the Government, had been excluded from the inner circle of the administration, Sir Warren Fisher characterized that Government as a 'set of inexperienced mediocrities'.[2]

Anderson duly entered Churchill's War Cabinet as Lord Privy Seal, with responsibility for economic coordination. From there, he progressed to

---

[1] John Terraine *The Right of the Line: The Royal Air Force in the European War 1939–1945* (Hodder and Stoughton, London 1985), p. 257.

[2] Sir Warren Fisher to Sir John Anderson, 29 September 1939, partially cited in Wheeler-Bennett *John Anderson*, p. 233.

the heights of the Exchequer when the Chancellor, Sir Kingsley Wood, unexpectedly died in September 1943. Sir Kingsley had been a key figure in the engineering of Churchill's accession to power in 1940, and had become as close to him as he had been to Chamberlain. Anderson's ultimate apotheosis was therefore to some extent accidental, but Churchill had in effect made of him his vicar in matters domestic, referring to him as the 'automatic pilot' and telling George VI that he should be regarded as next in succession to the premiership should anything happen to Churchill. It may be doubted if the professional politicians would have accepted the award of the supreme prize to a man who had always shied from the rough and tumble of politics; who sat for a Scottish university seat (he was a reputable successor to the disreputable non-graduate incumbency of Ramsay MacDonald); and who was never very happy under criticism. Nevertheless, though he had been far from successful in coping with the consequences of German bombing raids during his spell as Home Secretary, Anderson did effectively see off Clement Attlee as the overlord of the home front. Attlee served a a member of the War Cabinet until 1945, the only Labour politician to serve continuously in it, but he was deemed an uninspiring coordinator of committees when he was Lord Privy Seal in 1940–42. His post as Dominions Secretary after February 1942 was not a weighty one, and though he was Deputy Prime Minister from 1943 to 1945, his succession as Lord President in 1943 came just before that post lost the general oversight of post-war reconstruction plans.

The Government had taken effective steps to insulate itself from electoral pressures. At the outbreak of war, the Labour and Liberal leaders had made their support for it clear, and rapidly agreed on an electoral truce with the Government. Under it, seats in the Commons which fell vacant were to have a candidate nominated by the party in possession, and the other parties to the pact agreed not to oppose that candidate. Independents or non-coalition candidates were still free to run. Nobody could have expected them to be other than a joke. The electoral register was suspended, so people reaching the age of 21 ceased to be added, and the huge proportion of the population moving out of the constituency where they were registered were disenfranchised. Unopposed returns were commonplace. Even before 1939, MPs were profoundly unrepresentative as a cross-section of the population, whether judged by gender, class or occupation. Tory MPs were overwhelmingly from the wealthy classes, to the point where Duff Cooper remarked in 1939 that:

> It is as difficult for a poor man, if he be a Conservative, to get into the House of Commons as it is for a camel to get through the eye of a needle. This is not to say that it is impossible, any more than it is impossible, we hope, for a rich man to get into the Kingdom of Heaven, but in both cases entrance is attended with difficulty.[1]

It was a fair comment. When the aggressive young Beaverbrook journalist Peter Howard enquired about nomination for a pre-war constituency as a Conservative, the first question he was asked was what he proposed to

---

[1] Cited, from the *Evening Standard* of 14 March 1939, in Simon Haxey *Tory M.P.* (Left Book Club, Victor Gollancz, London 1939), p. 179.

subscribe to the local association. He offered all his prospective parliamentary salary. The reply was, 'We have already been offered £1,000 a year. If you can't do better than that, I'm afraid it is out of the question.'[1] The disproportionate number of retired trade union officials in Labour seats was another example of the fact that in 1939 MPs were elected but hardly representative. After 1940, new MPs' claims to be elected in the usual sense of the word were debatable. They were endorsed after having an appropriate label attached. The political class was ruling by divine right, indefinitely postponing general elections, and completely suspending local government elections. At that level, new councillors were co-opted by the party caucuses.[2]

Within this oddly self-contained world, there was movement. Balances of power shifted, partly in response to external shocks, but after 1940 more in response to the internal dynamics of the system. Of external shocks there were plenty after Churchill's accession. They were so appalling that they had a paralysing effect on politics. The fall of France totally undermined the central strategic assumption on which the British were fighting the war: that the French Army could effectively hold the German *Wehrmacht* at bay. Though the Germans held an important advantage in the superiority of their tactical air support for their army, most of the excuses subsequently manufactured for the defeat of France have proven bogus. Overwhelming numbers or superior equipment were not in fact decisive. France had more and better tanks than Germany. It was their misuse in small groups attached to the infantry, and the absence of any equivalent of the German armoured divisions, which made great central armoured thrust through the Ardennes such a potent weapon in German hands. Even so, the flanks of the astonishing penetration achieved by Hitler's panzer units were potentially very vulnerable, and in the last analysis the Battle of France was lost by the French High Command. Even the most francophile of British soldiers like Churchill's close friend, General Sir Edward Spears, were left aghast at the scale of the débâcle. There were technical reasons for the slowness of the French generals' response to the crisis, such as their gross neglect of field radio communication systems, but Spears watched horrified as generals like Weygand and military monuments like the aged Marshal Pétain began, even before France asked for an armistice, to forge a mythology which blamed defeat on anyone except its principal architects: the French commanders.[3]

Before the terrible summer of 1940, Churchill had been an activist, briskly exploiting the Admiralty's relatively sophisticated public relations system to publicize himself as the man who wanted to shift the war into higher gear. The trouble was that his vigour was not accompanied by any real insight. Though he knew that even his old mentor, Arthur Balfour, had late in life reached the conclusion that the Irish Free State would far better be treated as the foreign country which it clearly wanted to be, Churchill had early in the war argued for the forcible seizure of the naval bases in the

[1] Peter Howard *Ideas Have Legs* (Frederick Muller, 2nd edn, London 1945), p. 45.
[2] Angus Calder *The People's War: Britain 1939–45* (Granada, pbk, edn, London 1971), pp. 66–7.
[3] Sir Edward Spears *Assignment to Catastrophe* (Reprint Society edn, London 1956).

south of Ireland over which Chamberlain had waived the rights retained by Westminster in 1922. Churchill justified this policy by unconvincing theories about the lack of any right of secession from the Empire-Commonwealth. Fortunately, his colleagues refused to countenance a policy which British bases in Northern Ireland made ultimately unnecessary, and which would have been politically disastrous and militarily embarrassing.[1] There was less will to curb his role in the Norwegian fiasco, dubious though aspects of that role were. In the face of the fall of France, Churchill could offer little more than rhetoric and grand gestures. Both tended to annoy a French leadership already weaving Perfidious Albion into their apologetic tapestry of excuses for failure.

The supreme example of this was the offer of an 'indissoluble union' between the UK and France which originated in a discussion in a small group in London, including General Charles de Gaulle, then visiting the city, but was approved by the War Cabinet, and which Churchill was prepared to go to France to commend to its leaders. It was of course primarily a device to avert an armistice between France and Germany. Jean Monnet, who had worked on the draft with de Gaulle and Vansittart, clearly saw it as a way of persuading the UK to throw its remaining fighter squadrons into the battle in France. To the ministers of the new French regime led by Pétain, it was an irrelevance compared with the need to save by an armistice at least part of France from occupation; avert the slide into social chaos; and embark on a political revenge against those leftist forces which had produced such unspeakable horrors as the Popular Front government of 1936–38 in which Socialists and Communists had cooperated under Léon Blum. It was also a demonstration of just what the War Cabinet felt free to do without consulting any of the peoples involved.[2]

As a device to avoid an armistice, the union plan was a failure. By the summer of 1940, the Germans had occupied most of northern and western France. From Vichy in unoccupied France, a regime not recognized by the Westminster politicians, but at first recognized not only by the USA but also by two belligerent Commonwealth countries, Canada and South Africa, successfully removed both metropolitan France and the bulk of its overseas empire from the war. Attempts by the UK to run General de Gaulle and his 'Free French' as an alternative to Vichy proved totally unsuccessful outside a few unimportant territories in Equatorial Africa. De Gaulle had no serious support from either the right or the left of the French political spectrum. The Vichy regime was a genuine French option, embodying a strong, if ambiguous, right-wing backlash.[3] Churchill, the Government and the United Kingdom survived because of the fact that the hastily-constructed German invasion plan, Operation Sealion, could not be put into effect unless Germany had air supremacy over southern

[1] Martin Gilbert *Winston S. Churchill Volume VI: Finest Hour 1939–41* (Heinemann, London 1983). For Balfour's opinion that 'it would be much better for them to go out altogether', see Winston S. Churchill to Lord Salisbury, 5 April 1933, printed in Gilbert *Winston S. Churchill Volume V. Companion Part 2 Documents: The Wilderness Years* (Heinemann, London 1981), p. 413.

[2] *Ibid.*, pp. 558–61.

[3] Robert O. Paxton *Vichy France: Old Guard and New Order, 1940–1944* (Barrie and Jenkins, London 1972).

England, and the Royal Air Force Fighter Command under Air Chief Marshal Sir Hugh C. T. Dowding managed by a narrow margin to deprive Reichsmarshal Hermann Goering's *Luftwaffe* of that superiority.

It was in this period that Churchill emerged, as some of the earliest opinion surveys make clear, as an immensely popular symbol of a widely-shared popular will to battle on. After the evacuation of a large proportion of the British Expeditionary Force (though not their weapons) from Dunkirk, he had become the rhetorical voice of defiance, and by the time the Battle of Britain had been fought to a victorious conclusion in October 1940, he had become the embodiment of successful defiance. That public image covered a far more complex reality. Dowding had had to face him down in full Cabinet on 15 May to ensure that the vital remaining minimum of fighter squadrons was not frittered away in an already lost battle in France. From that moment Dowding was a marked man and, though he was undermined by insubordinate underlings ranging from the legless Group Captain Bader to the self-advertising Air Chief Marshal Sir Trafford Leigh-Mallory, the shoddy ungracious dismissal which he experienced in November 1940 remains a blot on the record of the supreme warlord who countenanced it.[1]

There was, in practice, no way of winning the war. That senior members of the Government started privately talking about a compromise peace merely showed that they were not fools. The option had to be faced, if not necessarily embraced. Churchill himself clearly preferred to fight on, not for victory at all costs, but in order to improve the politico-military situation by proving to Hitler that he could not successfully invade Britain. He was also probably influenced, as were all members of the War Cabinet, by the absurd delusion that Germany's (only partially-mobilized) economy was on the verge of collapse through overstrain. It seems that he was more than willing to concede Malta and Gibraltar to Mussolini, who was offering mediation, and return Germany's African colonies, if by so doing he could obtain a general settlement respecting the vital interests of the British Empire.

The public image, reinforced by set speeches in the Commons and immensely successful radio broadcasts, was pure resolution. It was undented by media criticism, not least because the media were thoroughly cowed by Government pressure. Attlee as much as Churchill regarded any criticism as 'irresponsible' criticism, and so told the BBC and other bodies capable of influencing the public. Privately, it was another story. Australia and New Zealand, which with Canada and South Africa had become belligerent in 1939, were pressing hard for a compromise peace. Churchill was still anxious to pull into belligerency De Valera's Ireland (better referred to as Eire after the approval of De Valera's thinly veiled republican constitution of 1937). His inability to understand any Irish point of view, Nationalist or Unionist, if it crossed his will was demonstrated by his secret offer to trade Northern Ireland against Eire's neutrality. De Valera became the embodiment of his own people by his refusal to play that game. Sir James Craig, the Northern Irish Premier, expressed understandable annoyance that his own Irish community was regarded as expendable without consul-

---

[1] Robert Wright *Dowding and the Battle of Britain* (Corgi, London 1970).

tation. He had a point, even if it did not become a practical issue then. Nor was De Valera the sole beneficiary of Churchillian appeasement policy in 1940. After a ferocious naval attack on units of the French fleet at Oran and Dakar in July 1940, when they refused to immobilize themselves or join with the Royal Navy, the Government appears to have reached a very secret understanding with the Vichy regime. Apart from certain French-Canadian channels, negotiations were conducted through Sir Samuel Hoare. That uncharismatic man had been the sole scapegoat when Chamberlain fell. Packed off to Madrid as ambassador, he helped to secure a *modus vivendi* whereby Vichy kept its fleet out of Nazi hands while the British kept de Gaulle on a leash, and desisted from verbal or physical aggression themselves.

There was therefore deep irony, which Churchill himself appreciated, in the huge increase in power and stature which came to him in the latter part of 1940. The cancer that forced Neville Chamberlain to resign office and the leadership of the Conservative Party in October 1940, and which killed him shortly afterwards, was Churchill's greatest ally. Having carried responsibility (as was not unreasonable given their monopoly of real power) for unprecedented diplomatic and military disaster, the Conservative Party was anxious to associate itself with Churchill's popularity by electing him to the leadership. From his point of view, control of a disciplined majority party would confirm him as an elective dictator more powerful than Lloyd George at his peak. On the other hand, Churchill still resented the attitude of the party towards him in the 1930s, and was well aware that he could in the medium term survive as Premier by balancing between parties. He accepted the leadership, as he virtually admitted in his acceptance speech in the Caxton Hall, because it was too dangerous in any other hands. The serried ranks of political escapologists before him had stood, cheered, and clapped relentlessly as he entered.[1] Standing ovations were something they could produce at will.

Political change at the top accelerated. When Chamberlain left the War Cabinet, Ernest Bevin and Kingsley Wood came in. By December 1940, Halifax, who would probably have been Tory leader if Churchill had refused, had been moved out and into the post of ambassador in Washington (with nominal War Cabinet membership, which fooled him not at all). His successor both at the Foreign Office and in the War Cabinet was Anthony Eden. Beaverbrook entered the War Cabinet where he quarrelled with the rival rough diamond, Ernie Bevin. Bob Boothby was later to argue that Churchill's Great Coalition was not a happy team, for he claimed ministers lived '. . . in constant dread of a red ink Minute from the Prime Minister, or the sack; and some of them got both.'[2] This is a comment by a man embittered by his own dismissal on charges of improper conduct from being Parliamentary Secretary to the Ministry of Food. It had been a promising first step on the ladder of preferment. The minister himself, the businessman Lord Woolton, was in the Lords, which gave Boothby responsibility in the Commons. Nevertheless, it has to be said that though Churchill did sack many politicians, particularly junior ones,

---

[1] Pelling *Churchill*, p. 459.
[2] Boothby *Recollections of a Rebel* (Hutchinson, London 1978), p. 169.

his record was not exceptional. Someone like Arthur Greenwood, despite his rank in the Labour Party, had eventually to be squeezed out of office because of chronic alcoholism. Halifax was obviously a marked man once Chamberlain left office. Yet Churchill could be deeply loyal, especially to old cronies. One of them, Beaverbrook, said that Churchill had in him the stuff of which tyrants were made, at least when on one of his manic upbeats. The principal sufferers were not so much politicians as air-marshals, generals and admirals.

The Premier was fascinated by problems of high command in war. He continually tended to intervene in such a way as to cut through the normal chains of command, starting with the Norwegian campaign. The fact that he was extremely upset when his behaviour during this particular episode was criticized in detail after the war does not alter the facts. It was perhaps significant that he maintained a worthy but not very strong Labour First Lord, A. V. Alexander, and, as long as he could, a First Sea Lord, Sir Dudley Pound, who was after 1941 physically unfit for his job, and never good at resisting the Premier. Churchill's grasp of the realities of modern naval warfare was imperfect, his grasp of the difficulties of amphibious warfare highly defective. Yet the sailors could hardly in the last analysis resist him. As one admiral later put it, 'Resignation is no answer. It is forgotten in a fortnight.'[1]

With generals the Premier had an almost bizarre love-hate relationship. He had always distrusted them, yet he saw himself as a generalissimo of supreme vision. Inured to the cut and thrust of party politics, he led by hectoring and provoking. It was a style which drove some of his ablest commanders, such as General Sir Archibald Wavell, into monosyllabic reserve. In the latter stages of the war, when the bulk of the German ground forces were tied up in Russia and American entry into the conflict made overwhelming force available, the Churchillian method of leadership by provocation worked quite well, because his indiscriminately aggressive instincts had to be filtered through his own advisers, and then through joint committees with the Americans. Even so, it was vitally important that General Sir Alan Brooke acted as a sort of strategic keeper for the Premier throughout the war, successfully arguing against American proposals for a premature invasion of western Europe, which would probably have handed Hitler a morale-boosting victory in 1942, though less certainly so in 1943. When, in 1957, as Lord Alanbrooke, he published his (at times intemperate) war diaries with the assistance of the historian Sir Arthur Bryant, Churchill was furious. By then, the ex-Premier's self-absorption was making him spend long hours reading about himself and Alanbrooke was going too far by chipping at the monument.[2]

After the Battle of Britain, the Government was handed two remarkable

---

[1] Stephen Roskill *Churchill and the Admirals* (Collins, London 1977). The quotation is from a letter by Admiral Sir Charles Forbes to Stephen Roskill, 1 December 1949, partially cited p. 296.

[2] Arthur Bryant *The Turn of the Tide 1939–43: A Study Based on the Diaries and Autobiographical Notes of Field Marshal the Viscount Alanbrooke K. G., O. M.* (Collins, London 1957). For Churchill's self-absorption and angry reaction to Alanbrooke's publication of his memoirs through Bryant, see Kenneth Young *Churchill and Beaverbrook: A Study in Friendship and Politics* (Eyre and Spottiswoode, London 1966), pp. 311–2.

bonuses. Chamberlain had endorsed a policy of trying first to knock Italy out of any future war. The Anglo-German naval agreement of 1935 limiting the German Navy to 35 per cent of the British (submarines 45 per cent), had only been repudiated by Hitler in 1939, after being observed by him. There were covert British agreements with President Roosevelt by 1939 that the bulk of the American fleet would be stationed in the Pacific where it was hoped it would deter Japan. It made sense to concentrate on Italy.[1] Mussolini's 'non-belligerency' therefore disconcerted UK strategic planning, but with Italy's entry into the war in June 1940, with a view to a share of easy spoil, it made sense to revert to pre-war strategy. The RAF in Egypt gathered that war had been declared on 10 June, by accident because a Squadron Leader was listening to a dance music programme on the radio from Rome. Shortly afterwards he was given permission to bomb surprised Italian military positions in nearby Libya, where the Italian regime had not yet alerted its warriors to the coming of war, and where apparently nobody had heard the newsflash in the music programme.[2] Thereafter, there were two remarkable feats of arms. Mussolini's strategically vulnerable empire in Abyssinia and Somaliland was destroyed by numerically inferior forces which, due to penetration of enemy codes and cryptographic devices, were knowledgeable about their opponents' intentions. Even more astounding was General Sir Richard O'Connor's offensive of late 1940-early 1941 which utterly routed vastly superior Italian forces in Libya and made British supremacy in the Mediterranean, with the confining of the German-Italian Axis forces within a sea cage, a feasible proposition.

The possibility was thrown away in 1941 by the catastrophic decision to intervene in Greece, which not only enabled the Axis to destroy vital British units and equipment, but also allowed Hitler to send General Erwin Rommel and his Afrika Korps to reinforce the Italians in North Africa. Though the violation of the basic principle of concentration of force by the decision to send air and army units to Greece was fiercely criticized by Staff officers like Sir Alan Brooke and Admiral Sir Tom Phillips, it was endorsed not only by Churchill but also by a wide spectrum of the political leadership, not to mention the regional commanders, military, naval and air force, whose units were to suffer unaffordable losses in Greece. Anthony Eden, the Foreign Secretary, led the charge, followed by Field Marshals Dill and Wavel, Air Chief Marshal Longmore, and Admiral Cunningham. The Prime Minister was among the first to show signs of returning to sanity as the *Wehrmacht* and *Luftwaffe* stamped out a highly predictable pattern of victory.[3]

It was too late. Between 1941 and 1942, Greece proved the harbinger of a series of disasters which demonstrated beyond question that, given a virtually free hand, the Westminster political complex was incapable of making a rational and effective use of scarce economic and military

---

[1] Lawrence R. Pratt *East of Malta, West of Suez: Britain's Mediterranean Crisis, 1936–1939* (Cambridge University Press, Cambridge 1975), pp. 175–7.
[2] Philip Guedalla *Middle East 1940–1942: A Study in Air Power* (Hodder and Stoughton, London 1944), pp. 83–4.
[3] Terraine *Right of the Line*, Part IV, Chap. 40, 'The Greek Fiasco, 1941'.

resources. The situation was actually worse than it appeared to the general public, for if high policy was deeply influenced by wishful thinking about the imminent collapse of the German economy, it was also profoundly enmeshed in the linked delusion of the bomber barons of the RAF that they could win the war—alone. The Italian General, Giulio Douhet, the American Colonel, Billy Mitchell, and the RAF's founder, Lord Trenchard, had upheld in the 1920s the dogmatic belief that bombers would win the next great war. After the fall of France, the RAF could exploit the emotional argument that it alone could hit back effectively at Germany. When, in February 1942, Air Marshal Arthur Harris became the chief of Bomber Command, a formidable and fanatical disciple of Trenchard began to demand more and more of the UK war economy for his hideously expensive bomber fleets. Nobody will ever know how much of the war effort they swallowed: possibly as much as a third. Harris even grudged long-range aircraft for the all-important task of convoy protection in the Battle of the Atlantic. Faced with evidence of the distressing inaccuracy of night bombing (day bombing had proved too costly), Harris went over the area bombing of German cities, with holocaust-like results, but remarkably little effect on German war production. It was selective bombing of key economic and military targets by night by the RAF and by the United States Army Air Force by day under long-range fighter protection in 1944–45 which ultimately made the bomber a key weapon.[1]

By then, the cost of the bomber offensive had done massive harm to the UK economy, as well as producing some strange by-products like the appointment of Admiral Sir Tom Phillips, out of favour with Churchill, to command the fleet sent out to the Far East. In 1940, Phillips had opposed bombing of German cities. In 1941, he finalized his breach with Churchill by opposing intervention in Greece. Strategically perceptive, he was tactically obtuse about the impact of developments in air warfare on naval operations. It was not inappropriate that he commanded the battleship and battle cruiser whose sinking by Japanese torpedo bombers off the Malay coast on Wednesday 10 December 1941 marked the unmistakable eclipse of the British Empire in Asia. The battleship, HMS *Prince of Wales* was at least fitted with modern anti-aircraft defences, though they malfunctioned due to electrical failure in the turret guns. The battle cruiser, HMS *Repulse*, originally launched in 1916, had as anti-aircraft armament only three sets of multi-barrelled 2-pounder 'pom-poms', and six unprotected, hand-operated 4-inch guns.[2] The bomber fleets had swallowed up funds which might have gone into adequate shipboard anti-aircraft defences, had the Admiralty been listened to. The idea that no other decision could have been taken does rather run against the fact that the Germans, with their superb anti-aircraft provision, had from the start been acutely conscious of the inaccuracy of horizontal bombing and the way a strategic bombing

---

[1] Max Hasting's *Bomber Command* (Pan Books, pbk edn, London 1981) is the best statement of the case against Harris, and its major points are largely accepted by Terraine, *Right of the Line*.

[2] Martin Middlebrook and Patrick Mahoney *Battleship: The Loss of the Prince of Wales and the Repulse* (Allen Lane, London 1977).

capability tended to eat up ever increasing amounts of funds and scarce materials.[1]

In North Africa, Tobruk had fallen, with the loss of 33,000 British soldiers to captivity. The defeats which followed the sudden Japanese attack on American and British positions in the Pacific in early December 1942 severely shook faith in Churchill's capacity as Minister of Defence, as well they might, for the Asian débacle was disgraceful. The loss of Hong Kong was not dishonourable. In Malaya, British land forces were routed by a much smaller, and vastly better, Japanese army, which then went on to a spectacular conquest of Burma. Churchill, arch-fugleman of the British Empire, had shown little interest in the details of its defence in Asia. Quite small numbers of appropriately-adapted modern fighter aircraft could have made all the difference. Heir to a naval strategy of 'main fleet to Singapore' which was pure wishful thinking, and sharing a misplaced racial contempt for the Japanese, the Premier reaped a whirlwind he only partially sowed.[2]

There was no political mechanism in the UK capable of reacting to his failure. Churchill romanticized about the Westminster parliament at the drop of a hat, but in practice he carried its castration well beyond the lengths Chamberlain had achieved. He ruled through Coalition whips. He deliberately encouraged MPs to seek employment incompatible with normal parliamentary activity. He sought power to grant certificates overriding rules about employments which were deemed to disqualify MPs from membership of the Commons. By early 1941, roughly 200 MPs were in some form of state employ, and another 116 were in the armed forces. Boothby joined the RAF (Ground Staff). Churchill privately expressed the view that a bomb disposal squad would have been more appropriate. As a mechanism for monitoring the activities of the executive, or of debating meaningfully major policy decisions, the Westminster parliament was ineffective. It was a measure of the frustration of MPs that the bi-partisan Select Committee on National Expenditure under the chairmanship of Sir John Wardlaw-Milne became one of few mechanisms for pursuing executive failure and incompetence and that by June 1940 Churchill was reprimanding its chairman for exceeding his remit.[3]

Churchill was in danger of being dumped only if his colleagues in the Government decided they needed a scapegoat for continued failure. The trouble was that the absence of light at the end of the tunnel encouraged doubts as to whether his huge zest for being Minister of Defence was matched by real talent, let alone achievement. Even the launching in June 1941 of 'Operation Barbarossa', Hitler's massive invasion of the Soviet Union, did not at first appear to hold out more hope. Both the British and American administrations had plenty prior intelligence about it, as had the Russians if Stalin had been prepared to believe it, but professional military opinion advised the Government that Russia would probably collapse quickly. It was not an unreasonable forecast. The capture of a manufactur-

---

[1] Cajus Bekker *The Luftwaffe War Diaries*, trans. and ed. Frank Ziegler (Corgi edn, pbk, London 1969), pp. 290–1 and Appendix 11.

[2] Russell Grenfell *Main Fleet to Singapore* (Faber and Faber, London 1951); and Adrian Stewart *The Underrated Enemy* (Kimber, London 1987).

[3] J. M. Lee *The Churchill Coalition 1940–1945* (Batsford, London 1980), pp. 40–2.

ing and communications centre such as Moscow would probably have crippled the Soviets after their early catastrophes, and we know that despite Hitler's ill-advised diversion of his armies into the Ukraine, Moscow was saved by that narrowest of margins: a winter of freak severity.[1] Churchill had spent much of 1940 buoyed by unrealistic hopes of the early entry into the war of the America he understood so little. If American belligerency was secured, the demographic and industrial resources opposed to Germany, especially if she was still fighting Russia, would be so overwhelming that victory could only be a question of time, and moderately competent management. Hence the enthusiasm with which Churchill greeted the news of the Japanese attack on the American fleet at Pearl Harbor, and of Hitler's subsequent declaration of war against the USA. Once he had heard of the Japanese onslaught, the Prime Minister retired to sleep 'the sleep of the saved and thankful.'[2]

Competent management of the vast resources of the combination of powers which President Roosevelt had by 1942 christened the United Nations was greatly assisted by the extent to which British and American intelligence sources had penetrated German and Japanese communication systems and codes. Of course, German and Japanese cryptanalysts had their own successes, but they in no way matched the results obtained by their foes. In the so-called 'Magic' operations the Americans cracked the 'Purple' codes used by Japanese diplomats. The success of the British in mastering the complexities of the German Enigma encipherment machines; in cracking the constantly-changing German military, air and naval ciphers; and in creating a worldwide secure system, based on their signals intelligence complex at Bletchley, for distributing useful intelligence, was not only a key to many of their successes, but also a central prop of Churchill's personal ascendancy. He was very careful until at least the latter part of 1944 to maintain an umbilical link with Enigma-based or Ultra (as it was often called) intelligence.[3]

The war inevitably saw a vast increase in the UK intelligence establishment. Apart from the police Special Branch, internal security and counter-intelligence were the responsibility of the Security Service (later known as Military Intelligence 5 or MI5 for short). Directed by Major-General Sir Vernon Kell in 1939, as it had been since 1909 when he had been Captain Kell, it had less than 30 officers, recruited on a conservative 'old-boy' basis, but meticulously vetted by Kell. Their political bias was such that Kell was known to have destroyed many files as a precaution when the first Labour Government came to power. Churchill brutally fired Kell in May 1940. Foreign intelligence was handled by the Secret Intelligence Service, or MI6,

---

[1] Russel H. S. Stolfi 'Barbarossa Revisited: A Critical Appraisal of the Opening Stages of the Russo-German Campaign (June–December 1941)', *The Journal of Modern History*, 54 (1982), pp. 27–46.

[2] Winston S. Churchill *The Second World War. Volume III. The Grand Alliance* (Cassell, London 1950), p. 540. For his over-optimism and failure to grasp the significance of America's complex heritage and traditional Anglophobia, see David Reynolds, 'Churchill and the British "Decision" to fight on in 1940: right policy, wrong reasons', in *Diplomacy and Intelligence During the Second World War: Essays in Honour of F. H. Hinsley*, ed. Richard Langhorne (Cambridge University Press, Cambridge 1985), pp. 161–3.

[3] Ronald Lewin *Ultra Goes to War* (Grafton pbk edn, London 1988).

which went through its own, less traumatic succession crisis in 1939. Both fell under decisive shaping influences from Conservative politicians, to the point where Labour members of the Government, who rightly feared the traditions of existing secret intelligence structures, insisted in placing at least part of what became a rapidly-growing empire in Labour hands. Hugh Dalton therefore became head of the Special Operations Executive (SOE) designed in Churchill's words to 'set Europe ablaze' by subversion. By the latter stages of the war, MI6 in particular had regained a high degree of operational autonomy, and was reverting with zest to older traditions of opposition to Bolshevism rather than Fascism.[1] The expansion of these services allowed 'moles' recruited by Soviet agents in an earlier recruiting drive in Cambridge University to penetrate British intelligence. Disillusioned and despairing converts to Communism, after Labour's 1931 collapse, they were the most ironic fruit of the Tories triumphant elimination of serious opposition.[2]

Parliament by 1942 was sitting only three days a week. So blunt an instrument was it that attempts to challenge Churchill's management of war production and the war proper culminated in guffawing farce in the Commons in the summer of 1942. The Premier was far more worried by signs of Conservative disaffection in 1942 than the threat of German invasion in 1940, but in practice dissidents had no viable alternative prime minister. Sir Stafford Cripps had built a bubble reputation on a successful embassy to Moscow. His Labour affiliation alone was a deadly handicap, and Churchill skilfully deflated him by exposure in an inappropriate job —Leader of the Commons—and an impossible mission: to reconcile competing Indian and British needs. The most important development in the Government, apart from its burgeoning secret sector, was the progressive insertion of the American federal administration as a potent element within the Whitehall decision-taking mechanisms.

That this was likely to happen if the war went on for more than two years had been known before war broke out. It was one of the most powerful arguments for trying to avoid war. When he became Premier, Churchill defined his policy, at least publicly, as 'victory at all costs', but the British did not have a bottomless purse. To be precise, the Chancellor of the Exchequer reckoned that the United Kingdom would run out of gold and dollar reserves by December 1940, and that only with 'abundant American help' could the adverse balance of payments with the USA be funded in 1941. The summer of 1940 saw the extraordinarily hard bargain whereby, in exchange for 50 ancient destroyers, the USA secured naval and air bases in Newfoundland, Bermuda and the British Caribbean and British Guiana, insisting on 99-year leases on the Caribbean and Guianese ones. The UK had no choice but to agree: by the end of 1940, its exports were down to a fraction over a third of the 1935 figure, even if exports of munitions to

[1] Nigel West *MI5: British Security Service Operations 1909–1945* (Bodley Head, London 1981) and *idem*, *MI6: British Secret Intelligence Service Operations 1909–45* (Weidenfeld and Nicolson, London 1983).

[2] Christopher Andrew 'F. H. Hinsley and the Cambridge Moles: Two Patterns of Intelligence Recruitment' in *Diplomacy and Intelligence During the Second World War*, ed. Langhorne, pp. 12–40.

the Commonwealth and Empire were included. By April 1941, UK gold and dollar reserves were a derisory $12 million. By March of that year to so-called 'Lend Lease' arrangements has passed the US Congress, enabling the UK to obtain credits for huge purchases of food, materials, and equipment in the USA, but at a long-term price of a massive surrender of independence. Economically, the Americans obtained terms which made it impossible to use Lend Lease funds to expand UK exports. By 1944, they were 31 per cent of those of 1938. A post-war UK was going to face robust competition from the US economy whilst heavily indebted to the US, and with deliberately crippled export trades.[1]

Since Churchill's personal survival strategy consisted of pulling and cajoling Roosevelt into belligerency at any price, there was little consciousness of the scale of surrender involved in these arrangements. His wartime correspondence with Roosevelt was an exercise in manipulative appeasement. Between 1941 and 1943, Churchill had travelled to the United States, Canada, and eventually North Africa to meet Roosevelt. He had also gone to Moscow to meet Stalin. From November 1943 when the tide of war visibly turned in North Africa with General Montgomery's victory at Alamein and Anglo-American troop landing in French North Africa, Churchill had become unassailable domestically. He was well on the way to deification, but in real terms his international stature was weak. The defeated Afrika Korps was a totally insignificant part of the German order of battle. The great bulk of Hitler's divisions were engaged against the Russians, whose losses were correspondingly appalling. The UK economy was propped up by, and increasingly in debt to, the USA. Not only was America an economic rival, but its leadership was acutely conscious of the need to avoid fighting the war in such a way as to prop up a British Empire to which they were historically and ideologically scarcely less hostile than the Russians. The British were very lucky that President Roosevelt stuck so firmly to the early agreement that priority must be given to the defeat of Germany. His principal naval counsellor, Admiral Ernest J. King, consistently argued for the primacy of the Pacific war against Japan. However, with tripartite meetings between Russian, American, and British leaders in Moscow and Tehran in 1943, trends emerged which were confirmed and sharpened by the final great tripartite conferences of the war at Yalta and Potsdam in 1945. The USA began to distance itself from the UK, moving closer to the Soviets, even at the cost of implicitly accepting future Russian preponderance in eastern Europe. Strategically, American preferences for direct attack on Western Europe replaced British preoccupation with the Mediterranean.[2]

There was more to this than the shifting balance of alliance politics. This shift was the beginning of the end for even the appearance of great power status for the UK. Churchill's only response was sustained, stubborn wishful thinking. The Westminster political system, including the bureaucratic empires of Whitehall, was much given to the habit. John Colville, who as

---

[1] Barnett *Collapse of British Power*, pp. 588–93.
[2] Keith Sainsbury *The Turning Point: Roosevelt, Stalin, Churchill and Chaing-Kai-Shek, 1943: The Moscow, Cairo and Tehran Conferences* (Oxford University Press, pbk edn, Oxford 1986).

a boy had once heard Ramsay MacDonald talk continuously for an hour and a half before breakfast, about himself, and who later witnessed Neville Chamberlain's violent resentment of any criticism, was of the view that 'vanity is a failing common to Prime Ministers'.[1] There were plenty of complaints by the end of 1940 of Churchill's arrogant way with colleagues, and his dislike of criticism, but by the standards of other prime ministers, he was no more than par for the course, and since he had the great virtue of never having quite grown up, his bullying titan act was intermittently lightened by flashes of impudent urchin. He was however an extreme example of the tendency of the closed and secretive administrative system he was part of to resent above all criticisms which suggested that a desperately wished-for reality was not a reality at all, or not the only possible reality. Though he seldom even approached reality on the topic of the Empire-Commonwealth, Churchill's supreme delusion was Anglo-American.

He hoped for a unique and permanent merging of at least the military and foreign policy directorates of the USA and the UK. It was to persist after the war. That its consequences would be beneficial Churchill and his Foreign Office supporters did not doubt. They also saw it as the only way in which the UK could preserve its great-power status.[2] So far from trying to preserve the resources of an over-mobilized society for post-war reconstruction, it was latterly Government policy to woo American goodwill by advertising the crippling scale of UK commitment to the war. After 1943, increases in the size of the UK's armed forces actually reduced war production in its factories. When the US used its loans as leverage to extract concessions for its civil aviation, Churchill took refuge in vacuous rhetoric about America's lack of 'vainglorious ambitions' (of which Americans had plenty),[3] and the Labour Government gave way with the Air Transport Agreement (1946). During the war, Churchill seized opportunities offered by his numerous trips to America to float, at the very highest level, ideas such as common US-UK citizenship and a common passport. Greeted by a deafening silence, he persisted long after the war, when Americans developed a highly selective ear and memory towards him. His famous 'Iron Curtain' speech delivered in Fulton, Missouri on 5 March 1946 is a classic example. To Americans, it was eventually a rousing warning of the dangers posed by the expansion of Communist power in Europe. To Churchill, it was primarily the last great public appeal for a special and fraternal association involving the merging of US and UK defence and foreign policies, and a common citizenship. After initially responding in a very mixed fashion for the appeal for a tougher line against Communism, the Americans chose in retrospect to exalt that aspect of the Fulton speech.

---

[1] Entry for Friday 2 February 1940 in John Colville *The Fringes of Power: Downing Street Diaries 1939–1955* (Hodder and Stoughton, London 1985), p. 79.

[2] Henry B. Ryan *The Vision of Anglo-America: the US-UK Alliance and the Emerging Cold War 1943–46* (Cambridge University Press, Cambridge 1987).

[3] For Churchill's theory that 'the American people under your reacclaimed leadership will not give themselves over to vainglorious ambitions' see Churchill to Roosevelt, 28 November 1944, Document No. 468 in *Roosevelt and Churchill: Their Secret Wartime Correspondence*, eds. Francis L. Loewenheim, Harold D. Langley and Manfred Jonas (Barrie and Jenkins, London 1975), p. 611.

The rest they tossed into oblivion. Churchill's proposals had always been complicated by his refusal to allow American control over the affairs of the dependent British Empire. By the 1950s, Americans were treating him as a living monument to their own ideological preconceptions: a mirror in which to admire themselves as they saluted him.[1] The honorary American citizenship which President John F. Kennedy bestowed on him in 1963 was the merest parody of Churchill's great design for a common citizenship.

If there were always weaknesses in Churchill's strengths, there was always an immensely impressive strength in his weakness. Unlike so many contemporary sycophants, he was well aware in old age that, judged by his own objectives, his life had not ultimately been a successful one. On the other hand, he never had any insight into his greatest failure politically, which was his failure to retain power in 1945. When attacked by Conservative critics in 1942, he had fumed that he alone had stood between the Tory party and extinction after their run of diplomatic humiliation and military defeat. He did however assume that apparent diplomatic triumph and military victory would reverse that electoral doom. The domestic front as such was not at the core of his interests. He did not seek the same control over it as he demanded over matters military and diplomatic. His main concern was to uphold a domestic political balance which suited him. As a result, when he struck out at former Chamberlain supporters who were critics of his conduct of the war in early 1942, he was prepared to replace some of them with Labour politicians. The Tory ex-Chief Whip David Margesson was sacked as War Minister, and given no other job, and Kingsley Wood, though retaining the Treasury, was removed from the War Cabinet, but Labour's Hugh Dalton advanced to the Board of Trade. This was a vital high-profile domestic post. Later in 1942, Churchill, whose political position had become impregnable with the successful invasion of North Africa, did demote Sir Stafford Cripps by displacing him as Lord President and a member of the War Cabinet, and packing him off to be Minister of Aircraft Production, but this was less because of Sir Stafford's left-wing politics, than because of his momentary delusions of grandeur about replacing Churchill. The Premier was even prepared to accept Ernie Bevin's veto on any all-powerful Minister of Production capable of trespassing on Bevin's Ministry of Labour. Apart from the need to sustain a political balance to which Bevin was central, Churchill was not as worried as most about production bottlenecks: his policy was to compensate for shortfall by buying on credit from America.

The fact that he allowed Labour ministers to occupy important domestic positions did not mean that Churchill agreed with them. Indeed, it is clear that, as after 1918, they were destined to be ditched, preferably after helping to ensure a smooth transition from war to peace. Despite an official rhetoric of mobilization on a basis of classless solidarity and equal sacrifice, which necessarily raised expectations of a less inequitable post-war society, the Coalition found it very difficult to turn concern with problems of reconstruction into agreed measures of social legislation. There was only one

[1] A good example of this is the record of *Proceedings of the Presentation of the Williamsburg Award by the Trustees of Colonial Williamsburg to the Rt. Hon. Sir Winston S. Churchill at Drapers' Hall, London, 7 Dec. 1955* (Colonial Williamsburg, VA 1957).

major achievement in this field: the Education Act of 1944. Drafted by the Board of Education, in close consultation with vested interests concerned, it was manoeuvred through the legislative process by Rab Butler, an unrepentant Chamberlainite who had been relegated to the Presidency of the Board. He was privately scathing about the ignorance of the (overwhelmingly privately-educated) Tory MPs on the subject, and the Act was ambiguous about the date on which the school leaving age would rise from fourteen to fifteen, and later sixteen, but it did represent a big expansion in state-funded education provision. Apart from the introduction of family allowances, no other significant measure of social reform passed. The Town and Country Planning Act of 1944 was a mere shadow of what had been hoped for. The Government dragged its feet on proposed extension of state-sponsored medical provision, and made it very clear in 1943 that it would not endorse the proposals for a comprehensive system of social insurance associated with the name of Sir William Beveridge, the civil servant who had chaired the relevant committee.

Churchill, in words not inapplicable to himself on a bad day, called Beveridge 'a windbag and a dreamer'. Beveridge was certainly a publicity hound. His egotism matched Bevin's and made the Ministry of Labour too small for both of them. Nevertheless, the debate in the Commons made it clear that 90 per cent of Tory MPs were hostile to the Beveridge Report and that the other 10 per cent in the Tory Reform Committee would finally vote with the Government when the Labour backbenchers divided the chamber on the issue of implementing the report. Churchill was as negative as anyone on social reform. Under his aegis, the home front was more and more dominated by the increasingly negative Treasury spirit of Sir John Anderson, and when, under heavy pressure from their party organizations, Labour ministers reluctantly withdrew from the Government in May 1945, the composition of the interim administration formed by Churchill to govern until a July election showed, if anything, a further swing to the right.[1]

Despite a disturbing anti-Conservative trend in by-elections, it is clear that the Labour victory in July came as an appalling shock to Churchill and the great bulk of Conservative MPs. In retrospect, with the help of contemporary opinion surveys, historians have concluded that the Conservatives would have had difficulty winning a general election after 1940, and that there may have been a slight swing back to them after 1943. In July 1945, a Conservative Party which in the 1930s had developed the habit of focussing its publicity machine on, and running behind, the reassuring image of Stanley Baldwin, naturally tried the same trick in every constituency with the image of Winston Churchill. The Premier fought his standard election campaign, unchanged since the mid-1920s. After seizing the public imagination with dramatic actions, and ensuring sympathetic press coverage (the *Daily Express*, for example ran its usual violent anti-Labour scare in June-July 1945), Churchill always told the electorate that if 'the Socialists' won, their savings would become worthless, and the full horrors of totali-

---

[1] J. M. Lee *The Churchill Coalition: 1940–1945* (Batsford, London 1980), and Kevin Jeffreys *The Churchill Coalition and Wartime Politics, 1940–1945* (Manchester University Press, Manchester 1991), *passim*.

tarian terror would shortly emerge from the Labour Trojan Horse. That he chose to use the word 'Gestapo' in 1945 was, as his wife told him, tasteless, but really only a substitute for his usual Russian reference. Many Tory MPs, as Chips Channon recorded, expected to return on the back of this appeal to their 1924 majority, if not their 1931 majority. That they did not was a tribute to the decreased gullibility of the UK electorate.[1]

It was less of a tribute to the electoral system that the Labour Party emerged with a large overall majority. Like most 'landslide' victories in UK politics after 1935, this was the bogus product of the vagaries of the voting system. With 48 per cent of the vote, Labour had 393 seats. The Conservatives plummeted from their vast old majority to a mere 213 seats, and the Liberals, who entered the election with 306 candidates led by Sir Archibald Sinclair and Sir William Beveridge, came out with 9 per cent of the vote and a risible twelve seats. Both Sinclair and Beveridge (who had become a Liberal MP at a 1944 by-election) were defeated. The Liberal Party had ceased to matter. Indeed, until 1947, the Tories hardly mattered. There had been no real political consensus within the Coalition, but there clearly was a consensus within the electorate, and the Conservative defeat was rooted in justified suspicion amongst voters as to the extent to which that party endorsed, or sincerely believed in if it nominally endorsed, certain widely-desired reforms.

Sir William Beveridge was an extremely ambitious man who miscalculated the ability of the Liberal Party to achieve a vote capable of yielding seats even faintly commensurate with support in 1945. That 'take-off point' was probably well over 20 per cent of votes cast. Yet he had been right in arguing publicly in 1943 that there was in effect 'a directive from the democracy of Britain' to the Government to endorse a social security system capable of checking the more obscene extremes of want. He was also correct at that time to tell the Government that there was a 'second directive' to the effect that 'the Government should take all necessary steps for the maintenance of employment after the war'.[2] The concept of such 'directives', except of course from an élite isolated from democratic pressures, was unlikely to appeal to Westminster politicians. Least of all would such language have been endorsed by the new Labour Prime Minister, Clement Attlee.

He was essentially a Victorian, an admirer, politics apart, of the prime-ministerial style of the great Lord Salisbury, and the last man to want to change any aspect of a political system which had so unexpectedly thrust such opportunities and powers into his hands. Nobody, including himself, had expected him to emerge victorious in the 1945 election. He had no visible personal ambition, and less vanity. To an unprepossessing appearance he allied a lack of oratorical talent calculated to make the most dramatic events sound banal. He had explained at some length to Churchill that he entered the War Cabinet purely because he was leader of the Labour Party, and not because of any personal qualities. In a hothouse full of

---

[1] Entry for 5 June 1945 in *Chips: The Diaries of Sir Henry Channon*, ed. Robert R. James (Weidenfeld and Nicolson, London 1967), p. 408.

[2] Sir William H. Beveridge *The Pillars of Security and Other War-Time Essays and Addresses* (George Allen and Unwin, London 1943), pp. 135–6.

egomaniacal blooms like Westminster, he ironically stood out precisely because he was such a plain plant. That did not make him ineffective. James Chuter Ede, a Labour schoolteacher from a radical Nonconformist background who would have liked to have been his Minister of Education, but in fact became the Home Secretary in 1945, remarked that if Attlee was 'no firework' he had helped display a solid backcloth against which Churchill's contrived extremism had shown up badly.

At the victory meeting in Beaver Hall in the City of London, Chuter Ede was also struck by the stress in Attlee's typical unemotional speech on the fact that he would have to be 'quite ruthless' in hiring and firing the ministers charged with executing Labour's programme.[1] And ruthless he was. He was given a warning of the dangers of weakness immediately after the election result was announced when Herbert Morrison, quite outrageously, tried to engineer a leadership contest in the hope of replacing the leader who had fought and won the election and whom George VI had asked to form an administration. Attlee viewed the episode as 'cockeyed', and stonily refused to give ground. As Lord President and Leader of the Commons, Morrison emerged as the second man in the Government, but his grasping egotism had brought disrepute on the 'constitutional' arguments he had used, or rather misused. After 1931, the Labour Party had in fact tried to check unbridled prime-ministerial patronage by arranging for the Parliamentary Labour Party to elect what Attlee called 'a body of three or four senior men to advise' the Premier in the formation of his Cabinet. Attlee regarded the whole idea as an 'Awful business', and remarked in retrospect, with undisguised satisfaction, that:

> The fact that I had to get over to Potsdam at once meant there was no time for lengthy confabulations or for going through a process of electing various people who admired each another. It wouldn't have worked.[2]

Throughout his term of office between 1945 and 1951, Premier Attlee presided like a rather remote but awesome headmaster over an administration whose members he hired and fired. Older ministers could have their sacking slightly softened by cricket metaphors about having had a good innings. Younger ones were just sacked, at times without warning. Apart from a limited number of old friends like Ernest Bevin, whom he made Foreign Secretary in 1945, Attlee was not well acquainted with the bulk of his colleagues. Supremely happy in a warm family life, he had no need of Commons smoking-room camaraderie. To have to break a career by swift dismissal placed in most cases no strain on him.[3]

His conversion to socialism, after a very orthodox upbringing in a devout upper middle class Anglican household, completed with the usual public school (Haileybury) and Oxford (University College) education, had been a moral conversion. He was delighted to have a large majority for the

---

[1] Entry for Saturday 28 July 1945, in *Labour and the Wartime Coalition: From the Diary of James Chuter Ede, 1941–1945*, ed. Kevin Jeffreys (The Historians Press, London 1987), pp. 228–9.

[2] Francis Williams *A Prime Minister Remembers: The War and Post-War Memoirs of the Rt. Hon. Earl Attlee* (Heinemann, London 1961), p. 85.

[3] Kenneth Harris *Attlee* (Weidenfeld and Nicolson, London 1982) is the most comprehensive biography.

programme laid down in the Labour election manifesto *Let Us Face the Future* but the case for that programme was that it was right and 'the embodiment of our Socialist principle of placing the welfare of the nation before that of any section'. In fact, there was little effective opposition to the implementation of the major proposals. Jim Griffiths, Minister of National Insurance, piloted through a National Insurance Act of 1946 which implemented a modified version of the Beveridge Report. The Bank of England was nationalized in the spring of 1946, with much less fuss than many had expected. The nationalization of coal mines in 1947, and of electricity, gas and the railways met only nominal opposition from the Conservatives. These were either public utilities or, like the coal mines and railways, so notoriously run down and under-capitalized that they were of debatable value to their owners, who in any case received substantial cash compensation. These industries were probably more valuable to the rest of the business community in public hands. Aneurin Bevan, the Minister of Health, was the most creative of the new ministers. He had been one of the few MPs who had tried to maintain an independent and critical spirit in the Commons in the heyday of Coalition ascendancy, perceptively underlining the relative unimportance of the desert war against the Afrika Korps in terms of German troop commitment, and even expressing scepticism about the sacred cow of area bombing of German cities. He earned from Churchill denunciation as a 'squalid nuisance'. In office, he refused to start from the premises of Coalition planning, and introduced a comprehensive National Health Service in July 1948. To do it, he grasped the nettle of the voluntary hospitals, and nationalized them. He also squared opposition from consultants and general practitioners by allowing them to practise private medicine whilst holding National Health appointments. Bitterly resented by the press barons, and by Churchill, the National Health Service was not a very socialist achievement.

Bevan's own crude neo-Marxist outlook,[1] picked up in the Welsh valleys and never much examined, let alone refined thereafter, was like Attlee's underlying vision of a socialist commonwealth—about as relevant to their actions in power as the Second Coming to the mainstream Christian churches. To put it the other way round: the ideology-obsessed minority of the Labour Party which insisted on viewing the world through the lenses of first principles, and of talking about first principles all the time were regarded by the Cabinet with the same enthusiasm which the Pope displays for Jehovah's Witnesses. Members of the Government, from Attlee down, talked frequently about planning the economy, but in practice they neither could nor did plan the UK economy. The Lord President's Committee, presided over by Herbert Morrison, failed to produce any coherent policy to cope with a coal shortage which, despite being foreseen as early as the spring of 1946, proved crippling in the winter of 1946–7. Calls for some form of wages policy, as a logical corollary to the extension of state intervention, came from politicians like Emanuel Shinwell when Minister of Fuel and Power and economists like Nicholas Kaldor as late as 1950. When not positively opposed by conservative trade unionists in the

---

[1] John Campbell *Nye Bevan and the Mirage of British Socialism* (Weidenfeld and Nicolson, London 1987).

Government, they fell on deaf ears. The nationalized industries were run by autonomous boards. MPs who, between 1947 and 1951, tried to ask questions about them often had their questions disallowed, as no minister was identifiably responsible.

The Government was buffeted by vast extraneous forces, over which it had little control. Economically, the post-war situation was described by J. M. Keynes as 'a financial Dunkirk'. The war had cost the UK a quarter of its total wealth (about £7,000 million). Indebtedness had soared as overseas assets were sold and exports artificially depressed. The latter stood at some £400 million per annum when £1100–£1200 million would be needed to sustain wartime consumption levels. Lease Lend facilities from America were cut by the new President, Harry S. Truman, on 21 August 1945, less than a week after Japan's surrender. An American loan alone could enable the Government to survive, and the negotiations for it proved difficult. Interestingly, the British Establishment, on a bipartisan basis, appears to have been prepared to face the unthinkable. Sir John Anderson magisterially warned the Republican Senator Vandenberg (a man not overflowing with sympathy for the Labour Party), that if the loan were refused, a National Coalition Government would be formed; it would impose acute austerity and real suffering on the UK for three years; and after that, the economy would recover, whilst acute hatred of America would linger long.[1] A loan of $3.75 billion at 2 per cent, repayable in fifty annual instalments after 1951, was arranged with provision for temporary relief in any year in which the UK failed to earn adequate foreign exchange. In addition, the UK agreed to ratify arrangements made at the Bretton Woods Conference of 1944 which would facilitate the erection of an International Monetary Fund and a World Bank, both ultimately formidable engines of American influence. Further undertakings to move towards full convertibility of the pound sterling into other currencies within a year; to run down sterling balances accumulated by Commonwealth countries in London during the war; and to pare away the structure of Imperial preference erected at Ottawa, underlined the scale of American influence over Westminster, as did the contrast between a hawkish US Congress pressing Truman to impose even tougher terms, and an unhappy House of Commons, many of whose members grasped well enough the scale of the political surrender involved, accepting the pressure of Government whips for a vote of acquiescence.

Attlee's own stature remained extremely high until 1947, when a combination of circumstances conspired to damage it seriously. The rise of the Cold War in the shape of a global confrontation between a liberal capitalist community of nations led by the US and a Communist block headed by Stalin's Soviet Union in some ways suited the Government well. American Anglophobia was muted by it, and in any case the original post-war confrontation had been primarily between British and Russian power. From central Europe to Greece, where British troops had intervened to check a coup by Communist insurgents, through the Middle East to Iran, Stalin's Russia seemed poised to dismantle the formal and informal structures of

[1] Entry for 28 January 1946, in *Harold Nicolson: Diaries and Letters 1945–1962*, ed. Nigel Nicolson (Collins, London 1968), p. 53.

British power. Not much wonder that both Churchill and Attlee were anxious to pull America into the struggle. Their success in so doing was assisted by the existence of US occupation troops in western Germany and by America's fear of Russian expansion in Asia, which had already been one of the factors motivating Truman to drop two atomic bombs on Japan in 1945 in the (ultimately unsuccessful) hope that Japan would 'fold up before Russia comes in'.[1] By 1947, the US was warming to the task, offering Marshall Aid to all cooperating European nations (affiliated eventually to the Organisation for European Economic Cooperation, or OEEC) on a scale which made Bevin grab at the idea and his share with both hands. By the end of 1950, when it terminated, Marshall Aid to the UK came to $2,694.3 million. It carried with it expectation that recipients would follow American urging to participate in some sort of western European political integration. The UK had signed a military alliance with France and the Benelux countries in the shape of the Treaty of Brussels of 1948, but the Russian blockade of West Berlin in that year acted as a catalyst to the creation of a North Atlantic Treaty Organization which linked America and Canada with the Brussels powers. On 4 April 1949, the NATO treaty, which owed more to Bevan than anyone, was signed.

By then, the price of locking the UK into international structures heavily dominated by America had become as apparent as the benefits. 1947 saw an exceptionally severe winter; a serious coal shortage; widespread, if temporary, industrial disruption and unemployment; and a devastating exchange-rate crisis rooted in the premature convertibility of the pound sterling forced on the UK by the US. Conservatives visibly perked up. On any usual calculation, the Labour majority of 1945 might have been expected to endure for not one but two more parliaments. Churchill was unrepentant and unreconstructed, refusing to speak to 'progressive' young Tory MPs at a banquet, and referring to them later as 'pink pansies'.[2] Harold Macmillan became unpopular for saying the Conservative Party, in what was likely to be a long period out of office, would have to moderate a political style basically rooted in the preferences of the very rich, and bid for that middle-class vote into which Labour, as witness many of its new MPs, had bitten so deeply in 1945.[3] When he went on to mutter about coalitions, Macmillan confirmed a reputation for unsoundness which he only lived down in the 1950s. Whatever incipient ideological accommodation between Labour and some Conservatives may have existed in 1945–6 vanished as a serious factor in 1947, when Tories smelled the unmistakable savour of recoverable power.

In fact, it was the Labour Government which recovered in the short run, with Attlee still in the saddle, but with the commanding presence of his Chancellor, Sir Stafford Cripps, setting the political tone.[4] It was a period of austerity in which the reliance on physical controls appropriate to an

---

[1] Richard Rhodes *The Making of the Atomic Bomb* (Simon and Schuster, New York 1988), p. 688.
[2] Entry for 19 December 1945, in *Nicolson: Diaries*, p. 45.
[3] Entry for 12 September 1945, *ibid.*, p. 35.
[4] Kenneth O. Morgan *Labour in Power 1945–1951* (Clarendon Press, Oxford 1984), Chap. 9: 'The Cripps Era'.

era of demobilization was largely abandoned, not least to head off Tory libertarian rhetoric. The young Harold Wilson, President of the Board of Control 1947–51, conducted a 'bonfire of controls' in 1948–49. Instead, demand management was substituted. Whether this constituted a 'Keynsian Revolution' is a contentious question.[1] Keynes, who had died in 1946, might well have approved of the policy, but Treasury mandarins certainly did not understand Keynsian economics in 1947. An older Treasury man like Sir James Grigg, unseated as an MP in 1945 but revitalized by Labour's troubles in 1947, simply regarded all post-1945 policy as evidence that 'Karl Marx had by 1945 captured the Labour Party'.[2] What his younger successors in the Treasury did understand was that by holding down domestic expenditure and consumption to encourage exports, they would go far to restore the ascendancy of their own negative traditions in central policy formation. Aided by a reluctant but overdue devaluation of the pound from $4.03 to $2.80 in 1949 which cheapened exports; relative wage restraint reinforced in 1949–50 by a fairly effective 'wage freeze'; and a formidable surge in exports to North America and elsewhere, Cripps contrived to bring the national trading account towards a healthy balance by early 1950.[3]

By the end of that year, he was dead, his end hastened by habitual gross overwork. Attlee worked a long enough day, in all conscience, but he could detach and pace himself. He did not become mired in the details of other mens' departmental duties, which was just as well, for his technical grasp of, say, economics, was minimal. He was a laconic but very firm chairman of the Cabinet, whose members he chose and then expected to get on with their current job. When they met as a Cabinet he made them produce necessary decisions in a clear form within a reasonable time. That he spoke little did not mean he was not in charge. He once told a carping Churchill who claimed to have settled an issue in a Coalition Cabinet that a monologue was not a decision. Attlee's were amongst the safest hands to hold prime-ministerial power, which did not mean that he did not increase it dangerously. The increase in state activity may not have made positive planning feasible, but it enabled central patronage to balloon. Nationalization of public utilities, for example, often removed them not from private hands but from vigorous innovative local government units. In Scotland, Churchill's profound lack of interest had allowed a Labour Secretary of State, Tom Johnston, to exercise a good deal of constructive initiative between 1941 and 1945, in fields ranging from health care provision to hydro-electricity. He was not a devolutionist in the later political sense, but he was a welcome break in an office traditionally occupied by the dreary and the dimly obedient. After 1945, centralization was the name of the game. Johnston wisely retreated into a career in quasi-autonomous government organizations or 'quangos'.[4]

[1] The academic debate on this topic can be followed conveniently in Alan Booth, 'The "Keynsian Revolution" in Economic Policy-Making' in *The Economic History Review*, 2nd series, vol. XXXVIII (1985), pp. 95–106.

[2] P. J. Grigg *Prejudice and Judgement* (Jonathan Cape, London 1948), p. 410.

[3] Apart from Morgan's *Labour in Power*, Henry Pelling's *The Labour Governments 1945–51* (Macmillan, London 1984) provides a lucid summary and analysis.

[4] Christopher Harvie *No Gods and Precious Few Heroes: Scotland 1914–1980* (Edward Arnold, London 1981), pp. 103–4.

There was a sinister side to the expansion of state activity in the field of atomic energy. Early British work summed up in the Maud Report of 1941 had been instrumental in persuading America to try to build atomic bombs. The entire project was transferred to North America and pursued as an Anglo-American enterprise with important Canadian participation. Predictably, the British hoped continued joint atomic research and development would be part of their much desired Anglo-America. When, by the McMahon Act of 1946, the US effectively annexed the atomic bomb projects, to which it had been the main contributor since 1941, and criminalized any sharing of information with other powers, the UK naturally considered the option of making its own bomb. With no American alliance, and facing Russian hostility, the idea was tempting. Yet in the long run what was truly significant was not the making and testing of a virtually unusable weapon, but the fact that the decision, like all future major decisions in the field, was taken in secrecy. The Premier with one or two ministers, plus the Chiefs of Staff, appear to have given the orders, which were concealed not just from the public and the Westminster parliament, but also from the Cabinet. As the Cold War developed, America became more willing to cooperate in the atomic field, but was shaken by a series of discoveries of Soviet spies within the UK programme. Tighter security by vastly expanded secret services was called for. No longer did a tiny UK Security Service oblige by recovering love letters written by Ramsay MacDonald to a 'Continental cocotte'. Now the structure and scope of security was expanding to a point where even within the Government there were those who worried about democratic values.[1]

Attlee's UK reached out for more control internally whilst becoming very vulnerable to external pressure, less from its declared enemies than from its professed friends. The Premier had never been a sensitive politician, in the broadest sense. Power had come to him. He, like most ministers, appears to have thought that it would come again, with an adequate but reduced majority in the election he called in February 1950. Despite a three per cent lead in votes over the Conservatives, Labour ended up with, literally, a handful of an overall majority due to its many irrelevantly huge majorities, especially in mining areas. Exhausted and with no positive programme, the new Labour Government self-destructed over the implications of the Korean War which broke out in June 1950 when the troops of Communist North Korea invaded South Korea, which lay in a grey area of doubt on the periphery of American power in Asia. On the back of the Communist seizure of power in China in 1948–49, which had enraged the powerful conservative 'China Lobby' in the US Congress, and the behaviour of Russia in Europe which had led to the formation of NATO, this latest offensive was seen, probably wrongly, as part of a global plot, indeed as a probing reconnaissance for World War Three. American pressure for increased defence expenditure mounted relentlessly. Backed by

[1] Margaret Gowing *Britain and Atomic Energy 1939–1945* (Macmillan, London 1964), and *Independence and Deterrence: Britain and Atomic Energy, 1945–1952*. Vol. 1. *Policy Making* (London 1974). Vol. 2. *Policy Execution*, of the same work quotes on p. 153 a memo to the Premier after the conviction of the spy Klaus Fuchs, querying whether some of the security measures being demanded were compatible with democracy.

the UK Chiefs of Staff, the American Chiefs of Staff kept escalating their demands with total disregard for the realities of the UK economy. By the start of 1952, it was Government policy to increase defence expenditure from a highish 7 per cent of gross national product to 14 per cent in two years. Hugh Gaitskell, who replaced Cripps as Chancellor, enthusiastically endorsed this physically impossible objective which halted a rise in productive investment, reduced exports, and placed an intolerable strain on the balance of payments.[1] The public symbol on which those opposed to this misguided enthusiasm chose to fight was Gaitskell's parallel obsession with introducing charges in the National Health Service, but the resignation of Aneurin Bevan, and two very able younger ministers, Harold Wilson and John Freeman, was a gesture of despair at a deeper level than teeth and spectacles. When Attlee, against the advice of many of his colleagues, called an election in October 1951, a divided Labour Party, led by exhausted old men and disconcertingly right-wing young ones, lost narrowly.

The Government lost partly through tiredness, but more through Attlee's economic illiteracy, and political or rather electoral amateurism. The pressures on him were appalling, and hubris rooted in poisonous vanity, the usual prime-ministerial weakness, was not his. Rather was it his combination of strength and manipulability which made his office the vehicle for the central paradox in the history of the UK after 1945. His Government had escaped from a series of thankless formal and informal imperial commitments. It had relentlessly accelerated the date of its withdrawal from the Indian sub-continent; accepted the partition into India and Pakistan which alone allowed an admittedly fragile consensus as to how this should be done; and then surrendered at midnight on 14 August 1947 not so much power as the burden of being blamed by those who could agree on nothing else. While the glittering, well-publicized Lord Louis Mountbatten performed the political rituals as last Viceroy and first Governor-General of the Indian Union, the last Commander-in-Chief, Claude Auchinleck grimly watched communal massacre in the Punjab between Sikh and Muslim, and the dissolution of the British Indian Army which had given the UK great-power status.[2] Burma was allowed to move to complete independence outwith the Commonwealth, and into chaos. In 1947, Attlee had told the USA that it would have to take over responsibility for Greece and Turkey. An impossible situation existed in Palestine, where the British Mandate was supposed to reconcile the irreconcilable ambitions of Zionist and Arab. President Truman repeatedly intervened to placate the American Jewish lobby and to make a bad situation worse. Bevin entirely failed to come up with a rashly promised solution. The decision to terminate the mandate in May 1948 and evacuate Palestine in August has been called shameful.[3] It was the sanest choice among evils.

Yet even as the Government was reduced to sending the British ambassa-

---

[1] Alec Cairncross *Years of Recovery: British Economic Policy 1945–51* (Methuen, London 1985), Chap. 8.

[2] John Connell *Auchinleck* (Cassell, London 1959), Chap. XXIX.

[3] John Connell *The 'Office': A Study of British Foreign Policy and its Makers 1919–1951* (Allan Wingate, London 1958), p. 303.

dor to ask President Truman to ask his Zionist protégés to stop shelling withdrawing British troops,[1] it was becoming clear that the peoples of the UK were being asked to continue to shoulder the burdens while losing the status of an imperial power. Not the least of these burdens was the smack of firm, fair, imperial-style government. Though used as a Conservative election slogan in the 1970s, the phrase 'firm, fair government' had been coined in interwar India.

---

[1] Henry Brandon *Special Relationships* (Macmillan, London 1989), p. 77.

10

Churchill's Indian summer, Eden's winter and Supermac's false dawn

All roads in the Constitution lead to the Prime Minister . . . Among his colleagues he is said to be *primus inter pares*, first among equals, but it is doubtful if this has been true at any time since Gladstone became Prime Minister in 1868. Harcourt said that he was a moon among lesser stars, but the lesser stars—as they seem to the naked eye—have no connexion with the moon: and the Prime Minister is much more like the sun among the planets.
Sir Ivor Jennings QC *The Queen's Government* (Penguin Books, London, 1954), p. 140.

This mesmeric fascination with the office of premier is one of the weaknesses of our system.
Hugh Thomas in *John Strachey*, p. 301.

Now that the Cabinet's gone to dinner
The Secretary stays and gets thinner and thinner
Racking his brains to record and report
What he thinks that they think they ought to have thought.
Anon.

The return of the Conservatives to power in late 1951 might have been expected to be the prelude to a dramatic counter-revolution against developments which that party had denounced in increasingly strident tones. The Labour 'Annus Horrendus' of 1947, and the rapid development of the Cold War after 1948 had created a situation in which it was both profitable and congenial for Conservatives to embrace the concept of a Manichean struggle between good and Communist evil, and to identify 'the Socialist Party' in snide but telling propaganda with the latter. Corrupted by Marxism, the argument went, 'The Socialists have taught the people to despise liberty, order and impartial justice'. Christianity was wheeled, slightly unwillingly, into a European rally of the right, compounded of 'the forces which accept Christian principles and profess faith in human responsibility and freedom.' The distinguished Liberal journal, the *News Chronicle*, which was by no means a blind admirer of the Labour administration, was rebuked for sometimes describing this noble rally against godless Communism as 'Reaction'.[1] Resistance to Communism was not to be expected from a Labour Party whose committed voters 'make no serious distinction between Socialism and Communism'.[2] This level of analysis is perhaps best explained by the traumas experienced by certain groups passing through an economically difficult time under a regime which for the first time in their experience was not primarily committed to them. There was however a much more profound vein of Conservative criticism.

The sheer power of Government over the legislature had been demonstrated again and again between 1945 and 1951. Private members' time in the Commons had been surrendered to the Government because of the weight of the legislative programme embedded in the Labour Party manifesto, which it was taken for granted would be passed. As one perceptive Conservative MP pointed out this was merely the culmination of a lengthy period of tightening party discipline and control by the whips over the Commons. It had become formidable in the 1880s with provision for forcible closure of debate. Yet the Government chose to preserve time-consuming and archaic procedures in the legislature. The technicalities of the legislation were often only comprehensible to a handful of ministers and bureaucrats. The result of votes often taken at absurdly late hours were so predictable that this particular critic very sensibly suggested that:

> As things are now, it would really be simpler and more economical to keep a flock of tame sheep and from time to time drive them through the division lobbies in the appropriate numbers. Absurd and excessive hours of meeting, constant all-night sittings, do not prove, as is sometimes superficially claims, that Parliament is working hard; they prove that Parliament is not working at all.

He went on to argue, again absolutely correctly, that the reason why this Government permitted MPs to express their opinions 'under such ridiculous conditions', was that 'the Government has already made up its mind that it is not going to pay attention to those opinions.' His proposed solution to this problem was the utterly unrealistic one of a separate 'Industrial Parliament' elected on a neo-syndicalist basis. Like a good Westminster man, he was very hostile to any suggestion of devolution to Welsh or Scottish regional assemblies.[3] His underlying motive was probably to make it impossible for any future administration easily to carry through such a nationalization measure as that proposed for the iron and steel industry, which had become a matter of bitter controversy.

The proposal had been in the 1945 Labour manifesto, but senior members of the Government were unenthusiastic about full-blooded nationalization for the industry. Herbert Morrison in particular would have preferred a compromise hammered out in agreement with Sir Andrew Duncan of the Iron and Steel Federation whereby a state board acquired extensive supervisory powers, but individual firms would normally remain privately-

[1] Colm Brogan *Our New Masters* (Hollis and Carter, London 1948), pp. 20–6.
[2] Colm Brogan *Patriots? . . . My Foot!* (Hollis and Carter, London 1949), p. 82.
[3] Christopher Hollis, MP *Can Parliament Survive?* (World Affairs Book Club, London 1950), pp. 64–5.

owned. When to mixed feelings in the Cabinet was added the absence of any detailed drafting of necessarily complex legislation, the eventual nationalization bill came so late as to be certainly interrupted by a general election if the House of Lords retained its two-year delaying power. In defence of a profitable industry, the Tories were distinctly revitalized.[1] The minister responsible for the measure, Gerald Strauss, was subsequently to remark that 'Nobody is ever convinced by a debate', but the timing of the iron and steel measure had made a reduction in the delaying powers of the Lords to a year a political necessity for the Government. This was duly achieved by a Parliament Act. The relevant bill was introduced in 1947. In early 1948, there was an attempt to achieve comprehensive second-chamber reform by agreement in inter-party talks. The attempt failed, which was hardly surprising, as both the Labour and the Conservative leadership were truly interested only in the timing of the iron and steel legislation. Nevertheless, in subsequent debate, Anthony Eden, who had by now emerged as the Tory heir-apparent, let slip the basic fact of life that no second chamber was less likely to make trouble for an executive with some sort of electoral legitimation than a hereditary chamber.[2]

When, therefore, Churchill crawled back into power at the 1951 election, he resumed a premiership whose potential had been raised to unprecedented heights. The power of whips had reduced the Commons to noisy powerlessness. Even the argument that its debates served the vital purpose of airing the major issues was bogus, for the press devoted little space to its interminable talk. Nobody read *Hansard*, its expensive official record. Radio and television were shunned by the Palace of Westminster like the plague. Party discipline was sharpened by electoral polarization, and the 1951 election showed almost total polarization between the violently antipathetic Labour and Conservative Parties. The Liberal showing at the election was pathetic. It was worse than it appeared, in fact, for of the five Liberal MPs in the old Commons who were returned, four had had no Conservative opponent. There was one freak gain in Bolton West against four losses. Had there been Tory opposition in all seats, perhaps only three Liberals would have been returned. The Conservatives had absorbed historic Liberalism, not least by adopting after 1947 an essentially Liberal rhetoric of principled opposition to all extension of state power. This very un-Toryish style sat easily on Churchill, an historic Liberal. He even offered Clement Davies, the Liberal leader, the Ministry of Education, to confirm the merging of two conservative streams, and was disappointed when Davies reluctantly refused.[3]

The Lords were more likely to make trouble for a Conservative administration, in terms of day-to-day revision of legislation, than for a Labour one, which could turn nasty on them, but the 1948 Parliament Act had reduced the upper chamber to a purely technical and advisory role. Churchill had publicly denounced what he saw as the totalitarian tendencies of

[1] Geoffrey Hodgson 'The Steel Debates' in *Age of Austerity*, eds. Michael Sissons and Philip French (Oxford University Press, Oxford pbk edn, Oxford 1986), pp. 285–304.

[2] The Rt. Hon. Anthony Eden, PC, MP *Days for Decision* (Faber and Faber, London 1949), pp. 99.

[3] Douglas *History of the Liberal Party*, pp. 263–6.

the Government's annexation of private members' time in the Commons He had thundered against iron and steel nationalization as a grab for power and patronage. Yet his relations with his own party were an illustration of his lifelong conviction that he was born to rule others. The office of Leader of the Opposition had been recognized and salaried in 1937, mainly, it must be presumed, to obscure the fact that the political realities of the day virtually eliminated any meaningful opposition to Government. In theory, as Leader of His Majesty's Opposition between 1945 and 1951, Churchill was expected to have a Shadow Cabinet of senior colleagues, with which he was supposed to consult regularly. In practice, the Tory Shadow Cabinet in this era was purely nominal. Churchill hardly bothered with it. He disliked several senior members of it, and knew full well that the Conservative Party, however much it muttered behind his back, was stuck with him. Once he sensed Labour was on the ropes, he provided intermittent but vigorous and rhetorically brilliant leadership in the Commons. He allowed younger men to try to update the ideas and organization of the Conservative Party. Two men made outstanding contributions. One was Lord Woolton, the businessman who had been Minister of Reconstruction 1943–45, and briefly Lord President. His formal joining of the Conservative Party after the 1945 election, though good dramatic stuff, was no Pauline conversion. Conservative he had always been, and vain enough to at least toy with the idea of being Churchill's successor before he actually joined Churchill's current party. The other, no admirer of Woolton and never much liked by Churchill, was Rab Butler, who revived Neville Chamberlain's brain-child, the Conservative Research Department.

Moribund in 1945, that body, along with the Tory Parliamentary Secretariat, gave a whole group of bright modern Conservatives their launch into active politics. Selection procedures were reformed to stop the worst abuses whereby candidates virtually bought seats in an auction for the benefit of constituency funds. In documents like the *Industrial Charter*, Butler and allies such as Harold Macmillan committed their party to full employment and a mixed economy with a significant public sector. Churchill went along, vaguely, with this, though Butler's impish tale to the effect that he did not really read the charter, and disagreed loudly with quotations from it when he happened upon them, rings true.[1] Churchill did approve of the policies of the last Labour Chancellor of the Exchequer, sending him in the early stages of the new regime a message of appreciation warm enough to have confirmed the views of Hugh Gaitskell's Labour critics, had they known of it. The message was so enthusiastic that Gaitskell wondered whether it was not the prelude to an attempt to form some sort of coalition.

The very structure of Churchill's new Government underlined the highly personal nature of his rule, not to mention the decidedly strained relations between the Premier and leading members of the Conservative Party, many of whom had been on very intermittent dining terms with him, and no more. The Government was a pastiche of Churchillian cronies and

[1] Anthony Howard *Rab: The Life of R. A. Butler* (Macmillan, London 1987), Ch. 11, 'Remaking the Tory Party'.

relatives, plus regular party professionals. As Hugh Gaitskell privately noted:

> Winston, of course, did exactly what one would expect and appointed his old friends and his family to many of the key jobs. In fact, one could say that the Government is broadly divided between them and the straightforward Tory Party candidates.

Gaitskell, like everyone else, was also struck by Churchill's ultimately unsuccessful experiment with coordinating 'overlords' whom he wanted to take responsibility for groups of departments.[1] As these jobs went to his old pals such as Lord Woolton, as Lord President; to Lord Leathers, as Secretary for the Coordination of Transport, Fuel and Power; and to Lord Cherwell, as Paymaster General, there was a built-in likelihood of conflict with the orthodox party ministers. Some of the latter, like Rab Butler, who became Chancellor of the Exchequer, had an unrepentantly Chamberlainite past. In the event, the overlord plan proved a fiasco and had to be wound up within a couple of years.

The Conservative Party had done so much to build up Churchill's image that it was in a very real sense the prisoner of its own public protestations. It was to discover after 1951 that there are snags in being led by a god, even if the latter Churchill was often a deity out of Offenbach rather than Wagner. Rab Butler was no economist. He may have been given the Treasury partly because Oliver Lyttleton, the Tory widely expected to be Chancellor, was regarded by the City of London as having been more of a financial adventurer than a sound businessman in former days. However, Churchill assured Butler that 'I am going to appoint the best economist since Jesus Christ to help you.' This turned out to be the elderly and pedantic former civil servant, academic and university MP, Arthur Salter. University seats having been abolished, Churchill had to wish Salter on the Ormskirk Conservative Association, whose MP was leaving the UK to go to Australia. The bemused Ormskirk Association had never head of Salter, but the Premier, sitting in bed 'in a gaudy bed-jacket' wafted Salter back into the Commons with waves of his cigar. The old rascal knew he could get away with it. Salter has been depicted as comically inept, despite being given the grandiloquent title of Minister of State for Economic Affairs. Promoted out to another non-job as Minister of Materials, he was finally pensioned off with a peerage.[2] It was all vintage late Churchilliana, but Salter was in fact briefly quite important.

Churchill claimed that he had gained 'not a crown of glory but a crown of thorns'.[3] The explanation for this maudlin and messianic view was part political, part economic. Though a revitalized and reorganized Conservative Party had fought well in 1951, it had won by an overall majority of a mere 17, and that by courtesy of the vagaries of the electoral system. With 13,717,538 votes and 48.6 per cent of the vote, it had received less support

---

[1] Entry for Friday 23 November 1951, in *The Diary of Hugh Gaitskell 1945–1956*, ed. Philip M. Williams (Jonathan Cape, London 1983), pp. 305–6.

[2] Howard *Rab*, p. 181.

[3] This phrase is recorded in Salter's unintentionally farcical account of Churchill's decision to restore him to the Commons and office in Arthur Salter *Slave of the Lamp: A Public Servant's Notebook* (Weidenfeld and Nicolson, London 1967), pp. 251–2.

than Labour, which had 13,948,605 votes and 49.2 per cent of the vote. There was nothing inevitable about Labour's defeat. Indeed, had Attlee displayed any serious electoral flair, or just imposed a modicum of realism on the very extreme 'moderates' who were pushing the Government as well as the economy into instability with physically impossible demands, there would have been no Conservative victory in 1951, and a 76-year-old Churchill would have come under irresistible pressure to retire. He had already had a stroke at Monte Carlo in August 1949, between writing the second and third volumes of *The Second World War*. After the completion of the third, he had a disturbance of the cerebral circulation in February 1950. The fourth and fifth volumes were completed before he resumed office, but the sixth and final one, which came out in September 1953 was preceded by serious strokes in July 1952 and June 1953. He had been miserable out of power. He was immensely glad to be back in office, despite the fact that his memory was failing and his old workaholism was impossible. That he survived as Prime Minister until April 1955 was a tribute to the power of the office, and to the heroic tenacity of the will which Churchill grimly pitted against the wishes of the professional leaders of the Tory Party.[1]

The economic situation in 1951–2 at first seemed bleak in the extreme, and many Labour politicians assumed that it might enable Labour to rebound into power on the back of Conservative failure within a couple of years at most. The outbreak of the Korean War had created a brief global boom, based on buoyant demand for strategic raw materials and strong American domestic demand. When it burst, many countries, including the UK, found their export earnings contracting while their overseas purchases and expenditures remained at the levels reached in the boom period. The UK was reducing its own productive investment and starving its engineering export sector of raw material as well as capital by persisting in a massive rearmament programme absorbing 11 per cent of gross national product. Its textile industries were in a slump. As well as bearing its own monetary burdens, the UK was the core of the vast and amorphous sterling area, membership of which had only been formally defined as late as 1940, but which by 1952 included not only all Commonwealth countries except Canada, but also the Irish Republic, Burma, Iraq, Jordan, Libya and Iceland. It was a system with fixed or relatively stable rates between the currencies in it, and a central reserve to which participants contributed gold and dollar surpluses, and from which they drew dollar supplies. The advantage to a UK chronically short of dollars of being able to draw on the large dollar surpluses earned by, say, the tin, rubber, and gold of Malaya was significant, but so were the stresses engendered by sterling's role as a reserve currency, and the UK's as banker of last resort. As it happened, many Commonwealth countries developed a severe balance of payments problem as the Korean war boom broke, and the gold and dollar reserves of the UK were draining away so fast in the early months of Churchill's new administration that a repetition of the devaluation crisis of 1949 seemed possible. Exports from the UK had risen by at least 50 per cent from pre-

[1] Lord Moran *Winston Churchill: The Struggle for Survival 1940–1965* (Constable, London 1966), pp. 786–7.

war. Imports had been held below pre-war figures. Yet changes in the terms of trade made imports more expensive, and a vast increase in Government expenditure overseas was crippling. But for the latter factor, there would have been a surplus in every year except 1947.[1]

The situation was so alarming at one point that the Treasury seriously pushed for a convertible and floating pound whose level would be market-determined. Neither Butler nor the bulk of the Cabinet appear to have understood the full implications of this scheme, code-named 'Robot'. It would have raised considerable difficulties with the Organisation for European Economic Cooperation, and the European Payments Union, both of which the UK had joined partly because of heavy American pressure so to do. The Commonwealth and the sterling area would both have been shaken. Bank rate and unemployment rates would have had to have been much more flexible. Intriguingly, it appears to have been two men in the Government purely as Churchill cronies, Lord Cherwell (the scientist F. A. Lindemann) and the elderly Salter, who alone grasped the potentially traumatic implications. They were not all necessarily bad. They might have involved a simultaneous loosening of American, European, sterling and Commonwealth shackles but the risks, once exposed, were too much for Churchill and the Cabinet. Nor were they necessary. Physical controls on imports, Commonwealth cooperation to cut dollar imports, and a spectacular swing in favour of the UK in the terms of trade, had by 1952 carried the Government through to an extremely favourable conjuncture in the shape of a strong boom and declining inflationary pressures. Necessarily secret at the time, 'Robot' remained secret until Cherwell's biographer breached yet another wall of silence in 1961.[2]

Thereafter, the Government could appease its own followers with some tax cuts, and the de-nationalization of iron and steel and most road transport. As temporary Minister of Defence, Churchill performed a great public service by insisting on cuts in a defence programme which he rightly regarded as utterly unrealistic. More use was made of bank rate, and most direct controls were removed by 1954, but the bulk of state economic activity and expenditure was left untouched, food subsidies apart. From 40 per cent, the Government's spending fell to 36 per cent of gross national product by 1958, and most of that was due to the fall in defence expenditure from 11 per cent in 1952 to 7.5 per cent by 1958.[3] Full employment was maintained. Walter Monckton was sent to the Ministry of Labour by Churchill with orders to avoid the massive industrial unrest forecast by Labour. Churchill was, in retrospect, blamed for 'buying off the unions', but this is an oversimplification. Attlee and Cripps had enforced draconian discipline in some ways. Troops had been used quite routinely not just to maintain essential supplies, but also to 'smash' strikes (to use a Gaitskell term). Eleven significant interventions by troops between 1945 and 1951 was unprecedented. Increasingly, Labour ministers saw 'Reds' behind awkward strikes, whether they were there or not. When Churchill spoke

[1] A. R. Conan *The Sterling Area* (Macmillan, London 1952), p. 7.
[2] The Earl of Birkenhead *The Prof. in Two Worlds* (Collins, London 1961), pp. 284–94.
[3] C. J. Bartlett *A History of Postwar Britain 1945–74* (Longman, pbk edn, London 1977), pp. 98–9.

of 'setting the people free', he romanticized, but not without having a point. People did need a break from a Cold War mobilization which was leaving common sense behind.[1] 1950 had been a year remarkably free of strikes. They did not become a real problem until 1955, the year in which Churchill finally left office in the spring.

If Attlee had, characteristically, told Francis Williams his Adviser on Public Relations, that he was allergic to the press (which admittedly was mainly poisonously hostile to him), Churchill could by 1951 usually count on adulation at the level of a royal. Oddly enough, the situation had a sobering effect on him. The old unbalanced hyperactive search for means of self-assertion had become an irrelevance. He was. That was enough, provided he was in power. He could not do a great deal of detailed administration, so his ministers were left to do their departmental work without undue interference, provided that work was primarily domestic. Of the 16 Cabinet ministers he appointed in October 1951, 11 were still in office three years later.[2] It was a very stable regime by normal standards. The principle of non-interference did not extend to foreign affairs. Any premier could exercise the prerogative of taking an active interest in any area which particularly interested him. Eden, being at the Foreign Office, was inevitably affected and not infrequently irritated by Churchillian sallies in his field, all the more galling as Eden was also the heir-apparent, with a vested interest in the old man's early retiral. He found it difficult to live with Churchill's publicly-declared enthusiasm for a three-power summit meeting between the leaders of the USA, Russia, and the UK, an enthusiasm which became even stronger after the death of Stalin in March 1953. Unscripted personal diplomacy between individual political leaders offended Eden's sense of the need for caution, preparation and diplomatic propriety. He was also deeply offended by Churchill's habit of breezily taking significant initiatives when Acting Foreign Secretary, a post he filled with gusto when Eden was incapacitated by factors ranging from illness to the honeymoon after his very happy second marriage. Eden was a fine technical diplomat, a skilled negotiator who had a particularly successful run at international conferences in 1954, when he facilitated an agreement between Italy and Yugoslavia over Trieste; played a key role in the Geneva conference which finally extracted France from her long colonial war in Vietnam; and skilfully negotiated agreements which allowed the rearmament within the Western alliance of the West German state formed out of the French, British and American occupation zones. By 1955, West Germany had been admitted as a member of the North Atlantic Treaty Organization.

Like West Germany, under the conservative rule of Chancellor Adenauer and his Christian Democratic Union, the UK was a 'penetrated' political system, in the sense that from 1941 forces outside the domestic political system had participated significantly in the taking of decisions which vitally affected the allocation of internal UK resources and priorities, and

[1] Justin D. Smith *The Attlee and Churchill Administrations and Industrial Unrest 1945–55* (Pinter, London 1990).
[2] Martin Gilbert *'Never Despair': Winston S. Churchill 1945–65* (Heinemann, London 1988), p. 1041.

in the attempts to mobilize opinion to support these decisions.[1] Unlike West Germany, the effects of this penetration were neither helpful in sustaining the economic recovery of the UK after the, in many ways remarkable, surge in production and exports between 1945 and 1951, nor did they indicate political objectives which were desired by the bulk of the UK political leadership, let alone by the peoples they ruled.

There was general agreement in both the bureaucracy and the Cabinet that the UK simply could not continue to sustain its existing scale of commitments. Not only did it lack the economic strength to do so, but the commitments were visibly undermining an economy already feeling competitive pressure from resurgent Japanese and West German economies, neither of which had hitherto had to carry any significant military burden. The UK was acquiring new politico-military burdens without sloughing off old ones, despite the fact that the new and the old were often logical alternatives. A classic example was the UK atomic weapons programme which Attlee had pushed forward steadily if secretly, hiding the true cost by devious accountancy which Churchill admired and continued when he came to power again. The prime function of the programme was political, and Churchill tried very hard to secure a degree of joint development and control of atomic weapons from President Harry S. Truman. However, with anti-Communist hysteria being whipped up in America by the likes of Senator McCarthy, and with Truman's Secretary of State Dean Rusk being denounced as the 'Red' Dean, the chances of such concessions were slim. The first British atomic bomb was exploded in Australia in October 1952. By 1957, the UK had exploded a hydrogen bomb, the even more lethal weapon which the Americans had tested in 1952, the Russians in 1953. This programme was, by UK standards, expensive as was the remarkable, and elegantly innovative V-bomber family of heavy jet bombers (the Valiant, Vulcan and Victor) designed as the delivery system.

When Harold Macmillan became Minister of Defence in 1954, he discovered that his new ministry was like the Foreign Office: it was one of the two departments with which Churchill habitually interfered. One result was a high level of articulation of problems, even if the insights were seldom followed up. Macmillan said at one point how impossible it was to prepare for both nuclear deterrence and a full-scale conventional European war. The logic of developing the H-bomb was to take a calculated gamble on its ability to deter rival powers, such as the USA and the Soviet Union, from taking the plunge into all-out war. Macmillan even pointed out the economic undesirability of having in 1954 800,000 men serving in the armed services, 300,000 of them conscripts, and all of this backed up by a reserve force of 600,000. Experience was to show soon just how unwieldy this vastly expensive establishment was.[2] Churchill himself could see that if it had been convenient to use the early stages of the Cold War to manipulate the US into joining the UK in its global confrontation with the Soviets, there was, by 1953, no British interest to be served by a further escalation in Russian-American conflict. He acted vigorously to encourage moder-

---

[1] Wolfram F. Hanrieder *West German Foreign Policy 1949–1963: International Pressure and Domestic Response* (Stanford University Press, Stanford 1967), pp. 228–33.
[2] Alistair Horne *Macmillan 1894–1956* (Macmillan, London 1988), p. 345.

ation in the two-year negotiation which finally brought the Korean War to a close, though only after a Chinese intervention which raised American anti-Communist zeal to fresh heights. The anti-Communist crusading zeal of his old friend General Dwight D. Eisenhower, who became President of the USA in 1953, and of his Secretary of State John Foster Dulles, spurred Churchill on in his vain search for a tension-easing summit meeting. There was, however, no mechanism to turn insights into informed debate and rational choice based on a broad view. Churchill's idea of Cabinet discussion tended to consist of long rambling monologues, interesting, but egotistical.

The Cabinet, as its members privately acknowledged, was quite incapable of an overview.[1] The regime was one of departmental administration under an aged, irascible monarch, and an increasingly frustrated crown prince. Cabinet contained some disgruntled courtiers, endlessly muttering and plotting, but never quite working up the nerve needed for a coup. They were very lucky that, once the economic situation improved, they were under no domestic political pressure. The Labour Party was torn by internal conflict which had been building up since 1947 but which polarized into a succession struggle between the candidate of the right, Hugh Gaitskell, and that of the left, Aneurin Bevan. Gaitskell behaved quite as badly as Bevan in terms of destructive vituperation against opponents he would have to live with, which gave Attlee an excellent reason for remaining leader. He was long past any constructive leadership, but he was a safe pair of hands, and on grounds of personal dislike, he was happy to keep Herbert Morrison out of the leadership until he was too old for it. Oddly enough, Labour had a poor housing record between 1945 and 1951, partly because Bevan had been responsible for both health and housing, and had had too little energy to spare for the latter. On 25 August 1953, Churchill ruminated that, 'The political situation is satisfactory. Labour is divided and uncertain of its theme. We are building three hundred thousand houses . . .'[2] It was by being responsible for meeting, and eventually surpassing that target that Harold Macmillan, as Minister of Housing, finally climbed into a position of great influence and stature within the Tory Party. He also became, in Churchill's eyes, the leader of his Praetorian Guard, shielding the old Premier against a world full of resentful colleagues, and rare but wounding press critics. Malcolm Muggeridge, editor of *Punch*, and a man whose flair for self-advertisement almost equalled Churchill's, was the most resented of these, because of his relentless harping on the decay of his victim's faculties.[3]

There was no serious criticism of the structure of power. Above all, there was no suggestion that public opinion should be allowed any serious role in policy debates. Sir Evelyn Shuckburgh, Eden's private secretary, was appalled by the way the US Congress was allowed to scrutinize and cross-question the executive branch of American government, and when told by

---

[1] This was the opinion of Kenneth Younger, the Minister of Labour, cited in *The Foreign Policy of Churchill's Peacetime Administration 1951–1955*, ed. John W. Young (Leicester University Press, Leicester 1988), Introduction, p. 21.

[2] Entry for 25 August 1953 in Moran *Churchill*, p. 461.

[3] Entry for 4 February 1954, in *ibid.*, p. 523.

an American that foreign policy must in future be subjected to 'continuous scrutiny by the masses', he angrily insisted that democracy could not survive 'if *issues*, as opposed to personalities, were to be put before the public'.[1] That was not just a Tory point of view. The Labour leadership was equally determined to screen the central processes of policy debate from the vulgar herd, and the group of younger, middle-class Oxford University educated ministers who had begun to make their mark in the later stages of the Attlee administration were perhaps the most arrogantly élitist of all in this respect. Hugh Gaitskell, for example, in a paper he seems to have written in late June of July 1952, complained that the American constitution 'creates trouble'. He went on to remark with satisfaction that 'English people' were used to being governed 'by an executive which in turn controls the legislature', and he concluded that: 'It is no exaggeration to say that if Anglo-American relations in these last few years had been left to the two governments alone, things would have gone much more smoothly.'[2]

Given the pervasiveness of such attitudes in the higher echelons of the executive and bureaucracy, what was remarkable about the second Churchill Government was the extent to which it was careful not to offend the susceptibilities of those it governed. There was no attempt to use the anti-Communist rhetoric of the Cold War, however useful it had been to some Conservatives in opposition, to cover a sharp lurch to the right in domestic politics, though of course there was a real if limited movement in that direction. The tight electoral balance here undoubtedly affected Churchill and his colleagues. Equally, they shunned any radical departures in the foreign policy which they had inherited. In so far as they modified it, it was in the eminently sensible direction of trying to decrease the over-commitment characteristic of the policies of the Labour right, which had largely crafted that policy. Australia and New Zealand had naturally turned to the USA as the only power capable of protecting them after the débacle of the fall of Singapore. In 1951, they signed a defence pact with the US (known by its acronym as the ANZUS pact), which Labour accepted with equanimity. Churchill could not conceal some emotional anguish at the exclusion of the UK from it. He was, after all, very upset when he heard that Royal Canadian Navy bands had ceased to play 'Rule, Britannia', and wept openly when the massed bands of the three Canadian services played it just once again, for him in Ottawa in 1954.[3] However, corporately, his Government after 1951 was very willing to accept the realities of the ANZUS pact. Eden's whole foreign policy was based on a judicious attempt to reduce overseas commitments to the point where they corresponded with a more realistic view of UK power.

On much of this the old Premier did drag his feet, but he was not dictatorial. Eden had to threaten to resign to have his way about the Anglo-Egyptian dispute over control of the Sudan. Eden's solution, which ultimately proved acceptable to General Gamal Nasser, the Egyptian military

---

[1] Cited in *Foreign Policy of Churchill's Peacetime Administration*, ed. Young, p. 25.
[2] *Diary of Hugh Gaitskell*, pp. 316–20.
[3] David Dilks *Three Visitors to Canada: Stanley Baldwin, Neville Chamberlain and Winston Churchill* (Canada House Lecture Series Number 28, London 1985), p. 27.

dictator, was to move the Sudan towards independence both of the UK and of Egypt. After 1953, Churchill was extremely unhappy about proposals to evacuate the large British military base in the Suez Canal Zone. His unhappiness was shared by a group of 30–40 'Suez Rebels' from the ranks of Conservative MPs. Their 1953–4 backbench revolt achieved nothing, of course, because Labour tacitly supported the Government by abstaining on votes on the issue. Nevertheless, the Prime Minister went along with the views of the bulk of his senior colleagues and advisers, and spoke the word 'obsolete' of a base he in his heart wanted to retain. With the support of Oliver Lyttelton, who eventually made it into the Cabinet as Colonial Secretary, Churchill did successfully wage colonial wars in Malaya and Kenya. He revitalized the war effort against Chinese Communist guerrillas in Malaya, and his Government broke the back of the Mau Mau rising amongst the Kikuyu tribe in Kenya. These were winnable wars. The British Army was at last showing a sharply upward learning curve on counter-insurgency techniques, and the rebellions were both rooted in only a minority of the populations involved.[1] Lyttleton was as flexible as he was energetic, and there was never any question of perpetuating direct imperial rule. The aim was to install a cooperative, independent post-war regime. Delusions of grandeur were few. Nobody, not even the Premier, had any desire to become re-involved in the Vietnamese mess, despite the fact that in 1945 it had been British Indian troops under General Douglas D. Gracey which had suppressed a widely-supported Vietnamese nationalist regime and allowed the French the opportunity to re-establish their colonial power.[2] During the Geneva negotiations, Eden agreed with his Russian opposite number, Molotov, that they must act together to moderate the attitudes of their Chinese and American allies, in order to avoid a direct Sino-US clash. Eden had no desire to yield to American pressure to break off these negotiations.[3]

Charges by enthusiasts for a united Europe, like Bob Boothby, that the Government was 'anti-European' and that Churchill in particular had 'betrayed Europe' by refusing to join in an attempt to create a federal European state were unreasonable. Churchill had delivered a few resounding but extremely vague speeches on the theme of a United Europe when out of office. He had always hoped rapidly to reintegrate Germany into the family of western nations, and he quite rightly regarded NATO and the Marshall Plan as forms of European unity. He was perfectly happy for the UK to be represented on purely consultative bodies, but clearly never envisaged it being part of an exclusively European political body. When Randolph Churchill was editing his father's speeches, he gave a volume published in 1950 the title *Europe Unite*. Very little of the contents, which are 52 Churchill speeches of the period 1947–8, have anything to so with

[1] General Sir William Jackson *Withdrawal from Empire: A Military View* (Batsford, London 1986) is an excellent analytical overview.
[2] George Rosie *The British in Vietnam: How the Twenty-Five Year War Began* (Panther Books pbk, London 1970).
[3] Melvin Gurtov *The First Vietnam Crisis: Chinese Communist Strategy and United States Involvement*, 1953–54 (Columbia University Press, pbk edn, New York 1968), p. 153.

Europe. It was a silly title.[1] Randolph himself made it clear in his preface that Europe was in his mind, as in his father's, only one of three props— the others were the Anglo-American Alliance and the Commonwealth— to continued British international stature. Boothby was a conceited man with a grudge against Churchill whom he blamed for his own wartime sacking from office. Like Harold Macmillan in the immediate post-war years, he had found the consultative assembly of the Council of Europe, which met regularly in Strasbourg from 1949 'a deeply satisfying oasis in an otherwise forlorn political desert.'[2] When, however, the Scottish fishing industry's interests (which were a crucial factor in Boothby's grip on his East Aberdeenshire seat) came up, brilliant cosmopolitan Bob turned instantly, as his distinguished biographer pointed out, into a total protectionist.[3]

Eden was also to be denounced in retrospect as 'anti-European' because he did not wish to see the UK permanently locked into an exclusive economic or political union with western Europe. Like Churchill, however, he accepted very close ties with the Continent within various frameworks. Both men could have said what Eden was to say of himself: '. . . I have never thought that my country need have any apprehension on account of a closer union between the nations of continental Europe.'[4] When the proposed European Defence Community, which was to enable a rearmed West Germany to contribute to a European Army rather than have its own army, collapsed due to French suspicions, it was Eden who preserved unity in western Europe. He extended the existing Brussels Pact of 1948 which linked the UK, France and the Benelux countries into one, including Italy and West Germany as well. Renamed Western European Union, this alliance enabled a West German army to become a component of the NATO order of battle. Eden himself envisaged it as far more than merely a military pact, and was disappointed when WEU failed to develop.

There was little support within the Government for any alternative to these constructive and cautious policies. The Board of Trade was virtually the only bureaucratic stronghold in favour of systematic economic integration with western Europe. Amongst the other ministries, the Foreign Office, later fanatically 'pro-European', was no such thing in the 1950s. The Treasury was much influenced by the Foreign Office, and Agriculture was downright hostile to proposals for joining a European bloc. In the Cabinet, only two figures wanted commitment to European integration: the predictable Harold Macmillan and Sir David Maxwell Fyfe, the Home Secretary. Macmillan, whose political instability had been notorious, but who always pulled back on the brink of disaster, considered resignation as a protest against the Government's European policy. Even he had to admit in retrospect that in the early 1950s there was 'no enthusiasm in the country whatever for Europe.'[5] Churchill had (quite reasonable) reser-

---

[1] *Europe Unite: Speeches 1947 and 1948 by Winston S. Churchill*, ed. Randolph S. Churchill (Cassell, London 1950).

[2] Alistair Horne *Macmillan 1894–1956* (Macmillan, London 1988), p. 314.

[3] Robert R. James *Bob Boothby: A Portrait* (Hodder and Stoughton, London 1991).

[4] *The Memoirs of the Rt. Hon. Sir Anthony Eden: Full Circle* (Cassell, London 1960), p. 32.

[5] Horne *Macmillan 1894–1956*, p. 351.

vations about the scale of military commitment which Eden made, virtually in perpetuity, in Europe to secure French support for WEU: four divisions and a tactical airforce. However, Eden was adamant, and with no senior colleague in support, Churchill gave way.

For all his physical incapacities, his was, as Anthony Seldon in particular has argued, not a undistinguished reign between 1951 and 1955.[1] He read less and less of the official papers, proving that this was not a fatal handicap. Far more important was his benign sway over a group of able co-workers. Quite a few, like Oliver Lyttleton, did not mean to stay in politics. Some, like Churchill's crony and favourite, James Stuart, who made a canny but effective Secretary of State for Scotland, had no further political ambitions. Sanity kept breaking through into this strange team led by an old man given to haranguing colleagues from bed, with a cigar in his hand and, on occasions, his pet budgerigar perched on his head. Neither in domestic nor in foreign policy did the Government use its undoubted power to force through measures unacceptable to a broad spectrum of UK public opinion. The MPs in the Commons were tightly controlled by the Conservative and Labour whips to the point where the most meaningful drama being staged there occurred during question time after the Premier's strokes, when Churchill put on bravura performances of wit and impudence, aimed in reality at those in the Conservative leadership anxious to drop him on grounds of senility. The odd principled backbench revolt, like that of the Suez Group, could be rendered innocuous by implicit collusion between the rival front benches. MPs were not allowed to interfere much with the activities of the amorphous policy-making élite of domestic and foreign lobbyists, ministers, and bureaucrats. Churchill himself intervened only very selectively, but he imposed on the whole regime the discipline he accepted, often grumpily, himself: never to try to override a clear consensus. Such humility did not come naturally to a Westminster Government.

His successor, who finally entered his political promised land in April 1955, was already a sick man, due to the failure of a major operation, and the strains of the extensive corrective surgery which followed. Eden came from an emotionally unstable family. He had always been highly strung, and though no vainer than the average professional politician, he was by normal human standards vain. Much more serious a handicap was his lack of any experience whatever of major domestic office. All his long career had been devoted to diplomacy and foreign affairs. As a result, he could be engagingly naïve compared with Churchill, who knew all the dirty tricks of domestic politics and was never, as Macmillan remarked, over-burdened with scruples. Eden was genuinely shocked to find that throughout Churchill's second Government, a small group of ministers had met regularly to discuss which secret pieces of information should be leaked, and to which newspapers and reporters they should be leaked. The Lobby system of unascribable briefing of selected reporters by Government representa-

---

[1] Anthony Seldon *Churchill's Indian Summer: The Conservative Government, 1951–55* (Hodder and Stoughton, London 1981) is not only a major work of history, but one of the few studies of recent British history which, by use of oral history amongst other devices, brings out the role of members of the Civil Service in political decision-taking.

tives had already been grossly abused in Chamberlain's day, but the systematic use of leaks was doubly odious, for the Government had no hesitation in using the tyrannical powers of the Official Secrets Act to preserve, in so far as it could, its monopoly of leaks. Curiously enough, the rage of certain journalists at the drying up of easily-obtained and privileged information after the accession of Eden was one of the factors which gave him, for a Tory Premier, a surprisingly poor press. The wrath of some influential people in the newspaper world hurt him more. Randolph Churchill, who loathed him, systematically attacked him in his column in the leading London evening newspaper, the *Evening Standard*, and Malcolm Muggeridge savaged him in *Punch*. Lady Berry, the wife of the proprietor of the *Daily Telegraph* turned very much against Eden, and it showed in the columns of the paper.[1] Some of this was personal spite. Some of it ran deeper. Particularly after he had secured a larger majority, there was considerable feeling at grassroots level amongst those who ran and funded the Conservative Party that the Government was dragging its feet over the need to curb trade union power. That feeling reached the offices of the press barons, who themselves sympathized with it. They were, after all, great experts on the abuse of privileged positions.

In the general election which he decided to hold shortly after he became Premier, Eden performed very well. The decision to hold an election on 26 May, just over seven weeks after his accession was, on the surface, a brave one. He proved a polished, well-briefed platform speaker; made good if limited use of the new medium of television (but then only limited use was available); and looked the happy and handsome man he was, in large measure because of his very successful recent second marriage to Clarissa Churchill, Winston's niece. Beneath the surface glitter, however, all was not well. The reason why a Premier who assumed office on 6 April chose to fight an election by 26 May was that he was receiving strong advice from his main economic adviser, from his Chancellor Rab Butler and from an imposing phalanx of Treasury knights that there was everything to be said for holding a quick election before the deteriorating economic situation compounded of a balance of payments problem and speculation against an increasingly convertible pound sterling plunged the Government into an exchange rate crisis. Given the Premier's arbitrary power of dissolution, it was therefore inevitable that Eden would opt for the earliest date compatible with dignity. Unfortunately, there was time for a budget between April and May, and Eden achieved the dubious distinction of being the first Premier to sponsor a budget designed to manipulate the economy in the short term in such a way as to encourage support for the Government at a forthcoming election. Butler was encouraged to put money into taxpayers' pockets by slashing income tax by 6d in the pound whilst removing purchase tax from all cotton goods as part of a 1955 inflationary package of £135 million (£155 million over twelve months). It was a cynical performance in the middle of a boom, with the reserves under pressure, and price and wage inflation escalating. One of the few excuses available to Eden and Butler in retrospect is that the Treasury advised them that they could safely do this, relying on firm monetarist

[1] Robert R. James *Anthony Eden* (Macmillan, Papermac edn, London 1986), p. 412.

measures, such as hire purchase restrictions, tighter bank lending policies, and higher interest rates.[1]

Real wages were rising faster than prices. Eden systematically built up hopes of sustained economic expansion during the electoral campaign. Labour was split not only by personal rivalries but also by emotive issues such as the desirability of the UK nuclear weapons programme. When challenged about his electioneering budget, Eden blandly denied that electoral considerations had ever crossed his mind. He was lying, though in all fairness it has to be said that it was only a question of time before some premier linked the power of dissolution to the power to manipulate short-term popular perceptions of material well-being. In practice, Conservative administrations were always able to tell themselves they were only doing what was needed to avert a collapse of business confidence at the prospect of 'socialist' government. This enabled them to behave with cheerful recklessness, whereas right-wing Labour leaderships in office tended to take masochistic pleasure in following paths of responsible rectitude calculated to lead to electoral disaster. The first electioneering budget worked. Buoyed by a gain of 783 seats from Labour in English borough elections on 12 May, the Conservatives increased their overall share of the vote on 26 May to 49.7 per cent against Labour's 46.4 per cent and increased their overall majority in the Commons to a more comfortable 59.

The inevitable, and oft-to-be-repeated corollary of the electioneering budget was an economic crisis manifesting itself in a dramatically worsening balance of payments deficit. In June, the deficit was £124 million, making a total deficit over six months of £456 million. Pressure on the currency mounted for two reasons. One was that foreigners saw no point in holding a threatened currency when they could sell it at a fixed parity. The other was that there was a great deal of loose talk in the highest official circles of moving not just to full convertibility, but also to a floating pound whose value would be market-determined. The Treasury, Bank of England and City were passionately in favour of convertibility which would encourage the use of the pound sterling as an international currency, and thereby enhance the scope and profitability of the City's financial operations. The trouble was that without a market-responsive currency, this policy was liable to involve the subordination of all other aspects of the economy, including investment and wage discipline, to the needs of the City. Foreign Secretary Macmillan archly dropped hints on the international circuit about imminent floating of the pound. It never came. Instead, Butler simply recovered, mainly in regressive indirect taxation in an October budget, what he had given away by cutting direct taxation in his April budget. He also, in a pattern to be repeated again and again, held down the capital investment programmes of the Government's two great captive sectors: local government and the nationalized industries. Allied to a firm statement that the existing $2.80 parity of the pound would be defended, this package stabilized the situation, but of course at the price of a slump in

---

[1] Richard Lamb *The Failure of the Eden Government* (Sidgwick and Jackson, London 1987), pp. 5–9.

Government support in polls and by-elections.[1] The public clearly thought it had been the victim of a confidence trick. It had.

Eden was a nervous, interfering prime minister, much given to pestering his ministers with phone calls. A resentful Churchill had said just before retiring that he doubted if Eden had the stomach for the premiership, and that as premier he would have to watch the antics of Macmillan, Butler's rival for the succession and a man of consuming ambition. Having clearly spotted Eden's underlying insecurity, Macmillan had started to bully him outrageously. In December 1955, he refused to move to the Treasury unless Eden promised not to give Butler, who became Leader of the Commons, the title of Deputy Premier. It was an impudent performance which a wise premier would have slapped down firmly. Macmillan later backed down from threats of resignation as Chancellor when he sensed that Eden was prepared to let him go. In December 1955, however, Macmillan had his way.

Nor was Macmillan the only politician crowding Eden. Western European supra-nationalism had by no means been destroyed by the collapse of the European Defence Community. The European Coal and Steel Community (ECSC), established in 1951 by the Schuman Plan proposed by the then French Foreign Secretary Robert Schuman, pooling the resources of France, Germany, Italy and the three Benelux countries, had proved successful. In 1955, those six countries met again at Messina to begin a process of discussion and legislation which by 1958 had created the European Common Market, which aimed at abolishing internal tariffs in favour of a common external one. In the same year, a Euratom Commission began to function. The UK was not a signatory of the 1957 Treaty of Rome which brought these developments into the realm of practical politics, nor had it ever been likely that it would be. Though trade with Europe was increasing at a time when trade with primary-producing countries was stagnant, the UK still did only about a third of its trading with Europe. It was argued retrospectively that UK participation might have allowed certain features of the Common Market to be modified at inception to suit British interests. The fact is that some of those which least suited those interests, then and later, like a common external tariff on food imports, were never negotiable. Eden was even clearer than Churchill in his opposition to sinking UK identity into a supranational structure. The whole point to his foreign policy since 1951 had been, by judicious reduction of overcommitment, to recover flexibility and room for manoeuvre. This did not really suit the American book.

Since 1953, Dwight D. Eisenhower had been the strikingly popular President of the USA. During his two-term incumbency between 1953 and 1961, he was to average 64 per cent on the monthly Gallup poll approval ratings. His Secretary of State, John Foster Dulles, looked to be in charge of foreign policy to an unprecedented degree. The reality was that he was an implementor of presidential policies. Eisenhower's was a 'hidden-hand' presidency, preserving popularity by deft obscuring of responsibility.[2]

---

[1] *Ibid.*, pp. 40–53.

[2] Fred. I. Greenstein *The Hidden Hand Presidency: Eisenhower as Leader* (Basic Books, New York 1982).

However, both Eisenhower and Dulles put personal pressure on Eden to take the UK into the Common Market, because they were at one on the subject. Dulles had been preaching European federation at Eden since 1942. By 1955, Dulles' contempt for the UK as an international factor was total. Both he and Eisenhower could, however, see it as a useful tool of American policy, inside the Common Market.[1]

Eden was therefore harassed from several angles as he faced up to his climacteric crisis over the Suez Canal. His domestic political base was eroding; the Americans were pressuring him for decisions with which he did not agree and for which there was little public support; and at least one member of the Cabinet, with his sights on the premiership, was deliberately testing the incumbent's nerve. That Eden felt obliged to assert himself has been seen as a weakness; it was in fact a political necessity.

Eden's policy of withdrawal from the Suez Canal base and cooperation with Egypt's military ruler, Gamal Abdel Nasser, had involved two disturbing corollaries. One was a search for an alternative base area in the Middle East. The selection of Cyprus, despite its lack of a deep-water port, implied the denial of the long-term prospect of self-government and union with Greece to its Greek-speaking majority, and triggered an embarrassing guerrilla war which by 1956 was tying down a large proportion of the British Army's commando and paratroop units. It also involved constructing a consortium of lenders to help Nasser build the Aswan High Dam, on which many hopes for material betterment for the Egyptian peasantry centred. The US, UK and World Bank came together, though the US was never very happy about its vast commitment. When Nasser persisted with virulent propaganda from Radio Cairo against British allies in the Middle East, sponsored murderous terrorist raids against America's protégé Israel, and finally circumvented a Western arms ban by buying weapons from Communist Czechoslovakia, the British and Americans withdrew from the consortium. On 26 July 1956, Nasser announced the nationalization of the Suez Canal, ostensibly to use its revenues to fund the Aswan Dam.

Eden had already allowed himself to be pulled by an ambitious Turkey into an attempt to create a NATO equivalent in the Middle East to fight a hypothetical war against Russian aggression. This Baghdad Pact, with three non-Arab members (the UK, Turkey and Iran), was a destabilizing factor for its fourth adherent, the unpopular Iraqi regime of the pro-British Nuri es-Said. A ham-handed attempt by Foreign Minister Harold Macmillan to bully Jordan's King Hussein into the pact, in the face of denunciation from Radio Cairo and riots in the streets, had failed. Even the Americans thought the British were showing too much Cold War zeal, though they remained supportive. For once Radio Cairo was in touch with reality when it denounced the objectives of the pact as fantastic and its underlying purpose as manipulative.[2]

[1] For Eden's long association with Dulles (like most people, Eden found him insufferable), see Leonard Mosley *Dulles* (Dial Press/James Wade, New York 1978), pp. 119–20, 347–8, 404–17.

[2] Brian H. Reid 'The "Northern Tier" and the Baghdad Pact', in *Foreign Policy of Churchill's Peacetime Administration*, ed. Young, pp. 159–79.

Nevertheless, the UK had vital long-term interests in Middle-Eastern oil. It had already seen the Anglo-Iranian Oil Company nationalized by the Iranian politician Dr Mussadiq without consultation or compensation. It proved possible to cooperate with the Americans in a Central Intelligence Agency plot to overthrow Mussadiq (code-named Operation Ajax) in 1953, but it was expensive and the UK retained only 40 per cent of its former monopoly, 6 per cent went to France, 14 per cent to the Dutch and 40 per cent to American companies. Since then an ebullient CIA had actually used force on behalf of its Saudi-Arabian clients (and their American oil company associates) against a British-protected ruler in a dispute over the Buraimi Oasis. When that failed, the CIA tried equally unsuccessfully to bribe the international arbitrators at Geneva.[1] America had become a more immediate threat to the independence and identity of the UK than the Russians. There was a very strong case for some assertion of independent powers of initiative by the UK within the framework of the Anglo-American alliance.

It was also possible to put together an alliance with the French, whose transport planes could compensate for the lamentable failure to develop a similar capability within the Royal Air Force, and with the Israelis, whose army would have no difficulty in obliterating the Egyptian ground forces, provided RAF bombers first eliminated Nasser's air force. The Anglo-French collusion with Israel, denied at the time, has been fully documented since. Eden exaggerated the impact of the loss of control of the canal on western European economies. Supertankers were becoming so large that they could not use the Suez Canal. These ships voyaged round the Cape of Good Hope instead. There was a case, insistently urged by the Americans, for inaction by the UK, to drain the scene of the drama on which Nasser throve. That would not have precluded the eventual emergence of the USA by a mixture of alliances, bribery and force as the new Middle East hegemon, which is indeed what happened. From the UK point of view, there was only one course which had nothing to be said for it from any point of view. This was the course followed by Her Majesty's Government and its armed forces. Delay was a leading characteristic of both, even after Eden had taken the decision in principle to use force if Egypt refused, as surely it would, to accept an internationalization of the Suez Canal. Force was on the cards from July. Chancellor Macmillan was 'highly belligerent', but it rapidly became clear that the UK, despite crippling expenditures of defence, did not possess the sort of substantial mobile forces with an amphibious capability capable of quickly moving into position to fight the only kind of conventional war the UK was at all likely to fight. To quote Macmillan's earlier words of March 1956: 'It is defence expenditure which has broken our backs. We also know that we get no defence from the defence expenditure . . .'[2]

The truth of this was demonstrated in the summer of 1956 as an Anglo-French force was creakingly put together. Outrageous delays were added by total changes of plan on the part of the Chiefs of Staff. Even more time was lost on political missions doomed to failure. Eden needed to act swiftly and win a decisive victory if he acted at all. That would have created a

---

[1] Mosley *Dulles*, pp. 348–54.
[2] Horne *Macmillan 1894–1956*, p. 381.

massive surge of popular support in the UK which would have rendered his position unassailable. Opposition views in the Commons were, in practical terms, an irrelevance, as was the small, incoherent group of Conservative critics. Subsequent critics became excited by the idea that the Suez crisis had seen 'a breakdown of Cabinet government'. Conservative apologists for the existing system like the Labour politician Patrick Gordon Walker argued ingeniously that in placing the management of the expedition in the hands of a committee of seven ministers (the Premier, Lord Salisbury, and Messrs Butler, Macmillan, Selwyn Lloyd, Head and Lennox-Boyd), Eden had merely moved over to a 'partial Cabinet' system.[1] The concept of a 'partial Cabinet' is about as useful as that of a 'partial horse'. Cabinet government had not been a particularly sensible description of the British executive long before 1956. Matters tended eventually to reach the Cabinet, though often in so final a form as to leave the Cabinet no options, because Cabinet minutes were the normal way of notifying and activating the administrative bureaucracy. During Suez, the ministerial committee liaised with the Chiefs of Staff, but not with the Foreign Office, which was opposed to the invasion. What stopped the operation was a run on the pound and American action on the International Monetary Fund Board to stop the UK withdrawing enough capital to sustain its currency. Israel had attacked Egypt on 29 October. By 5 November, British and French paratroopers were being dropped at the northern end of the Canal, but when those on the spot thought 48 hours more would give the allied troops total control of the canal, Macmillan threatened resignation if the war was not stopped. He appears not to have thought of the possibility of the run on the pound. Before Christmas, the Anglo-French withdrawal was complete. By early January 1957, an Eden broken in spirit and health had resigned.[2]

Macmillan's seizure of the succession came as a great surprise to public opinion. Nearly the entire press assumed that Rab Butler would succeed, but there was no set procedure for the Tory succession when the party was in office. Since 1937, there had been an electoral college of all MPs and peers, plus all prospective candidates and the executive committee of the National Union, but this only when Tories were in opposition. Butler had picked up the pieces after Suez. Macmillan had shown arrogant overconfidence before, total technical incompetence during and something like funk towards the end of the operation, but all in private. He had the peerless indifference to the consequences of his own actions which was a characteristic trait of his class and its culture, as well as an aggressive appetite for power. In theory, the Queen chose her premier. In practice, the Crown was effectively manipulated by the senior Conservative politicians to ensure that neither the bulk of Conservative MPs, nor constituency opinion was consulted. A straw poll of the other fourteen members of Eden's last Cabinet conducted by Lords Salisbury and Kilmuir showed

[1] The debate is summarized in *Documents on Contemporary British Government 1: British Government and Constitutional Change*, ed Martin Minogue (Cambridge University Press, Cambridge 1977), pp. 83–91.

[2] The best introduction to the Suez episode is probably Hugh Thomas *The Suez Affair* (Weidenfeld and Nicolson pbk reissue, with a new Introduction, London 1986).

overwhelming support for Macmillan. Butler's evasively apologetic public manner had alienated his colleagues. Salisbury's recommendation to the Queen was reinforced by Churchill's advice that Macmillan was the 'more decisive' of the candidates. His track record during the Suez crisis hardly bore that out, and at least one hard-liner, the Secretary of State for Scotland, James Stuart, was of that opinion. He had told Eden that 'I did not object to our going IN: what I did object to was our coming OUT'. He opposed Macmillan for premier and was dropped from his Cabinet. His own statement that he was not unduly grieved, for 'I had lost interest',[1] is probably true. Macmillan publicly stressed that though he meant to stay close to America 'we don't intend to be satellites'. That was of course precisely what he did intend to be. He had been chosen by 'the magnificos' of his party to manage large-scale surrender—to the US.

How long Macmillan expected to last as Premier is an interesting question. Parliament was the least of his worries. In March 1957, a highly-publicized meeting with Eisenhower in Bermuda confirmed the willingness of the new UK Government to go along with the main thrust of American policy in both the Middle East and Europe. Once that was established, Eisenhower was positively interested in building up a Conservative premier for fear of a Labour one, and worked hard at doing so. The fact that the conference was held in what was still a British colony was a tactful gesture. To veil the sheer scale of British subservience, minor differences were not just tolerated but also subtly stressed, as with the question of trade with Communist China. Macmillan was prepared to apply the same strategic restrictions to Chinese as to Russian trade (where the American-sponsored list of forbidden goods ran to no less than 250 items), but not to apply an even more stringent list to China as the US was doing. Eisenhower protested publicly, whilst making it privately clear that he quite understood.[2] There was no danger of the Westminster parliament securing any sort of enquiry into the Suez fiasco, for the Conservative parliamentary majority remained 'very steady', and all that ever appeared before the archives opened were memoirs. Eden's were rushed out early, because the poor man needed the money they fortunately did indeed earn, but he was disingenuous about such matters as collusion with Israel. Labour's zest for an enquiry did not survive that party's re-entry into office in 1964. The only realistic threat to the Government was panic and demoralization from within. With bad by-election results punctuating the summer, the Tory press predictably supplied the panic. In July, the Premier made a note in his diary which shows retrospectively how fragile he originally thought his grasp on power had been: '. . . The Party in the country is *not* in a good mood. But I think we shall get through to the end of the session without disaster. If we *can* do that, it's more than I thought possible six months ago.'[3]

However, once it was clear that Macmillan could sit the crisis out for the couple of years before he was legally obliged to hold an election, it did not

---

[1] James Stuart *Within the Fringe: An Autobiography* (The Bodley Head, London 1967), p. 177.
[2] Harold Macmillan *Riding the Storm 1956–1959* (Macmillan, London 1971), pp. 317–8.
[3] *Ibid.*, p. 350.

greatly matter that when he came to power Labour was thirteen points ahead in Gallup polls, and commentators were busy explaining that this corresponded to a majority of 100–150. Lord Swinton, who was a personal friend, later believed that 'the election in 1959 was a mere formality' and that 'the question was the size of Macmillan's majority'.[1] It was an extraordinary turn-round, but the path to it was not at all straight. Wages had for a lengthy period been rising ahead of prices, as they were almost bound to do in conditions of full employment, when there were often two vacancies for every person genuinely looking for employment, and when Churchill, Eden and Macmillan all believed strongly in avoiding a head-on clash with the unions. The Treasury *Economic Survey* for 1954 was one of the first publications to indicate alarm at the erosion of price competitiveness and the decline in the UK's share of world trade. Peter Thorneycroft, who succeeded Macmillan as Chancellor when the latter became Premier, was able to make significant cuts in taxation in his spring budget in 1957. Macmillan's fiscal expertise was not very great, but he had an almost mystical faith in reducing taxes. Then, in the summer, there was a burst of technical speculation against the pound, triggered by a partial devaluation of the French franc which was expected to initiate a general adjustment of western European currencies. In September, Thorneycroft responded by a deflationary package which hit the economy as wage inflation was falling as the result of the fading of the post-Korean War business boom. As a natural expansionist, Macmillan went along with this a little reluctantly. His positive contributions to policy were exhortatory, like his much-quoted (out of context) remark that 'most of our people have never had it so good', which was an appeal for restraint in the face of inflation. As long as he was unchallenged as Premier, he interfered with colleagues much less than Eden.[2]

But Thorneycroft and his two junior ministers, the brilliant if bitter Nigel Birch, and the intense young Enoch Powell, simply went too far when they embarked on a crusade to hold down the Government's expenditure and they resigned in January 1958 over a gap of £50 million which their colleagues refused to cut. Their motives remained obscure to most observers. There was division in the Treasury. Sir Roger Makins, the Permanent Secretary, had advised against the September package. Now the ministerial team seemed to be quitting over a trifle. They were isolated. Macmillan promptly appointed his Minister of Agriculture, Derick Heathcoat Amery, as Chancellor and departed for a Commonwealth tour referring to the episode as 'a little local difficulty'. His insouciance or 'unflappability' as it was called masked incomprehension. He blamed Birch and Powell for infecting Thorneycroft with 'fanaticism'.[3] His political sense told him the three were no immediate threat, and their attempt to impose rectitude on him ironically handed him a programme for coordinating the business cycle with the next election. Amery was of course cautious in the extreme

[1] The Earl of Swinton (with James D. Margach) *Sixty Years of Power* (Hutchinson, London 1966), p. 185.
[2] Samuel Brittan *The Treasury under the Tories 1951–1964* (Penguin, London 1964), p. 170 and pp. 185–96.
[3] Macmillan *Riding the Storm*, p. 372.

after such a succession, so there was little Keynsian counter-cyclical funding in the 1957–58 recession. When 620,000 unemployed in early 1959
provided an ideal justification, it was possible to introduce an overdue
expansionist budget which cut income tax and purchase tax, repaid post-
war credits and restored investment allowances, all to the tune of some
£360 million, just as the business cycle swung sharply upwards.

Macmillan had privately been afraid that if the three Treasury ministers
who resigned became active critics, they might destroy the long-term
ability of the Government to survive by undermining party morale. In fact
they were silent, but as late as 3 April 1959, Conservative Central Office
forecast a majority of only thirteen in an immediate election. That was
before the budget. It was also well within the margin of error of forecasting.
Because managerial groups and organized labour tended to cope better
with the problem of keeping their incomes ahead of mild inflation than
the salaried middle class, there had been a middle-class backlash. It had
benefited the Liberals as a party of protest and, in February 1958, they
had driven the Conservatives into a humiliatingly bad third place in a
by-election won by Labour in the admittedly very volatile Lancashire seat
of Rochdale. Even after the budget in 1959, Macmillan needed a long, good
summer of boom and prosperity to be sure that he could not lose his
election.

In the meantime, he had cheerfully exploited every opportunity for personal publicity offered by his office. He had had a pretty miserable life
until he was nearly 60, compounded of political miscalculation and personal tragedy due to his son's alcoholism and his wife's protracted public
affair with, of all people, the egregious Boothby (who was to have the gall
to ask for and accept a peerage from Macmillan). Suddenly, he was at the
top of the greasy pole. Well-publicized foreign tours, like his trip round
the Commonwealth, his two visits to Eisenhower, and his visit to Russia
in February and March 1959, helped to build a 'statesmanlike' image. The
white fur hat he wore on the Russian jaunt was a solecism. It was typically
Finnish (he had bought it there during the Winter War). However, it went
down well back home, which was what mattered. With his teeth straight-
ened, and neat suits replacing the Edwardian upper-class tramp image
which he had hitherto cultivated, he became an astute performer on the
ever more important television. He even shamelessly roped in Eisenhower
for an ostensibly non-partisan television performance during the latter's
brief visit to London in August 1959. It was seen at the time, rightly, as
the first shot in the election campaign.

If Eisenhower wanted a Tory victory, he equally wanted the UK incorpor-
ated into a federal Europe. The two aims were not wholly compatible, as
Macmillan surely indicated as early as Bermuda. The whole point of the
European issue in domestic UK politics, from the Conservative point of
view, was to provide the party with a lifebelt, not a lead weight. Evelyn
Shuckburgh, Eden's Private Secretary until May 1954, when he became an
Under-Secretary at the Foreign Office, has recorded gossip at the Office
on 4 October 1956, when it was known that Macmillan was sponsoring:

> . . . serious study of our joining some sort of European confederation system.
> The Tories are beginning to think that something of this sort is essential for
> their own electoral prospects, which are at present very dim. Kirkpatrick [Sir

Ivone Kirkpatrick, the Permanent Secretary] has the idea we might get Western Union into the Sterling Area (we would describe it as creating a common currency thus getting the vast German capital reserves pooled with our own).[1]

What emerges from this record of informed gossip is the dual stress on electoral advantage and escape from exchange crises by sleight of hand rather than economic reform. The Treasury team which resigned in 1958 was much more radical than Macmillan in the sense that it wanted a funda-mental assault on what it saw as the UK's failure to accept fiscal, cost and wage discipline. Enoch Powell in particular looked for discipline through a freely convertible, floating pound, an idea which Macmillan toyed with in theory but rejected when in power.

All three Treasury rebels were sceptical about the so-called 'independent' British nuclear deterrent. Macmillan valued it as giving leverage with the US, and also hoped that reliance on it could cut the costs of conventional forces. The abrasive Duncan Sandys became Minister of Defence. He issued a White Paper envisaging the rapid implementation of ideas which had been around since the early 1950s. Sandys drove them through, con-cealing their precise form from his colleagues and civil servants until the last minute, and then backing his proposals with long spells of detailed work, often at the utterly unreasonable hours he had learned from his father-in-law, Churchill. The results were disappointing. Conscription was phased out by 1960. There was some reduction in ground forces in Central Europe, compensated for by the introduction of tactical nuclear weapons, but there was no reconsideration of the UK's pattern of global commit-ments. Worse, the nuclear deterrent proved an increasingly expensive complication in Anglo-American relations. A genuinely independent British deterrent lasted at most three years.[2]

A politician like Macmillan whose opening gambit had been to hang on and hope could always hope, as indeed he did, that the only conceivable alternative basis for an administration—the Labour Party—would self-destruct in factional feuding. Since 1955, it had been lead by Hugh Gait-skell, very much the candidate of the centre and right, and of the old right-wing union leadership, but the balance of union power was changing with the rise of more left-wing figures like Frank Cousins of the Transport and General Workers Union. The explosion of the first British hydrogen bomb in 1957 added emotional edge to the party's deep divisions over defence policy. Neither the Labour nor the Conservative Party cultivated any great degree of internal party democracy. Candidates for seats virtually in the party's pocket were habitully chosen by tiny cliques of party activists. The Conservative annual conference was far more stage-managed by the executive than the Labour annual conference, but in the last analysis, the Tories had stronger tendencies towards populist democracy at local level than Labour. Nigel Nicolson, a rebel against the Suez invasion and rejected by his constituency for that, narrowly failed to regain the nomination two

[1] Entry for 4 October 1956 in Evelyn Shuckburgh *Descent to Suez: Diaries 1951–56*, ed. John Charmley (Weidenfeld and Nicolson, London 1986), p. 361.
[2] Michael Dockrill *British Defence since 1945* (Basil Blackwell, Oxford 1988), Chap. 5: 'The Sandys White Paper and its Consequences, 1957–1963'.

years later, but only after a postal ballot involving over 76 per cent of association membership. Labour had the lethal combination of a structure giving special interests, especially trade unions, great power at all levels, and a genuinely open forum in conference where the unrepresentative products of the system could fight furiously over issues of marginal interest to the general public.[1]

It followed that Macmillan's approach to the emerging European Common Market could only be cautious. He was unlikely to risk a split in his own party when he lived in hope that Labour would split. He knew that Westminster had underestimated the drive behind the Common Market, and he was anxious to square the circle of British reluctance and American over-enthusiasm by negotiating for a wider European Free Trade Area. To depict this as an attempt 'to wreck the Common Market'[2] is grossly unfair. Macmillan was genuinely looking for a creative compromise to enable the UK to coexist aimiably with the Common Market, and he more than most British people would have been perfectly happy to build provision for expanded political cooperation into any such arrangement. As it was, he lost any chance of success in this policy when in 1958 General Charles de Gaulle was returned to power in France on the back of a rising by the professional French Army in Algeria, and by the white settlers there. Both groups were desperate to secure a regime in Paris committed to continuing the long colonial war being waged for a 'French Algeria'. De Gaulle was a man for whom ambiguity was the height of statesmanship, but he unequivocally terminated the negotiations for a wider free trade zone in Europe embracing the six Common Market Countries, the UK and all the OECD nations. To him, the UK under Macmillan was a rival, objectionable as such and as an American satellite.

In the short run, this hardly mattered. Rising material prosperity at home in the first era of widespread availability of consumer durables in the UK, plus peace abroad and the advantages of incumbency, were enough to ensure electoral victory. Prosperity was a theme heavily stressed in the advertising campaign mounted for the Conservatives by Messrs Colman, Prentis and Varley. It would have boomeranged with even a mild recession, which is why Macmillan kept such an iron grip on the incipiently deflationist tendencies of Heathcoat Amory and the Treasury knights. The Premier had his own Keynsian guru in the shape of the Oxford economist Roy Harrod, but the prime determinant of policy was politics. Macmillan the expansionist of 1959 had already been bitterly denounced, and rightly, as an econocidal deflationist during the 1957–8 recession.[3] Gaitskell went into the election after a long run of polls had shown the Conservatives comfortably ahead, and with Macmillan's image assiduously burnished by a press which gave the Premier six times the coverage of his Labour rival Briefly, Gaitskell conducted his campaign with such energy and professionalism that the tide in the opinion polls began to turn. Gaitskell then dug

---

[1] Peter Paterson *The Selectorate: The Case for Primary Elections in Britain* (MacGibbon and Kee, London 1967), pp. 129–30.

[2] Alexander Werth *De Gaulle* (Penguin, London 1965), p. 315.

[3] Philip M. Williams *Hugh Gaitskell: A Political Biography* (Jonathan Cape, London 1979), p. 488.

deep into the rich seam of political ineptitude in his nature and uttered phrases which enabled his opponents' propaganda machine to harp relentlessly on his 'fiscal irresponsibility' in the last days of the campaign. It was an ironic theme for a fiscal opportunist like Macmillan, but it put the election back on track. The Liberal revival achieved little. With one gain and one loss, the Liberals retained six seats while increasing their share of the vote from 2.7 per cent to 5.9 per cent. Their precise political position was vague. Their new leader, Joe Grimond, perhaps only made his basic political stance on some central issues clear many years later from the safety of the Lords, when he showed considerable sympathy for the economic tenets of the Thatcher Government. In 1959, he dashed around, occasionally by helicopter, peddling that most vacuous of political pabulums, 'moderation'. With 49.4 per cent of the vote, the Tories had an overall majority of 100. Their percentage vote was slightly less than in 1955, but Labour fell more, returning with 258 MPs to the Conservatives' 365.[1] Having lifted the nightmare of loss of power which had haunted his party since Eden's post-electoral economic crisis of 1955, Macmillan (or Supermac) became the most over-rated of post-1945 premiers, and walked on into his own self-induced economic débacle.

[1] D. E. Butler and Richard Rose *The British General Election of 1959* (Macmillan, London 1960).

11

1959–70: 'Not Amurath an Amurath succeeds, but Harold Harold' *(with an interlude for baronial usurpation)*

This is the English, not the Turkish court; Not Amurath an Amurath succeeds, but Harry Harry.

King Henry IV, Part 2

Up to now the 64,000 dollar question has been 'How to Boom without Busting'. With the help of the experts and the *Times* newspaper it seems that our immediate future may be to Bust without Booming.

Harold Macmillan, March 1963

Greater love hath no man than this, that he lays down his friends for his life.

Jeremy Thorpe MP on 'The Night of the Long Knives'

In terms of sheer visibility, Macmillan had raised the prime-ministerial office to unprecedented heights, greatly aided by television and by the application of commercial advertising techniques to politics. Both influences encouraged a simplified presentation of issues or institutions most easily obtained by focussing on a personality. Macmillan himself had lost the intellectual interest in domestic problems which had characterized him in the 1930s. Being a publisher and living to a great age after reluctantly relinquishing the premiership, he published many volumes of memoirs through whose pages shines a profound lack of enthusiasm for matters outside the glamorous field of foreign affairs. Despite the rapid emergence of acute internal problems, his self-satisfaction seems to have remained undented until the latter part of 1960 at least. In November of that year, a number of by-elections happened to come together. This might well have been embarrassing for the Government, with a swing away from their high general election vote. In fact, they held everything comfortably, and the election of the supposedly very left-wing Michael Foot for a safe Labour constituency pleased Macmillan even more, as he recorded: 'The "little General Election" is over—with considerable success for Conservatives. We have held every seat. Foot has been elected with an immense majority —not very pleasant for Gaitskell.'[1]

---

[1] Harold Macmillan *Pointing the Way 1959–1961* (Macmillan, London 1972), p. 308.

Thereafter, things fell apart. After the 'go' of the pre-election consumer spree came the 'stop' of deflation. Amory had to raise profit tax, impose severe credit restrictions and raise bank rates. The exercise destroyed his personal credibility, but his successor in 1961 was also hand-picked by the Premier for bidability. This was Selwyn Lloyd, a lonely man with no charisma and little grasp of economics. Macmillan displayed what was to become a recurring political reflex. He was extremely reluctant to face up to the brutal truth that, having allowed a substantial increase in consumption to ensure electoral victory, he was now being forced progressively to dampen down demand to cope with the resulting balance of payment problems. In retrospect, he saw it all as 'A Touch on the Brake'.[1] The analogy with driving a car was both comic and false. It was comic because, as it happens, Harold Macmillan was never capable of driving a car. It was false because the real analogy was with a roller-coaster to which he was clinging desperately and luckily. By delaying action, the Premier probably made the final crunch worse. It came in the spring of 1961 when much of the large volume of short-term capital or 'hot money' attracted to London by high interest rates started to flow out due to an upward revaluation of the West German mark and rumours of a general realignment of currencies.

By 25 July, Selwyn Lloyd was producing a mini-budget which used regulatory power to increase consumer taxes by a fierce ten per cent, raised bank rate to seven per cent, and placed drastic curbs on Government spending and bank loans. The upshot was two years stagnation in industrial production, but in fact Lloyd had with difficulty won a, needless to say, secret battle against even more dramatic and destructive deflation. The protagonists came from three major players in the game of UK economic decision-taking. The Treasury was now headed by Sir Frank Lee, a man whose zeal for Common Market entry, which he saw as an opportunity for bracing, salutary competition for British industry, still outran that of the bulk of Treasury bureaucrats. His instinctive deflationism was, however, almost a form of Treasury tribalism. The Earl of Cromer, the new Governor of the Bank of England, had just begun a long and aggressive career of trying to influence Government policy by demands for deflation. In the background, Per Jacobsson, the Managing Director of the International Monetary Fund, could be found voicing demands that Government spending be cut by £500 million, to restore 'confidence'. This Greek tragic chorus did not get its way, but of course it did as it intended, profoundly influence the atmosphere in which final decisions were made.[2]

If 'King Harold' seemed somewhat preoccupied, the reasons were not far to seek. He had, after all, done this before. A sharp recession was not necessarily electoral suicide. Coming up fast out of it provided an ideal springboard to a pre-election boom, like that of 1959. His search for a conspicuous triumph in foreign affairs was closely related to calculations about domestic politics. He was, for example, always afraid that the Labour Party would gain advantage in the struggle for the much-discussed centre ground in British politics by exploiting allegations of Conservative inflexibility in the Cold War. That was one reason why, despite private reser-

---

[1] *Ibid.*, Chap. 8.
[2] Brittan *The Treasury under the Tories*, pp. 232–3.

vations, he had paid his well-publicized visit to Russia in early 1959. By September 1959, the Russian Premier, Nikita Khruschev, was paying a very successful visit to the United States. American opinion began to share Macmillan's optimism about a summit meeting scheduled for May 1960, which the Premier saw as potentially a 'wondrous moment' when 'we seem on the threshold of genuine, practical steps toward peace'.[1] Alas, the summit meeting between Eisenhower, Khruschev, Macmillan and de Gaulle in Paris blew up on 16–17 May, when the Russian leader used systematic violation of Russian air-space by American U-2 spy planes (which, with characteristic diplomatic insensitivity, the Americans had not suspended) as an excuse to abort a conference which was clearly not going to give him the concessions he wanted over Berlin, and which exposed him to hard-line domestic critics.

The Common Market was the next possible trump card. The failure of the negotiations for an enlarged Free Trade area had prepared domestic and more particularly Conservative opinion for a straight UK application for membership. The failure had positively pleased the Americans who much preferred full UK membership of the Common Market. At the annual conference of the Conservative Party in October 1961, a motion of support was easily passed for an application for membership of the Common Market, subject to the negotiation of appropriate terms and conditions of entry. Politically, attempts to secure concessions over Commonwealth exports to Britain were unavoidable. So were promises that a long transition phase during which British farmers would continue to receive Exchequer grants would be requested. Some of the leading Tory enthusiasts for the Common Market, like the former Chief Whip Edward Heath whom Macmillan was to put in charge of the entry negotiations, were professional machine politicians formed by war and post-war party service. Many of the other early enthusiasts were from the old protectionist, Imperialist wing of the party, like Leo Amery and Duncan Sandys, who was Commonwealth Secretary at the time.

There was strong pressure for a UK application from the young US President, John F. Kennedy, who had won the November 1960 presidential election by a vote plurality so narrow as to be within the margin of error ascribable to the dirty tricks practised by his campaign, or indeed that of Richard M. Nixon, his rival. Kennedy's Under Secretary of State for Economic Affairs at the State Department, George W. Ball, had worked as a lawyer in the headquarters of the French Planning Commission with Jean Monnet, a pioneer of European political integration and a father of the Common Market. Ball's account of Macmillan's visit to Washington to meet Kennedy in April 1961 makes it clear that an excitable Macmillan, overimpressed as most people were by his sparkling but deeply flawed host, was flapping around soliciting approval for his resolve to take a decision pregnant with long-term political consequences by moving the UK into the Common Market. The Premier even turned on what was to become of his favourite long-playing record, an emotional account of why the horrors of his own First World War experience made this the only way.

---

[1] Eric F. Goldman *The Crucial Decade—and After: America, 1945–1960* (Random House, Vintage Books edn, New York 1960), p. 334.

The Americans listened with fascinated approval, as also they did often enough to West German Chancellor Konrad Adenauer's equivalent record, which was a monologue about how the British had lost an empire and also the will to work. In both cases, the approval was understandable: they were hearing what they wanted to hear. Ball had long talks with Sir Frank Lee and Edward Heath to assure himself that the Treasury and party leadership was committed to what Ball relentlessly stressed was a political option. Great was his fury when Macmillan went home and with typical chicanery 'reminded' the Commons on 31 July that 'the EEC is an economic community, not a defence alliance or a foreign policy community, or a cultural community.'[1]

Ball's intolerance of opinions which differed from his own on points of political substance was on a par with Monnet's denunciation as 'anti-European' of anyone who failed to embrace his integrationist aims. Under-Secretary Ball looked angrily at countries like Sweden and Switzerland which in his view 'defined "neutrality" to suit their own purposes'. Their refusal to join the Western alliance was to him 'casuistry'.[2] Ball was all for Macmillan shouting political commitment to the EEC at the top of his voice. It would not only have been political suicide but also probably a waste of time. General de Gaulle was not susceptible to self-righteous American pressure or to seduction by the expensive English flummery which Macmillan staged for him during a state visit to London. He simply looked at the facts of life. Macmillan's commitment to an 'independent' British nuclear deterrent provided unmistakeable evidence of the nature of the Anglo-American relationship. To extend the effective life of the V bomber force, the UK had purchased the air-launched American Skybolt missile which Kennedy's cost-conscious Secretary of Defense, Robert McNamara, promptly cancelled on 7 November 1962. By 20 December, Macmillan was in Nassau in the Bahamas for an urgent meeting with Kennedy at which he grimly underlined the 'shaky position' of his administration and the imperative need for the Government to bring back something from Nassau which would restore faith in a special relationship with the US.[3]

The Prime Minister himself probably believed vaguely in the destiny of the Westminster élite to act as civilizing Greeks within the raw power structures of America's new Roman Empire. His condescension apart, the rootless and cosmopolitan Kennedys, 'Boston Irish' purely for electoral purposes, were attracted by the British ruling élite, with whom Ambassador Joseph P. Kennedy had been intimate in London between 1938 and 1940. His son, President John F. Kennedy, was on particularly good terms with Sir David Ormsby-Gore, personal friend and a relative by marriage who was also a relative of Macmillan, and who became a highly successful British ambassador in Washington DC in 1961.[4] At Nassau, Kennedy eventually agreed to supply the UK with the submarine-launched long-

[1] George W. Ball *The Past has Another Pattern: Memoirs* (W. W. Norton, pbk edn, New York 1982), pp. 213–8.

[2] *Ibid.*, p. 219.

[3] *Ibid.*, p. 267.

[4] Garry Wills *The Kennedys: A Shattered Illusion* (Orbis, London 1983), chap. 6, 'Semi-English'.

range ballistic missile system known as Polaris. It was assigned to NATO by its prospective new owners, subject to a strategically meaningless but politically vital reservation by Macmillan that the UK could use it independently in an emergency. Financially, the bargain was not a bad one, if the UK had to have such a thing. Politically, Kennedy had little choice. There was nothing special about the American relationship with the UK in the sense that the US cooperated very closely with other countries and had even more power and influence in some of their political systems than it had in the UK. Yet Kennedy could hardly destroy so obliging an ally as Macmillan by refusing Polaris. It was not just British membership of NATO which was at stake. As Macmillan stressed, it was the survival of the Government.

Once survival was secured, the Premier was counting on Common Market entry to turn the tide. His Chancellor Selwyn Lloyd, who was as aware as most people of the low levels of investment and comparatively slow growth rate of the UK, was counting on entry to unleash a vast investment boom. His was the stubborn faith of the politician trying to conjure up a much needed escape-hatch. Macmillan himself went round making notably vague speeches about entry having all the stimulant qualities of 'a bracing shower'. This reflected accurately enough the hazy nature of his economic thinking. Most professional economists who examined the matter concluded that the economic imperatives of entry were much exaggerated. Indeed, they concluded that the case for and against was balanced about fifty-fifty. It was a political decision. In retrospect, the most prescient remark made in the course of an increasingly partisan debate was an early one by Labour's Harold Wilson, who said on 25 July 1960: 'If a middle-aged, portly man seeks to join a bunch of athletes lapping round a track, it may make him more athletic, or alternatively, he may drop dead or, at best, retire panting from the track.'[1]

In the event, General de Gaulle on the afternoon of 14 January 1963 vetoed the UK application for membership of the Common Market. By so doing, he did not greatly endear himself to the other five members of the Market. He enraged the UK and US administrations, and secured a notably hostile press from the strongly pro-Market British liberal media representatives like Nora Beloff, the *Observer* correspondent. Yet the General was substantially accurate in his view that the UK was likely to be both a rival to France for leadership within the Market, and an agent of the political and economic interests of the Americans. He was very conscious of the American sponsorship behind Macmillan's application, and his forecast that the UK would press for 'Atlantacist' and free trade policies was to be wholly vindicated by the behaviour of the UK after it was eventually admitted.[2] For Macmillan the veto was a catastrophe. He talked about de Gaulle returning to Napoleon's Continental system (an attempt to block all British trade with Europe). De Gaulle rightly dismissed this as the arrant rubbish it was: UK trade with the Common Market was rising and

---

[1] Cited in Bartlett *History of Postwar Britain*, p. 189.
[2] W. W. Kulski *De Gaulle and the World: The Foreign Policy of the Fifth French Republic* (Syracuse University Press, Syracuse, NY 1966), pp. 234–45; Nora Beloff's wrath emerges in *The General Says No* (Penguin, London 1963).

continued to rise after the veto. The distraught response of the Prime Minister was much more explicable in terms of his lack of any alternative escape plans from his domestic toils.

Even the support he was given by Kennedy carried a price. The President had squeaked into office partly as a Cold War hard-liner, with a record of McCarthyite zeal for harassing alleged 'reds' like the historian Owen Lattimore (whose main fault was realism over China),[1] and a much advertised concern about a (non-existent) 'missile-gap' against the Russians. Even so dedicated a Kennedy supporter as the historian Arthur Schlesinger Jr was prepared to admit in retrospect that Kennedy's inaugural speech, which threw down the gauntlet to global communism, contained 'extravagant rhetoric'.[2] The trouble was that the rhetoric tended to turn into expensive reality such as the concept of 'flexible response' in Europe, which made it difficult for the UK to run down its conventional military commitment there. This rather destroyed the point of the Sandys White Paper, and indeed of a whole line of strategic thinking going back as far as 1945 when the scientist Sir Henry Tizard, then a member of the Air Council, had argued that the UK's aim should be 'maximum insurance against war', and not 'maximum contribution to' a possible Russian-American conflict.[3] Equally, the US was an ardent supporter of an expensive British military presence 'east of Suez'.

In so far as he was free to act without encountering serious political checks, Macmillan did eventually liquidate commitment. Most of the remaining colonies were in Africa, and an ambivalent but significant cost-benefit analysis conducted discreetly as early as 1957 had cast some doubt on their value. By the early 1960s, with Colonial Secretary Iain Macleod, a politician as uncertain as he about where to go in Africa, Macmillan was prepared to follow the line of least resistance. Churchill and Eden had not greatly concerned themselves with colonial matters in the 1950s, but had just assumed, quite correctly, that there was no immediate threat to British control in most of the remaining colonies.[4] Retreat before pressure had not seemed likely in Africa before 1961, but it was a general principle. Suddenly, it began to be applied in the face of not very formidable black African nationalist movements. After a spasm of protest about the transfer of power to black nationalists in Kenya and Northern Rhodesia (now Zambia) early in 1961, the Conservative Party at Westminster acquiesced, despite the consequent break-up of the white-settler dominated Central African Federation. Indeed, the low level of resistance within the party to every change from the subsequent flurry of decolonization to the Common Market application has led imperial historians to ruminate on 'the generally docile acceptance by the Conservative party of the external policies of the

---

[1] Peter Collier and David Horowitz *The Kennedy's: An American Drama* (Summit Books, New York 1984), p. 198; Owen Lattimore *Ordeal by Slander* (MacGibbon and Kee, London 1952).

[2] The admission appears in an article by Schlesinger entitled 'The Kennedy Legend', in *The Observer Review*, Sunday 20 November 1983

[3] Ronald W. Clark *Tizard* (Methuen, London 1965), p. 402.

[4] David Goldsworthy 'Keeping Change Within Bounds: Aspects of Colonial Policy during the Churchill and Eden Governments, 1951–57', *Journal of Imperial and Commonwealth History* 18 (1, 1990), pp. 81–108.

leadership'. They have even been tempted to conclude that: 'it may have been due to the centralised and hierarchical character of the party, which made dissent difficult.'[1] By 1965, from the Caribbean to the tiny Maldive Islands in the Indian Ocean, the UK had ditched a great deal of useless real estate. Pre-planned, this probably was not; nor did it save much money.

Macmillan saw himself as preserving the Great Power Britain he had done more than most to undermine. He successfully saw off an Iraqi threat to oil-rich Kuwait in 1961, with limited naval and marine forces (though the carriers carried atomic bombs which contemporary UK tactical doctrine saw as battlefield weapons). He supported Kennedy in the hair-raising 1962 Cuban missile crisis, when the post-1945 world probably came closest to nuclear war. Yet domestically there was little left to do except try to stoke up the economy again and win the next election on the back of a consumer boom. We know that at strategy talks at Chequers, the official country residence of the Premier, in April 1963 the assumption was that a satisfied consumer was a Tory voter.[2] In Reginald Maudling, Macmillan was to find a Chancellor who was, as a clever chancer, very much a kindred spirit, but to install him in office the Premier had to pass through an episode which left his own image pretty threadbare.

He was well aware that what he needed was economic expansion without inflation, which might most easily, from his point of view, be achieved by some form of control on wages, tying them to the annual calculated rise in real national wealth, which for many, many decades had in normal times been what it was in 1962–63, to wit about 2–2.5 per cent. Hence the great explosion in 'planning' devices such as the National Economic Development Council ('Neddy') and the National Incomes Commission ('Nicky'). French 'indicative' planning, whose efficacy was much exaggerated, had for some time been fashionable in Treasury circles. At the core of all this lay such concepts as a 'guiding light' on incomes, and confrontations with public sector unions. Churchill may have practised appeasement through his Minister of Labour, Walter Monckton, but Macmillan's record was far more mixed. The trouble was that there was no particular reason why interest groups politically opposed to him should cooperate in generating a boom which all experience suggested would promptly be reversed by spending cuts and increases in highly regressive indirect taxes after it had served its electoral purpose. Nor was there any reason for people to be happy with the period of restrictions which always preceded a Macmillan boom. Indeed, during a period when the working class was restive in the face of an inevitably inequitable Government-sponsored 'pay pause', and the middle classes unhappy with credit restrictions, Macmillan's never very strong political nerve was severely shaken by a sensational Liberal by-election victory in March 1962 in the prosperous suburban constituency of Orpington.

---

[1] John Darwin *The End of the British Empire: The Historical Debate* (Basil Blackwell for the Institute of Contemporary British History, London 1991), p. 32. There is a useful near-contemporary survey in Colin Cross *The Fall of the British Empire 1981–1968* (Hodder and Stoughton, London 1968).

[2] Reginald Bevins *The Greasy Pole: A Personal Account of the Realities of British Politics* (Hodder and Stoughton, London 1965), p. 101.

The upshot was the extraordinary 'Night of the Long Knives' in July 1962, which seems to have been triggered by a typically feline leak by Rab Butler, but in which Macmillan sacked not just Selwyn Lloyd, but a third of the Cabinet, and that with a graceless brutality which hurt deeply. He made such a botch of the interview with Lloyd that he forgot to toss in the poor consolation prize of the Companion of Honour title, and had to have someone else phone him the next day to offer the C.H., a tarnished piece of political tinsel by then. Victims like the admittedly pompous Lord Chancellor Kilmuir, dismissed like an unsatisfactory housemaid, hit back in their memoirs. Kilmuir described a windy Premier slaughtering friends in an attempt to refurbish his image. Macmillan spat back at the 'beta minus' Kilmuir, the 'stupidest Lord Chancellor ever'. There was much to be said for both men's views. The massacre has been seen as deeply damaging to the Premier, indeed as 'suicide'. It was no such thing. With Maudling as Chancellor, the usual tax cuts in the budget with which Macmillan fed an upswing in the economy (they totalled nearly £300 million) were reinforced by new incentives for relatively depressed areas such as Scotland and Wales (where purely co-incidentally the Conservatives were under electoral pressure). In March 1963, polls showed 62 per cent of the public wanted the Premier to resign. It mattered not, for he was in control of a party he thought could eventually win a general election.[1]

That may explain the tragi-comedy of the Profumo affair. That the Secretary of State for War, John Profumo, lied to the Commons about his affair with a call-girl he turned out to be sharing with the Russian naval attaché was not what destroyed his career. It was being found out, partly due to the venom of his Labour opposite number George Wigg, which finished him. The UK secret state had developed rapidly in the Cold War, in cooperation with the American Central Intelligence Agency (CIA) founded in 1947 and given to feuding with its principal American rival, the Defense Intelligence Agency (DIA), though not with the insane zeal with which the two principal British intelligence agencies MI5 and MI6 fought one another. CIA confidence in British intelligence (at one point much admired by the Americans for its alleged 'style') had been dented by a recent series of security fiascos. There is reason to suspect that British intelligence had set a 'honeytrap' for the Russian attaché in blissful ignorance that the girl was also sleeping with Profumo. Stephen Ward, the pimp involved, appears to have been the patriot who realized the mistake; tried to rectify it; was framed as fall-guy for his pains by the security establishment; and committed suicide in despair and shock. As usual, secrecy was used less to protect secrets than to spare specific parts of the executive embarrassment (in this case the intelligence services). The snag was that the exercise was unconvincing. It did not hang together, and the general public smelled more than just moral decay: it smelled a rat.[2]

---

[1] Alistair Horne *Macmillan 1957–1986* (Macmillan, London 1989), pp. 338–50 and 470.
[2] Anthony Summers and Stephen Dorril *Honeytrap* (Hodder and Stoughton, Coronet pbk edn, London 1987) brings out many of the complexities obscured at the time. John Ranelagh *The Agency: The Rise and Decline of the CIA* (Hodder and Stoughton, Sceptre pbk edn, London 1988), pp. 235–7 and 289–91 shows the odd love-hate relationship between the CIA and British intelligence.

With an over-stimulated economy and a series of image-wrecking disasters which ruled out a quick dash for the polls, it was the last straw when the elderly and shaken Macmillan, on the eve of the October 1963 annual Conservative Party conference, was struck down by prostate trouble requiring an operation. He decided, possibly wrongly, that he could not carry on and turned with zest to the task of rigging his own succession. He himself had snatched the succession on the back of a straw poll of the Cabinet. His problem in late 1963 was that a similar procedure would undoubtedly have handed the supreme prize to Rab Butler whom Iain Macleod and many others were convinced Macmillan was determined to stop at all costs, despite having given him the uniquely honorific, if meaningless, title of First Secretary of State. He himself appears to have initially preferred Quintin Hogg, Lord Hailsham, as his successor, and Hailsham promptly announced he would take advantage of recent legislation to renounce the title which stood in his way. Regrettably, the prospective Mr Quintin Hogg then cavorted before the full blaze of publicity at the party conference at Blackpool in a way which which convinced the bulk of his senior colleagues that he was at best incorrigibly unbalanced, if not slightly insane. The prospect of supreme power did not so much excite him as intoxicate him. It was partly a product of an emotional switchback with Macmillan himself who had first promoted his career from Minister of Education to Lord President and Chairman of the Tory Party, then after the 1959 election triumph, because of a private misunderstanding, cast him into disfavour, giving him the new portfolio of Science and Technology and a very cold shoulder personally. Hailsham was deeply hurt by this 'almost Borgia-like behaviour',[1] and understandably felt an enormous surge of relief when the misunderstanding (whose basis he had never been aware of) was put to rights. The sun shone on Hailsham again, which made the way he promptly pushed the self-destruct button doubly sad. The Premier had to cast his net wide in a series of 'consultations' conducted mainly by his elephantine Lord Chancellor Dilhorne. Macmillan inserted into the list of possible successors about whom Conservative peers, MPs and constituencies were to be consulted one nobody had thought possible: his Foreign Secretary, the Earl of Home. The arithmetic whereby Macmillan concluded on the strength of the responses that only Home could hold the party together finally struck even Home as bizarre,[2] but by then it was too late. Queen Elizabeth, advised by Macmillan from his hospital bed, gave the commission to form an administration to Home.

It was, by common consent, an outrageous performance but the real problem lay in defining precisely what was outrageous. There had been angry comment when Macmillan had promoted Lord Home from Commonwealth Secretary to Foreign Secretary, because Home was a peer. That was unreasonable criticism. By its own choice, the House of Commons had become a time-wasting rubber stamp on major issues. One former

---

[1] *A Sparrow's Flight: The Memoirs of Lord Hailsham of St Marylebone* (Collins, London 1990), p. 324.
[2] Patrick Cosgrove *R. A. Butler: An English Life* (Quartet Books, pbk edn, London 1981), p. 138 brings out the fact that at a late stage Home 'suspected Macmillan of playing around somewhat with the figures'.

Conservative minister quite seriously suggested in 1965 that it would be a desirable reform to cut the parliamentary week from five days to three, and the parliamentary year to twenty weeks in order to 'liberate ministers from the crippling claims of the House of Commons', with its absurd hours, regular pantomimes like Question Time (where in the last analysis questions could be ducked), and occasional lunacies like all-night sittings. Interestingly, he urged this to give ministers more time and energy to devote to the real business of decision-making, especially in contacts with senior civil servants. The balance between minister and civil servants was, he knew, fluid but he was clear that many mandarins 'visibly dislike the idea of a minister making up his own mind and rejecting their own advice'.[1] Since this bracingly honest approach to the Commons was impractical, there was much to be said for having a senior minister in the less taxing, more civilized Lords. Home promptly shed his peerage on becoming Premier. As Sir Alec Douglas-Home he was shoed in for the Kinross and West Perthshire constituency whose Tory allegiance was of so rock-ribbed a character as to survive even the experience of being represented after 1974 by 'Dandy Nick' Fairbairn, lawyer, lover, beau and poet (the worst since William McGonagall, according to an unkind critic).

The new Premier was perfectly sincere in seeing himself as the consensus candidate whose job it was to hold the party together. The most intelligent and independent-minded Conservative ministers, like Iain Macleod, the Commonwealth Secretary, and Enoch Powell, the Minister of Health, were appalled by the way the succession had been fixed. Both were staunch supporters of Rab Butler for premier. In a famous *Spectator* article of 17 January 1964, Macleod declared his conviction that there had been a plot by an inner 'magic circle' to stop Butler. He was too much a Conservative to raise the issue of the hasty royal concurrence, but a week later Paul Johnson raised it in the *New Statesman* of 24 January 1964. The point was substantial but never pursued,[2] because Butler, whose refusal to serve would have made him prime minister, did not fight. By accepting the Foreign Office, under Home, he confirmed the latter in power, and left his own supporters, among them the brightest and best of the party, scuppered. If political power be the ability to bend the will of others to one's own, Macmillan had won an unrepeatable trick. The Tory MPs, with few consolations for the ambitious among them other than office, were unlikely to risk a repeat performance over the supreme office. After a brief spell as Premier, Home in opposition bowed to internal party pressures and produced on 25 February 1965 an agreed procedure whereby future Conservative leaders were to be selected by ballots of Conservative MPs and the ballots were to be organized by the backbenchers' 1922 Committee.

Home therefore assumed his new office at a time when its powers had been probably abused, and certainly stretched to the point of undermining the minimum of tolerance from the Conservative parliamentary élite without which they could not be effectively used at all. As it happened, the

---

[1] Bevins *Greasy Pole*, pp. 60–4.

[2] Anthony Howard *Rab: The Life of R. A. Butler* (Macmillan, Papermac edn, London 1988), pp. 316–20; Robert Lacey *Majesty: Elizabeth II and the House of Windsor* (Hutchinson, London 1977), pp. 247–63.

new Prime Minister's personality helped handle the situation. A smoother, not a shaker, charming and conciliatory, he did the job every Tory MP wanted done. By prostate gland rather than dagger, they had been freed from a leadership under which few thought they could win an election. In a manoeuvre which was to be repeated, they rallied behind a new face in the hope of disassociating themselves from the unpopularity of the later Macmillan administration and turning the polls round in time to win the impending election. Home naturally tried to present an image utterly different from that of his predecessor. If Macmillan was widely perceived as devious, Sir Alec was anxious to appear a transparently honest Border laird. He even claimed to do his economic calculations with matchsticks. A Border magnate he was. Transparent he was not. He was an experienced professional politician, having been parliamentary private secretary to Chancellor Neville Chamberlain before the war. Churchill had sent him to Edinburgh in 1951 as Minister of State with orders to 'see if you can get rid of this embryo Scottish nationalist thing'. A friendly press had splurged the word 'statesmanlike' over his very average performance as Foreign Secretary, but he was competent, and it may be doubted if a man who subsequently decorated gatherings of the Mont Pélerin Society, an economics club for the super-rich addressed by such conservative gurus as Milton Friedman, ever needed matchsticks to help his understanding of the economic issues. Indeed, anyone visited regularly by a Sir Alec exuding charm and bonhomie despite acknowledged differences was wise to assume that he was being set up for something less than wholly to his advantage. Be that as it may, in his first five months as Premier he was wheeled around to make 64 full-scale formal speeches, not to mention 150 or so whistle-stop performances. If the 330,000 words he spoke were a little repetitive, it was hardly surprising. Above all, it seemed to work. Conservative Central Office calculated it would have lost an election by 100 seats in November 1963. By April 1964, the calculated prospective margin of loss was 50. Though doomed to be remembered as the Prime Minister who lost, Sir Alec's real significance lay in how close he came to victory.[1]

His style of leadership within the Government was necessarily more collegiate than that of his predecessor. In any case, the Conservative leadership naturally tended to hang together when the alternative was to hang separately. Areas of potential controversy like the Common Market were temporarily on ice, which obscured the fact that Home was not much less of an enthusiast for entry than his close associate Edward Heath, who had been principal spokesman on foreign affairs in the Commons when Home had been Foreign Secretary. Later Heath had been principal negotiator in the first bid for entry. Home's zeal seems to have been based on a mixture of despair at the undynamic nature of the UK economy, and conviction that the UK could lead Western Europe towards a great Atlantic free-trade

[1] Kenneth Young *Sir Alec Douglas-Home* (J. M. Dent, London 1970), though a partisan piece by the then Political Adviser to Beaverbrook Newspapers, is so sure of the righteousness of its subject, not to mention the iniquity of his opponents, that it provides a good deal of first-hand material on the private calculations of Home and Lord Blakenham (the Conservative Party chairman).

area. His immediate hopes in 1964 hinged on the effect of the reflation of the economy which his Chancellor, Reginald Maudling, had embarked on in 1963.

It was a less cynical reflation than was later believed. There were to be very few clinically efficient pre-election booms in the twentieth-century UK. Much commoner was incompetence in counter-cyclical management compounded by low cunning towards the end of a parliament. Maudling's 'dash for growth' seems to have begun as an excessively delayed attempt to counter a protracted recession by £250 million of tax reliefs in the 1963 budget. This boost to consumption (equivalent to a 2 per cent wage increase for many workers) worked through into an economy which was already making a sharp natural recovery from the trough of recession. It was also an economy in fundamental imbalance in that growth above a comparatively modest level tended to suck in imports beyond any compensatory rise in experts. Macmillan's various planning bodies had all talked about growth, which was a current buzz word with economists. Maudling cared little for the 'statistical theology' indulged in by the different schools of thought debating how to achieve growth, but he liked the sound of 4 per cent. Such annual growth was not uncommon in western Europe, though informed observers doubted if the UK could possibly achieve the 5 per cent annual increase in exports needed to sustain it. The main point was that the 1964 budget was never likely to dampen demand adequately as a huge balance of payments deficit emerged. A 'voluntary' incomes policy was of course peddled by Maudling, but the unions were as clearly confrontational as his consumer boom was electoral and unsustainable.

There were only two conceivable and feasible means of sustaining the boom. The short-term device, useful only for holding the line while other measures were taken, was physical restriction of imports to ensure they increased no faster than exports. The other was devaluation to make imports dear, exports cheaper. Devaluation was also an effective wages policy, but only if combined with a demonstration that attempts to compensate for dearer imported goods with unrealistic wage increases spelled bankruptcy and higher unemployment. Neither of these options was mentionable. William Armstrong, the new Permanent Secretary of the Treasury from July 1962 was much less dogmatically political than his predecessor, Sir Frank Lee, but physical controls would have been almost as unpopular with the Treasury as with the Foreign Office. Devaluation was an obscene word in Treasury circles, and neither the Labour nor the Conservative Party was prepared to let it cross its collective lips.[1] The fact was that Japan's spectacular re-emergence as a rival in world markets owed not a little to the way the American-imposed Dodge Plan had deliberately devalued the Japanese yen (at 360 to the US dollar) in such a way as to 'facilitate exports'.[2] France had devalued sharply as preparation for Common Market entry. Sir Alec preferred to go round talking about the Communist menace; the need for an independent nuclear deterrent (which

[1] Samuel Brittan *Steering the Economy: The Role of the Treasury* (Secker and Warburg, London 1969), pp. 173–184.
[2] Takafusa Nakamura (with Bernard R. G. Grace) *Economic Development of Modern Japan* (Ministry of Foreign Affairs, Japan 1985), p. 60.

would hopefully help split Labour); and how he would go in for simple, honest talk (not necessarily about every significant field).

The major decision of his premiership was when to call the general election. It could not be later than Guy Fawkes Day (5 November) 1964, but understandably Home was not attracted by that precise date. His colleagues differed, some being for the spring, like Maudling, some for the summer, but the key adviser was Lord Blakenham, the party chairman, who, operating on Central Office polls, persuaded Home to call the election as late as mid-October. Though low unemployment and rising real wages clearly helped swing the pendulum back towards the Tories, they did have a problem in the shape of the unexpected cohesion of the Labour Party and the shrewd effectiveness of its new leader, Harold Wilson. Having made little mileage out of Suez, and having failed unexpectedly badly at the 1959 election, Attlee's right-wing successor, Hugh Gaitskell, had then embarked on a deeply inept campaign to persuade the Labour Party to jettison some of its socialist shibboleths. His close ally, Roy Jenkins, who was even less of a socialist, if that was possible, than Gaitskell, admitted in retrospect that Gaitskell's tactics were simply appalling. He denounced clause four of the Labour Party's constitution which envisaged common ownership of the means of production. By so doing he revitalized a long-neglected idol which even the Conservative *Speakers' Handbook* failed to mention.[1] He did not secure the repeal of the clause, but did divide the party deeply and helped the left to win a party conference majority for unilateral nuclear disarmament which Gaitskell and his supporters, organized in the Campaign for Democratic Socialism (CDS), had to fight hard to reverse, though they did so by 1961. Benefiting by a deep yearning in his own ranks for unity, and the disarray of the Conservatives, Gaitskell at last displayed political sensitivity when he came out firmly against Common Market entry in 1962. He had an emotional commitment to the Commonwealth. He thought the terms being offered indifferent, which they were. He increasingly distrusted people like Monnet, but above all he knew he would split his party. Even the CDS was divided, and the party would have refused to be railroaded into the Market. As it was, his stance attracted former Conservative voters.[2] His sudden death in January 1963, followed by the victory of Harold Wilson in a contest for the succession, determined solely by the votes of Labour MPs, might have been the prelude to division and faction fighting in the party. It was not. Wilson held the Labour Party together and entered the general election with his defeated right-wing rival for the succession, George Brown, as an active and loyal Deputy Leader.

It was a hard and close contest. Home did not prove a natural performer on the enormously important new medium of television. He talked endlessly of modernization, but was hoist with his own petard when Wilson, making equally specious claims to spearhead a new scientific forward-

[1] Philip M. Williams *Hugh Gaitskell: A Political Biography* (Jonathan Cape, London 1979), pp. 547–8.
[2] Kenneth O. Morgan 'The High and Low Politics of Labour: Keir Hardie to Michael Foot', in *High and Low Politics in Modern Britain*, eds. Michael Bentley and John Stevenson (Clarendon Press, Oxford 1983), pp. 307–8.

looking wave of progress, taunted him with his 'grouse moor' image. Home could hardly reply with the truth: that it was as much camouflage as reality. Indeed, reality at one stage bid fair to be excluded almost entirely from the campaign. Neither Home nor Maudling, naturally enough, wished to talk about the massive balance of payments crisis building up behind them. Maudling made 'responsible' noises about the need for a big surge in exports, on the assumption presumably that he could call spirits from the vasty deep. Labour's prospective Chancellor did not want any discussion on the subject. Jim Callaghan might have had at best a bright fifteen-year-old schoolboy's grasp of economics (if that), but he knew that talk of crisis meant flight from the pound, which he would face as soon as he entered office. Blakenham had expected a narrow Tory victory by ten or fifteen seats. Wilson, in the latter stages of the campaign, began to suspect Blakenham might be right. He blew the whistle on the conspiracy of silence by highlighting bad quarterly trade figures. As a result, a drain on UK gold reserves began at once. Yet without that issue it is difficult to see how Labour could have emerged, as it did, with 317 MPs and a working majority of four, the smallest since 1847.[1] If 900 people in eight constituencies had voted Tory or just abstained, Sir Alec would have remained Premier.

Wilson, with 44.1 per cent of the vote to the Tories 43.4 had the right to assume all the prerogatives of executive office. It was an historic moment. Both leaders had done very well in a highly personalized campaign focussed on their contrasting personalities. The main loser in the campaign was arguably the public, despite the fact that it had acquired quite the cleverest of post-1945 premiers. Though he had a somewhat spurious reputation as a left-winger, mainly because of a long-standing opposition to Gaitskell, Harold Wilson was probably never very different from the radical Liberal he had been at Oxford University. In many ways, he was profoundly traditional. His Congregationalist religion, monarchist convictions, patriotic reverence for British 'greatness', and commitment to the Western Alliance were all unexceptionable. The real problem is why such a man became one of the most controversial, denounced and, beyond question, the most viciously smeared of modern UK prime ministers.

It was not as if the Labour Party was bent on any fundamental change in the structure of politics. Though excluded from office for thirteen years, it still had found memories of the pre-1951 days when the Westminster system had delivered to its leader a gratifying measure of power. In 1954, Herbert Morrison had published a textbook significantly entitled *Government and Parliament*. It had been sponsored by Nuffield College, Oxford, and was published by Oxford University Press. Sales were good. From start to finish the book (which really revealed very little inside political information) is a monumentally self-satisfied paeon of praise.[2] Nor was

---

[1] Anthony Howard and Richard West *The Making of the Prime Minister* (Jonathan Cape, London 1965), pp. 175–6.

[2] Herbert Morrison *Government and Parliament: A Survey from the Inside* (Oxford University Press, London 1954). The circumstances of its composition, and the important role of Norman Chester are described in Bernard Donoughue and G. W. Jones *Herbert Morrison: Portrait of a Politician* (Weidenfeld and Nicolson, London 1973), p. 528–9.

Labour altogether short on that other traditional attribute of the ruling élite: metropolitan condescension. John Strachey, one of the last active politicians who had held senior office in the Attlee Government, and who would have been offered senior office by Wilson had he not died suddenly in 1963, hardly tried to conceal his distaste for his Dundee constituency (he and his wife cheered up when the train bearing them south entered England). At one stage, he even employed an agent who quite openly loathed the constituency, which predictably went, over time, from a safe Labour seat to a marginal.[1] Gaitskell in 1961 was privately rebuked for his taste for socializing with an essentially Tory smart set by, of all people, Anthony Crosland, one of his rising young supporters. Crosland (who had himself when younger been intimately associated with certain wayward female scions of the nobility) defended his rebuke by citing the offensive degree to which swanning around in Conservative circles, especially in country houses, had already alienated Roy Jenkins from his nominal Labour loyalties.[2]

Nor was the Labour leadership less pro-American than their Conservative counterparts. In the 1950s and '60s, a steady stream of Labour leaders like Gaitskell, George Brown, Patrick Gordon Walker, Anthony Crosland, Douglas Jay, Michael Stewart, John Strachey and Denis Healey crossed the Atlantic at the expense of the American 'Foreign Leaders Program', or the Rand Corporation, or the Institute for Strategic Studies. Strachey and Healey were left with their early Communist associations as a skimpy fig-leaf over their rising right-wing tendencies. Increasingly, these men wrapped themselves by association in the glamour surrounding President John F. Kennedy, whom Patrick Gordon Walker, Wilson's shadow Foreign Secretary described as 'the man they trusted to hold the thunderbolt'.[3] Given what emerged after his assassination in November 1963 about the unstructured nature of Kennedy's decision-taking, and his instinct for confrontation, this was simple faith indeed.

Despite an amiable disposition and an accent which made it clear that, unlike Jenkins, he did not mean to assimilate unconditionally to the social style of the Establishment, Wilson did not believe that the public should intervene in serious decision-making. When Gordon Walker was defeated at the general election by a Conservative candidate who dared to voice the considerable concern in the constituency about the scale and implications of sustained large-scale coloured immigration from the Commonwealth, the new Premier nevertheless appointed him Foreign Secretary and described his opponent as a 'parliamentary leper'. The time-honoured procedure for restoring Gordon Walker to the Commons involved levering an established Labour by-election candidate out of the 'safe' constituency of Leyton, where the Foreign Minister then ran in such lordly style that he did not even deign to mention immigration in his manifesto. Early in 1965,

[1] Hugh Thomas *John Strachey* (Eyre Methuen, London 1973), pp. 221–4; 274–5 and 282–3.

[2] Susan Crosland *Tony Crosland* (Hodder and Stoughton, Coronet pbk edn, London 1983), pp. 107–8.

[3] Coral Bell *The Debateable Alliance: An Essay in Anglo-American Relations* (Oxford University Press, London 1964), p. 129.

he lost, narrowly but deservedly, to the Tory candidate. Even the Liberal candidate advocated stricter control of immigration on a 'strictly non-racialist basis'. The phrase has been denounced as meaningless, but it had (whether that candidate knew it or not) a precise meaning. Churchill in his last spell as premier had been willing to legislate to control immigration, but had been told that it could not be done on a racialist basis. Since there was no substantial immigration from the white communities of the Commonwealth, Churchill was not unduly deterred, so the last obstacle had to be unmasked. There was substantial immigration from the Republic of Ireland, which was not even a Commonwealth member. These people enjoyed not just right of entry but also immediate full voting rights. The case for armed resistance to Westminster could hardly have had a better demonstration, for even Conservative politicians were fanatically reluctant to touch those rights.[1] The Treasury certainly regarded every immigrant from the West Indies or India as a damper on wage inflation. Ever since India had remained in the Commonwealth as a republic in 1947, the already confused and potentially mischievous state of nationality law in the UK had headed for the realms of the absurd. In 1952, the backbench Tory, Enoch Powell, had described the Commonwealth (no longer the British Commonwealth) as 'a fortuitous aggregation of a number of separate entities'.[2] As ever, he was the skeleton at the feast of self-satisfaction, but he was right. The fact that a great many who alleged that here was a Government conspiracy to conceal the scale of coloured immigration were racists, did not mean that there was no such conspiracy. The studious avoidance of any collection of statistics on the subject alone showed there was. Powell was to be dismissed from the Shadow Cabinet by Home's successor, Ted Heath, in 1968 for a violent speech on immigration. Both major party leaderships moved reluctantly to establish controls on Commonwealth immigration, but Labour was to move, to its cost, the slower of the two.

There was thus much of the traditionalist in Wilson, but after thirteen years of ruling, Conservatives had come to regard any non-Conservative government as somehow illegitimate. It was very much the attitude Tories had shown to pre-1914 Liberal Governments. They had, however, two reasonable hopes. The first was that the scale of the balance of payments crisis and run on the pound would compel Wilson to abandon any radical legislation in a bid to restore business confidence. That scenario would, almost certainly, lead to serious splits in the Labour Party. On the other hand, the pressure was fierce. The deficit had been £35 million in 1963. The new Government was advised that the 1964 figure was likely to be £800 million. Nor was a domestic consumer-boom the sole engine of disaster. Between 1957 and 1967, the maintenance of large and expensive armed forces in both Germany and the Far East helped new Government spending abroad rise from £147 million in 1957 to £499 million in 1967. The situation was not helped by the policies of the Kennedy administration in the US which practised deficit financing and tax-cutting at a time of sharp economic growth (when orthodox Keynsianism recommended the opposite),

[1] Lamb *Failure of the Eden Government*, pp. 15–24.
[2] Patrick Cosgrove *The Lives of Enoch Powell* (The Bodley Head, London 1989), p. 128.

and tried to maintain the value of the dollar by high interest rates, attracting funds from countries like the UK.[1] The second Conservative hope was not unconnected with the first: economic crisis might make Wilson seek some sort of national coalition, guaranteed to split Labour as well as restoring Conservatives to power.

In a sense, the new Premier's prime achievement was to avoid both traps. As the exchange crisis deepened, the Tories were, in Wilson's words, 'cock-a-hoop' and Maudling 'unhelpful', in that his remarks encouraged rather than dampened speculation. The voice of the City, Lord Cromer, demanded, with increasing violence the abandonment of the social programmes in the Labour manifesto, and domestic deflation so drastic as to involve suspending work on schools and roads under construction. That this was instant political suicide for a Government with a majority of four, later three, seemed to distress the City not at all. Wilson eventually taxed Cromer to his face with trying to negate an unpalatable election result, and his lordship '. . . had to admit that that was what his argument meant, because of the sheer compulsion of the economic dictation of those who exercised decisive economic power.'[2]

One possible escape from this nightmare situation was instant devaluation which could then be blamed, quite fairly, on the men who more than any others had allowed the situation to get out of hand: Home and Maudling. Though the Treasury mandarins led by Sir William Armstrong regarded even the contemplation of devaluation as a moral lapse, the upper bureaucracy was not solid on this topic. Some of its younger members could see clearly enough that a Labour Government which did not devalue might have no room for manoeuvre. In fact, the decision not to devalue was taken almost at once and presented as a *fait accompli* to the Cabinet, whose influence on economic decisions at this point and for some time ahead was zero. Ostensibly, it was taken by three men: the Premier, who considered devaluation would be a political gift to the Conservatives; James Callaghan, who echoed Conservative Treasury hostility to devaluation; and George Brown, who had come up through the Transport and General Workers Union, and who represented union hostility to devaluation as a means of lowering real wages (which had for some time been rising ahead of production). In fact, Wilson and Callaghan had already in 1964 reached an understanding with Alfred Hayes, President of the New York Federal Reserve Bank, to the effect that if Labour agreed not to devalue the pound (seen as an outwork defending the equally over-valued US dollar), massive American support would be given to the pound sterling. The US administration was told about Chancellor Callaghan's first, deflationary budget before the Labour Cabinet. Cromer and the City were outflanked. Cromer was bitterly resentful. In January 1966, he actually threatened to resign when he heard that Callaghan had, without consulting him, invited the Vice President of the New York Federal Reserve to London for talks. There

[1] Alan P. Dobson *The Politics of the Anglo-American Economic Special Relationship 1940–1987* (Wheatsheaf, Brighton 1988), pp. 208–10.
[2] Harold Wilson *The Labour Government 1964–70: A Personal Record* (Weidenfeld and Nicolson, London, 1971) p. 37.

was, however, a price: the Government could not go against American political and diplomatic objectives.[1]

The Americans were routinely consulted about changes in UK bank rate. Callaghan, who had the impudence to tell the Cabinet that informing them in advance about the contents of his budget would constitute 'subverting the Constitution', automatically informed the US government about all proposed major economic initiatives long before he revealed them to the Cabinet. Gordon Walker's successor at the Foreign Office, Michael Stewart, and Wilson himself crossed to America as soon as possible to meet the new President Lyndon B. Johnson. The Americans themselves had no illusions. Their courtly ambassador to the UK through most of the 1960s was the Virginian David Bruce. He was one of a long succession of US ambassadors to cut a swathe through London's social life, but in 1967 he told the US State Department that, 'The so-called Anglo-American special relationship is now little more than sentimental terminology.'[2] By the 1960s, both the French and West German economies were larger and growing much faster than that of the UK, but Wilson was a useful ally, and in late 1965, a deal was hammered out under which the US organized multilateral central bank support for sterling, in exchange for no reduction in the UK global defence effort, guarantees against reflation, and an undertaking to have some sort of statutory incomes policy. Concealed from the public, Parliament and most of the Cabinet, this deal underpinned Wilson's short-term electoral strategy.

If the most important decisions were kept secret, some of the most highly publicized decisions were to prove less important than they looked. Despite being essentially an old-style manipulative party boss, Wilson had talked much about the 'white heat' of a technological revolution which he implied he would facilitate. The one concrete proposal related to this in the 1964 Labour manifesto was for the establishment of a new Ministry of Technology. It achieved little more than a grouping of pre-existing Whitehall functions under a new umbrella. So far from conjuring up the 'new science-based industries' (about which Wilson had talked so confidently on television), it never seems to have had a clear remit. The other major institutional innovation was the Department of Economic Affairs, set up under George Brown with the highest hopes that it would mark a radical break with Treasury dominance of economic policy-making. Wilson himself seems to have shared a widespread perception that the essentially negative spirit of the Treasury was one reason for the UK's failure to break out of the 'vicious circles' of low growth and 'stop-go'. Brown, with typical hyper-enthusiasm for any cause he made his own, saw it as 'the opening campaign of a major social revolution'.[3] It was always likely to face grim hostility from the Treasury. Bizarrely, a significant proportion of its staff came from the Treasury. Its functions were never defined. Wilson used it

[1] Stephen Dorril and Robin Ramsay *Smear: Wilson and the Secret State* (Fourth Estate, London 1991), Chap. XI: 'Wilson and the Bankers'.

[2] Clive Ponting *Breach of Promise: Labour in Power 1964–1970* (Penguin edn, London 1990), p. 43.

[3] George Brown *In My Way: The Political Memoirs of Lord George Brown* (Victor Gollancz, London 1971), p. 95.

as a parking place for one of his two rivals. The other headed the Treasury. The two loathed one another, egged on by Wilson, a great divider and ruler. Before it became extinct in 1969, it produced an electorally useful National Plan in September 1965. Its targets were quite unrealistic, and the Premier did not have mechanisms to implement them.

He did have the wit to reject approaches for a coalition early on from the Liberals, who had shortly before been trumpeting their destiny as gravediggers of Labour hopes. Far more important, as the economic crisis grew in intensity in 1965, was his negative response when Home and Maudling approached him, oozing bonhomie, with offers of coalition. This was regarded as a serious possibility within the Establishment. Harold Macmillan, for example, speculated that 'might not a situation be developing when a coalition government could be set up?' He even contemplated being drafted for high office in it. He would then have taken a life peerage which could be fixed 'in a matter of hours'.[1] Wilson was no Ramsay MacDonald. He knew he had the economic underpinnings to survive and go to the polls in his own time. That doomed Home, who hardly bothered to fight when Edward Heath seriously challenged for the Tory leadership. After losing the next election, Home knew he would have to go anyway. Graceful surrender guaranteed the reversion of the Foreign Office. Meantime, Wilson urbanely collected credit for his early handling of the unilateral declaration of independence by white settlers in Rhodesia led by Ian Douglas Smith. The Premier was firm but conciliatory. Economic sanctions were organized to try to bring down the Smith regime. The Conservative Party's sympathies were divided. There was no discernible enthusiasm amongst the public to use force in Africa.

The whips had enabled the Government to survive on a majority of three, though they were greatly helped by the fact that a post-election swing to Labour in the polls made the Conservatives anxious not to defeat the Government by voting in the Commons. When the polls turned adverse, it happened that parliament was in recess, and when it resumed they swung back in Labour's favour consistently up to the March 1966 election in which, with 48 per cent of the vote compared with the Tory 42 per cent Labour won 363 seats and a comfortable majority of 98 over all parties. Incumbency (summed up in the slogan 'You Know Labour Government Works'), plus obvious competence and widespread perception that the economic problems were a Tory heritage explained the triumph. It is true that only three-quarters of the electorate voted, but power not participation was the professionals' criterion. Wilson was enshrined in right-wing demonology, having foiled the bankers, avoided the coalition trap and manipulated a window of electoral opportunity. It was his great misfortune that leading figures in the CIA like its counter-intelligence chief, James Jesus Angleton, and Peter Wright of the UK's MI5 were deeply paranoid. Rumours that the Premier was a Russian spy flew around the Anglo-American security complex. MI5 was the source of a crazy theory that Gaitskell has been assassinated to clear the way for Wilson. Wild rumours flew around about the Premier's (rather dull) private life. System-

[1] Harold Evans *Downing Street Diary: The Macmillan Years 1957–1963* (Hodder and Stoughton, London 1981), p. 303.

atic surveillance of his colleagues and Government was facilitated by the fact that senior Labour party figures were CIA or MI5 agents. In the case of the outrageous homosexual MP Tom Driberg, there is every reason to think he was at least a double agent, feeding rubbish to both sides in exchange for effective immunity from arrest for soliciting outside public lavatories. Wright really saw himself as struggling to stop the Russians from taking over the Government. The Bank of England Director and newspaper tycoon, Cecil King (a Harmsworth on his mother's side) was from mid-1966 onwards talking obsessively about the impending economic collapse and the prospect of three million unemployed (a figure only approached under Conservative rule in the early 1990s). To defend 'the British way of life' he wanted what Home, Maudling and Cromer had all tried to peddle: a National Government. King was however clearly prepared to obtain it via some sort of coup. Lord Louis Mountbatten, warhero, royal and Chief of Defence Staff 1959–65, was his chosen figurehead, but Mountbatten refused to play this deranged game.[1]

Though there were acute economic difficulties in 1966–68, it was precisely in this period that the profound conservatism of Wilson came to the fore. He had never 'sold out' to the Americans. When they pressed him for politically damaging concessions, like surrendering the nominal independence of the British deterrent to NATO, or supporting their war in Vietnam physically rather than verbally, he refused. Their other demands, listed in a briefing for President Johnson in 1967, like staying in the Far East, deflation to control the balance of payments, no thinning of forces in Germany or 'giving up on entry to Europe' were acceptable to him anyway. His defence of sterling had been depicted by sympathetic commentators as heroic, and that is how he saw it.[2] With a large majority and five years to make an early devaluation work, he had no desire to follow that path until swept traumatically down it by irresistible economic crisis in November 1967. His innovations such as the DEA were foundering. George Brown, though endowed with a naturally quick mind, was a deplorable colleague, endlessly drunk in business hours, jealously resentful of Wilson, and subject to violent mood swings even when sober. His transfer to the Foreign Office in August 1966 was the final demonstration that under a Premier who had himself the mentality of a senior bureaucrat, Treasury ascendancy was unchallengable. It was also the prelude to another attempt to join the Common Market. Brown himself was a genuine 'Euromaniac' to use the contemporary term (i.e. he regarded the desirability of entry as an article of faith). He could and did rationalize it brilliantly, but ultimately his commitment was absolute and emotional. It did not matter. De Gaulle vetoed the application in May 1967. All his objections to Macmillan applied doubly to the Wilson regime.

If forcible devaluation plus drastic internal deflation as the price of support from the International Monetary Fund destroyed the Premier's self-created image, it also compelled the UK into long-delayed choices. Wilson's

---

[1] Dorril and Ramsay *Smear*, Chap. XXIV: 'The Cecil King Coup'.
[2] Henry Brandon *In the Red: The Struggle for Sterling 1964–1966* (André Deutsch, London 1966). This is a revised and extended version of Brandon's influential *Sunday Times* reporting on 'How Sterling Came in from the Cold'.

new Chancellor Roy Jenkins hardly chose devaluation by 14.3 per cent from $2.80 to $2.40. It had been forced on his predecessor, Callaghan, but he did try to make it work by sustained internal deflation whilst repaying sterling balances (effectively debts held by foreign countries) as a prelude to winding up the Sterling Area, which was clearly beyond the powers of the UK to uphold. In defence, despite American objections, Wilson gave up the attempt to maintain an east of Suez presence, announcing in January 1968 that the British retreat from Singapore, Malaysia and the Persian Gulf would be complete by 1971, and that the Royal Navy would cease to operate carriers by 1972. It was less a decision than a snapping of an over-stretched piece of string. The UK had very successfully waged a 'confrontation' with Indonesia (at a cost of £250 million, £100 million of it in foreign exchange) in 1963–6 to protect the federation of Malaysia. Critics of the January 1968 announcement pointed out that in terms of military achievement for money spent, the amphibious operations east of Suez compared well with either an expensive deterrent whose sole functional value was to increase leverage with the Americans, or vastly expensive forces in Germany waiting to fight an unlikely and debatably sustainable conventional war with Russia.[1] However, with loans from American and Continental bankers sustaining the pound, and Common Market entry desperately desired, critical reassessment was unlikely. When American critics like Dean Acheson had complained about the post-imperial UK's failure to 'find a role' they actually meant 'adopt the role which would suit America'.

Wilson was effectively the prisoner of his new Chancellor, whose resignation would so shake confidence as to destroy the Government. Brown's resignation in March 1968 was a positive relief, and his complaint that the Premier was high-handedly ignoring the Cabinet was comic for two reasons. Brown himself had a truly despicable taste for high-handedly pulling rank on and publicly insulting people whose position did not allow them to reply. Secondly, the balance of power had altered dramatically. The Tories were so far ahead in the polls that few Labour politicians believed they could win the next election. Young people who had joined the Labour Party in the early 1960s were abandoning it in droves. Disillusionment was rampant. What saved the Premier was the venomously bad atmosphere which existed between his potential rivals. The diaries which were being kept, with a view to publication, by Dick Crossman, who was Lord President and later Secretary of State for Health and Social Security, bring out the intricacy of the infighting between Cabinet members, but as one well-informed bureaucrat remarked in retrospect, they do not convey the sheer loathing which poisoned the air between Wilson, Brown and Callaghan.[2]

[1] C. J. Bartlett *The Long Retreat: A Short History of British Defence Policy, 1945–70* (Macmillan, London 1972), pp. 220–7.

[2] The emphasis on 'how much they all hated each other' can be found in comments by Lord Bottomley, a Cabinet member as Secretary of State for Commonwealth Affairs 1964–66; Sir Richard Powell, Permanent Secretary at the Board of Trade until 1968; and Sir Trevor Lloyd Hughes, Press Secretary to Wilson 1964–69, which can all be found in the record of a symposium 'The Crossman Diaries Reconsidered', in ·*Contemporary Record*, Vol. 1, No. 2, Summer 1987, p. 29.

For Wilson, this ensured that there could be life after political death, though life of an unpleasant kind. His Chancellor had no real sympathy with the Labour Party. He was not averse to condescending to use it as a vehicle for his ascent to the post of prime minister, but as the other and better Cabinet diarist, Barbara Castle, pointed out (and it was common knowledge), he could not hope to do so if Wilson won the next election.[1] Government policies could no longer be automatically implemented, as became clear in 1968 over what was dubiously called the 'reform' of the House of Lords. It was a scheme sanctioned by Wilson and the Tory leader Heath, but in fact drawn up by Crossman and Heath's spokesman, Lord Carrington. It would have deprived existing peers of their vote whilst adding about 230 new peers nominated by the prime minister, but roughly in proportion to the balance of parties in the Commons. In short, it was additional silver lining on party-leader Heaven, for the minority nominations would also have come from party leaders. Defeated by a wholly reasonable alliance of the right, led by Enoch Powell, and the left, by Michael Foot, the bill's failure to pass made no real difference. Heath's Government simply implemented it by royal prerogative, minus only the deprivation of existing peers. More serious was the rout of proposals for imposing a legal framework on industrial relations.

Conceived as a means of defusing an electoral issue raised by the Conservatives, the Government proposals were sponsored by Wilson and his optimistically-named Secretary of State for Employment and Productivity, Barbara Castle. They were embedded in a White Paper, 'In Place of Strife'. Every conceivable tactical blunder was made by the sponsors. Callaghan led a revolt in Cabinet, designed to topple Harold the Second in favour of King Jim. The Trade Union Congress was implacably hostile to Government intervention, but the proposals were not defeated by the TUC. They were defeated by Cabinet members and backbenchers, all of whom expected to lose the next election. Castle received the impression that in his heart of hearts, Wilson expected to lose it. His colleagues could see no sense at all in having the Labour movement tear itself apart over the issue when the Conservatives were sure to legislate on it, and face whatever problems legislation created. After trying to force legislation through by threatening resignation, Wilson grasped that nobody cared if he did resign, and surrendered on the whole issue.[2]

That he subsequently thought he would win the 1970 election was in itself an extraordinary phenomenon, though at the time he had grounds for optimism. By May 1970, the lead which the Conservatives had held in all reputable opinion polls for three years quite suddenly began to shrink. Because the Jenkin's Chancellorship made the balance of payments the test of economic rectitude, the fact that after deficits of $461 million in 1967 and nearly $400 million in 1968, it swung into a positive balance of £387 million in 1969 altered perceptions of the Government significantly. Even more telling after years of 'freezes' and 'severe restraint'; the abandonment of price and income controls in April 1969 saw real wages surge ahead. The

---

[1] Entry for Wednesday 5 November 1969 in Barbara Castle *The Castle Diaries 1964–70* (Weidenfeld and Nicolson, London 1984), p. 726.
[2] Ponting *Breach of Promise*, Chap. 22: 'Breach of Promise'.

well-funded, carefully prepared Conservative campaign had been designed for a time of crisis and gloom. Now under the uncharismatic Heath, they faced the twin threats of perceived prosperity and Wilson's reassuring imitation of Stanley Baldwin. That the Labour Party in key marginals had virtually ceased to exist under the shocks and disillusionment of the three previous years was less apparent. The 266 Labour paid election agents of 1966 were down to 144 in 1970. In 468 constituencies Labour had only volunteer agents.[1] Misleadingly bad trade figures in the last week of the campaign hurt Labour, but widespread distrust of the artful dodger Wilson and his 'presidential' if soporific style probably hurt more. On a low 72 per cent turnout the Conservatives benefited from an average 4.8 per cent swing to them to capture 330 seats. With 46.4 per cent of votes cast, they had an overall majority of thirty. Labour, with 43 per cent of the vote had 287 seats. The Liberals, the Welsh Nationalists and the Scottish Nationalists, who had been the principal by-election beneficiaries of Labour's years of spectacular unpopularity, all suffered setbacks at this general election. The new Liberal leader, Jeremy Thorpe, saw seven of his party's thirteen seats lost. The Scottish National Party (SNP) was left clinging precariously to a single seat in the Outer Hebrides.

The result was scarcely a ringing endorsement for the Tories. It was an expression of disillusionment both with the economic record of the 1960s, which had turned out to be a heightened version of the much-denounced 1950s, and with the political system in general, which was clearly viewed with deep if vague scepticism by much of the electorate. There was no chance that the latter point would be taken up by major politicians. The only political agenda which truly interested them was their own one, and they remained addicted to the vision of faster growth mainly because it would facilitate that agenda and produce a quiescent electorate. The best political commentators of the era agreed that the traditional functions of the Commons had become meaningless, but they also agreed that executive dominance was inevitable and irreversible, because only the executive had the power to reverse this trend. That executive was visibly not coping, but could be relied upon to assume that the bad situation would be better if it had more exclusive control over possible responses to it. In the words of perhaps the brightest of young right-wing Labour MPs of the period in an extremely perceptive commentary written just before the 1970 election:

> As a result it is likely that the solutions adopted will be mixed but will, on the whole, confirm the present drift towards centralised executive power controlled only by the reference of the government and the Prime Minister's overall record to the voters at infrequent general elections.[2]

---

[1] Robert Rhodes James *Ambitions and Realities: British Politics 1964–1970* (Weidenfeld and Nicolson, London 1972), pp. 250–1.

[2] John P. Mackintosh *The Government and Politics of Britain* (Hutchinson University Library, pbk edn, London 1970), p. 188.

12

Humpty Dumpty and the Queen's Men.
Heath, Wilson and Callaghan 1970–9

The prime minister of the day need pay no attention to his ministers, nor to the House of Commons, as long as nothing goes seriously wrong. If it does, he is removed and almost immediately forgotten, while someone else takes his place. All the talk about Wilson's—or Home's or Macmillan's—mastery of the House of Commons is meaningless. While he is PM, he automatically masters the House. The day he leaves 10 Downing St he ceases to matter.

Entry for 9 October 1966 in *The Cecil King Diary 1965–70*
(Jonathan Cape, London 1972), p. 93.

We English gentlemen hate the name of a lie; but how often do we find public men who believe each other's words?

The final sentence of Chapter 13 of Anthony Trollope *Barchester Towers*.

Humpty Dumpty sat on a wall,
Humpty Dumpty had a great fall,
All the King's horses and all the King's men,
Couldn't put Humpty together again.

Traditional nursery rhyme

If the 1970 general election marked the failure of a Government appeal heavily focussed on the personality of the Premier, it did not mark any reduction in the status and centrality of his office; rather the contrary. Heath could claim an unusual degree of credit for the general election result. He had gone into the election aware that if he lost he could not expect to survive on the grounds he had fought well, as he had in 1966. A twice-defeated pretender was wisest to leave the field of battle, and it was a measure of the initial pessimism of his party during the campaign that, out of kindness, a meeting had been arranged for just after the declaration of the result, to help Heath pick another career.[1] Instead, he became Prime Minister at a time when it was becoming commonplace to describe

---

[1] Margaret Laing *Edward Heath: Prime Minister* (Sidgwick and Jackson, London 1972), pp. 1–2.

the political system as presidential. Cecil King had believed this to be so by 1966. In 1970 Dick Crossman, whilst a Cabinet member, delivered three Godkin Lectures at Harvard in which he argued that cabinet government in the UK had been effectively replaced by what he called prime ministerial government. Though such a description was not inappropriate for Harold Wilson's position before 1966, it may be doubted if it was a realistic assessment of his powers in 1969–70. Crossman was much more realistic in his description of the boredom and futility of backbenchers' lives in the Commons, and their role as mere lobby-fodder for whips. He was maliciously precise in calibrating the inability of the Commons to remove a minister, arguing that the bigger the mess in a ministry, the more anxious the Government usually was to cover it up by insisting all was well.[1]

Edward Heath's succession to power was nothing like the sharp break in political continuity which Harold Wilson had tried to imply it would be during the election. Wilson had seized on the results of a Shadow Cabinet session in the Selsdon Park Hotel in Croydon in January 1970 to denounce Heath as 'Selsdon Man', a primitive capitalist creature hell-bent on dismantling state-sponsored welfare systems and introducing the crudest forms of capitalist market economics as an alternative to the substantial state involvement which had characterized the management of the UK economy since the Second World War. It had proved difficult to shift the proportion of gross national product absorbed by state expenditure towards a lower figure. It stood at about 41 per cent in 1951, dipped to 36 per cent in 1958 but was back at 41 per cent by 1963.[2] There had of course been intellectuals such as F. A. Hayeck who as early as 1944 had argued that any serious expansion of state activity led straight to totalitarian tyranny. There were undoubtedly echoes of Hayeck in Churchill's 1945 'Gestapo' speech. It was a creed with a strong potential appeal to the right, just as the crass over-simplifications of Marxist or Trotskyite theory had a recurring fascination for the extreme left, but it had been so belied by events in the UK as to possess little inherent power to change the pattern of developments.

This did not mean that the Conservative and Labour Parties had converged on a non-ideological compromise christened 'Butskellism' by the media (after Gaitskell and Butler). Anthony Sampson, author and journalist, interviewed Heath for his *New Anatomy of Britain*, published in 1971. It was a revised version of a successful *Anatomy of Britain* he had published in 1962. That book had come out of a welter of volumes provoked by the evidence that the UK was failing to match the growth rates of her principal rivals. They all had titles stressing words like 'suicide' and 'stagnant', and they all latched onto the somewhat glib idea that it was the insular and archaic nature of British society which explained the 'failure'.[3] Sampson's

---

[1] Richard Crossman's *Inside View: Three Lectures on Prime Ministerial Government* (Jonathan Cape, London 1972), is the UK-published version of three Godkin Lectures 'on the Essentials of Free Government and the Duties of the Citizen' delivered in Harvard University in April 1970. See pp. 59 and 101.

[2] Bartlett *History of Postwar Britain*, p. 208.

[3] The archetypal example of this literature is Michael Shanks *The Stagnant Society* (Penguin, London 1961).

first revision of the 1962 *Anatomy* bucked the trend by stressing, correctly, how much social change had already occurred under cover of old labels being plastered over new contents. Wilson, who had just become Premier when the revised version (entitled *Anatomy of Britain Today*) appeared in 1965, received a eulogistic write-up as 'the first Englishman outside the traditional middle or upper class ever to have become prime minister' (Lloyd George was Welsh and Ramsay MacDonald Scots). Wilson was also praised for his 'austere and lonely dynamic'.[1] By 1971, after the sixties had turned out much like the fifties, Sampson was visibly falling back on the old platitude about archaism, in the Dean Acheson style, comparing the UK to seventeenth-century Imperial Spain. Presumably this helped to explain why the even more insular, and socially even more (in some ways) archaic, society of Japan was making such a bad job of adjusting to a post-imperial industrial role. However, there was a commendably perceptive note in Heath's replies to Sampson's questions about consensus:

> There never was a consensus . . . The parties never came together in their policies. Even the idea of 'Butskellism' was sloppy and inaccurate; it bore no relation to the facts . . . The Conservatives did manage to do quite a lot between 1951 and 1964 . . . Now we have to get back to the traditional British attitude of independence from the state . . . Of course, our view is not an extreme one; we accept that there are many fields, like pensions, defence and aviation where the state must be involved.[2]

That summed the situation up neatly. Conservatives had a basic bias towards lower taxes, less welfare expenditure and a smaller state sector. On the other hand, their political antennae told them that the window of opportunity to move dramatically in this direction did not exist. They faced the formidable ex-Premier Wilson, at the head of a more-or-less coherent Labour Party. Their majority was only 30: enough to see them through a parliament but easily wiped out by quite a small adverse swing at a general election. Furthermore, everyone knew that a Premier clearly heading for defeat by mid-term could have a difficult and unstable two years ahead of him. The threat was from his own party. The Commons remained almost as ineffective as ever, despite considerable efforts dating back to the period 1965–9 to develop and expand its select committee structures. This had been a favourite project of Dick Crossman. As early as 1969–70, 254 MPs had served on select committees, which compares well with the 291, or nearly half the total, who so served in 1974–75. They had a certain investigative capability and helped fill the lives of MPs out of office, but whips chose the committees and the Government could, in the last analysis, refuse to produce evidence, a bureaucrat or even a minister. None of this activity was allowed to bear on the serious business of decision-making, let alone on proposals for legislation. Ritualized party conflict remained the dominant political theatre. One commentator at the end of the 1970s remarked that it was difficult to persuade students to take parliament seriously, adding: 'Any why should they? From the outset one is bound to confess that even as an observation platform from which to survey the

[1] Anthony Sampson *Anatomy of Britain Today* (Hodder and Stoughton, London 1965), pp. 86 and 104.
[2] *Idem The New Anatomy of Britain* (Hodder and Stoughton, London 1971), p. 100.

places where real decisions are taken the House of Commons has limited value.'[1]

As Leader of the Conservative Party before 1970, Heath had taken advantage of the control he had over the composition of the Shadow Cabinet to get rid of some of the leading figures in the 'new right' of the party. Angus Maude and Enoch Powell were both peremptorily sacked from the Shadow Cabinet, and with more difficulty (because he fought back by enlisting support from Conservative area chairmen) Edward Du Cann had been forced out and replaced as Chairman of the Conservative Party by a Heath trusty, Anthony Barber. Heath was therefore not ideologically driven on the subject of market economics, though he believed in them, and he clearly detested the attempt sponsored by thinkers like Powell to stimulate a public debate on the post-imperial meaning of British identity. The populist edge to this attempt ran totally counter to the oligarchic and authoritarian core of Heath's personality.[2] The irrelevance of his humble origins to anything but his social insecurity was striking. He had moved up the system from Chief Whip to Premier and he was what the system had made him.

He was pragmatic about many matters, but utterly dogmatic on two issues, one more obvious than the other. The obvious one was the Common Market. Heath was a convinced believer in a politically integrated western Europe. The precise form of such a structure was perhaps not something he would have been prepared to be drawn on in 1970, but then that was true of other English enthusiasts for a politically unified western Europe, like the former ambassador to France, Lord Gladwyn. The latter was the supreme Establishment presence in such bodies as 'Britain in Europe', which he chaired. His detestation of de Gaulle's EEC policy was not confined to the two vetos against the UK. Gladwyn angrily rejected the General's confederal vision of a 'Europe of states', and was clearly most anxious that a neo-Gaullist policy towards the EEC should not be allowed to become a serious option in the UK. At the time of the Labour application for entry he had organized what he described as 'a large number of MPs, peers and distinguished people' to sign a declaration for 'a political Europe', and his rage over the second veto made him allege that the 'Bonapartist bombast' of de Gaulle was leading France into a future 'as a sort of Soviet satellite'.[3] It was an oddly American misapprehension, but with Heath at the helm after 1970, Gladwyn, a recent Liberal convert, had a Premier after his own heart. De Gaulle had fallen from power in April 1969, and the Wilson Government had resumed its application for entry.

Heath was therefore following a bipartisan policy when he picked up the application. As Foreign Minister, Labour's George Brown had appointed a Tory politician, Churchill's son-in-law, Christopher Soames, to the Paris

---

[1] *The Commons in the Seventies*, eds S. A. Walkland and Michael Ryle (Collins, Fontana edn, London 1977), Chaps. 9 and 12. The quote is from p. 240.

[2] Laing in *Edward Heath* (a biography compiled with help from the subject, and very much in favour of him) describes on p. 215 his 'predilections' as 'oligarchic, rather than democratic'.

[3] Lord Gladwyn *The European Idea* (Weidenfeld and Nicolson, London 1966); *The Memoirs of Lord Gladwyn* (Weidenfeld and Nicolson, London 1972), pp. 358 and 361.

Embassy, in the hope the appointment would facilitate Market entry. It was not the only area of policy on which there was a thinly-disguised compact among the Westminster party leaderships. The Northern Ireland or Ulster problem was another. The province had a devolved administration based at Stormont outside Belfast between 1921 and 1972, and had fought off quite a serious IRA offensive in the 1950s. However, the arrival of a Labour Government in 1964 encouraged the formation of a Campaign for Democracy in Northern Ireland and the emergence of a Civil Rights Movement in Ulster designed to marshal mass protests against long-standing discrimination against the large Roman Catholic minority. Wilson's dislike of the Ulster Unionists, who took the Conservative whip, was undisguised. He made noises about reducing the number of Ulster MPs at Westminster, and encouraged Labour MPs to join the Campaign for Democracy in Northern Ireland. Terence O'Neil, a mildly reformist Northern Ireland Premier, ended up in the classic position of such politicians. He was caught between revolt in his own power-base within the Protestant community and his inability to attract enough compensating support from a radicalized Catholic community. Rioting on a scale beyond any powers the Royal Ulster Constabulary possessed to contain it swept Ulster. Sectarian terrorism reared its head. In 1969, the Westminster Government took the, in retrospect, very debatable decision to introduce its regular troops into Ulster to protect the minority. Whatever the Westminster politicians may have thought, Irish politics were less about justice than about winning, and the long-run winner would be the group which most successfully manipulated Westminster by the mixtures of force and cajolery which had paid such big dividends so often. The killing of regular army troops in Ulster started in 1971. Bombs in London were merely a question of time.

Both Heath and Wilson were determined to keep ultimate control in the hands of the Westminster élite, and to make it clear to Unionist politicians that they would not be divided by the issue. When Terence O'Neil visited Wilson, then Premier, he was whisked round to Heath's Albany apartment immediately after visiting Downing Street, for a display of solidarity. After 1970, Heath as Premier moved to the view that Ulstermen would be less of a pain if they all wanted to unite with the Republic of Ireland. He started characteristic moves to 'encourage' them to think the right way. Wilson made even more militant speeches on the same lines. By 1972, Heath was determined to reduce Stormont to a facade by the transfer of all responsibility for law and order to Westminster. Stormont would have survived as a mere scapegoat, so Brian Faulkner and the Northern Ireland Unionist administration he led preferred to resign. By late 1973 Heath had, after elaborate and exhausting negotiations involving both the London Government and the Republic of Ireland at Sunningdale near London, contrived to set up a 'power-sharing' administration of both Unionists and Nationalists in Belfast, primarily as a cooperative partner in a Council of Ireland behind which he was clearly anxious to put political impetus. Most Ulster Unionists could see perfectly clearly where he was headed and became yet another group in revolt.

By 1974, there was an impressive collection of them. The Government's initial economic policy had been mildly Selsdonish. Interventionist bodies set up by Labour like the Industrial Reorganisation Corporation had been abolished, and the Chancellor, Anthony Barber, had introduced a first budget which cut welfare expenditure and taxes. By 1971, it was clear that the business cycle was turning down into a recession, with low business profitability, low liquidity and low investment. By 1972, the situation was alarming. Inflation was accelerating; between 1970 and 1973, the average rise in retail prices was 8.6 per cent annually. Weekly earnings had risen by 249 per cent between 1963 and 1975, but productivity improvements lagged and prices passed on the difference. Wilson may have exaggerated the strength of the economic position he handed over in 1970, but there was a balance of payments surplus of £300 million in 1971. By 1972, it had become a deficit of £700 million.[1] In June of that year, Barber allowed the pound sterling to float. It was not a voluntary decision. No Westminster government was capable of that degree of rationality. Barber, pressured by exchange crises, fell over backwards into the water and found he floated. Huge increases in world commodity prices exacerbated the situation. In March 1972, with unemployment approaching a million, a highly reflationary Barber budget signalled a total reversal of policies to a reflationary and interventionist pattern which necessarily involved an attempt to control prices and incomes, and which was justified by the old mirage of five per cent annual growth. About a fifth of the parliamentary Tory Party was permanently alienated by the abandonment of the over-hyped 'quiet revolution' against Wilsonian interventionism. What was most offensive of all was the wooden arrogance with which Heath demanded acquiescence. The charming private man was deceptive. A small circle of deferential and supportive friends who are careful not to contradict brings out the best in anyone. The high-handed authoritarian who appeared in public was the real Heath. He believed he had a divine right to rule, whether in accordance with a specific policy, or next week with the precisely opposite policy. It was only a question of how long it would be before his wages and incomes policy brought him into mortal conflict with an equally stubborn *apparatchik* who had come up through the authoritarian hierarchies of the trade union movement rather than those of the Tory Party and Westminster.

The Government had passed an Industrial Relations Act which made collective industrial bargains enforceable by a National Industrial Relations Court. Like the preceding Labour Government, it was anxious to curtail strikes. The next two years saw more than ever before, including a miners' strike and a dockers' strike which represented massive defeats for the Government. It was however a confrontation with the National Union of Mineworkers from November 1973 which proved decisive. The NUM was determined to breach the third stage of the Government's statutory counter-inflation policy. They mounted their assault just as the consequences of American and Israeli policies in the Middle East came home to roost. In 1967, the Israelis had rerun their Suez campaign in the shape of a pre-emptive strike against Nasser. The Egyptian dictator was as irresponsible a windbag as ever, but both the Israelis and their American backers, with whom they cleared the operation through CIA channels, knew he was in

[1] Alan Sked and Chris Cook *Post-War Britain: A Political History* (Penguin, 2nd edn, London 1984), p. 256–7.

no position to attack them. Israel ended up occupying a great deal of Egyptian, as well as some Syrian and Jordanian territory.[1] In October 1973, Nasser's successor, President Anwar Sadat, in alliance with Syria, launched the Yom Kippur War against Israel, one of whose consequences was a decision by Arab states to pressure the western powers by restricting production, and vastly increasing the price of crude oil. The UK's bill for imported oil went up by a factor of roughly four.

One reason for the reckless extremes of the reflation process was undoubtedly the Premier's desire to see the UK economy surge into the Common Market in immensely dynamic shape. Whether Heath made any great difference to Common Market entry is a debatable question. The negotiations were long and difficult. Special transitional terms for Commonwealth sugar producers and New Zealand dairy products were an emotional necessity (and probably recognized as such, even by the French). In May 1971, Heath had held a summit meeting with President Pompidou in Paris in which most remaining problems were solved, but since they were 'solved' mainly by the UK surrendering the basic principle on every issue, the cynic who remarked that 'Soames' chauffeur could have done it' had a point. It was agreed that there should be series of transition periods of up to six years before the main provisions such as the common external tariff, the common agricultural policy, and contributions to the Community budget were fully applied. Nevertheless, the structure of the CAP and the budget in particular meant that the UK was joining West Germany as one of the two main positive contributors. A common fishery policy was rapidly outlined just before UK entry, undoubtedly to prepare the way for an assault on the UK fishing industry and its very substantial proportion of North Sea fish stocks.

None of this could Heath, given his commitment, do much to modify. His problem was that, though his own motives and those of other ardent marketeers like Gladwyn or Roy Jenkins were almost entirely political, there was a consensus among most such advocates that entry should be sold to the public as economically beneficial due to its 'dynamic' effect on the UK economy. Puzzled commentators remarked that there had been 'remarkably little public discussion' of the political dimension of entry. Indeed that was so, and deliberately so. On the other hand, a thoroughly misleading economic confidence was assiduously advertised. The implication was that by associating with faster-growing economies, the UK, presumably by a process of osmosis, would acquire their characteristics, thereby making politicians' lives much easier. Those who pointed out that it was 'not clear what basis there was for optimism'[2] about accelerated growth rates, did not commend themselves to their political masters. Heath, like Ignatius Loyola in this at least, that he was primarily obsessed with the will, did his best to will the desired effect, by means calculated to ensure its opposite. He was desperate to secure a surge in investment. Real interest rates (discounting inflation) were reduced to the historically

[1] Andrew and Leslie Cockburn *Dangerous Liaison: The Inside Story of the US-Israeli Covert Relationship* (HarperCollins, London 1991), pp. 150–5.
[2] Peter Donaldson *Guide to the British Economy* (Penguin, 3rd edn, London 1971), p. 225.

low level of 1.2 per cent by late 1972. Money supply is notoriously difficult to quantify, but by current calculations it rose by 25.6 per cent between January 1972 and January 1973. Wartime excepted, such increases were unheard-of. The resulting boom was based more on consumption and property speculation than investment in manufacturing capacity. Price controls attenuated already poor profit ratios. A splendid outburst of rage by the Premier directed at the Institute of Directors, on the grounds that after many concessions and a promise of 5 per cent growth in 1974 'still you aren't investing enough', did not really help.[1]

There was a certain irony in the way that it was the aftermath of Market entry which destroyed Heath. It was entry which showed him at his most intolerant, literally refusing to speak to Conservative MPs who differed from him on the issue. Of course he added another hostile constituency to the many others in the shape of anti-Market Tory MPs, one of whom, Enoch Powell, felt strongly enough to urge Conservatives to vote Labour at the 1974 election. Yet entry was never in real danger. The Foreign Office was believed to have encouraged the Labour bid for entry in 1967 (in full awareness of its likely failure) mainly to commit Labour to a policy ardently desired by the Foreign Office.[2] In opposition, Labour drifted back to arguing over details (to the extreme anger of Heath, who once shouted to Wilson, 'you ratted'), but there was always a committed core of conservative senior Labour figures prepared to offset Tory anti-Marketeers. The narrowness of some votes in the Commons probably reflected their need to vote with the Government on a rough rota, minimizing individual exposure. When the Shadow Cabinet voted to back an amendment tabled by one of the shrewdest and most amiable of Conservative anti-Marketeers, Neil Marten, calling for a referendum before entry, Labour's deputy leader Roy Jenkins resigned and with close friends openly supported the Government. Both he and George Thomson, a younger Labour marketeer, argued that Wilson in office would have swallowed entry terms he criticized in opposition. Jenkins had no Labour loyalties and Thomson was blatantly cultivating Tory goodwill with hopes of future patronage (which were to be gratified), but they were probably right. That did not make the terms other than rather bad.

Heath's final grapple with the miners was vastly more dangerous. Even before the NUM went to all-out strike, the Government had put industry on a three-day week. (Ironically, production only fell by a fifth, and did not recover until long after the return to normal working.) Every possible expedient offering an escape from the confrontation was tried, from a secret afternoon tea with only the NUM President Joe Gormley, Heath and Sir William Armstrong present, to a full-scale attempt at a corporatist tripartite social pact between Government, the TUC and the CBI.[3] The

[1] Keith Middlemas *Power, Competition and the State. Volume 2: Threats to the Postwar Settlement: Britain 1961–74* (Macmillan, London 1990), pp. 375–6.

[2] Jock Bruce-Gardyne *Whatever Happened to the Quiet Revolution?* (Charles Knight, London 1974), p. 163.

[3] For a survey of the crisis, with comments by several senior participants, see the symposium on 'The Trade Unions and Fall of the Heath Government' in *Contemporary Record*, Vol. 2, No. 1, Spring 1988, pp. 36–45.

alternative was an election and the Government, though confident it would win, hesitated. The final decision was clearly corporate. Heath was a lonely figure and an unusually dominant Premier, but the Cabinet was very much involved in the decision and choice of date.

The machinery of Whitehall fascinated Heath to the point where he was continually tinkering with it. One of his innovations had been the setting up of a central policy review staff within the Cabinet Office. It worked for the Cabinet as a whole, underlining the general implications of proposals so as to provide a balance to the departmental brief prepared for a specific proposal and supplied only to the relevant minister. In practice, Heath's personality inhibited general discussion. Abrupt and intolerant of dissent he had difficulty asking for advice and no capacity for conciliation, let alone compromise. Sitting in the later Macmillan Cabinet had been likened to chatting at court with Henry VIII. Heath was not a chatterer. Certain matters he thought too important for Cabinet, like his partial nationalization of a bankrupt Rolls Royce in 1970. His self-isolation was relentless. Tory backbenchers deemed it plain rudeness. Inevitably, the Premier was forced back on senior mandarins like Sir Douglas Allen, Head of the Treasury, and Sir William Armstrong, Head of the Civil Service Department. It was a tragedy that Iain Macleod, Heath's first Chancellor, had died prematurely. He was one of the few ministers of genuinely independent stature, though Powell's fate does not suggest that Macleod would necessarily have survived politically if he had lived.[1]

There was a hawkish faction in the Cabinet which pressed for an early election. Its spokesmen were Lord Carrington, who was responsible for energy, Anthony Barber, the Chancellor, and Jim Prior, the Minister of Agriculture. Pressure for a hard line (which implied an early election to legitimate it) came also from Conservative Central Office, the Treasury and with considerable emotional thrust from Sir William Armstrong. Opposed to an early election were Robert Carr, the Home Secretary, and William Whitelaw, currently serving in the new post of Secretary of State for Northern Ireland. As such, he had finagled into existence a 'power-sharing' provincial executive which he knew full well had little support in the province, and which he did not want to see exposed at the polls. A reluctant Heath might have won an early February election, which was what the hawks wanted. He eventually called one for 28 February. He needed to win well, and to his own and his party's horror, he failed. The narrowness of the margin was unimportant. He had tried to focus the election campaign on the question 'Who governs?'[2] As he believed he had the right to indicate to the public appropriate modes of thought, he and his colleagues started full of confidence. However, they were essentially a self-righteous liberal oligarchy which had trod on the toes of one constituency after another. Wilson, fighting for his life against an Establishment which clearly meant to exclude him from power for good after his 'ratting' during the Common Market debates, fought stubbornly and successfully to widen the agenda to all the other issues worrying the electorate. The answer which

[1] Middlemas *op. cit.*, pp. 301–2.
[2] Jim Prior *A Balance of Power* (Hamish Hamilton, London 1986), pp. 88–95, gives an admirably succinct account of the Cabinet's divisions and hopes.

emerged to the Government's question may be paraphrased as 'We are not very sure, but not particularly happy about someone as distant and unsympathetic as yourself'. It was a not unreasonable answer. In concrete terms, the Labour Party, with 37.1 per cent of the vote, won 301 seats while the Conservatives, with 37.9 per cent, due to the vagaries of the voting system, fell to 297. The vehicles of protest all did rather well. The Liberals returned fourteen MPs; the Scottish Nationalists, seven; their Welsh equivalent, Plaid Cymru, two; and in Ulster, eleven out of the twelve were Ulster Loyalists opposed to Sunningdale and the power-sharing executive.

There was clearly likely to be another election soon. That alone made Liberal MPs reluctant to ally with the discredited Heath. The new Liberal leader, Jeremy Thorpe, was avid for office (he very much fancied himself as Home Secretary), but bowed reluctantly to his colleagues' views and declined Tory offers of coalition. To everybody's astonishment, and not least his own, Harold Wilson found himself forming a minority Government after Heath finally resigned. The new Government inherited an apparently desperate situation. The economy was in chaos, not to mention massive external deficit. It had a draft legislative programme for a full parliament, because the Whitehall mandarins always prepared two Queen's Speeches based on the manifestos of the Conservative and Labour Parties, but there was no guarantee that the new Government would survive the vote at the end of the debate on the Queen's Speech, which opened parliament. Indeed Heath at one stage made noises about striking the new administration down forthwith. He soon backed off, for it became apparent that Wilson and his experienced team would do better in a second election, especially if they seemed to have had it unreasonably foisted upon them. The Conservative whips worked quite hard at maintaining an appearance of active opposition, without actually winning any significant vote. The Government was not in real danger in parliament. Nor were its early economic decisions agonizing: they were self-evident. The NUM had won its battle. There was nothing left to do but settle broadly on its terms. In just over two days, the strike was settled. In under three, the State of Emergency which had been declared by the Conservatives three months before had, to general public relief, been wound up, and normal daily life resumed. In a conciliatory gesture to the unions, Wilson appointed Michael Foot, from the left wing of his party, as Secretary of State for Employment. Foot's Trade Union and Labour Relations Act, which repealed most of the Conservatives' Industrial Relations Act, reached the statute book in slightly modified form before the summer recess, which was the prelude to the second 1974 election.

Beyond these moves, the situation was extremely difficult. 1972–3 had been the peak of a world boom during which the previous Government had followed recklessly expansionist fiscal and monetary policies. The system of fixed but adjustable rates of exchange set up under the Bretton Woods Agreement of 1944 had dissolved in 1973. Inflation was over 10 per cent by late 1973, and commodity price increases which were sharpened by the depreciation of sterling ensured that further price rises were inevitable. Even the Heath regime had tried to deflate the upward spiral in late 1973 by means of expenditure cuts and restrictions on bank lending. The incoming Labour Government had no really thought-out policies. The Labour Party had a document on economic policy called Labour's Programme 1973, which proposed extensive planning agreements, price control, and a decisive shift in the political allegiance of the main economic muscle in the country through the public ownership of 25 top companies. The overwhelmingly right-wing leadership of the Government at Cabinet level seems to have had no intention of implementing any significant part of this document. Policies were ad hoc decisions taken by experienced ministers in consultation with the Prime Minister. One well-placed observer was struck by 'the infrequency of collective Cabinet discussions on economic policy'. Indeed, in the first twelve months of the Government, he could not recall any sustained discussion of economic policy in the Cabinet or in its committees.[1]

Harold Wilson was absolutely central in the effective decision-taking mechanisms of this Government. He set the parameters of its real agenda. Access to him was crucial, but difficult in the sense that access to his presence was a very different matter from access to the mind behind the enigmatic smile. There had already been trouble about this, most entertainingly during his first reign when Postmaster General George Wigg had fallen out violently with the Premier's long-standing political secretary, Marcia Williams. As his autobiography made only too clear, Wigg was extremely jealous of Williams' growing influence over Wilson (who later ennobled her as Lady Falkender).[2] This sort of squabble was in one sense an inevitable consequence of the monarchical role of the Premier, since in any monarchical system the politics of access matter. In Wilson's case, the inner circle of personal political advisers was more important than usual. When he came back into office in 1974, he authorized the systematic appointment of political advisers by Cabinet ministers. There were about thirty of them spread over fifteen ministries. The Premier had his own unit under Dr Bernard Donoughue which, because it had coordinating functions, was seven strong. There were precedents from previous Conservative administrations, but this systematic development made sense. It was not, as Wilson said, 'going to overturn our powerful government machinery' but it provided an additional source of policy options and above all, perhaps, it helped sieve the huge flow of paper which burden all ministers, and not least the Premier.[3] Wilson, though only in the second half of his fifties, was visibly ageing under the overload of commitment which went with his job. Ronald Reagan was to show, at least during his first term in office after 1981, that it was possible to be a highly effective chief executive of the United States without working the grotesque hours expected of a UK Premier. One of the reasons for the gravity of the problem was the amount of time which was consumed in the Commons, especially

[1] Bernard Donoughue *Prime Minister: The Conduct of Policy under Harold Wilson and James Callaghan* (Jonathan Cape, London 1987), p. 51.

[2] Edward Short *Whip to Wilson* (MacDonald, London 1989), pp. 247–8.

[3] Harold Wilson *Final Term: The Labour Government 1974–1976* (Weidenfeld and Nicolson and Michael Joseph, London 1979), p. 19. The best general survey of the private adviser system is in a paper which Wilson produced for the Commonwealth Premiers meeting in Jamaica in 1975, and reproduced as Appendix V, in his *The Governance of Britain* (Weidenfeld and Nicolson and Michael Joseph, London 1976).

when episodes like late-night sittings occurred. Whips regarded ministerial presence as essential to encourage weary MPs and to give him his due, Wilson did not, as some ministers did, plead his long office hours as a reason for not turning out in the Palace of Westminster.[1]

The short-term objective of the Government was simple: to win another election. The only choice lay between June and October. The Government had of course suffered minor defeats in the legislature as the result of the abnormal situation in which it had no majority, but Wilson was re-running his 1964–6 pattern in which he could use incumbency and the ability of the Government to create its own publicity to offset the violent hostility of most of the press and the bulk of the Establishment, and win the normal working majority at a second election. In October 1976, he failed. Labour had 43 seats more than the Conservatives. The Labour percentage of the vote was 39.2, the Conservative 35.9. Despite their usual high hopes, the Liberals fell back from 15 to 13 and it was the disgruntled periphery, in the shape of 11 Scottish and three Welsh Nationalists, plus 12 very disgruntled Ulster MPs (albeit disgruntled for rather different reasons), which held Wilson to a majority of three guaranteed to be eroded by by-elections or defections.

The brief remaining period of Wilson's second reign seems to have been governed by three factors. One was understandable weariness. The job was crippling. He was still being viciously rubbished in the bulk of the press. The lunatics of the security services were still convinced that he and his close associates were Russian agents. They fed their bizarre theories into media circles through favoured journalist contacts. One of these, who made no bones about his close relationship with MI5 and MI6, even published a thriller in which the central character (very much a Harold Wilson look-alike) is a Labour prime minister, and the central question is whether he is a Russian spy.[2]

The second factor was his general view of what politics were about. He had always been noted for a tendency to search for formulae of a sufficiently embracing character to reconcile the often fiercely antagonistic positions to be found within the Labour Party. That such formulas tended to be bland to the point of being meaningless worried him not at all. He had become an accomplished greasy-pole climber who pragmatically played with the pieces on the political board with a liberal conservative bias, but no other discernible ideological load. Very conscious of the role of luck and the fact that a week was a long time in politics, he knew that geological discoveries in the North Sea meant that 'North Sea oil, we knew, would one day bring our balance of payments into surplus'. It was a characteristically opportunist view of politics, and the widest field of vision he had is best summed up in his own words:

> For years, in fact, Government and Opposition had played a macabre game of musical chairs, in the hope of being in possession of the chair when the oil began to flow in quantity. This lent urgency to the Outs, now led by Mr Heath, to force us to vacate the chair.[3]

[1] Short *Whip to Wilson*, p. 35
[2] Chapman Pincher *Dirty Tricks* (Sidgwick and Jackson, London 1980).
[3] Wilson *Final Term*, p. 16.

In a nutshell: politics was a system of musical chairs played by two groups: the Ins and the Outs. It was a vision worthy of Dean Swift, but not, in Wilson's mouth, consciously ironic.

The third factor appears to have been the one issue in which he retained any great interest, albeit a characteristically oblique one. He wanted to put the Common Market issue permanently to sleep. It threatened the unity of his party. Though most Conservatives were genuinely worried as to where the new Premier stood on the issue in 1974, they rapidly sensed that he in fact wanted to stay in the Market. To remove the issue from the political stage would be Wilson's supreme service to an Establishment whose broken pieces he had spent much of his life repairing. His problem was that the Labour Party was unenthusiastic and had reserved the right of withdrawal. To cap that awkward fact, it was widely recognized that events since entry on 1 January 1973 had 'brought little comfort to the Marketeers and opponents of entry claimed ample justification for their forebodings'. Gallup polls showed that public opinion was consistently hostile in 1972, 1973 and early 1974.[1] Labour's October manifesto guaranteed an appeal to the public within a year. 'Renegotiation' of terms of accession was set in motion. Much of this was pure rhetoric. In April, a contemporary source solemnly recorded: 'Callaghan tells EEC Britain's renegotiation policies: speech regarded as tough, uncompromising'.[2]

The only feature of any significance whatever in the bulk renegotiation package settled with other member states by early 1975 was one providing, in theory, for rebates for a member state whose contributions were out of line with its prosperity. Wilson was clear that the controversial proposal for monetary union was, in practice, a non-issue. He was also happy to establish heads of governments, under the title of the Council of Europe, as a non-statutory but powerful rival to the long-established Brussels Commission of the EEC. Armed with an almost entirely cosmetic document, he then had no difficulty in securing a two-to-one vote in the 1975 referendum, for his new terms. Full Government support was placed behind the call for a 'Yes' vote. All three main party leaderships were enthusiastically behind a well-funded campaign supported by the CBI and the City. The anti-Market minority of the Cabinet and the dissident Tories, led by Michael Foot and Enoch Powell respectively, had little chance. The Premier intoned the end of the issue. Given the nature of his victory, it was unremarkable that this did not happen. The problem of the UK's relationship with the EEC re-emerged under the next Premier and remained, rightly, near the heart of political debate in the late twentieth century. Even before Labour left office in 1979, it was becoming clear that the UK was faring badly in the 'redistributive game' within the Community.[3]

On the domestic front, Labour inherited an almost impossible problem.

---

[1] David McKie and Chris Cook *The Guardian/Quartet Election Guide* (Quartet Books, London 1974), pp. 81–97. This is a guide to issues published after the first 1974 election in the correct expectation that another would follow fast.

[2] *Ibid.*, p. 191.

[3] Andrew G. Scott 'The Labour Government and the European Communities' in *Labour's Economic Policies*, eds. Michael Artis and David Cobham (Manchester University Press, Manchester 1991), pp. 125–6.

The full impact of the oil-price rises was reserved for their period of office, and the brutal fact was that the consequent shift in global economic power required a fall in real wages in the UK Unfortunately, the new Government had inherited from Heath's pay policies a series of 'threshold agreements' which automatically triggered large wage increases as inflation passed certain bench-marks. Ideally, these agreements should have been repudiated, though it is doubtful if the Government was in a position to do so. What is clear is that these agreements were a total disaster. Whereas in 1972–3, inflation had been 9.2 per cent, it rose to 16 per cent in 1973–4, and a horrendous 24.1 per cent in 1974–5. Wages were going up by some 25 per cent annually in 1973–4, which, given the usual two per cent annual growth in output, meant that unit labour costs were soaring. In many ways, the extent to which this economic hurricane was brought under control in 1975–6 was impressive. The Chancellor, Denis Healey, brought in, in April 1975, a 'rough and tough' budget which aimed to cut public deficit spending by a quarter from 1975–6 to 1976–7. Direct and indirect taxes were raised. Subsidies and spending, including the sacred cow of defence spending, were cut.

There was much ribald comment on the 'Social Contract' which Wilson claimed would enable the Government and the unions to cooperate. In a sense, all regimes rest on an implicit social contract, and what was remarkable about this one was the way it permitted the Government to impose mandatory wage restraint. In July 1975, a £6 limit was set on weekly wage increases (10 per cent of average wages). Above an annual income of £8,500 there were to be no increases. The TUC endorsed the proposals. It had no real power over its constituent unions, but the fact that it went along with the policy mattered, and there was a real sanction in the form of a Price Code which made it impossible for firms to pass on increases in wages. Before April 1976, the new wage guidelines were not violated. The Government was helped by a sharp growth in world trade in manufactures in the relatively liberal atmosphere ushered in by the General Agreement of Tariffs and Trade signed originally in 1947 and amplified in 1949 and 1951. By 1953, the 33 signatory countries, all pledged to tariff liberalization, accounted for 80 per cent of world trade. World trade in manufactures rose by 12 per cent in 1976 and soared by 17 per cent overall in the period 1975–7. North Sea oil came on stream in significant amounts by 1977. Wage bargaining was undoubtedly sobered by Government policy, but also (and perhaps more effectively) by a rise in unemployment to 1.125 million in the last quarter of 1975. The current account balance of payments moved into surplus in 1978.[1] Overall, it was a substantial achievement.

Wilson himself turned out to be the stablest of the three major party leaders in 1974–6. Jeremy Thorpe, the Liberal leader, had quite competently projected the mandatory if vague image of himself and his party as an island of sanity in a sea of 'extremism' at both 1974 elections, though with modest success. Anyone active in Liberal politics at the time knew that privately Liberal activists who saw a good deal of him thought there was precious little to chose in terms of lifestyle and ambitions between

[1] Paul Ormerod 'Incomes Policy', in *Labour's Economic Policies*, eds. Michael Artis and David Cobham, pp. 56–72.

Thorpe and Heath and Wilson. In a tangled web of allegations about a homosexual affair, devious misuse of party funds, and involvement with shady businessmen, Thorpe's career collapsed. Perhaps the most damaging aspect of the episode was the hit-man who shot at the alleged lover and hit his Great Dane dog instead. Given the curious mentality of the middle classes in the Home Counties, this was beyond the pale. Thorpe was replaced as leader in the summer of 1976 by the Scotsman David Steel, a photogenic dog-lover. What emerges unequivocally from Steel's judicious account of the episode is that Thorpe made Harold Wilson look almost straightforward.[1]

Heath, by comparison, truly was straightforward. Having lost three elections out of four, he meant to cling to the leadership. In conversation with Jim Prior, he had made it clear that he regarded the leadership as a sort of freehold in perpetuity. Politicians, who as a breed were passionately hostile to safeguards for the public against assertions of unbridled authority by politicians, now began to erect safeguards for themselves. Steel was elected by a most elaborate procedure. Sir Alec Douglas-Home presided over a committee which, late in 1974, called Heath's bluff by proposing successfully that in opposition the party should elect its leader annually, with the need for a 15 per cent majority of those eligible to vote. In some ways it was, as critics pointed out, a 'coward's charter'. It had to be, for with a leader like Heath, whose supporters threatened sanctions against defeated opponents, it was too dangerous for party grandees to run until a second ballot, by which time an expendable front-runner would have established that the leader's throne was toppling. Amongst the ranks of his declared enemies Heath must have recognized in Airey Neave a unique personal venom. It was allied to great organizing talent. Neave first tried to persuade William Whitelaw, Heath's trusty lieutenant, to run. When he refused, he had hopes of the more right-wing Edward Du Cann. Du Cann withdrew, and Margaret Thatcher became Neave's third choice.[2] The former Secretary of State for Education was, in the words of a politician who knew her well, 'the only one man enough in the Conservative Party to stand for the leadership'.[3] Heath, going into the first round confident, came out beaten, and withdrew. The accelerating Thatcher bandwagon then routed Whitelaw in round two.

Wilson, by comparison, cruised blandly on. He did not always have his own way. He would, for example, have preferred to keep the power-sharing executive in Northern Ireland despite the verdict of the polls against it, but it was brought down by the Protestant Ulster Workers' Council strike in May 1974. Whitelaw, who had set the executive up, criticized the decision to replace it by another indefinite period of 'interim' direct rule, but then Whitelaw had done much to create the atmosphere

[1] David Steel *Against Goliath: David Steel's Story* (Weidenfeld and Nicolson, London 1989), Chap. 5.
[2] Kenneth Harris *Thatcher* (Weidenfeld and Nicolson, London 1988), pp. 25–32.
[3] Patricia Murray *Margaret Thatcher* (W. H. Allen, London 1980), p. 92, citing Lord Pannell, who, as Labour MP for West Leeds, was her pair (an MP from another party who agrees to absent himself or herself from the same divisions as their partner) between 1959 and 1974.

of distrust surrounding the executive, not least by such ploys as holding not-very-secret secret talks with representatives of the militant Provisional IRA and trying to conceal that he was doing so. He deserved the nickname of 'Woolly Whitewash', and Wilson had to accept that political strikes were a game two could play.[1] Deviousness became second nature to the Premier, perhaps as the result of the scale on which he was committed to ensuring that large sections of the electorate, and indeed of his own party, had to be foiled and baffled, but not driven to resistance. He modernized the Polaris nuclear delivery system with new multiple warheads, but secretly. Testing was underground in Nevada by courtesy of the Americans who necessarily knew what was going on. Parliament did not, nor did the Cabinet. It was the old story of a clique of senior ministers and civil servants, called a committee. The cost of some £1,000 million by 1980 was hidden in the maintenance budget. This 'Project Chevaline' cost double what it should have, partly due to the sheer inefficiency dictated by secretive procedures.

Needless to say, Harold Wilson had no intention of allowing the National Enterprise Board, set up by the 1975 Industry Bill, to become the vehicle of a radical interventionist strategy. This was the decidedly naïve hope of his Secretary of State for Industry and Minister of Posts and Telecommunications, Tony Benn, who was also an anti-Marketeer. Defeated and humiliated by the referendum (an idea he himself had floated), Benn was moved to the Department of Energy. It was a marginalization exercise not wholly devoid of malicious wit. Despite being about to exercise his sense of humour at Benn's expense, Wilson had had enough. He resigned, unexpectedly, in March 1976. There is no reason to query his statement that he had taken the decision two years earlier and had then told Queen Elizabeth, for whom he had a genuine reverence. This did not prevent him from imposing on her a resignation honours list of so disreputable a nature as to elicit a protest from the committee which nominally vetted such candidates, but which patently could not stop the real sovereign from asserting his will. Among the few who suspected Wilson was about to go were Government car pool drivers, when they heard he had arranged for all retired premiers to have a car and driver for life. He did not take an earldom but a knighthood, though in the prestigious Order of the Garter. His resident bane, Tony Benn, himself a successful escapologist who had freed himself from the shackles of a hereditary peerage, had once calculated that in one six-and-a-half year period, Tory MPs had received 27 peerages, 30 baronetcies and 48 knighthoods. Nearly a third of them had been given titles, and that did not include the bucketfuls of OBEs and MBEs emptied on constituency chairmen and agents. Benn concluded, correctly, that honours were primarily cheap political payoffs.[2] Wilson's was not. It was the least the Establishment owed to a man who had restored 'normalcy' in a way few would have thought possible in early 1974.

His successor, Jim Callaghan, was different. He won the premiership in the end against a good fight by the candidate of the left, Michael Foot, in an election still determined by the parliamentary party. If Wilson was a

---

[1] William Whitelaw *The Whitelaw Memoirs* (Aurum Press, London 1989), pp. 100–1.
[2] Anthony W. Benn *The Regeneration of Britain*. (Gollancz, London 1965), p. 87.

devious exhausted closet Liberal, Callaghan, though four years older than Wilson's 60 years, was a robust working-class conservative. A teetotal Baptist family man with a naval background and a long history of close association with the trade unions, he ruled by assertion when Wilson relied on subtlety. It was not at all the case that he inherited an impossible political and economic situation. There were likely to be difficulties, but his reign as Prime Minister was shaped by his own decisions. His pragmatic political sense enabled him to spin out its duration far beyond what anyone expected. His profound misjudgements in three major decisions ensured it ended in catastrophe.

Most UK premiers had no concept of politics as an integral part of the administrative and legislative process. The peoples of the UK were their lieges. They ruled them until an infrequent general election transferred the ruling prerogative to another. Callaghan was operating in a quite abnormal situation where the rubber-stamping Commons majority did not exist. Technically, it had vanished, due to a run of disastrous Labour by-election performances, by early 1977. To cope with this situation, Callaghan structured a Cabinet which leaned more to the right, with the exception of Michael Foot, whose strong showing in the leadership election was reflected in his Leadership of the Commons and Lord Presidency. Barbara Castle, left rather than right, and an old foe from 'In Place of Strife' days, was sacked. Healey and Jenkins were strongly conservative fiscally, and though Jenkins soon accepted nomination to the European Commission (of which he became President), the sudden death of Tony Crosland was the occasion for the introduction as Foreign Minister of another strongly right-wing figure, David Owen. Callaghan was consciously tough with his own party to extract the concessions which enabled him to deal with other interests. So abnormal was the situation that concessions even had to be made to the Commons. In pursuance of promises made by the Labour Government in 1975, a Select Committee on Procedure reported in July 1978, recommending a new and much more elaborate system of specialist select committees. Foot, a devout traditionalist, wanted to shelve the report, but the idea was forced past him and even survived the 1979 election, to be implemented early in the Thatcher era. As the committees made no serious impact on the predictability of legislation, they had a comparatively small effect on events.[1]

What kept Callaghan going was his remarkable, and very sensible, willingness to wheel and deal with minor parties. 1977 saw a Liberal-Labour pact which was almost ideal from the Premier's viewpoint. The Liberals were facing falling ratings in the polls. They were as unenthusiastic about an election as Labour. To obtain the Lib-Lab pact, Callaghan surrendered nothing to which he was not already committed. That the Liberals were given a virtual veto over future legislation hardly worried a conservative Premier who had no immediate desire for further contentious legislation. Futhermore, there was the bonus that once the pact was announced, the Liberals became virtually prisoners, because their ratings in the polls plum-

---

[1] Stephen J. Downs 'Structural Changes: Select Committees: Experiment and Establishment', in *Parliament in the 1980s*, ed. Philip Norton (Basil Blackwell, Oxford 1985), pp. 48–68.

meted. This was wholly predictable: their activists were left of centre but their electoral appeal was primarily to disgruntled Tories, who of course detested the pact. A Liberal leadership still interested in power for its own sake was therefore forced to cover its embarrassment by a ridiculous procedure whereby Liberal MPs 'shadowed' certain ministers and, of course, it also waited eagerly for a favourable chance to slip out of the pact.

That possibility became imminent in late 1977, when it became clear to the Liberals that they were gaining no real concessions from the Government. Callaghan then adroitly moved over to dealing with the Scottish and Welsh Nationalists and the Ulster Unionists (who by the grim logic of events were becoming a species of nationalist). Together, they had enough MPs to replace the Liberal prop. In Ulster, Callaghan's obvious lack of any delusions about 'solving' its continuing crisis served him well, and in Roy Mason he had the only Secretary of State whom most inhabitants of the province did not more or less automatically assume was lying to them when he spoke publicly. The support of the Unionists was obtained by a simple measure of political justice: the redressing of the under-representation of the province in parliament. The measure was unpopular with that substantial element within the Labour Party which would much have prefered to push Northern Ireland into the Republic. Bernard Donoughue, for example, was furious at it. He was not furious about the bills providing for devolution of political powers to Scottish and Welsh assemblies, which Callaghan had inherited from Wilson, but he shared the overweening metropolitan arrogance of the political élite towards manifestations of discontent in Wales or Scotland. To him the SNP was 'eccentric'. To the Commons, as Wilson rightly said, the devolution bills were 'a bore'. They were also a life-raft, but a dangerously unbalanced one.

Before that fact became central, Callaghan had, by three decisions, destroyed the medium-term viability of the Labour Party. The first was in September 1976 during the so-called IMF crisis, when an unexpectedly heavy run on the pound made necessary further borrowing from the International Monetary Fund to deal with what was essentially a short-term speculative crisis. There was a fundamental problem with the public sector borrowing requirement in the sense that a sluggish economy could clearly not sustain the levels of borrowing to which the Government had initially committed itself. On the other hand, more significant cuts had already been made in expenditure, and the way in which the Government swallowed American and West German pressure through the IMF (strongly backed by the overseas, though not the domestic, side of the UK Treasury) for a large measure of overkill both in borrowing and in cuts, deeply alienated large sections of the Labour movement.

Initially, there was a large Cabinet majority for resistance, and a straightforward mechanism to hand for bargaining hard with the IMF. Benn's alternative siege economy may have been a non-starter, but it was a basic principle of negotiations, especially Irish ones, that one had to have an extremist with which to threaten the other party. Benn was a potential asset and very moderate members of the Cabinet like Crosland and Peter Shore believed that temporary import controls to guard the balance of payments were desirable and feasible, despite the distraught hostility of the Foreign Office to any proposal so disliked by foreigners. Besides, Crosland argued, if the UK meant its counter-threat, it need never implement it, for the IMF was as frightened of import restrictions as the Devil of holy water.[1] In the event, Callaghan and Healey forced through the overkill package. A Premier and Chancellor united usually carry the day, and a Premier whom his senior colleagues do not wish to assassinate can, as Callaghan demonstrated, use Cabinet to demonstrate prime ministerial power by turning a minority into a majority. Callaghan did try to secure moderation of the IMF terms, but by the unlikely route of the West German Chancellor Helmut Schmidt, whom he relied on to defend the Government in Washington. He had well-authenticated reports of Conservative lobbying there, designed to persuade President Ford to tighten the screws on the Labour regime. In fact, Schmidt, with whom Callaghan became very friendly, was increasingly influenced by the new and virulently anti-Keynsian monetarist fashion in economics. He declined to help the UK on the grounds that German currency reserves were largely committed to propping up the US deficit.[2] It did not help that Presidents Kennedy, Johnson and Nixon had funded their costly Vietnam involvement not by the politically difficult method of raising taxes, but by the inflationary path of deficit funding and borrowing.[3] Ironically, though the press gleefully depicted the episode as 'national bankruptcy', less than half the IMF loan was ever drawn; the economy and exchange rate recovered rapidly; and within six months, the Government was trying to dampen an unwelcome appreciation in the currency.

The two other destructive decisions came together. In October 1978, Callaghan, to universal amazement, announced on television that he was not calling a general election that year. The pay restraint which had been so crucial was wearing thin by 1977, but a Government 10 per cent norm more or less set the pace. TUC 'acquiescence' helped though the winter of 1977–8, but 1978 was a difficult year in which the changing balance of power within the union movement, and the pent-up resentments of the public sector unions, whose members had of course been more directly affected by Government pay policy than private sector workers, promised a difficult winter. Government popularity was peaking and very likely to go into decline. Arguably, Callaghan was of all Labour premiers the one least likely to be able to cope with an all-out clash with the unions. His own career had been based on union power. He had used it to defeat 'In Place of Strife' and to shake Harold's throne. His conservatism in the highest office was so extreme as to have offended and alienated a huge part of the political movement he led. Under pressure, behind the smiling mask reserved for the media, he had become a cantankerous old man, with no real vision, apart from vague, Schmidt-influenced, homilies about West German tripartite cooperation between Government, industry and unions. At a TUC-Labour Party Liaison Committee when Benn said he feared the de-industrializing UK was going to become 'the Merseyside of the EEC',

[1] Susan Crosland *Tony Crosland*, pp. 376–82; Kathleen Burk and Alec Cairncross *'Goodbye Great Britain': The 1976 IMF Crisis* (Yale, New Haven 1992).
[2] James Callaghan *Time and Chance* (Collins, London 1987), p. 431.
[3] Paul Kennedy *The Rise and Fall of the Great Powers* (Vintage Books, New York 1989), pp. 434–5.

Callaghan's replay was: 'I share his fears, but the state can't do much to stop it. Nobody knows the answer. I cannot offer a plan. It does not exist.'[1]

Callaghan's attempt to impose a five per cent pay limit, which led to massive revolt by public service unions in the 1978–9 'Winter of Discontent', compounded his folly in ducking an election, which he would probably have lost, but not by much. Five per cent was apparently the figure produced by Donoughue's advisory unit as the one guaranteeing no rise in inflation. The Premier's endorsement of it was rash. A more politically realistic figure like eight per cent might have been roughly enforceable. As it was, he handed the Conservatives a usable past in the shape of strikes and picketing which enraged the general public because they affected their lives. His own luck ran out over the referenda on Welsh and Scottish devolution. Both bills were quite extraordinarily bad, being designed solely to save Labour seats from further SNP or Plaid Cymru challenges. They conceded as little as possible, which was hardly unexpected given the corporate presumption of Westminster. The two new assemblies were to be on block grants from Westminster, like county councils, and the Secretaries of State for Wales and Scotland were to remain as powerful watchdog-satraps of the premier. In March 1979, the Welsh electorate turned down its version of devolution by four to one. English-speaking Wales, middle and working class, had little time for a measure seen as a sop to an unpopular Welsh-speaking militant minority. The Scottish vote yielded a small positive majority, but that had been provided against by an amendment requiring 40 per cent endorsement by the electorate. That this would have ruled out the Callaghan and the Wilson Governments in 1974–9 was irrelevant. The subsequent alienation of the minority parties and narrow defeat of the Government in a vote of confidence merely marked the final collapse of a spent force.

Callaghan had been a more dominant premier than Wilson in the sense that he repeatedly threw his weight around within his party and the Government, freely threatening resignation and dissolution to have his way.[2] As the shrewder members of Cabinet grasped, once they had allowed him to lock them into disaster, they were stuck with him, because his avuncular conservative image alone could prevent defeat becoming obliteration. Joel Barnett, Chief Secretary to the Treasury, reckoned that Callaghan's combination of assertiveness and no very firm views made the regular weekly meetings of the Permanent Secretaries, the top mandarins, very potent indeed.[3] The Labour election campaign of 1979 was very heavily focussed on Callaghan, who insisted on a manifesto bland in the extreme. He performed well, and lost. With 43.9 per cent of the vote and 339 seats, the Conservatives had an overall majority of 43. Labour fell to 36.9 per cent and 268 seats. The swing to the Conservatives on a roughly

---

[1] Entry for Monday 26 March 1979, in Tony Benn *Conflicts of Interest: Diaries 1977–80*, ed. Ruth Winstone (Hutchison, London 1990), p. 477.

[2] A careful reading of Brian Sedgemore's. *The Secret Constitution: An Analysis of the Political Establishment* (Hodder and Stoughton, London 1980), brings out how much more personally offensive this former Parliamentary Private Secretary to Tony Benn appears to have found Callaghan to be than Wilson.

[3] Joel Barnett *Inside the Treasury* (André Deutsch, London 1982).

three-quarter turnout of the electorate was strongest in the south of England. The Liberals fell to eleven seats and the SNP collapsed to two. Even in defeat, Wilson and Callaghan had helped put the pieces together again. They not only handed Mrs Thatcher the old political system to play with, but also the old polarized party system. Perhaps in the deepest sense that was what their long delaying action had been all about.

13

Thatcherite epilogue: *Reductio ad absurdum or Plus ça change . . . ?*

> But now a party can be elected on a minority vote, and in spite of that gain a Parliamentary majority, and use it to force down the throats of the electorate policies which the majority do not approve. This is a caricature of democracy. It was never meant to be like that. Mr Solzhenitsyn has called it the 'strangled silence' of the majority.
>
> from *The Way the Wind Blows: An Autobiography by Lord Home*
> (Collins, London 1976), p. 282.

> A pathological belief first observed in Cook County that only the rate of growth of the money supply can affect significantly the rate of inflation or the level of employment.
>
> Paul Samuelson, 1971 Nobel Laureate in economics, on monetarism

> Déjà vu all over again
>
> ascribed to Yogi Berra

It was common for late twentieth-century British premiers to reach office convinced that they had some sort of mission, or to convince themselves that this was the case shortly after assuming power. Heath had been going to conduct a revolution, even if it was to be the quiet one of 'action not words'. The phrase was an explicit critique of the very high profile sustained by Harold Wilson in his first reign. As the technocrat and interventionist *par excellence*, 'King Harold' would come in by helicopter from his Scilly Isles retreat in a blaze of media publicity to settle a threatened strike by meeting the interested parties over beer and sandwiches in Number 10 Downing Street. It was a measure of his shrewdness that during his relatively brief second reign between 1974 and 1976, he eschewed this style, which would have made his task of holding the political and social order together without splitting his own party more difficult. Jim Callaghan had moments when he saw himself as a sort of British Moses, a fact revealed to an incredulous world by his then son-in-law, Peter Jay, the economist and journalist whom Callaghan made, at 40, the youngest-ever British ambassador to the United States. It was not a happy appointment, personally or professionally. Jay was mercilessly parodied in a 'factional' best-selling novel and firmly recalled by Prime Minister Thatcher in 1979.[1]

Yet Margaret Thatcher was herself to be the beneficiary of an image which tended to the Mosaic. Norman St John Stevas, Leader of the House and an independent-minded colleague until she sacked him, referred to 'the apotheosis of the Blessed Margaret' at a Conservative Party conference. It was not altogether a happy phrase. The nearest analogue was perhaps the much-used Renaissance symbol of Astraea, the corn-bearing virgin whose return to earth signifies the end of the cycle of decline through the ages of brass, iron and lead, and the coming again of the golden years.[2] Most Tory premiers are assured, at least at the start, of a favourable press, but so anxious were the press proprietors that she succeed that there was a period when the parameters of sycophancy were set at absurd levels. In distinguishing between continuity and change during her reign, it is therefore more difficult than usual to separate myth and reality, not least because the myth is an important part of the reality.

What is clear is that in opposition, the Conservatives kept their options open until they were quite clear that the Callaghan–Healey axis would not succeed in reaching 1979 on a conservative fiscal platform capable of making Labour a serious contender for power or, if defeated, so short a distance behind the Conservatives as to constitute a major brake on any Conservative government's freedom of action. Hence the vague and general nature of *The Right Approach*, the official statement issued for the 1976 Conservative Party Conference. There were of course increasingly vocal right-wing ideologues around in the party, but then there always had been. Sir Keith Joseph, an early convert to emphasis on rigid control of the money supply, and a sharp reduction in the role of the state in the economy, set up a Centre for Policy Studies which, along with the Institute of Economic Affairs run by Lord Harris and Arthur Seldon, assiduously propagated 'monetarist' views. Very similar views had never died out in the Conservative Party since the 1930s, and could be heard in the 1960s in such bodies as the Institute of Directors or Aims of Industry. After all, Milton Friedman was a monetary radical because he was a political conservative. Many of these doctrines were shorthand statements of the personal interests of the numerous groups now resentful of the income transfer element in state welfare. It was quite crucial for electoral purposes that those groups included skilled working class groups in stable employment, especially in the Midlands of England.

In 1978, when most observers thought an election was fast approaching, it was clear that the Conservatives wanted to cut state expenditure and direct taxes (probably partly by increasing indirect ones), but it was not at all clear that they had entirely turned their backs on such 'corporatist' programmes as a wages and incomes policy.[3] The campaign of 1979 did

---

[1] There is an entertaining entry for Peter Jay in Compton Miller *Who's Really Who* (Sphere, London 1984), p. 121.
[2] See 'Queen Elizabeth I as Astraea' in Frances A. Yates *Astraea: The Imperial Theme in the Sixteenth Century* (Routledge and Kegan Paul, London 1975), pp. 29–87.
[3] David McKie, Chris Cook and Melanie Phillips *The Guardian/Quartet Election Guide* (Quartet, London 1978), p. 52.

not exactly help clarify matters. Mrs Thatcher said the Tories two priorities were to cut taxes and restore the UK's defence power. Her final broadcast was as general and as vaguely patriotic as could be, including appeals to 'make this a country' safe to do sundry things like 'safe to work in' and 'safe to walk in'. Given the levels of unemployment which lay ahead, the first point was ironic. The second was simply standard. All Conservative candidates ran on a 'law and order' ticket at all elections, either explicitly or when challenged. It was pure rhetoric. They were as incapable of affecting the reality as anyone else. Crime statistics were to rise relentlessly in Mrs Thatcher's reign.[1]

Despite a ritual declaration that she had no time for internal arguments within her party, Thatcher's new Government had to balance the factions, because only a small percentage of senior Tories were convinced adherents of her hard-line economic policies. These 'dries' were outnumbered by traditional politicians with varying shades of conviction and pragmatism. They were all to be lumped together by their leader and others as 'wets'. Her first objective was clearly to isolate her open enemy, Heath. This she had already partially done. If Heath had had any intimates towards the end of his premiership, they were Whitelaw and Lord Carrington. Whitelaw had come to terms with Thatcher already, acting as her deputy in exchange for a guarantee that he would be consulted on Shadow Cabinet appointments. This carried on into the Government, where Whitelaw became the essential oiling can in often rapidly-changing Cabinets. Now Lord Carrington, Heath's other former close ally, was given the Foreign Office, and Heath offered only the Washington embassy, which he angrily rejected. It was an elegant manoeuvre: Heath was 'European' to the point of deliberately cultivating a lack of rapport with the Americans.

The 'dries' clustered round the levers of economic policy, with Sir Geoffrey Howe as Chancellor, Sir Keith Joseph Secretary of State for Industry; John Nott at Trade and David Howell at Energy. John Biffen, in the long-run clearly much the most balanced and sensible of this group, became Chief Secretary at the Treasury. Their policies were pushed through in two budgets which severely slashed public spending, reduced direct taxation (though value added tax went up to 15 per cent to compensate), dismantled all exchange controls by October 1979, and set up a Medium Term Financial Strategy to establish targets for the money supply for several years ahead. The main practical drive behind this was undoubtedly inflation, and the need to reduce it. The rate of inflation in retail prices was 10.3 per cent when Mrs Thatcher assumed office. A year later, it was 21.9 per cent, which mercifully represented a peak. The 1981 budget followed the same course as those of 1979 and 1980, reducing public sector borrowing. Indeed, the target set was undershot by £2 billion in 1981–2. By spring of 1982, inflation was in single figures.[2]

The problem was that the political consequences of these policies were as suicidal as their industrial repercussions. With the beginnings of really substantial income from North Sea oil, the pound sterling became a petro-

[1] David Butler and Dennis Kavanagh *The British General Election of 1979* (Macmillan, London 1980), pp. 185 and 195.
[2] Sked and Cook *Post-War Britain*, pp. 329–36.

currency, much too highly valued to make many exports competitive, and encouraging deep penetration of domestic markets by foreign manufacturers. Unemployment soared to 2.5 million by July 1981, a figure which more than any other halted wage inflation. Gross domestic product by the same date had fallen by 3.7 per cent; the index of industrial production had slumped by 9 per cent. It is thought that the UK industrial base shrank by 17 per cent between 1979 and early 1982.[1] Domestic investment slumped. Overseas investment rose. That there were riots in disadvantaged areas of London and Liverpool in 1981–2 is unremarkable. Commentators, aware of what was happening, assumed that the Thatcher Government was in an irreversible spin down to disaster.[2]

That appears to be what saved it. The right wing of the Labour Party agreed that the Tories were probably doomed. Roy Jenkins had moved to a lucrative job in Brussels, but he was an archetypal Westminster politician who missed its ambience and kept in touch through a small circle of friends, one of whom, the historian and MP David Marquand, he had taken to Brussels with him as an adviser. In November 1979, Jenkins delivered for the BBC the televised annual Dimbleby Lecture. He delivered it just when the Bank of England pushed minimum lending rate up to an unheard of 17 per cent, sustaining the rise in the pound and the ruthless deflation of the economy. The simultaneous announcement that Anthony Blunt, Keeper of the Queen's Pictures, had been unmasked as a Russian spy did little to improve the Government's corporate image, as it also emerged that he had confessed in 1956 and that for 15 years the Crown and successive premiers had connived at his prominent public role.[3]

Jenkins urged the formation of a new centre party, and argued for the proportional representation voting system which alone could guarantee its success. Apart from *The Times*, his reception was civil rather than rapt. He had been in touch with the Liberal leader, David Steel, to discuss joining that party. It was Steel who saw the long-term advantages of first destroying Labour. That possibility did not really exist until Michael Foot defeated Denis Healey in the contest for the succession to Callaghan as Leader of the Labour Party, and presided in January 1981 over a special conference which adopted a new electoral college to select the leader and agreed that votes in it should be distributed 40 per cent to the trade unions and other allied bodies, 30 per cent to the constituency parties and 30 per cent to the parliamentary party. This was the last straw for three figures who, with Jenkins, formed the so-called 'gang of four' and eventually launched a new Social Democratic Party, which promptly formed an alliance with the Liberals. The three were Shirley Williams (who had lost her seat at the election), David Owen and Bill Rodgers. The two latter were, prior to resigning the Labour whip, Shadow Cabinet spokesmen for Edu-

[1] Keith Middlemas *Power, Competition and the State. Volume 3: The End of the Postwar Era: Britain Since 1974* (Macmillan, London 1991), p. 253.

[2] See, for example, the comments by Wynne Godley of the Cambridge University Department of Applied Economics, 'The Siege has begun' in *The Observer* Business section, Sunday 10 August 1980.

[3] Barrie Penrose and Simon Freeman *Conspiracy of Silence: The Secret Life of Anthony Blunt* (Grafton, rev. edn, 1987).

cation and Defence respectively. For Williams and Jenkins, the most important specific issue was probably the Common Market from which Labour
was threatening to withdraw. For Owen (though a keen Marketeer), it
was probably the party's move towards a unilateral repudiation of nuclear
weapons. More profoundly, the 'gang of four' bitterly resented the assault
on the prerogatives of the parliamentary party. There were certain issues
they did not want to see offered as options on the UK political agenda.
That agenda was for the philosopher kings and queens of Westminster to
define, especially if endowed with their own qualities of manifestly
superior intelligence, urbane cosmopolitanism and informed insight.

Launched with massively favourable media coverage, the new SDP,
aided by impressive by-election performances was recording 28.5 per cent
support by December 1981 in voter intention polls. Given the Liberal vote,
which brought the combined total over 50 per cent, it was probably true
that Labour simply could not have won an election even before the events
of 1982 revitalized the Thatcher Government. That, in a sense, was what
the SDP was all about.[1] In 1982, it not only began to experience checks in
the polls, but also faced radically different circumstances. The first of these
was the outbreak of war in the South Atlantic when on 2 April Argentina
invaded the British Falkland Islands, to which, as the Islas Malvinas, it had
long asserted a claim. It happened that David Owen had written to the
Foreign Secretary protesting about a decision, announced in June 1981, to
withdraw the ice-patrol vessel HMS *Endurance*, the sole Royal Navy vessel
in the South Atlantic. In January 1982, John Nott, the Defence Secretary,
replied to the effect that the ship represented no real deterrent, and that
British sovereignty in the Falklands was secure and would be defended.
In 1977, Owen had secretly despatched a small naval force to the islands
to reinforce diplomacy trying to avert threatened Argentinian action. The
1982 invasion was therefore not by any means without previous precedent.
What pushed the Argentinian junta finally into military action seems to
have been a combination of two factors. One was the need to divert attention from the domestic failures of military rule. The other was the clear
impression that Westminster did not really wish to uphold its rights. To
the deep annoyance of the islanders, Nicholas Ridley, a Foreign Office
minister, had suggested a surrender of sovereignty followed by a
'leaseback' (i.e. for a period the UK would lease the islands from Argentina). *The Times*, a few days before the invasion, talked of 'These paltry
islands which separate us', meaning by 'us' the UK and Argentina. Like
the IRA earlier, the Argentine ruling junta had reason to expect only a
limited resistance for form's sake, by a Westminster anxious to ditch a
liability.[2]

Lord Carrington had clearly followed the Foreign Office line on the
subject apart from refusing in 1981 to sanction a large-scale 'educational'
campaign to persuade domestic opinion that the islanders must not have

[1] Hugh Stephenson *Claret and Chips: The Rise of the SDP* (Michael Joseph, London 1982),
Chaps. 1–6.
[2] Christopher Dobson, John Miller and Ronald Payne *The Falklands Conflict* (Hodder
and Stoughton, Coronet pbk, London 1982), has useful material from Owen on this on
pp. 4–6.

the last word on any deal negotiated between the Foreign Office and Argentina. He did this because he did not think the Premier and Cabinet would buy it. The Foreign Office was in fact so wilful about what it wanted to happen that it did not condescend to read the Argentinian newspapers which told about an invasion which was about to happen. The Argentines could have had the islands, in some thinly-veiled hand-over, with a little patience. Had they waited six months, Nott's defence cuts designed to concentrate effort on Armageddon with Russia would have left no Royal Navy aircraft carrier capability and therefore no capacity to fight back. It was the desire of the Argentinian government for an immediate political pay-off from humiliating the British that precipitated war. Thatcher fought or fell. Heath clearly thought she would fall and raced back from a Chinese trip to advocate 'tough' negotiations (i.e. surrender to the Argentinians and toughness with the Falkland Islanders). He underestimated his archenemy. She fought back with massive American assistance and by mid-June had soundly trounced the Argentinians. It was the junta which lost the zero-sum game. Carrington resigned as dignified scapegoat, taking two junior ministers with him. He was rewarded for doing the decent thing with the Secretaryship-General of NATO in due course. What was extraordinary was that the permanent officials of the Foreign Office, who above all others had displayed a combination of violent political prejudice allied to professional incompetence, sat stolidly and safely at their desks throughout. Their credit with the Prime Minister sank below the horizon, of course. Nevertheless, the only practical sanction, for what it was worth, was that the Permanent Under-Secretary Foreign Office in the period leading up to the invasion, Sir Michael Palliser, had to wait some time after his retirement before the routine peerage was bestowed on him.[1]

There is argument that the 'Falklands Factor' was not decisive in Mrs Thatcher's subsequent 1983 electoral victory. Inflation was down to 5 per cent by the spring of 1982. On the other hand, unemployment was up to three million, a figure not seen since the 1930s. But it cannot be denied that the Falklands victory was a crucial part of the springboard to political recovery.[2] In a sense, the Conservatives did what Macmillan had been trying to do in 1964: they exploited the general sense of improved economic expectations as the economy climbed out of a recession. However, their reputation for hawkish views on defence was made much more of a political asset by Mrs Thatcher's rampant patriotism over the Falklands. Labour's intelligent scepticism about the reality of the threat of a 'standing-start' Russian onslaught in central Europe, and that party's doubts about the alleged vast Russian superiority in conventional weapons, which was being used to justify demands for big increases in American and British defence spending, did not prove major electoral assets,[3] especially when combined with a desire to jettison nuclear weapons. Ironically, the solid support to the Falklands war effort offered by Michael Foot and the bulk

---

[1] Patrick Cosgrove *A Life and a Policy* (J. M. Dent, London 1985), chap. 6.
[2] Helmut Norpoth 'The Falklands Factor: The Latest Blast', *Contemporary Record*, Vol. 2, No. 4, Winter 1988, pp. 26–7.
[3] *Sense About Defence: The Report of the Labour Party Defence Study Group* (Quartet, London 1977).

of the Labour leadership did not prove particularly rewarding either. The impact of the obsessively anti-war Scots Labour MP Tam Dalyell, as he relentlessly hounded the Premier about details of the campaign, details which bored the public profoundly, was to put it mildly counter-productive. He may have been right in saying she had misled the Commons, but then what Prime Minister did not?[1]

Deep division within the opposition was still quite fundamental to the Conservative victory in the 1983 election. That election yielded them 397 seats and a huge majority of 144 on a reduced vote compared with 1979. Only 42.4 per cent of votes cast went to the Tories. The Alliance (as the SDP–Liberal front was known) polled no less than 25.4 per cent of the vote for a paltry 23 seats, and a divided, shaken Labour, led by an honourable but uncharismatic figure, retained 209 seats for 27.6 per cent of the vote. Michael Foot had no flair for media-oriented electioneering, despite being photographed with his dog at the start of the campaign. Even then, he failed to grasp that the key to English hearts was to stand still, looking as much like one's dog as possible. He had earlier turned up to the annual wreath-laying at the Cenotaph war memorial wearing a smart but informal donkey-jacket. It made him look less like an undertaker's deaf-mute than the other party leaders, but it did not go down well with the public. Yet arguably his achievement was real. There was never any doubt who would win the election. What was a stake was the survival of the Labour Party under the most visceral assault ever launched against it by an Establishment which, since 1981, had hoped to narrow the political agenda decisively by replacing Labour by the Alliance. Narrowly, Labour survived.

The remainder of the Thatcher decade was an apparently paradoxical era, in which the Prime Minister was in many ways a singularly detached and critical member of her own Government, occupied at one and the same time with rolling back the frontiers of the state and extending them to a degree which was widely condemned as offensive. At Westminster itself there was little serious questioning of the existing structures of political power. The new Labour leader, Neil Kinnock, a friend and protegé of Foot, elected in October 1983, had been a very active opponent of Welsh devolution. Though elected as a man of the 'soft' left, his leadership marked the culmination of a defeat of left-wing ideas in the party which had started when John Silkin had narrowly defeated Tony Benn in a bitter struggle for the deputy leadership in 1981. After election in 1983, Kinnock soon faced a ferociously hostile press anxious to stereotype him either as 'the Welsh windbag' or 'frustrated' because a mere puppet of Trotskyites and anarchists. Tempted to sign himself 'frustrated of Ealing', he concentrated on resisting left-wing 'entryism' at local level in the party.[2] An image of being 'against the Militant Tendency' and pretty malleable on everything else was probably the best he could hope for. Nor did the SDP, despite its rhetoric about 'breaking the mould', in functional terms represent a new departure. On the contrary, the leadership of the SDP was an extreme case

---

[1] Tam Dalyell *Misrule: How Mrs Thatcher has Misled Parliament from the Sinking of the Belgrano to the Wright Affair* (Hamish Hamilton, London 1987).
[2] Michael Leapman *Kinnock* (Unwin Hyman, London 1987), pp. 18 and 182–3.

of a group of Westminster's 'Great and Good' who invited people to vote them into power because they were very Great and very Good. The party was full of gimmicks like holding its annual conference in three slices in three towns, but the reality of its power-structure was a very strong grip by the parliamentary party on anything it might say or do.

The mentality of the SDP made cooperation with the Liberals difficult, because, however ambitious and pragmatic David Steel might be, his MPs were mostly in their seats for local reasons, and the party was genuinely devolved and into 'community politics'. This made negotiations over seat-allocation between the parties extraordinarily difficult. SDP leaders like Bill Rodgers simply did not understand why a recalcitrant Liberal association might have to be cajoled into withdrawing a candidate in a long-nursed constituency, in order to clear the way for the SDP candidate to whom it had been allotted by intra-Alliance agreement. The SDP leadership believed in orders from the centre and obedience in the constituencies.[1] Even the most socially radical of the original SDP leadership, Shirley Williams, in a slightly unfortunately titled book, *Politics is for People* (there can have been few who thought it for sheep or ducks), produced little more than a vague call for a more 'open' Government.[2] By the time the best brains available to the SDP were producing concrete plans for a neo-Keynsian 'developmental state',[3] the party had failed even more decisively to make a real breakthrough in the 1987 election, and the enormous personal rivalries between the leaders of the Alliance had accelerated the subsequent decline. Roy Jenkins had fought the 1983 election with the ridiculous title of 'Prime Minister elect' hung round his neck. David Owen turned out on defence and economic affairs (though not social policy) to out-Thatcher Thatcher. By 1990, the SDP was defunct, and the Liberals had a slightly different name. Given the incompatibility and rivalry rife in its leadership, and their high view of their own prerogative, this was an unsurprising end to the Alliance, but a fearful waste of the talents, money and idealism of thousands of its supporters.[4]

What 'the Great and the Good', including very many in her own party, most disliked about the Thatcher style was the note of radical populism in it. On the EEC, for example, she turned the cosmetic Wilson re-negotiation into a real one by the only approach which would have made any difference, which was an aggressive one. The UK had been financing an excessive 20 per cent of Community spending, which was out of line with the relative size of its gross domestic product. To the chagrin of the Foreign Office, the amazement of several members of Cabinet, and the anger of the ultra-communitaire Ted Heath, the Premier secured a series of massive rebates, as the price of literally thumping the table and demanding 'Britain's own money back'. She secured a rebate of over 60 per cent of unadjusted net contributions in 1980–3, defusing the Market issue for the

---

[1] Steel *Against Goliath*, p. 229.

[2] Shirley Williams *Politics is for People* (Penguin, London 1981), pp. 185–9.

[3] David Marquand *The Unprincipled Society: New Demands and Old Politics* (Jonathan Cape, London 1988).

[4] David Owen *Personally Speaking to Kenneth Harris* (Pan Books, London 1988), Chap. 10, brings out the sustained jockeying for position at the top of the Alliance.

1983 election.[1] Her neo-Gaullism was precisely the sort of approach which might long before have created a popular consensus on the EEC. It was also a point of view that ardent Marketeers had always been anxious never to hear enunciated by anyone in authority in the UK. In the end, she and her Chancellor, Nigel Lawson, were effectively locked in battle before and after the 1987 election over the issue of whether the UK should join the European Monetary System. Under a different Chancellor, John Major, she did, very much as a deathbed repentance, allow the Treasury to join it, but it was clear by the end of her reign that she was a Euro-sceptic more acceptable to a broad band of public opinion than to many leading members of the Westminster élite.

The Premier had much the same populist backing in her assault on what she regarded as the bloated and econocidal role of trade unions in the economy. For the TUC, she had no time. It was not to be included in the consultative process. Her approach to legislation was cumulative, starting with a very modest measure from Jim Prior, a Heathite Secretary of State for Employment, but after half a dozen pieces of legislation culminating in the 1989 Employment Act, her Governments had profoundly changed the legal framework of labour relations. Broadly, they had severely restricted the picketing rights which had led to violent scenes during the 'winter of discontent'; removed union immunity to liability for damages for unlawful actions; and compulsorily democratized, by means of secret ballots, a whole range of decisions from strikes to selection of officers, to the decision to have a political fund.[2] To some extent, the Government was favoured by circumstances. A reassertion of managerial capacity to manage was overdue and this had to some extent been recognized before 1979. A new breed of aggressive managers willing to cut costs by de-manning and attacking restrictive practices had begun to emerge with such figures as the South African Michael Edwardes, who became chairman at the car firm British Leyland in 1977. He was eloquent on the theme that in 20 years the UK's share of world trade had halved and that every additional one per cent lost from that figure meant 250,000 lost jobs, just as every one per cent of the home market lost to imports involved a loss of 80,000 jobs.[3] Mass unemployment weakened unions and led to falling memberships.

In the coal industry, Thatcher was the first premier simply to prepare to win a confrontation with the National Union of Mineworkers, laying in fuel stocks and building a police coordination system to cope with widely-spread picketing problems. In the elderly Scots-American Ian MacGregor, who was Chairman of the Coal Board during the fierce 1984–5 strike, she had a personal acquaintance whose politics were perhaps Reaganite rather than Conservative but who, like her, blamed the unions for industrial decline. The clash between MacGregor and Arthur Scargill, the miners' leader, was symbolic. The price paid was heavy, but in the last analysis the Premier's resources much exceeded those of the miners. If she could

[1] Peter Riddell *The Thatcher Government* (Martin Robertson, Oxford 1983), pp. 211–5.

[2] B. C. Roberts, 'Trade Unions' in *The Thatcher Effect: A Decade of Change*, eds. Dennis Kavanagh and Anthony Seldon (Clarendon Press, Oxford 1989), pp. 64–79.

[3] Michael Edwardes *Back from the Brink: An Apocalyptic Experience* (Pan edn, London 1984), p. 305.

not be shaken, MacGregor was bound to win. Interestingly, hopes of replacing the NUM by the break-away Union of Democratic Mineworkers were only partially fulfilled.[1] In fact, the Government ended up making unions much more democratic than Westminster. It was a great public service, and the irony perhaps only struck home when, to the Government's manifest disappointment, union after union voted to keep its political fund.

If in the end the Premier had most of her desired measures in dealing with the unions, even her dominant personality could do no more than continue the traditional fluid three-cornered struggle for control of policy in other fields. In some areas the mandarins, whom she instinctively distrusted and on whom she persistently tried to impose a more entrepreneurial culture, continued on track with long-standing policies. Tam Dalyell, as he pestered her with questions about the sinking of the Argentine cruiser *General Belgrano* at the start of the Falklands War, noted with glee that under the byzantine complexities of the 1981 British Nationality Act, a substantial minority of Falklanders were not the British citizens the Premier had spoken about so much during the war, but non-patrial British Dependent Territories Citizens (BDTC) with no absolute right of abode in the UK.[2] The Anglo-Irish agreement of 1985, which gave the Republic of Ireland legal status in the administration of Northern Ireland, ran contrary to almost everything the Premier had been saying up to 1984. It fitted in well enough with known Foreign Office preferences. If Tom King, the Secretary of State, passionately denied in public that it involved surrender of sovereignty, he was simply not credible. As a device for discouraging terrorism, it had some effect in the US, where a Supplementary Treaty making it easier to extradite IRA terrorists was ratified by the Senate in 1986, partly because of Thatcher's support and provision of facilities for President Reagan's air strikes against Libya in that year. In the province itself, the tempo of terror fell briefly, then predictably picked up again, encouraged as ever by political ambiguity.[3]

In many ways, the Thatcher years were an exaggerated version of the trends of the 1970s in the UK, despite desperate attempts to suggest a clean break with a lamentable past. Breaks there were, but the functional framework of politics remained, with appropriate modifications for long-term Tory operation. Levels of abuse of the Official Secrets Act were probably worse than ever, partly because of the self-righteous crudity with which they were applied. The height of folly was reached with Government attempts to suppress *Spycatcher*, a not-very-readable account by an embittered ex-assistant director of MI5, partly to stress past Soviet penetration of MI6, and partly to argue that Sir Roger Hollis, Director-General of MI5 from 1956 to 1965, had been a Russian agent. When the UK Government heard that the author Peter Wright, who had retired on inadequate pension to Australia, had found a publisher in Australia, it tried to sup-

---

[1] Martin Adeney and John Lloyd *The Miners' Strike 1984–5: Loss without Limit* (Routledge and Kegan Paul London, 1986).

[2] Tam Dalyell *One Man's Falklands* (Cecil Woolf, London 1982), p. 128–9.

[3] Jack Holland *The American Connection: US Guns, Money and Influence in Northern Ireland* (Poolbeg, pbk edn, Swords, Co. Dublin 1989), pp. 194–5.

press the book by legal action alleging breach of implied contract between itself and Wright. For once the Government exposed its use of its discretion on security matters to neutral scrutiny. The result was devastating. Sir Robert Armstrong, the Secretary to the Cabinet, flew out in 1986 to testify, briefed by a Government which, at the end of a long legal fiasco, stood effectively convicted of dishonest testimony and shameless bias as between Wright and the politically trusty Chapman Pincher, whose not dissimilar *Their Trade is Treachery* had been tacitly approved by the Government.[1] Already there was a campaign for a freedom of information act in the UK launched in 1984 on the grounds that there were over 100 statutes making release of information criminal, and that the UK was the most secretive 'democratic' country in the world.[2] The Official Secrets Act had to be 'reformed' but the ferocity with which the Government slapped down attempts by backbench Conservatives to advance private bills genuinely aimed at reform underlined its determination to substitute, as critics said, an armalite rifle for an unusable blunderbuss.[3]

Clive Ponting, a civil servant charged in 1985 under the Official Secrets Act for passing documents (which showed ministers were lying to the Commons) to Tam Dalyell, went much further in a book, published after a jury refused to convict him. He argued secrecy was a disease of a professional 'political class', used to cover its low calibre and its lack of experience outside the artificial world of Westminster. He was aware that Whitehall was as addicted to secrecy as Westminster.[4] Because Thatcher had comparatively few true believers in some of her economic policies in her Cabinet, all the old complaints so common under Wilson about key decisions being made in secret Cabinet committees surfaced again. It came to a head in 1985–6 over the so-called 'Westland scandal'. It was an extremely complex business revolving round the procedure to be followed to keep the Westland helicopter company alive when it became clear that its financial structure was radically unsound. Government policy initially appears to have been wholly pragmatic, but eventually a 'private enterprise' solution (involving, of course, Government funds and crony capitalism, as such things do) was put together with Mrs Thatcher's approval by Sir John Cuckney, Chairman of Westland, and a well-known 'company doctor'. Cuckney was an ex-MI5 man with intimate connections with Government. It involved, in practice, the taking over of Westland by the American firm Sikorsky. Michael Heseltine, the increasingly restive Minister of Defence, tried to put together later a 'European' alternative to Sikorsky, in a consortium designed to monopolize a closed EEC market for military helicopters. It was a straight challenge to all the Premier valued, for his scheme was interventionist, protectionist and ultra EEC-oriented.

[1] Peter Wright *Spycatcher* (Dell, New York, 1988); Malcolm Turnbull *"Spycatcher" Trial* (Heinemann, London 1988).

[2] *The Secrets File: The Case for Freedom of Information in Britain Today*, ed. Des Wilson (Heinemann, London 1984).

[3] In 1988, a Home Office official said, 'The Government's intention was to make secrecy legislation more effective.' See report 'SAS tactics on Secrets Act' in *The Guardian*, Wednesday 6 January 1988, p. 1.

[4] Clive Ponting *Whitehall: Tragedy and Farce* (Hamish Hamilton, London 1986), pp. 242–3.

Both sides fought dirty. Both peddled threats and disinformation. Scup-pered, predictably, in a Cabinet committee, Heseltine stalked out of the Cabinet early in 1986. Mrs Thatcher's close associate, Leon Brittan, had to resign as Chief Secretary at the Treasury when it became known he had leaked a document to influence Westland shareholders. It was all abso-lutely standard practice. Government had been leaking like a sieve for decades.[1] What was odd was how tolerant the Premier had been for so long in the face of a brash challenger.

The assault on local government under the Thatcher premiership was violent, because ideologically edged. Much of local government was Labour-controlled. By starving it of central funds, the Government achieved two ends. First, it tightened its control over public expenditure. Second, by forcing local government to increase the rates of its own residual taxation to compensate, it made it possible for ministers to denounce 'high-spending' non-Conservative local authorities (though, of course, not a few Conservative ones went through the same mill). With the abolition, after the 1983 election, of the Greater London Council and the six metropolitan counties which had survived the reorganization of English local government under Heath, Thatcher became clearly identified with an assault on a power-centre, the GLC, which had roused her ire as a bastion of political defiance under its left-wing leader, Ken Livingstone. The latter had originally built up his position by catering to highly-motivated activist minorities which were not popular with the general public, but his cheeky defiance of the imposition of direct rule (which is what it amounted to) caught a more general current of concern. Under Heath, Scottish local government had been totally reorganized on a regional basis, at about twice the predicted cost. Thatcher was to endow the Secretary of State for Scotland with near dictatorial powers over local-authority funding levels. None of this was at all unprecedented, only extreme. The systematic destruction of local authority tax bases dated from Churchill's budgets of the 1920s.

As John Silkin so wisely pointed out before his premature death, there had been for decades under either party a systematic campaign to eliminate what little substance was left in a local-government system trivialized by lack of power, dominated by minorities because of a well-founded lack of general interest, and dependent on the centre for some 70–80 per cent of funding. Silkin was clear that Whitehall mandarins were convinced they could run the whole country, and wanted to, especially after their close association with the immensely powerful bureaucratic traditions of the Continent through the EEC. Admiration of the French mandarins who saw themselves as 'the permanent government of France' was widespread in Whitehall.[2] Even Ken Livingstone, who made a living by personalizing the abolition of the GLC as a struggle between himself and Margaret Thatcher, knew well enough that this particular assertion of the will of Government

---

[1] Magnus Linklater and David Leigh *Not with Honour* (Sphere, London 1986), is defini-tive but curiously moralistic. Julian Critchley *Heseltine: The Unauthorised Biography* (André Deutsch, London 1987), pp. 129–68, is more realistic about political *mores*.

[2] John Silkin *Changing Battlefields: The Challenge to the Labour Party* (Hamish Hamilton, London 1987), chap. 9.

against the wishes of the majority of Londoners was simply the logical conclusion of a campaign which predated both protagonists.[1]

In areas of policy which appeared so radically different from her Labour predecessors, such as the privatization of nationalized industries and the encouragement of home ownership, especially by sale of local-authority housing, Premier Thatcher was below the surface following policies whose effects were not dissimilar to those of Premier Wilson. Nationalized industries had, from the start, been run to some extent as a service to consumers and the private sector. They always bore the brunt of deflation, whether in the shape of savagely reduced investment plans, or front-line status in pay-policy conflicts. Though Government could not efficiently control public corporations, it could and did, especially after 1961, continually interfere to hold prices down. Coal, for example, was available for many years, to the private sector well below world prices. The deficits of the industries were to some extent due to the fact that nationalization concentrated on declining industries, but where opportunities for substantial profit and healthy diversification on the back of those profits existed, they were fiercely and successfully resisted.[2] In 1979, the Tories were only committed to reversing Harold Wilson's two significant acts of nationalization, which were British Aerospace and shipbuilding, and to selling off the National Freight Corporation. 'Privatization' was invented in office as a dramatic way of cutting down public-sector borrowing requirements at the cost, of course, of stripping assets and of creating private monopolies in place of state ones.[3]

Apart from the first, not wildly successful, privatization, all the sell-offs were structured to encourage small investors and priced so as to allow them guaranteed gains in the shape of sharp rises in share values. These were eminently accessible gains for there was substantial subsequent selling by small investors to institutions or large investors. Liquidity was being pumped into the economy and directed at natural supporters of Government. The soaring house market in the south and east of England was another example. With Wales, Scotland and Ulster virtually enemy territory where satraps called Secretaries of State held sullen peoples in check, and Labour confined to an English electoral ghetto north of a line from Plymouth to Hull, it was gratifying that house prices in the area which produced most Government MPs appreciated up to 100 per cent between 1983 and 1987 when inflation was in single figures and the increased equity was increasingly available in such forms as a second mortgage.[4] Tax relief on mortgages, a debatably defensible subsidy, was the subsidy the Premier

---

[1] Ken Livingstone *If Voting Changed Anything They'd Abolish It* (Collins, London 1987), p. 246.

[2] John Hughes *Nationalised Industries in the Mixed Economy* (Fabian Tract 328, The Fabian Society, London 1960); R. Kelf-Cohen *Twenty Years of Nationalisation: The British Experience* (Macmillan, London 1969), pp. 317–8; Richard V. Saville 'Economic Advice and Nationalisation, 1945–65', review article in *Scottish Economic and Social History* (10, 1990), pp. 82–8.

[3] Christopher Johnson *The Economy under Mrs Thatcher 1979–1990* (Penguin, London 1991), Chap. 5.

[4] R. J. Johnston, C. J. Pattie and J. G. Allsopp *A Nation Dividing?: The Electoral Map of Great Britain 1979–87* (Longman, London 1988).

did not wish to discuss. Oil and gas revenues peaked in this decade, helped by a second hike in oil prices in 1979–80. It was oil which enabled the Government to pursue a tight fiscal policy by sustaining revenues which would otherwise have collapsed with industrial contraction and soaring unemployment. The subsequent surplus revenues derived from becoming a net exporter of oil during the period of economic recovery were not ploughed into industrial investment or infrastructure in the UK. They were invested abroad.[1] Wilson propped up the economy. Thatcher relied on a highly selective consumerism directed towards the minority which, due to unusual political circumstances, could create large majorities for her. Both left difficult heritages.

By 1990, with rising inflation; rising unemployment; a sagging stock market; the disappearance of the once-predictable 'invisible' surplus earned by the City for the balance of payments; and a manufacturing sector starved of investment, the UK was in trouble again. Headlines like 'Back to 1979 and all that' were incredibly damaging after all the talk about a 'Thatcher miracle'.[2] That the slide into recession was slow was remarkable, especially after the spectacular collapse of an overheated stock market in 1987. It gave the Government time to become intensely unpopular because of widespread distrust of its plans for the National Health Service and state education which were, after all, the product of a group of people rich enough not themselves to use either. Above all, the proposal to replace rates, the admittedly inadequate main source of local government revenue, by a poll tax which was arguably one of the few taxes even less desirable than rates, proved a political disaster. Tried out on the natives of Scotland (where the Tory party was in apparently terminal decline) as a prelude to its introduction to England, it was the last straw. Thatcher's throne could not stand when polls showed her unpopularity was so deep that she would surely sink her party in an election in 1991 or 1992. Challenged by Heseltine, she fell before an electoral mechanism which worked as intended (rather than as in 1979). After Heseltine, an unacceptable leader, broke the Thatcher myth of invulnerability, Chancellor John Major, an acceptable political chameleon, stepped into the second ballot to win easily. He could appeal to all tastes as he had shown in 1987 when, as Minister of Social Security, he had authorized extra expenditure on the old and infirm, and then clawed it back when appointed Chief Secretary to the Treasury.[3]

Thatcher, as ever, had a point when she angrily stressed that she had never lost an election or a vote in the House, yet she was expelled from Number 10 on 48 hours notice. It was ritual slaughter of a magic monarch, whose time was up. Major's job was to save the party and the system with a more acceptable 'caring face'. The actual statistics of the 1980s for the UK show a 2.2 per cent per annum growth rate, more or less the same as the

[1] *Oil: The Price of Power* ed. Adrian Hamilton (Michael Joseph/Rainbird, London 1986), pp. 158–61.
[2] Robert Tyerman 'Back to 1979 and all that' *The Sunday Telegraph*, 23 September 1990, p. 11.
[3] 'Chameleon Man', reprinted in *John Major: Prime Minister*, ed. John Jenkin (Bloomsbury for the Press Association, London 1990), p. 196.

1970s[1] but at the cost of the destruction of over a third of the manufacturing base. Alarmingly, within a European Community which increasingly left deflation as one of the few economic policies open to the UK, there was every reason to expect the deficit in manufactured goods trading to become an accelerating rather than a shrinking problem. Whether the absolute increases in living standards which had masked the alarming nature of the fundamental trends could continue was a nice question.[2] What was not debatable was the degree of disaffection with the political system. The vast majority of voters had voted against the administrations of the 1970s and 1980s. Ulster had reached the point where, in the middle of a barely suppressed civil war, there was unanimous discontent with the existing system (if no agreement as to its replacement). In Scotland, the Nationalists had survived. More important, demands for devolution became, outside an isolated Tory rump, universal. The younger Labour MPs were sincere in their conversion to it, and there was wide agreement that its tax base must be provided by an irreversible transfer from Westminster of the right to collect specific taxes in Scotland. Due to spectacular revelations of corruption in virtually one-party Labour local government redoubts in South Wales, and new industrial development there, the Conservatives did exceptionally well in Wales between 1979 and 1983, peaking with fourteen Welsh seats in that year. Yet between 1976 and 1990, the Labour leader sat for a Welsh seat, and Labour remained the ascendant regional party.[3]

The professional politicians, increasingly members of a specialist guild with little real grasp of outside realities,[4] remained basically unreformed and intransigent. Intelligent and moderate requests for long-overdue democratic reforms from bodies like Charter 88, which transcended national and regional limits within the UK, were initially just as unpalatable to Labour right-wingers like Roy Hattersley (Deputy Leader of the Labour Party after 1983), as they were to the Tory leadership. Much that was most bitterly denounced in the Thatcher style of executive rule was no more than a logical progression from well-established usage, when indeed it was not old hat. For ideological reasons, there were long periods when she tried successfully to keep major decisions away from the Cabinet, one of whose members is reputed to have claimed that he and his colleagues were like mushrooms: kept in the dark most of the time until a door suddenly opened and a load of manure was thrown on them. Yet the good lady was infinitely more careful to be accessible and pleasant to backbench Tory MPs and their spouses than Ted Heath, who latterly had little time and less civility for such lobby fodder.[5] Nor had the bulk of the Cabinet been better served on Irish and foreign affairs under Asquith in 1913–4.

Perhaps the most depressing aspect of a system in which polarization in

[1] Johnson, *op.cit.*, p. 13.

[2] Douglas Jay *Change and Fortune: A Political Record* (Hutchinson, London 1980), pp. 497–504.

[3] Philip Jenkins *A History of Modern Wales* (Longman, pbk edn, London 1992), pp. 364 and 380–3.

[4] See, for example, David Butler and Michael Pinto-Duschinsky 'The Conservative Élite 1918–78. Does Unrepresentativeness Matter?' in *Conservative Party Politics*, ed. Zig Layton-Henry (Macmillan, London 1980), pp. 186–209.

[5] Simon Hoggart *On the House* (Pan, London 1982), pp. 100–1, and 162–4.

the constituencies often facilitated bipartisan behaviour at Westminster, was its reluctance to grant civil rights to its subjects. It had always been much readier to surrender power to outsiders. A Freedom of Information Act, for example, which would finally bury the iniquities of the Official Secrets Act, was more or less promised by Harold Wilson in 1974. A Cabinet committee, chaired by Roy Jenkins, was eventually set up to investigate the recent American legislation which had suggested the idea. After the mandatory junket to Washington to talk to bureaucrats who regarded the legislation as a defeat, Roy and his colleagues predictably concluded that a right to know for the public would just make life difficult for enlightened chaps trying to govern. The proposed legislation was allowed to lapse. As befitted a short-tempered reactionary, Premier Callaghan was simply opposed to the idea. Despite much talk about police states when in opposition, the Conservatives under Thatcher were, if anything, anxious to make the culture of secrecy more effective. They were assisted by judges who ruled that 'the public interest' meant the political convenience of whoever controlled the executive. They tried to extend political protection to such hitherto debatable activities as wiretapping, and pressed by bodies like the European Court in Strasbourg, they replied with what *The Times* called 'dumb dog insolence' in the shape of legislation which observed the letter and mocked the spirit.[1]

The UK's long and complex involvement with the politics of the Common Market, or EEC, by the 1990s the European Community, is a saga in itself, and not a theme which can be appropriately pursued for its own sake in this book, especially at this point. However, it is important to grasp that that involvement complicated rather than fundamentally changed the principal political and economic problems which had long faced the inhabitants of the UK. To put it more bluntly: it offered no easy escape from these apparently insoluble problems. By definition, British policy towards the Community was an extreme case of, rather than an exception to the generalization that the ruling élites in the UK were extremely anxious to keep policy formulation as far as possible from exposure to popular pressures. They correctly judged popular opinion to be far less enthusiastic about participation in an increasingly centralized Community than some of the most powerful elements in the political élite and the Foreign Office. Mrs Thatcher had deliberately drawn strength from anti-EEC populist support for her aggressive demands for concessions from other members on the problem of the UK's spiralling contributions to the Community budget in the early 1980s. Without that support, the European Commission in Brussels might never have released accurate figures for the UK contribution, and the leaders of the other member states would certainly have persisted in their initial response, which combined lofty calls for more European 'commitment' from the British, with derisory concessions to a very real problem. Yet Thatcher herself, despite a subsequent

---

[1] Clive Ponting *The Right to Know* (Sphere, London 1985), chaps 1–2, may usefully be supplemented by Patrick Fitzgerald and Mark Leopold *Stranger on the Line: The Secret History of Phone Tapping* (The Bodley Head, London 1987), and *The Secrets File: The Case for Freedom of Information*, ed. Des Wilson (Heinemann Educational, pbk edn, London 1984).

rush of enthusiasm for a range of initiatives from the Channel Tunnel to the single internal Community market, paid a heavy price in embittered resentment amongst senior colleagues at her, in their eyes, vulgar lack of Community spirit.[1]

The European Commission in Brussels, which was the most important single force behind the drive to create a centralized Community with a single currency and a strong, activist regulatory executive, carried the attitudes of the Whitehall mandarinate to extremes. This was because it was so convinced of the utter righteousness of its basic crusade for a superpower Europe, but it was only one of a succession of effectively unaccountable bodies which had over the years tried to pre-empt UK policies towards the Community. In the administration of America's President Lyndon B. Johnson, Under-Secretary of State George Ball had in the 1960s tried to use the leverage afforded by American loans to the British Labour administration of Harold Wilson to push Wilson towards the Common Market, partly to stop him reducing expensive UK military commitments in Germany. Wilson did, far too late, disappoint Johnson by devaluing the pound and abandoning a UK east-of-Suez military presence, but he left the British forces in Germany intact, because he had become a Common Market enthusiast. Dollar diplomacy needed a cooperative element at the top of the British élite to secure its objectives on the Common Market, but that élite was far readier to accept input from America than from domestic opinion on such issues.[2] Accountability did not look like becoming less of a problem within the Community, and control was clearly going to be largely one-way. The Brussels Commission in the 1990s showed every sign of following the federal government of the United State of America down the pathway which led to exaggerated levels of over-regulation of details of domestic and business life.

Nor did membership of the Community seem likely to offer escape from the basic UK economic problem of a sluggish economy which was not paying its way in the world. As membership worked after 1973, if anything it exacerbated the problem. Towards the end of the 1970s, as the Labour government was losing its majority and limping towards highly predictable electoral disaster the Confederation of British Industry produced its 'Programme for Action '77' in which it advocated the cutting of direct taxes on the grounds that 'lack of incentive has held back productivity in manufacturing industry'. Here lay one origin of what was to be the Conservative Party's central policy in its long period of ascendancy after 1979—to cut direct taxes. That they probably always intended to increase the overall tax burden by raising indirect taxes is beside the point: the argument was that cutting direct taxes was one of several ways of restoring vigour to a declining manufacturing sector. Top tax rates were undoubtedly too high in 1977 (as was the widespread evasion of them by various quite legal devices), but the argument was flawed. Between 1909 and 1914 most taxable earned income had paid the historically low figure of under four per cent in tax. Yet industry had been stagnant, as had been wages and productivity. Most

[1] Hugo Young, *One of Us: a Biography of Margaret Thatcher* (Macmillan, London 1989), pp. 183–91.

[2] Diane Kunz 'Lyndon Johnson's Dollar Diplomacy', *History Today*, April 1992, pp. 45–51.

British investment had been abroad. The emergence of a heavy adverse balance of trade in manufactures for the UK within the Community after 1979 was therefore unsurprising. The 'trickle-down' theory to the effect that the rich would necessarily produce investment in industrial capacity as their surplus wealth trickled down through the rest of British society was one which had been proven bogus by 1914.[1]

The only period in the twentieth century when the UK's long relative decline in growth rates and export market share compared with other major industrial powers had been reversed had been the period between 1932 and 1957, when UK industry enjoyed protection. In the five years before the outbreak of the Second World War the UK even headed the table for industrial growth. After 1945, the new western hegemon, the USA, was passionately opposed to protection, especially if British, and after 1973 the already unsatisfactory British growth rate slumped within the Common Market to about two-thirds of its former figure. All of this was of course masked by the greatest absolute increase in real living standards in history. While economists and politicians beat their breasts about low growth, as a prelude to adopting policies which made it even lower, the consumer happily bought more and more imported food, drink, and consumer durables. North Sea oil drove the value of the pound up, enabling overseas countries to pay for their imports of UK oil by buying less of now more expensive UK goods, and exporting more of their now relatively cheaper goods to the UK.[2]

The Thatcherite New Jerusalem, the heavenly city of the mid-Victorian entrepreneur, was never likely to descend on England's green and pleasant land. What the Conservatives succeeded in erecting was much more like an Edwardian citadel upon a hill, where the indispensable 40 per cent or so of the electorate needed to sustain a working majority in the Commons for the executive had to be provided with a rather better standard of living than was warranted by the performance of a stagnant economy locked into union with far more efficient rivals like France and Germany. That alone ensured that in 1992, in the depths of a profound recession, with not far short of three million unemployed, the UK was running an annual deficit of five or six billion pounds. Any significant recovery was likely to see that deficit soar. Since Premier John Major's successful electoral strategy in 1992 included borrowing heavily to cut taxes, it is clear that the problem of deficit-funded consumerism was a fundamental part of the political structures which endowed him with his otherwise vast domestic power.

One Conservative publicist rashly stated that Mrs Thatcher's message to her social enemies was 'Yobboes or morons either conform or go under'. A more restrained Conservative voice had some years before argued in much the same vein that it was 'the balance of operative power' which determined social structures.[3] Political power is a socially-defined struc-

---

[1] Sir Henry Phelps Brown 'What is the British Predicament?', *The Three Banks Review*, December 1977, No. 116, pp. 12–13.

[2] Nicholas Kaldor *The Economic Consequences of Mrs Thatcher: Speeches in the House of Lords 1979–82*, ed. Nick Butler (Duckworth, London 1983).

[3] The quotations, respectively from Peregrine Worsthorne (rash), and his friend Maurice Cowling (restrained), are cited in John Rentoul *The Rich Get Richer: The growth of inequality in Britain in the 1980s* (Unwin paperback edn, London 1992).

ture, and UK prime ministers were constrained by their friends as much as their enemies. External buttresses of their political citadel like the US Treasury and Federal Reserve or the German Chancellor and Bundesbank, were almost as much of a problem as the Tory voter. The Germans and Americans had used the sterling crisis and IMF loan of 1976 to press heavily for changes in UK domestic policy in what would later be called a Thatcherite direction. They failed to convert, but did help discredit the Labour government of that time.[1] Yet the bottom line for both the Americans and Germans had been a desire to avoid serious change in either the UK's NATO defence commitment, or the UK's relationship with the EEC. In a situation where the long-term prospect was deeply worrying, internal and external pressures effectively narrowed the range of possible responses. By the end of her reign Mrs Thatcher seems to have had the gut instinct that inability to lower the value of the overvalued currency would deprive her of a crucial escape route from accelerating relative decline within the EEC. Sir Alan Walters, one of her most influential economic advisers, thought that her reluctant acceptance of membership of the European Exchange Rate Mechanism, which confined the value of the pound sterling to a narrow band, was in retrospect her greatest defeat.

Economic inadequacy was an Anglo-American predicament. At the very moment President Lyndon Johnson and his advisers were pressing the Labour government for what that Democratic American administration saw as fiscally responsible measures, the United State had long been following fiscally irresponsible and very inflationary policies by refusing to bite on the bullet of the need for higher taxes to pay for the unpopular Vietnam War. In the 1980s the Republican administration of President Ronald Reagan tripled the US national debt, and borrowed more than $20,000 per American family of four on the way to building an annual trade deficit of over $100 billion per annum. Such profligacy was not characteristic of British governments in the 1980s, but they did in practice transfer unearned purchasing power to their political supporters, and the deficit basis on which they were running the UK economy by the early 1990s was, like the similar American system, a device for enabling the consumer to send the bills to his or her children.[2]

For both the US and the UK a day of reckoning was bound to come, when the mortgaging of the future turned into present calamity. As the weaker of the two powers, the UK possessed less room for manoeuvre, and indeed less will to try to manoeuvre. Sir Nicholas Henderson, a former Assistant and then Principal Private Secretary to five Foreign Ministers, and a former UK ambassador to Washington, was a sharp critic of David Owen's public denunciation of the Foreign Office as a wilful department bent on imposing its own policies on ministers. Henderson painted an improbably meek Foreign Office, far too reluctant to give advice when it had good advice to give, but blandly stated that any radical policies on NATO or the EEC would 'impose a severe strain upon the code of loyal service to politi-

---

[1] Kathleen Burk and Alec Cairncross *Goodbye, Great Britain: The 1976 IMF Crisis* (Yale University Press, New Haven and London 1992).

[2] Benjamin M. Friedman *Day of Reckoning: The Consequences of American Economic Policy Under Reagan and After* (Random House, New York 1988).

cal masters'. Bipartisan consensus was the UK elite's preferred weapon for restricting political access and public debate.[1]

The European dimension added another layer to the web of domestic and overseas interests which both sustained and imprisoned the contemporary UK political system. Though it was a commonplace among informed observers that the role of the prime minister fluctuated with changes in both personality and circumstances,[2] the basic structures of the political regime remained very stable after it became clear in the late 1970s that even in office the Labour Party lacked the will or capacity to wield power. Any substantive proposals for political or economic change tended to run into lethal hostility from one of the major conservative vested interests, overseas or domestic, built into the system. By early 1992 UK manufacturing output was actually below the level achieved in the second quarter of 1974. The City of London's share of international lending fell from 27 per cent in 1980 to 18 per cent in 1990. In many of the most promising of the new technologies the British industrial presence was nil or contracting. As to the future: investment was by 1992 below 1970 levels. A backward offshore island appeared to be the UK's likeliest European future.[3] Without political change of a fundamental kind, necessarily allowing the natives more continuous say in their own governance, no change in this long-established drift was remotely likely. Absolute monarchies are devices which provide the keystone to an arch of privileged interests. The structure of prime-minsterial monarchy in twentieth-century Britain was therefore too precious to be dismantled, even by those who occasionally felt obliged to assassinate a given premier. It was the guarantee of stability in a long-term decline which was not unprofitable to some domestic interests, and preferred to change by many external ones.

[1] Nicholas Henderson *Inside the Private Office: Memoirs of the Secretary to British Foreign Ministers* (Academy, Chicago 1987), p. 122; Neil Stammers *Civil Rights in Britain During the 2nd World War* (Croom Helm, London 1983), p. 236.

[2] This is the theme of Lord Blake *The Office of Prime Minister* (British Academy, Oxford 1975), and James Barber, *The Prime Minster since 1945* (Institute of Contemporary British History, Blackwells, Oxford 1992).

[3] John Eatwell 'Heseltine and the Curse of "Common Sense"', *The Observer*, Sunday 26 April 1992, Business Section. p. 28.

Name Index

284 *The e*